D0231378

NEGRO EMPLOYMENT
IN RETAIL TRADE

*A Study of Racial Policies in the Department
Store, Drugstore, and Supermarket Industries*

INDUSTRIAL RESEARCH UNIT
WHARTON SCHOOL OF FINANCE AND COMMERCE
UNIVERSITY OF PENNSYLVANIA

Founded in 1921 as a separate Wharton Department, the Industrial Research Unit has a long record of publication and research in the labor market, productivity, union relations, and business report fields. Major Industrial Research Unit studies are published as research projects are completed. Advanced research reports are issued as appropriate in a general or special series.

Recent Industrial Research Unit Studies
(Available from the University of Pennsylvania Press or the Industrial Research Unit)

No. 40   Gladys L. Palmer et al., *The Reluctant Job Changer*.   1962. $7.50

No. 41   George M. Parks, *The Economics of Carpeting and Resilient Flooring: An Evaluation and Comparison*.   1966. $5.00

No. 42   Michael H. Moskow, *Teachers and Unions: The Applicability of Collective Bargaining to Public Education*.   1966. $8.50

No. 43   F. Marion Fletcher, *Market Restraints in the Retail Drug Industry*.   1967. $10.00

No. 44   Herbert R. Northrup and Gordon R. Storholm, *Restrictive Labor Practices in the Supermarket Industry*.   1967. $7.50

No. 45   William N. Chernish, *Coalition Bargaining: A Study of Union Tactics and Public Policy*.   1969. $7.95

No. 46   Herbert R. Northrup, Richard L. Rowan, et al., *Negro Employment in Basic Industry: A Study of Racial Policies in Six Industries*. (Studies of Negro Employment, Vol. I.)   1970. $15.00

No. 47   Armand J. Thieblot, Jr., and Linda P. Fletcher, *Negro Employment in Finance: A Study of Racial Policies in Banking and Insurance*. (Studies of Negro Employment, Vol. II.)   1970. $9.50

No. 48   Bernard E. Anderson, *Negro Employment in Public Utilities: A Study of Racial Policies in the Electric Power, Gas, and Telephone Industries*. (*Studies of Negro Employment*, Vol. III.)   1970. $8.50

No. 49   Herbert R. Northrup, Richard L. Rowan, et al., *Negro Employment in Southern Industry: A Study of Racial Policies in Five Industries*. (Studies of Negro Employment, Vol. IV.)   1971. $13.50

No. 50   Herbert R. Northrup, et al., *Negro Employment in Land and Air Transport: A study of Racial Policies in the Railroad, Airline, Trucking, and Urban Transit Industries*. (Studies of Negro Employment, Vol. V.)   1971. $13.50

No. 51   Gordon F. Bloom, Charles R. Perry, and F. Marion Fletcher, *Negro Employment in Retail Trade: A Study of Racial Policies in the Department Store, Drugstore, and Supermarket Industries*. (Studies of Negro Employment, Vol. VI.)   1972. $12.00

NEGRO EMPLOYMENT IN RETAIL TRADE

A Study of Racial Policies in the Department Store, Drugstore, and Supermarket Industries

(Volume VI—Studies of Negro Employment)

by

GORDON F. BLOOM
Senior Lecturer
Sloan School of Management
Massachusetts Institute of Technology

F. MARION FLETCHER
Associate Professor of Management
College of Business Administration
Louisiana State University

CHARLES R. PERRY
Assistant Professor of Industry
Wharton School of Finance and Commerce
University of Pennsylvania

INDUSTRIAL RESEARCH UNIT
Wharton School of Finance and Commerce
University of Pennsylvania

Foreword

In September 1966, the Ford Foundation began a series of major grants to the Industrial Research Unit of the Wharton School of Finance and Commerce to fund a series of studies of the Racial Policies of American Industry. The purpose has been to determine why some industries are more hospitable to the employment of Negroes than are others and why some companies within the same industry have vastly different racial employment policies.

Studies have proceeded on an industry-by-industry basis under the direction of the undersigned, with Dr. Richard L. Rowan, Associate Professor of Industry, as Associate Director. As of June 1972, twenty-seven industry studies have been published with three more being written.

This volume is the sixth in our series of books combining industry studies and analyzing the reasons for different racial policies and Negro employment patterns among various industries. The present volume includes studies previously published as Report Nos. 22, 24, and 25 plus a new introduction and a final section analyzing and contrasting the Negro employment situation in these three retail industries.

Volume I, *Negro Employment in Basic Industry*, published early in 1970, contains an introductory section which sets forth the purpose and hypotheses of the overall project and a brief overview of the position of the Negro in American industry. Volume II, *Negro Employment in Finance*, Volume III, *Negro Employment in Public Utilities*, Volume IV, *Negro Employment in Southern Industry*, and Volume V, *Negro Employment in Land and Air Transport*, have also been published. Volumes dealing with maritime industries and building construction are in the planning stage. These eight volumes and the various industry reports should contain the most thorough analysis of Negro employment available in the United States.

Dr. Gordon F. Bloom, Senior Lecturer at the Sloan School of Management, Massachusetts Institute of Technology and former chairman of the National Association of Food Chains, wrote the introduction and conclusion of *Negro Employment in Retail Trade* and served as co-author of Part Four. An economist and attorney, as well as a successful business executive, he has brought a rare blend of objective analysis and practical understanding to these studies.

Part Two (department stores) is the work of Dr. Charles R. Perry, assisted by Mrs. Marie R. Keeney and Miss Elsa Klemp of the Industrial Research Unit. Dr. Perry is Assistant Professor of Industry, Wharton School of Finance and Commerce, currently on leave as Assistant to the Director of the U.S. Office of Management and Budget. His study focuses particularly on the opening of sales and managerial level positions to Negroes. Part Three (drugstores) is by Dr. F. Marion Fletcher, Associate Professor of Management, College of Business Administration, Louisiana State University, with the assistance of Mrs. Keeney. A detailed chapter on the availability of black pharmacists explores the possibilities for black ownership and management in this industry. Part Four (supermarkets) was written by Dr. Bloom and Dr. Fletcher. This study relates the extensive civil rights pressures on this industry to changes in employment policy and reviews reasons for the lack of success to date of black-owned supermarkets.

Many others have contributed to this volume. The fine cooperation of numerous industry and government personnel made it possible to obtain material and data not otherwise available. Dr. John R. Coleman, President of Haverford College, made the initial grants possible as a staff member of the Ford Foundation, and later Mitchell Sviridoff, Vice-President, and Basil T. Whiting, Project Officer, assured continued Foundation support and interest. Major editorial and research assistance was provided by Mrs. Marie R. Keeney, and Miss Elsa Klemp; Mrs. Margaret E. Doyle, our Administrative Assistant and Office Manager, handled the administrative details. The manuscripts were typed by Mrs. Rose K. Elkin, Mrs. Veronica M. Kent, and Miss Mary McCutcheon.

As in most previous reports, the data cited as "in the author's possession," have been carefully authenticated and are on file in our Industrial Research Unit library.

HERBERT R. NORTHRUP, *Director*
Industrial Research Unit
Wharton School of Finance and Commerce
University of Pennsylvania

Philadelphia
June 1972

CONTENTS

PART ONE

INTRODUCTION

by

GORDON F. BLOOM

Introduction

The post-World War II era brought a shift from an economy where more workers produced goods than services to one in which service industries such as government, transportation, public utilities, trade, finance, service, and real estate took the lead in the number of jobs. These industries continued ahead of goods in the 1960's. This employment trend is expected to continue so that by 1980, according to U.S. Department of Labor predictions, service-providing industries will employ twice as many workers as goods-producing industries.[1]

Future employment opportunities for Negroes, like employment opportunities for all workers, lie primarily in the area of service industries. An understanding of the opportunities as well as the problems which the Negro worker faces in the decade of the seventies depends upon knowledge of the peculiar demand and supply conditions for labor which characterize the service industries.

The single most important category of the service-producing industries is trade—wholesale and retail. It is estimated that by 1975 over 20 percent of the labor force will be earning a living by buying and selling.[2] If Negroes are to make progress in number of jobs in the years ahead, it is of critical importance that the stores where they and countless other Americans shop also open their doors to Negroes as job applicants at every level of business.

This book examines black employment experience in three of the major components of retail trade—department stores, drugstores, and supermarkets. It is hoped that the detailed analysis of Negro job experience in these industries will cast some light upon the factors which influence Negro employment in the growing service sector of the job market. Although many studies have been made of black employment in manufacturing, transportation, and public utilities, the service area—and particularly the area of wholesale and retail trade—has been relatively neg-

1. U.S. Department of Labor, *U.S. Manpower in the 1970's: Opportunity & Challenge* (Washington: Government Printing Office, 1970), p. 14.

2. U.S. Department of Labor, *Manpower Report of the President, January 1969* (Washington: Government Printing Office, 1969), Table E-9, p. 235.

lected, despite its growing importance as a source of job opportunities.[3]

The Importance of White Collar Employment

Retail trade is important to the Negro job applicant not only because of the number of jobs provided, but also because of the nature of the employment opportunities which are offered. In each of the industries examined, the proportion of white collar jobs is between 74 and 79 percent of the total. White collar jobs are growing at a significantly faster rate in our economy than blue collar jobs. By 1980 white collar jobs will outnumber blue collar jobs by more than 4 million.[4] It is important to the upgrading in status and income of black labor that it be fairly represented in this growing proportion of white collar employment.

Unfortunately, despite considerable progress during the past decade, Negroes are still heavily underrepresented in white collar employment. In 1970, for example, only 27.9 percent of Negroes and other nonwhites held white collar jobs compared to 50.8 percent of employed whites.[5] In that year, Negroes constituted 11 percent of the total labor force but accounted for only about 6 percent of white collar employment.[6]

The Negro today still holds a disproportionate share of jobs at the lower end of the occupational ladder. In 1970, despite years of occupational upgrading, about two-fifths of all Negro male workers were employed in service, labor, or farm occupations. For Negro women, the percentage was even higher because of the high proportion of such women still engaged in service work. In 1970, 44 percent of Negro women were engaged in such occupations; 26 percent were employed as service

---

3. Two other studies dealing with service industries were presented in Armand J. Thieblot, Jr. and Linda P. Fletcher, *Negro Employment in Finance*, Studies of Negro Employment, Vol. II (Philadelphia: Industrial Research Unit, Wharton School of Finance and Commerce, University of Pennsylvania, 1970).

4. U.S. Department of Labor, *Manpower in the 1970's, op. cit.*, p. 13, (farm workers not included).

5. U.S. Department of Labor, *Manpower Report of the President, April 1971* (Washington: Government Printing Office, 1971), Table A-10, p. 217.

6. *Ibid.*

workers, excluding household, and 18 percent were employed in private households.[7]

Because of the changing structure of the job market, employment in the occupations in which Negroes are now concentrated will be growing more slowly than in other fields. As a consequence, if Negroes are to continue to improve their employment situation in the future, they will have to gain a larger proportion of the jobs in the white collar and skilled occupations even faster than heretofore. Projections made by the U. S. Department of Labor indicate that if Negroes merely continue to hold the same proportion of jobs in each occupation that they held in 1965, nonwhite employment would grow to 9.1 million in 1975, but the nonwhite proportion of total employment would decline because of the slower growth rate of occupations in which they are concentrated. The result of maintaining the status quo in occupational distribution would be an estimated nonwhite unemployment rate of about 15 percent—which would, of course, be intolerable. Even if the proportion of nonwhite workers in each occupation should continue to change between 1965 and 1975 at the same rate as during the 1958-1965 period, employment of nonwhites would rise only to 10.2 million in 1975, and the 1975 unemployment rate for nonwhites would still be twice that of the total labor force as a whole.[8]

It is obvious that there must be an acceleration in the rate of transfer of Negroes from blue collar to growth-oriented white collar occupations if any substantial improvement is to be made in reducing the already high black unemployment rate.[9] The degree of success achieved by Negroes in obtaining white collar employment in retail trade in recent years may provide some indication of the likelihood of such an acceleration in transfer becoming an eventuality.

---

7. U.S. Bureau of the Census, *The Social and Economic Status of Negroes in the United States, 1970*, Special Studies, Current Population Reports, Series P-23, No. 38 (July 1971), Table 48, p. 60.

8. J. L. Russell, "Changing Patterns in Employment of Nonwhite Workers," *Monthly Labor Review*, Vol. 89 (May 1966), pp. 508-509.

9. In 1970, the Negro unemployment rate averaged 8.2 percent compared to 4.5 percent for whites. U.S. Bureau of the Census, *op. cit.*, Table 36, p. 48.

Characteristics of Jobs in Retail Trade

Retail trade would seem to provide attractive employment opportunities for black workers because many of the job characteristics conform to the pattern of Negro labor supply.

Low Skill. The great majority of jobs in retail trade require relatively little skill. Furthermore, except in the meat cutter trade in the supermarket business and in the pharmacy field in the drugstore industry, there are no long apprenticeship training programs required which could act as a barrier to Negro entry. Although the objective of manpower planning must be to move an increasing proportion of Negroes into higher-skill better-paying jobs, the fact of the matter is that in the immediate future the bulk of the Negro labor force—and in particular many of the new entrants into the labor market—will be relatively unskilled but nevertheless require employment at jobs which provide stability with opportunities for advancement.

Despite marked gains made in the last decade, the average Negro job applicant still lacks the educational training of his white counterpart. In 1970, for example, only 54 percent of Negro males between the ages of 25 and 29 had completed four years of high school or more compared with 79 percent of white males in the same age group.[10] Since in many cases the quality of education received by Negroes is inferior to that of whites, reading ability, comprehension of mathematics, and other basic skills are sometimes deficient even though the Negro has his diploma. The availability of jobs in a pleasant working environment with relatively low skill requirements would therefore seem to be important for the future employment of a significant segment of the Negro labor force.

Youth. Retail trade has historically been a major source of job opportunities for youthful entrants to the labor market. Many older members of the labor force began their working careers as carry-out boys in supermarkets, sales clerks in department stores, or fountain clerks in drugstores. A significant characteristic of the Negro labor force today, and in the balance of the decade of the seventies, is its youthful composition. The Negro population itself is young—the median age among males in 1970 was 21.7 years compared with 27.8 years for whites.[11]

---

10. *Ibid.*, Table 66, p. 80.

11. *Ibid.*, Table 14, p. 20.

Furthermore, since the Negro birth rate has exceeded the white birth rate, the decade of the seventies will witness a sharp increase in the number of young Negro entrants to the labor market. From 1969 to 1980 it is estimated that the number of whites in the labor force aged 16 to 19 will increase by only 9 percent whereas the number of blacks in the same age group will increase by 43 percent.[12]

The employability problems which this influx of young Negroes will create can better be appreciated when it is considered that in 1970, when the major increase in rate of entry was still ahead, the rate of unemployment among Negroes aged 16 to 19 already amounted to 29.1 percent compared to an unemployment rate for whites in the same age bracket of 13.5 percent.[13] Retail trade can provide a critically important safety valve by enabling these youthful job-seekers to find profitable employment. The alternative may be an escalation of delinquency, violence, and disaffection with our basic institutions.

Part-time Work. Retail trade represents a major source of part-time jobs for those participants in the labor force who for various reasons cannot work full-time. This is particularly true for women who have household duties and for youth in school. The proportion of workers employed part-time by choice in our economy increased rapidly during the past decade—from about 7.5 percent of the nonagricultural labor force in 1959 to about 11.5 percent in 1969.[14] The U. S. Department of Labor has estimated that if this trend continues, by 1980 one out of every seven persons will be a part-time worker.[15]

In view of this trend, part-time job opportunities such as those provided by retail stores play an important role in satisfying the employment needs of a growing portion of the labor force, both white and black. However, part-time work is of special importance to the Negro labor force because of the high proportion of working mothers with household responsibilities.

Although about one-half of all the women who were heads of families were in the labor force in March 1970, regardless of

---

12. U.S. Department of Labor, *Manpower in the 1970's, op. cit.,* p. 5.

13. U.S. Department of Labor, *Manpower Report, April 1971, op. cit.,* Table A-5, p. 209.

14. U.S. Department of Labor, *Manpower in the 1970's, op. cit.,* p. 15.

15. *Ibid.*

race,[16] a much larger proportion of black families are headed by females—in 1969, 28 percent as compared to 9 percent for whites.[17] The labor participation rate for Negro females is significantly higher than that for white females. In 1970, 50 percent of all nonwhite women were in the labor force compared to only 43 percent of white women.[18] Therefore one might expect that many Negro women would seek part-time employment as clerks, cashiers, and sales personnel in the three industries which are the subject of this text.

Central City Location. Although manufacturing establishments have to an increasing extent migrated from the cities to less congested suburban areas, retail trade is still heavily concentrated in our central cities. The growth of suburban shopping centers has siphoned off a growing share of retail sales, but nevertheless the cities, because of their concentration of resident population and transient office workers, will probably always provide a market for a significant amount of retail activity.

This fact has significant implications for Negro job opportunities in the future because an increasing proportion of the Negro population is becoming concentrated in the central cities of the metropolitan areas of our nation. The population increase among Negroes since 1960 has been almost entirely in the central cities, accounting for 3.2 million of a total increase of 3.8 million in the last decade. By contrast, among whites the population increase in the suburbs (outside of central cities) accounted for 15.5 million of a total increase of 18.8 million.[19] By 1970, about 58 percent of the Negro population lived in central cities compared to about 44 percent in 1950. In these 20 years, the proportion of whites living in central- cities declined from 35 percent to 28 percent.[20]

Retail trade and other service industries hold the key to Negro employment opportunities for the future in our central cities. Examination of the employment policies of companies in the department store, drugstore, and supermarket industries can throw valuable light on the prospects for Negro employment in central cities in the decade ahead.

---

16. U.S. Bureau of the Census, *op. cit.*, Table 43, p. 55.

17. *Ibid.*, Table 88, p. 109.

18. *Ibid.*, Table 41, p. 53.

19. *Ibid.*, Table 6, p. 12.

20. *Ibid.*, Table 7, p. 13.

Research Methodology

The studies contained in this text focus attention on **manage-ment** employment policies toward Negroes. Although both gov-ernment and union attitudes and regulations affect management policy in varying degrees, employers still have considerable dis-cretion in their hiring, training, and promotion policies with respect to minority groups. The research outlined in the follow-ing pages attempts first to describe the employment policies in each industry and then to seek an understanding of the many influences—company, industry, environment, etc.—which shape these policies and which may account for variations among firms and among the three industries.

As in previous volumes, a selected list of hypotheses will be examined against the background of factual data for each in-dustry. To what extent does an increasing demand for labor explain the changing pattern of Negro employment? To what extent has the nature of the work attracted, or deterred, appli-cations for employment by Negro labor? How have employers reacted to community mores, to union policies, and to govern-mental pressures? These and other relevant considerations will be discussed in detail in the following pages.

In each industry studied, statistics have been compiled from census sources, Equal Employment Opportunity Commission data, and from original survey material compiled by individual authors. The resultant statistical tabulations provide a unique overview of three major areas of retail trade with respect to which rela-tively little information has heretofore been available.

Although this study is an integral part of a broader series which has already analyzed racial employment practices in some thirty industries, retail trade must be viewed as more than "just another industry" in any assessment of the future employment prospects of Negro labor. For the reasons enumerated in this introductory chapter, retail trade, in a very real sense, repre-sents a harbinger of the future of Negro employment opportuni-ties in our central cities. In view of their concentration in such areas, black experiences in obtaining satisfactory employment in retail trade will have a major impact upon the Negro em-ployment situation in the economy as a whole.

PART TWO

THE NEGRO
IN THE DEPARTMENT STORE INDUSTRY

by

CHARLES R. PERRY

with the assistance of
ELSA KLEMP *and* MARIE R. KEENEY

TABLE OF CONTENTS

LIST OF TABLES

CHAPTER I

Introduction

The basic rationale for the investigation of the Negro employment policies of any specific industry is the contribution which an analysis of the nature and basis of those policies can make to an understanding of the past, present, and potential labor market status of this currently restive minority group and of minority groups generally. In this context, there are four fundamental reasons for the inclusion of the department store industry in the study of the racial employment policies of American industry.

First and foremost, the department store industry is a large and growing, urban-based industry with a substantial demand for relatively low skill blue collar and white collar labor. It can provide in the near future a large number and wide range of employment opportunities to Negroes.

Second, it is a service-oriented industry composed primarily of moderate price retail stores which cater to a predominantly white, middle class clientele. This should be an excellent setting for analysis of the impact of real and imagined customer biases and changing social attitudes on Negro employment policies in service industries.

Third, it is a competitive industry composed basically of high cost retail stores which depend on sales volume to generate profits. It should provide an interesting field for analysis of the impact of increasing Negro purchasing power and changing urban residential and retail patterns on Negro employment practices in retail trade.

Finally, the department store industry is a relatively low wage industry composed of units which are characterized by high turnover and continuous employment activity. The industry, therefore, should provide an appropriate setting for analysis of the impact of relative labor market position and changing labor market conditions on Negro employment patterns in low wage industries.

RESEARCH FRAMEWORK

Prior to 1960, the department store industry was heavily concentrated in the city where it drew on a basically white, but increasingly Negro, clientele and supply of labor. Two obvious

questions arise in an analysis of industry Negro employment policies over this period. First, to what extent was this white middle
class oriented service industry willing to hire Negroes, particularly in customer contact positions? Second, to what extent did
this "willingness" change with the increasing concentration of
Negro population in central cities during the 1950's?

The civil rights revolution of the 1960's coincided with two
highly significant structural changes in the department store industry. The first was a dramatic change in the locational structure of the urban segment of the industry in response to the sustained flight of the white middle class to the suburbs. The second was an increased reliance on part-time labor in response to
the application of higher minimum wage requirements and the
overall reduction in unit sales volumes associated with the addition of suburban units. In this context, the questions which must
be answered in an analysis of Negro employment policies during
the 1960's are: (1) to what extent was the industry, by virtue
of its center city base and high visibility, subjected to and responsive to pressure for equal opportunity and/or equal employment? and (2) to what extent was this low wage industry which
offered an increasing number of suburban and part-time job opportunities able to contribute to an improvement in the economic
status of the urban Negro?

There are clear and compelling reasons to anticipate intracity
differences in Negro employment practices and patterns based on
Negro access to units either as customers or employees. These
differences would be a function of prevailing residential patterns
and transportation systems. The diversity and complexity of urban residential patterns and transit systems, however, makes an
intensive analysis of such differences impractical and will dictate
reliance on a simple urban-suburban dichotomy.

Finally, attention must be directed to recent developments and
trends which are not yet, and may not be for some time, fully
reflected in industry employment statistics, but which may significantly influence the future position of the Negro in the department store industry. Foremost among these developments
are the continuing decline in center city retail activity which
accelerated in most cities after the riots of 1965-1968, the prolonged tightness of most urban labor markets from 1965 to 1968
and their loosening somewhat thereafter, and the emergence of
social pressures and economic incentives to hire the hardcore
unemployed.

Within this chronological framework, a cross-sectional analysis will be undertaken in an effort to isolate some of the more important institutional forces which have shaped the establishment and evolution of Negro employment policies in department stores. Three basic variables will be used in this analysis: (1) geographic location, (2) scope and structure of the firm, and (3) market position and image of the unit.

There are clear and obvious reasons to anticipate regional differences in Negro employment policies and practices based on cultural and social variables. It is also important, however, to recognize that there may be demographic and economic bases for regional differences in Negro employment patterns.

It is quite possible that systematic differences will exist between firms on a national, regional, and/or local basis which are related to the scope and structure of the firm. The scope of a firm may influence its sensitivity to tradition and local mores and, therefore, the willingness of its top management to accept equal opportunity. The structure of a firm should determine the locus of control over employment practices and, therefore, the ability of top management to encourage or enforce either equal opportunity or equal employment.

It is not unrealistic to expect differences among firms or divisions of the same firm with respect to Negro employment patterns which are related to the local market image or position of those firms or divisions. The real or desired image of a department store may influence its willingness to employ members of minority groups and/or its ability to recruit minority group employees. For the purpose of testing this possibility, the firms and divisions in the industry will be divided into three categories: (1) bargain stores serving a predominantly lower middle class clientele; (2) moderate price second line stores catering to a broad middle class clientele; and (3) carriage trade stores dedicated to a service-conscious "upper class" clientele.

RESEARCH METHODOLOGY

This study is based on an intensive investigation of the Negro employment policies, practices, and patterns of leading department stores in a limited number of major cities, with particular emphasis on downtown units. The nature of the subject made in-depth investigation and analysis imperative. The number and dispersion of units, however, made intensive study of the en-

tire industry—or even of the largest firms in the industry—
impractical and necessitated use of a sample. The concentration of industrial employment in urban areas coupled with the
concentration of Negro population in the central cities of such
areas dictated the nature of the sample.

Selection of the Sample

Twelve of the twenty-five largest urban retail sales markets
were chosen on the basis of size and location to serve as the
focus of field research. Over the postwar period, these twelve
cities have generally accounted for approximately 30 percent of
total employment in general merchandise stores, but 50 percent
of total Negro employment in such stores. The standard metropolitan statistical areas selected and some of their more relevant
characteristics, in terms of this study, are presented in Table 1.

In each of these urban areas, an attempt was made to enlist
the cooperation of several downtown department stores, including all units affiliated with the major national federations and,
where possible, at least one prominent local firm. In addition,
an attempt was also made to secure the cooperation of the three
largest national chains with respect to their units within the
twelve metropolitan areas. This approach produced an initial
sample encompassing well over 500 units, operating under 45
relatively autonomous managements and controlled by 25 firms.

Four of these firms refused to participate in the study. Several
others were willing to discuss Negro employment, but reluctant
to provide data on the number and occupational distribution of
Negro employees. This reluctance was most pronounced among
the large national chains and local carriage trade firms—a phenomenon which will be discussed and analyzed in greater detail
in the body of this report. Once anonymity and confidentiality
were assured, however, most firms did agree to cooperate fully in
the study.

The final sample encompassed 406 units with total 1968 employment of almost 300,000. Some of these units did not qualify
as department stores under the census definition, but entered and
were retained in the sample because they were affiliated with a
major department store firm. The locational distribution of the
units and employees in the final sample is presented in Table 2.
These units were controlled by 26 firms and operated through 37
autonomous managements. The corporate structure and market
image of these firms and divisions are presented in Table 3.

TABLE 1. *Department Store Industry*
Selected Characteristics by Location
Twelve Metropolitan Areas

Metropolitan Area by Region	1967 Rank in Retail Trade		Units	Sales (Millions)	Employees	1970 Percent Negro Population	
	SMSA	Center City				Center City	Suburbs
Northeast							
New York	1	1	130	$2,338.8	83,886	21.2	5.9
Philadelphia	4	4	85	373.7	34,091	33.6	6.6
Pittsburgh	10	19	55	486.9	18,960	20.2	3.5
Border							
Baltimore	13	11	57	420.2	18,284	46.4	6.0
St. Louis	9	18	55	517.3	20,700	40.9	7.2
Washington, D.C.	8	10	63	696.6	23,625	71.1	7.9
South							
Atlanta	19	14	36	363.2	13,882	51.3	6.2
Houston	15	7	60	436.4	14,888	25.7	8.8
Midwest							
Chicago	3	2	180	1,943.6	72,355	32.7	3.5
Detroit	5	5	118	1,135.8	34,336	43.7	3.6
West							
Los Angeles-Long Beach	2	3	176	1,637.3	53,564	17.9	6.3
San Francisco-Oakland	6	6	74	703.6	23,217	13.4	5.4

Source: *U.S. Census of Business, 1967*, BC67-RA1, Retail Trade, United States, Table 4; Table 10, and State Volumes, Table 4; and *U.S. Census of Population, 1970*.

TABLE 2. *Department Store Industry
Employment and Units by Region and Location
Sample Companies
Twelve Metropolitan Areas, 1968*

Region	Urban	Suburban	Total
Northeast			
Units	30	66	96
Employees	51,950	30,335	82,285
Border			
Units	20	41	61
Employees	22,081	24,662	46,743
South			
Units	15	18	33
Employees	19,557	10,530	30,087
Midwest			
Units	50	53	103
Employees	41,028	30,199	71,227
West			
Units	43	70	113
Employees	27,869	35,122	62,991

Source: Data in author's possession.

TABLE 3. *Department Store Industry
Operating Structure
Sample Companies
Twelve Metropolitan Areas, 1968*

| | Type of Firm | | |
Sample	Chain	Federation	Independent
Number of firms	2	7	17
Number of divisions	2	18	17
Market image			
Budget	2	3	5
Moderate	—	9	7
Carriage	—	6	5

Source: Data in the author's possession.

Data Sources

Two types of data provide the basis of this report. Qualitative data on Negro employment policies and prospects were secured primarily from corporate and/or divisional management in the firms studied and secondarily from local civil rights agencies and organizations. Quantitative data on Negro employment practices and patterns were derived from a variety of sources including the census, data published by the U.S. Equal Employment Opportunity Commission (EEOC), existing studies of minority group employment in individual firms and local labor markets, and highly confidential corporate statistics on Negro employment.

The qualitative data were secured through structured interviews with corporate and divisional managers—generally the corporate vice president for personnel and the divisional personnel director. In many cases, it was also possible to interview the employment manager of the downtown store and/or the divisional specialist in minority group employment. In combination, these interviews were designed to gain information on the history and present status of organizational philosophy and policy with respect to minority group employment; the existence and nature of any internal control devices or incentive programs in the area of minority group employment, and the history and current status of Negroes in the firm and operating division, with emphasis on sales and management positions, in general, and on the key positions of "big ticket" sales and "merchandise buyer," in particular. Also examined were the basic staffing policies and practices of the organization including recruitment, selection, training, placement, and promotion; the nature of and experience with any special minority group or hardcore employment programs; and the percentage of recent job applicants which was Negro and the basic characteristics of those Negro applicants. The self-image and market position of the firm or division, in terms of its clientele and competitors, and the basic employment trends and prospects in the organization, including planned new units and projected changes in staff size or structure, were also studied.

No attempt was made to contact unit managers, first line supervisors, or Negro employees. This restriction on the sources of qualitative data raises some questions as to the accuracy and adequacy of the data secured, particularly with respect to the more subjective "why" and "how" questions regarding the establishment and evolution of Negro employment policies and practices. In general, however, the managers interviewed were willing to discuss frankly Negro employment issues, attitudes, and practices and many were critical of their own organizations. In most cases, the divisional managers interviewed were able to provide fairly detailed historical and contemporary information on Negro employment at least for the downtown store, the unit of greatest interest and importance, where divisional managers were normally located. In addition, the existence of minority group or hardcore employment coordinators in a substantial number of firms and divisions enhanced access to both intensive information on and critical insights into Negro employment policies within the constraints on the scope of interviews.

In the course of interviews, considerable information was obtained on idiosyncratic forces which shaped the establishment and evolution of minority group employment policies and practices in individual firms, divisions, and units. With the exception of actions taken by local civil rights agencies and groups, such forces could not be anticipated or incorporated into a basic analytical framework. The information gained about such forces can make a significant contribution to an understanding of the determinants of racial employment policies in the industry and will be interwoven into the structured analysis of Negro employment policies and practices.

Data Restrictions

Quantitative data on Negro employment in Chapters III and IV rely primarily on two sources, the U.S. Census of Population in the former and the U.S. Equal Employment Opportunity Commission in the latter. Unfortunately, with one exception data on minority employment from these sources are not available for the department store industry as a distinct group. The broader category used by the census and EEOC, "general merchandise stores," includes limited price variety stores, limited line discount houses, and mail order operations along with department stores. Staff structures and market positions of these other operations vary significantly from that of department stores and therefore may lead to very different Negro employment policies and practices.

Census data on Negro employment must be viewed with these restrictions in mind. Fortunately, it was possible to check the accuracy of EEOC general merchandise data, since a breakdown for the department store segment in 1969 was made available by the EEOC. A comparison of the larger group with its smaller subunit showed that characteristics of department store employment so dominated the general merchandise group data that the larger category can be used with confidence to assess racial employment patterns.

Sample data in Chapters IV and V must also be viewed with some caution. Most of the firms in the sample were able to supply comprehensive occupational and locational data on minority employment only for years since 1966. In most firms, Negro employment data were based on informal sight surveys or the memory of the most senior person in the personnel records office. There was evidence of significant variability among units, divisions, and firms with respect to the assignment of specific jobs to an occupational category. Aggregation may compensate for some of these weaknesses in the data, but it will not cancel out any systematic bias toward overstatement of the number and occupational level of Negro employees. The existence of such a bias cannot be proven, but must be suspected in the context of the current public and private pressures in the civil rights area. Thus, the survey data give an approximate estimate, not an accurate measure, of Negro employment in the department stores studied.

It must also be recognized that the data provide only a point estimate of Negro employment and not an estimate of average annual Negro employment in the department stores studied. All of the units studied were characterized both by high turnover and by large weekly, monthly, and seasonal fluctuations in employment. Either of these phenomena may produce dramatic fluctuations in the number and/or percentage of Negro workers in a unit or occupational category, particularly if the number of Negro employees is small. Fortunately, most of the firms studied gathered data on Negro employment at about the same time of year and during a non-peak, non-slump season—the late winter. Thus, the data should provide a basis for assessing and comparing modal Negro employment.

CHAPTER II

The Department Store Industry

The Bon Marche established in Paris in 1852 is generally regarded as the original department store. There is no comparable consensus as to the first department store to emerge in the United States, but there is basic agreement that the departmental form of organization had been adopted in some large general merchandise stores in this country as early as 1870 and had achieved widespread acceptance in such stores by 1890.

In 1930, when the department store was first recognized as a distinct type of general merchandise store in the U.S. Census of Business, there were nearly 4,200 department store units in operation and the industry accounted for slightly over 60 percent of total general merchandise store sales and employment with total 1929 sales of almost $4 billion and total employment of 508,249. By 1948, when the current census definition of a department store was adopted, the number of department store units had declined to 2,580, primarily as a result of the application of a more restrictive minimum size criterion. Department store sales, however, had grown to over $10 billion and employment to 843,479, and the industry still accounted for more than 60 percent of total sales and employment in general merchandise stores. The most recent census of business (1967) listed 5,792 department store units with total annual sales of $32.3 billion and total employment on mid-March payrolls of 1,174,351. These department stores constituted only 8.6 percent of all general merchandise stores, but contributed nearly three-fourths of total sales and employment in general merchandise stores. The pattern of industry growth from 1930 to 1967 is presented in Table 4.

INDUSTRY STRUCTURE

The department store historically has been and generally remains a relatively large, labor intensive retail sales unit. The operation of such high cost retail units requires both sizeable

TABLE 4. *Department Store Industry*
Units, Sales, and Employment
Selected Years, 1930-1967

| Year | Units[a] | Sales (Billions) | Employment | Percent of All General Merchandise | | |
				Units	Sales	Employment
1930	4,190	$ 3.9	503,249	7.7	60.9	61.4
1939	4,074	4.0	637,189	8.1	70.2	66.0
1948	2,580	10.6	843,479	4.9	66.3	62.4
1954	2,761	10.6	734,920	3.6	59.2	58.4
1963	4,251	20.5	970,802	6.8	68.3	66.1
1967	5,792	32.3	1,174,351	8.6	74.3	71.3

Source: *U.S. Census of Business:*

1930: Vol. I, *Retail Distribution*, Part 1, Table 1A.

1948: Vol I, *Retail Trade*, General Statistics, Part 1, Table 1C.

1958: Vol. I, *Retail Trade*, Summary Statistics, Tables 2 and 2A.

1963: Vol. I, *Retail Trade*, Summary Statistics, Part 1, Tables 2 and 3.

1967: BC67-RS4, *Retail Trade*, Single Units and Multiunits, Table 2.

[a] Does not include mail order business. Definition of a department store was revised between 1939 and 1948, see text.

markups and substantial sales volume to generate a profit.   In the postwar period, gross margins in department stores consistently averaged around 35 percent, but after tax net margins generally averaged under 3 percent.[1]   Thus, the department store traditionally has been and typically remains a moderate-high price retail store which competes for consumer loyalties and expenditures primarily on the basis of such non-price factors as shopping convenience and customer service and caters to a predominantly middle class clientele.

1. Malcolm P. McNair and Eleanor G. May, *The American Department Store, 1920-1960* (Boston: Harvard University Graduate School of Business Administration, Division of Research, 1962), pp. 24-25.

Many of the firms which operated department store units also had non-department store retail operations. Most firms operated fewer than four department stores, but the larger multiunit firms accounted for most of the units, sales, and employment in the industry. The breakdown by corporate structure is shown in Table 5. The twenty firms which operated 101 units or more together accounted for more than 40 percent of all industry units, sales, and employment in 1967.

Types of Firms

There are four basic types of department store firms. The first is the small local firm which operates from one to three units in a single trading area, usually other than a major urban area. The second is the large local firm which operates from four to ten units in a single trading area, generally centered in a major city. Firms such as John Wanamaker (Philadelphia) and Carson Pirie Scott (Chicago) fall into this category. The third is the regional or national federation which controls sev-

TABLE 5. *Department Store Industry*
Employment by Company Structure and Sales
United States, 1967

	Firms	Units	Sales (Millions)	Employment[a]	Employees per Unit
Single unit firms[b]	611	611	$ 1,799,734	75,640	124
Multiunit firms					
2 to 5 units	223	522	2,339,043	104,708	201
6 to 25 units	101	877	5,625,801	208,016	237
26 to 100 units	29	1,039	7,850,134	290,068	279
101 or more	20	2,743	14,729,307	495,919	181
All multiunit companies	373	5,181	$30,544,285	1,098,711	212
All companies	984	5,792	$32,344,019	1,174,351	203

Source: *U.S. Census of Business, 1967*, BC67-RS4, *Retail Trade*, Single Units and Multiunits, Table 2.

[a] During week including March 12.

[b] Including companies which operate only one department store although they have other types of business units.

eral multiunit divisions, each of which approximates a large local firm and operates on an atonomous basis under a locally established trade name.   Allied Stores, Associated Dry Goods, Federated Department Stores, and May Department Stores are leading examples of this type of firm.   The fourth is the regional or national chain which operates units over a wide range of local trading areas under a single trade name and fairly centralized management policies.   The largest such chains are Sears, Penney's, and Montgomery Ward (now Marcor), all of which also maintain large catalogue sales operations.   Sales, employment, and other 1970 data on ten of the largest department store companies are shown in Table 6.

Store Definition

Department stores can be distinguished from other retail stores on the basis of three criteria.   First, a department store must normally employ at least 25 persons.   Second, a department store must have sales of apparel and "softgoods," combined amounting to 20 percent or more of total sales, and sell some items in each of three basic merchandise groups: (a) furniture, home furnishings, appliances, and radio and television sets; (b) a general line of apparel for the family; and (c) household linens and dry goods.   Third, a department store must have substantial sales volume in each of the basic merchandise groups, in terms of the following standards: (a) 85 percent of total sales or less in any single group, if annual sales volume does not exceed $5 million; or (b) total sales of at least $500,000 in each group, if annual sales volume does exceed $5 million.[2]

The department store industry, thus constituted, encompasses a diverse group of labor intensive, full line general merchandise stores ranging from "discount houses" to "carriage trade" stores, but is composed primarily of large, moderate price, service oriented retail sales units.   In this respect, it is important to note that the definition cited above excludes from the industry not only specialty shops but a significant number of large, moderate or high price, limited line general merchandise stores normally perceived by consumers to be "department stores."   Also excluded are limited price variety stores, limited line discount houses, and nonstore general merchandise retail sales organi-

---

2. *U.S. Census of Business, 1967,* BC67-RA1, *Retail Trade,* United States, Appendix A, pp. 1-157—1-158.

TABLE 6.   *The Ten Largest Department Store Companies, 1970 Statistics*

Company and 1970 Rank among Retailing Companies		Headquarters	Sales	Assets	Net Income	Stockholders' Equity	Employees	Net Income as a Percent of	
			($000)					Sales	Stockholders' Equity
Sears, Roebuck	1	Chicago	9,262,162	7,623,096	464,201	3,708,279	359,000	5.0	12.5
J.C. Penney	4	New York	4,150,886	1,627,055	114,096	753,256	145,000	2.7	15.1
Marcor[a]	6	Chicago	2,804,856	2,459,730	59,637	896,015	127,100	2.1	6.7
Federated Department Stores	9	Cincinnati	2,096,935	1,165,770	82,169	692,474	75,700	3.9	11.9
Gamble-Skogmo	16	Minneapolis	1,296,704	771,896	15,066	193,672	24,275	1.2	7.8
Allied Stores	18	New York	1,225,070	921,506	14,801	311,251	50,000	1.2	4.8
May Department Stores	21	St. Louis	1,170,383	925,380	31,873	421,625	56,000	2.7	7.6
Dayton Hudson	22	Minneapolis	969,287	691,357	18,970	289,560	27,000	2.0	6.6
R.H. Macy	25	New York	907,029	579,264	20,660	234,633	37,500	2.3	8.8
Associated Dry Goods	29	New York	795,278	496,285	28,042	278,145	42,000	3.5	10.1

Source: *Fortune*, Vol. LXXXIII (May 1971), pp. 196-197.
[a] Formerly Montgomery-Ward.

zations such as mail order houses. These other retail organizations define the boundaries of the industry and identify its major competition.

Location

The volume requirement of department stores consistently has dictated the concentration of units in urban mass middle class retail markets. The convenience orientation of the institution has made it sensitive to changes in the residential and commuting patterns of the urban middle class while the low net margin character of the industry has made department store firms responsive to such changes. The structure of the urban segment of the industry and of urban department store firms, therefore, historically has paralleled the residential and retail patterns of the white middle class majority.

Prior to World War I, the limited scale of the urban middle class retail market, coupled with the dispersion of middle class population within urban areas, dictated the concentration of units in the central business district and fostered the emergence and dominance of the large single unit firm. Between World War I and World War II, the growth of the cities and of the urban middle class, coupled with increased reliance on the automobile, resulted in a partial fragmentation of urban retail markets and a decline in the popularity of the downtown department store. The extent of this decline and the scale of the emerging "neighborhood" markets were too limited to force or encourage expansion by existing firms, but were sufficient to support somewhat smaller, less labor intensive units. The result was the appearance and growth of the chain store.

Urban-Suburban Shift

Prior to 1945, there had been little industry expansion outside the city and in 1948 most urban units and nearly all urban sales were in central cities. Given this locational structure, the postwar flight of the urban white middle class to the suburbs, coupled with the high and increasing cost and inconvenience of central city shopping for a suburban resident, created a crisis in the industry and in individual firms. This was reflected in a drop in industry market share from 7.3 percent of total retail trade in 1948 to 6.2 percent in 1954.[3] This crisis eventually

---

3. *U.S. Census of Business, 1954,* Vol. I, Part 1, p. 13.

resulted in the addition of suburban branches by existing firms. Consequently, the multiunit local firm replaced the single unit firm as the basic ownership unit in the urban segment of the industry. Some companies, however, were unable to undertake effective expansion into the suburbs and were absorbed by other firms. As a result, the multidivision federation has become a major factor in the industry.

These trends have continued under the impact of the continuing decline in the accessibility and desirability of central city shopping areas as a result of both sustained residential and industrial migration to the suburbs and enhanced economic, social, and psychological barriers between the "safe" suburbs and the "congested," "riot-torn," "crime-ridden" cities. There is little reason to anticipate any dramatic change in this pattern of industry growth in the near future as most of the firms studied reported both a sharp drop in downtown sales volume after the riots of 1965-1968 and a strong commitment to adding new units in high median family income areas.

The continued migration of Negroes into the cities, coupled with the rapid expansion of the industry into lower density suburban retail markets, has created a new set of economic problems for firms in the industry. In the city, department stores increasingly are forced to choose between unit shutdown or active competition for the economically limited Negro market. In the suburbs, department stores increasingly are faced with strong competition for a geographically "thin" white market. To date, the basic response of firms in the industry to both challenges has been an increase in store hours—including night and Sunday openings—and store services, rather than price competition or movement toward discount house operation. The inevitable outcome has been an increase in cost and an acceleration of the historical trend toward consolidation in search of economies of scale within the industry.

MANPOWER

Over 1.5 million people worked in department stores and related corporate and other activities by 1970; almost 70 percent of these were women. Employment growth, from 1960 to 1970, based on U.S. Bureau of Labor Statistics data, is presented in Table 7.

TABLE 7. *Department Store Industry*
Total, Female, and Nonsupervisory Employment
United States, 1960-1970

Year	All Employees (000)	Female Employees (000)	Percent Female	Nonsupervisory Employees (000)	Percent Nonsupervisory
1960	917.2	652.7	71.2	846.3	92.3
1961	924.6	654.8	70.8	850.4	92.0
1962	971.4	684.7	70.5	892.3	91.9
1963	1,021.2	708.2	69.3	936.6	91.7
1964	1,087.8	753.4	69.3	998.0	91.7
1965	1,173.0	809.8	69.0	1,077.6	91.9
1966	1,255.0	859.9	68.5	1,153.6	91.9
1967	1,324.3	910.2	68.7	1,219.2	92.1
1968	1,406.3	970.7	69.0	1,293.8	92.0
1969	1,484.4	1,026.5	69.2	1,366.9	92.1
1970	1,517.0	1,053.7	69.5	1,394.5	91.9

Source: U.S. Bureau of Labor Statistics, *Employment and Earnings Statistics for the United States, 1909-70*, Bulletin No. 1312-7; and *Employment and Earnings*, Vol. 17 (March 1971), Tables B-2 and B-3.

Department store employment reported to the EEOC in 1969 is shown in Table 8. The large scale nature of this retail industry results in few employees outside of firms with less than 100 employees, the EEOC minimum. A comparison of 1969 figures in Tables 7 and 8 reveals that about 77 percent of employment recorded by the U.S. Bureau of Labor Statistics is represented in EEOC material.

Almost one-half of all employment is in sales and another one-quarter of all employment is accounted for by managerial and clerical employees in this heavily white collar industry. The blue collar group, which comprises only one-fifth of all jobs, is dominated by service work. Since traditionally Negroes have been excluded from sales positions in many industries, a sales-dominated industry such as department stores might be expected to have offered extremely limited opportunities to black workers until very recent times.

TABLE 8. Department Store Industry

Total Employment and Percent Distribution by Sex and Occupational Group
United States, 1969

Occupational Group	All Employees		Male		Female	
	Total	Percent Distribution	Total	Percent Distribution	Total	Percent Distribution
Officials and managers	128,079	11.0	83,924	21.5	44,155	5.7
Professionals	12,774	1.1	7,779	2.0	4,995	0.7
Technicians	9,994	0.9	7,102	1.8	2,892	0.4
Sales workers	533,775	46.0	118,564	30.3	415,211	53.9
Office and clerical	234,903	20.2	28,450	7.3	206,453	26.8
Total white collar	919,525	79.2	245,819	62.9	673,706	87.5
Craftsmen	38,508	3.3	31,805	8.2	6,703	0.9
Operatives	65,446	5.7	40,767	10.4	24,679	3.2
Laborers	45,542	3.9	30,202	7.7	15,340	2.0
Service workers	91,667	7.9	42,237	10.8	49,430	6.4
Total blue collar	241,163	20.8	145,011	37.1	96,152	12.5
Total	1,160,688	100.0	390,830	100.0	769,858	100.0

Source: U.S. Equal Employment Opportunity Commission, 1969.

Note: Companies with 100 or more employees.

Theoretically, mobility between occupational categories is possible in department stores and is encouraged by the widespread existence of "promotion-from-within" policies. Such mobility has been an important factor in staffing in the industry and it is not uncommon to find managers who began their careers as stockboys. Presently, however, such internal occupational mobility is extremely limited and, for all practical purposes, there are five distinct occupational groups within department stores: managerial, sales, clerical, general blue collar labor, and service.

Managerial Personnel

The broad occupational categories of officials and managers, professionals, and technicians are characterized by low entry or base level salaries, but high potential or upper level income in the department store industry. Historically, management personnel have come largely from within the department store organization, generally through informal progression from sales positions. Currently, however, management personnel come primarily from formal management training programs.

The basic source of management trainees has been smaller colleges. Low entry level salaries coupled with the prospect of irregular working hours as dictated by store hours and customer traffic has made it difficult for firms in the industry to recruit at major universities and has effectively precluded large scale recruitment of graduate degree holders.

In recent years, some of the firms studied have experienced real difficulty in securing an adequate supply of management trainees from their traditional sources and have begun to turn to junior colleges and, in a few cases, to the top ranking graduates of local high schools who do not intend to go on to college. Most firms have not yet greatly enhanced efforts to identify and develop managerial potential among nonsupervisory employees.

Management training is largely on-the-job training and involves a series of assignments in sales departments beginning with assistant department manager or assistant buyer. Promotional progression varies among firms, but generally involves movement to department manager and to either merchandise manager and merchandise buyer or to service manager and store manager. Both the buyer and store manager positions involve substantial responsibility. Firms in the industry have not been uniformly successful in developing candidates for these positions through internal progression, as evidenced by considerable hiring of experienced people into these positions.

Higher level management positions are filled by promotion from within. Interunit, interdivision, and intercity transfers and promotions are limited and confined to top levels of management. As Table 8 shows, 11 percent of all employees are officials and managers, and another 2 percent are professionals and technicians. Over two-thirds of these positions are filled by males and more than one-quarter of all men in the industry hold jobs in these positions as compared with 7 percent of all female workers.

Sales Workers

Department stores utilize three types of sales workers: (1) regular full-time personnel who generally work a 37.5 hour week; (2) regular part-time personnel who work a fixed short hour schedule based on hours of the day or days of the week; and (3) contingent personnel who are called in on an ad hoc basis as required to meet short run shortages in personnel or peaks in customer traffic such as those associated with special sales and Christmas season. Most sales workers are paid an hourly rate and many still receive a small commission on sales, although this practice is diminishing. Sales workers in "big ticket" departments such as furniture and appliances, on the other hand, work a full commission basis and may earn in excess of $10,000 per year as compared with about $5,000 for full-time workers in other departments. All employees receive some merchandise discount privileges, but only regular employees who work more than 20 hours a week normally enjoy a fringe benefit package.

Sales workers are hired at the unit level and are generally assigned to departments in consultation with and on the approval of the department manager or buyers. The basic source of potential sales workers is walk ins and most units do little active recruiting beyond encouraging existing employees to make referrals and advertising inside the store. External advertising and search activities are limited to openings in "big ticket" departments where experienced personnel are strongly preferred, and to openings during the Christmas rush.

In general, a newly hired sales worker receives little formal training. About ten hours are spent in classroom training designed to familiarize the individual with store procedures and acquaint him with the operation of a cash register and sales slip systems. The major burden of training falls on the department manager and/or the established employee assigned to work with the novice. Few firms conduct ongoing training programs or attempt to encourage or develop superior performance on a formal or systematic basis. Routine merit reviews are made in most stores, but identification of managerial potential or special ability is a responsibility of the department manager.

Turnover among sales workers in department stores is high, but is heavily concentrated among part-time and contingent employees. Most stores indicated that they had a solid core of long service full-time workers in most areas and in all "big ticket" departments. Thus, much of the replacement demand for sales workers in the firms studied is in the lowest earnings potential segment of the sales force, particularly since most stores also indicated that part-time employees are given the first opportunity when full-time openings arise. This overall limitation on the structure of entry level demand for sales workers, however, is partially offset by the fact that there is little interdepartmental movement within the sales force in most stores.

Over three-quarters of all sales personnel are female and approximately 30 percent of all men and 54 percent of all women in the department store industry held sales positions in 1969 (Table 8), making sales the most important employment category among both groups in terms of size.

Clerical Workers

The clerical labor force in department stores is closely related to the sales labor force. Both are composed primarily of women and both draw on the same labor pool. They are, however, distinguishable on two grounds. First, clerical jobs are generally not customer contact positions. Second, clerical workers normally are full-time employees and work regular business hours. The former factor tends to segregate the clerical and sales forces on the demand side of the employment relationship; the latter, on the supply side.

Department stores have been at a competitive disadvantage in recruiting clerical workers in most of the cities studied and have generally experienced high turnover among such workers. Most of the firms studied indicated that they were unable to rely on walk-ins to provide an adequate supply of clerical workers. In general, the firms reported active recruiting in local high schools supplemented by advertising for more skilled clerical job openings. One fifth of the total work force was in office and clerical occupations in 1969, and nearly 88 percent of these workers were women (Table 8).

Craftsmen, Operatives, and Laborers

In department stores, blue collar employment other than in service work is limited and concentrated in material handling operations requiring semiskilled and unskilled workers. There is, however, a sizeable craftsman population in most stores due to both basic maintenance requirements and recurrent construction work associated with display activities.

Craftsmen, operatives, and laborers receive relatively high wages by internal industry standards because department stores have been unable to compete as effectively in this labor market on the basis of location, image, and employee discounts as they have in the sales and, to a lesser extent, clerical areas where female secondary wage earners are the basic element in labor supply.

The recruiting and retention problems faced by department stores in the clerical area extend to the upper level blue collar work force. Most firms reported consistent recruiting activity at this level and many have had to establish formal apprenticeship programs in order to meet their needs for skilled craftsmen. These programs have met with varying degrees of success, but virtually all have served to significantly inhance opportunities for upward mobility among blue collar workers in the industry and particularly in downtown stores and central service familities.

Craftsmen, operatives, and laborers comprised just over 20 percent of the work force in 1969. Men held about 70 percent of all such jobs, but this percentage was much lower in suburban stores than in urban stores as suburban stores have been forced by labor market conditions to use women in blue collar jobs traditionally filled by men. Men held about 70 percent of all craftsmen, operative, and laborer positions.

Service Workers

The service labor force encompasses a wide range of low skilled workers, many of whom are either seen by or interact with customers. This segment of department store employment is of interest for two reasons. First, it contains many of the jobs which might be expected to have been and/or remain "Negro" jobs—elevator operators, maids, and custodians. Second, there is some potential for movement between this occupational group and the sales force.

Unfortunately, data on the number and composition of service workers in department stores are not highly reliable. There was good evidence in the firms studied of great variability in the jobs included in this occupational category and of a systematic understatement of the number of service workers in favor of inclusion of them in other blue collar or even white collar jobs.

Companies reporting to the EEOC in 1969 reported 91,667 employees in the service worker group, just 7.9 percent of the total work force. Service work was about evenly divided between male and female, in contrast to all other department store occupations which were dominated by members of one sex or the other.

Female Employment

Women predominate in sales and clerical positions in the department store industry—the 621,664 women in these two occupations in the 1969 EEOC data make up over one-half of the total department store work force (Table 8). As mentioned above, the sales force is characterized by numerous part-time employees and low turnover in the full-time staff. Stores generally do not need to recruit actively to fill these positions; given the pleasant working conditions and purchasing benefits they offer, there is a large supply of secondary wage earners available to fill both full-time and part-time sales jobs. If there is strong competition for these jobs, Negro women may be at a disadvantage, particularly for those sales positions in suburban shopping areas where few Negroes live.

An unusually large number of women hold managerial positions in this industry. Over 34 percent of all officials and managers are women, although only 7.5 percent of the female work force is in this category, compared to 21.5 percent of the male work force.

Wages

The department store industry has traditionally been a low wage industry which drew heavily on a marginal labor force composed predominantly of women. Over the postwar period, entry level wages in department stores have clustered near the prevailing wage rate. In 1968, most of the firms studied were paying $1.65 per hour for inexperienced entry level employees. In 1970, the average weekly wage in the industry was $79.38 and average hourly pay was $2.52.[4]

The low wage character of department stores has made them sensitive to changes in the legal minimum wage rate. The labor cost conscious nature of the industry has made it responsive to such changes. Thus, the series of increases in minimum wage rates since 1958 has forced some adjustment in the industry and is at least partially responsible for the decline in the ratio of payroll costs to sales from a postwar high of 16.6 percent in 1958 to 14.4 percent in 1967.[5]

The basic service orientation of department stores has limited their ability to adjust employment in response to changes in wage rates. Instead, they have undertaken two other courses of action. The first is movement toward the abolition of sales commissions in all but "big ticket" departments in which commissions rather than hourly wages are the basic determinant of employee income. This movement has resulted in relative stability in the absolute differential between the minimum wage rate and average hourly earnings for nonsupervisory employees in the industry, i.e., in a slight compression of the relative earnings structure rather than the absolute wage structure. The second, and more significant, response to rising wages has been a reduction in employee hours in the form of increased reliance on short hours personnel.

Part-time Personnel

The department store industry historically has utilized large numbers of part-time workers to meet basic weekly, monthly, and seasonal fluctuations in customer traffic. In recent years, however, increasing wage rates have led department stores to extend their reliance on part-time labor in accordance with hourly and daily fluctuations in customer traffic as well as longer swings in store activity. The result has been a consistent decline

---

4. *Employment and Earnings*, Vol. 17 (March 1971), Table C-2.

5. *U.S. Census of Business, 1958*, Vol. I, *Retail Trade*, Summary Statistics, Table 2; and *1967*, BC67-RS3, *Retail Trade*, Employment Size, Table 1.

in median hours worked by nonsupervisory employees in the industry from 35 in 1958 to 31.5 in 1970.[6]

Thus, much of the recent growth in employment in the industry has been in part-time jobs—particularly in the suburbs where store hours are longest and customer traffic most concentrated. The inevitable result has been a localization of the department store labor market and an increased reliance on secondary wage earners. In very recent years, this latter trend has been accelerated by the tight labor market which has made it difficult for many stores to recruit even full-time male employees.

There is strong evidence that the shift toward part-time labor will continue, at least in suburban units. Most of the firms studied indicated a desire to increase the ratio of part-time to full-time nonsupervisory employees to three to one in the near future. Most also expected to be able to achieve this goal in the suburbs within a few years, but were not so optimistic regarding downtown units because of constraints on the supply side of the labor market. Failure to increase part-time employment in city units can only increase the extent to which suburban branches will have to subsidize city units and, thereby, increase pressure to abandon such units or to convert them into clerical headquarters. In any event, the trend toward increased reliance on part-time labor has and will continue effectively to limit the attractiveness of suburban job opportunities in the industry to all Negroes and the attractiveness of urban job opportunities to Negro males.

UNIONIZATION

The department store industry historically has been and currently remains largely unorganized. The preponderance of white collar employees and the dominance of female secondary wage earners and young transitory workers in the industry has made it relatively immune to organization in all but such high cost of living, highly unionized areas as New York City and San Francisco. With the exception of these two cities, white collar organization in the units studied was confined to those budget stores outside the South which had early accepted and/or encouraged organization in the hope of capturing the "union mar-

---

6. *Employment and Earnings*, Vol. 5 (May 1958), p. 53 and Vol. 17 (March 1971), Table C-2.

ket." Blue collar organization tends to be similarly confined in terms of geography and market orientation.

Two AFL-CIO unions divide what membership exists in the field. The Retail, Wholesale and Department Store Workers, a former CIO affiliate, has long organized several of the major department stores in the New York City area, including Macy's and Gimbel's. Its membership outside of this area in all fields is small. The much larger and older Retail Clerks International Association is the bargaining agent in most other areas where department stores are unionized. In addition, a number of craft unions represent small groups in the industry, such as elevator operators, electricians, or plumbers.

The unions have not had any discernible effect on black department store employment. Their lack of strength and general tendency to allow management to handle such matters preclude their having a significant impact on racial policies.

CHAPTER III

Negro Employment to 1960

Department stores and other general merchandise stores have long provided job opportunities for Negro workers, but the number and occupational range was traditionally severely limited. Where this was true in other forms of retailing, Negro entrepreneurs started their own stores, thus allowing blacks opportunities in the full range of occupations available. The nature of general merchandise retailing, however, requires such a large capital investment and substantial customer market that few Negroes could enter this business as owners. Thus, the general merchandise industry in general, and department stores in particular, offered perhaps the most limited early employment opportunities in retail trade.

EMPLOYMENT BEFORE WORLD WAR II

Studies of Negro employment early in the twentieth century point out that Negroes were generally not hired for sales positions at that time. John Daniels wrote that the sales occupation in department stores was one from which Negroes were practically excluded in Boston.[7] He did point out that a few Negro salesmen and saleswomen found employment in smaller shops, and that there was one Negro buyer in a large store. "The reason given for the non-employment of members of this race in department stores," he wrote, "is that both white employees and the white patrons would object."[8] Greene and Woodson's study of Chicago also found that jobs in stores as clerks and salesmen were generally not open to Negroes during this period.[9]

---

7. John Daniels, *In Freedom's Birthplace* (1914; reprint ed., The American Negro, His History and Literature Series, New York: Arno Press, 1966), pp. 321-322.

8. *Ibid.*

9. Lorenzo J. Greene and Carter G. Woodson, *The Negro Wage Earner* (Washington: The Association for the Study of Negro Life and History, Inc., 1930), p. 116.

Negro-owned department stores were extremely rare during the early 1900's. According to Richard Wright, Jr., the Philadelphia Colored Directory for 1908 did list one department store among other Negro businesses,[10] and Greene and Woodson also mention one in Chicago in 1906.[11] The stores, however, would probably not fulfill the current definition of a department store. An extensive study of Negro businesses in Cincinnati during the 1920's showed no Negro department stores, and reported that black workers were not even employed as clerks in stores in that city.[12] Although it was reported that Negroes were being hired as sales personnel in Chicago department stores by the 1930's,[13] the prevailing pattern throughout the first half of the twentieth century was to exclude Negroes from these jobs.

A study of Negro women in industry in fifteen states based on 1920 census data found only 161 Negro females employed in 61 general merchandise stores.[14] The occupational distribution of these 161 Negro women was as follows:

Maids	121
Seamstresses	11
Stockgirls	10
Pressers	8
Soda fountain attendants	4
Other	7

Subsequent data on Negro employment in general merchandise stores—which include five-and-dime stores and more limited retail units as well as the department stores—suggest little real change in the scope or structure of job opportunities open to Negroes within the industry. Specifically, 1940 census data indicate both a relatively limited number of Negro employees in general merchandise stores and a strong concentration of those

10. Richard R. Wright, Jr., *The Negro in Pennsylvania: A Study in Economic History* (1912; reprint ed., The American Negro, His History and Literature Series, New York: Arno Press, 1969), p. 86.

11. Greene and Woodson, *op. cit.*, p. 115.

12. Wendell P. Dabney, *Cincinnati's Colored Citizens* (1926; reprint ed., The Basic Afro-American Reprint Library, New York: Johnson Reprint Corp., 1970), p. 77.

13. Green and Woodson, *op. cit.*, p. 314.

14. Mary Pidgeon, *Negro Women in Industry in Fifteen States*, Bulletin No. 70, Women's Bureau, U.S. Department of Labor (Washington: Government Printing Office, 1929), p. 26.

employees in the service sector of blue collar jobs, although a
few held sales and clerical positions. The number and occupations of Negro and other nonwhite employees in general merchandise stores for eleven of the cities studied [15] are presented
in Table 9.

Nonwhites (primarily Negroes) in the eleven selected cities
were only 0.7 percent of the white collar work force in 1940.
Since four-fifths of all occupations were white collar, the substantial proportion of service jobs held by Negroes and other
nonwhites (33.9 percent) did little to improve their overall representation, which stood at 3.1 percent in 1940. Particularly important is the fact that there were less than 600 Negroes among
the 105,590 female sales workers in that year, while almost 83
percent of all female jobs were in that category in an industry
already dominated by female employment. Black men were better represented in general merchandise stores at this time, largely because they held over 40 percent of the male service jobs.
Their total employment was 5.7 percent of the male work force
in these cities in 1940.

These census data, as explained above, are for the larger category of general merchandise stores. Interviews with managers
in the firms and divisions chosen for this study indicate that
census data give a fairly accurate picture of the department
store industry itself for this period. A general picture of Negro
department store employment prior to World War II emerged
from company legends and employment records.

In those firms or divisions which existed prior to World War
I, the first Negro employee generally was hired before 1920; in
those which emerged after World War I, the first store opened
with Negro employees. In both cases, the first Negro employee
or employees were assumed to have been or were identified as
working in the laborer or service occupational categories. In
only a few of the firms or divisions had Negroes entered clerical
jobs by 1940; and in none of the firms or divisions was management certain that Negroes had been placed in sales positions by
1940. Thus, fieldwork seems to confirm the previously cited study
on Negro female employment in 1920 which indicated that these
women did not hold sales position at that time.[16] It also agrees
with another study done in New York City prior to World War

---

15. No data were available for San Francisco in 1940.

16. Pidgeon, *loc. cit.*

TABLE 9. *General Merchandise Industry Including Department Stores Employment by Race, Sex, and Occupational Group Eleven Cities, 1940*

Occupational Group	All Employees			Male			Female		
	Total	Nonwhite	Percent Nonwhite	Total	Nonwhite	Percent Nonwhite	Total	Nonwhite	Percent Nonwhite
Officials and managers, professionals, and technicians	27,383	165	0.6	19,330	122	0.6	8,053	43	0.5
Sales workers and office and clerical	142,091	1,044	0.7	36,501	456	1.2	105,590	588	0.6
Total white collar	169,474	1,209	0.7	55,831	578	1.0	113,643	631	0.6
Craftsmen	9,040	134	1.5	7,349	115	1.6	1,691	19	1.1
Operatives	14,153	564	4.0	7,551	495	6.6	6,602	69	1.0
Laborers	2,890	256	8.9	2,425	193	8.0	465	63	13.5
Service workers	12,440	4,219	33.9	7,488	3,201	42.7	4,952	1,018	20.6
Total blue collar	38,523	5,173	13.4	24,813	4,004	16.1	13,710	1,169	8.5
Total[a]	207,997	6,382	3.1	80,644	4,582	5.7	127,353	1,800	1.4

Source: *U.S. Census of Population:* 1940, Vol. III, *The Labor Force,* Parts 2-5, Selected States, Table 20.

Note: Cities are listed in Table 1. No data available for San Francisco.

[a] Totals exclude employment figures where occupation was not specified.

II which showed that large department stores hired Negroes only for such behind-the-scenes jobs as stock, receiving, and packing, and in traditional service occupations such as restaurant work and elevator operation.[17]

FAIR EMPLOYMENT EFFORTS IN THE 1940's

Negroes began to be hired as salesmen and saleswomen during the 1940's, as several civil rights organizations and state agencies put pressure on the department store industry to open these positions. The National Urban League, among others, decided to put a major emphasis on department store employment during the period.

An Urban League survey of Negro employment in New York, Boston, and New Jersey department stores [18] found black workers generally confined to clerical occupations and working as maids, elevator operators, and wrappers. A small number of black saleswomen were reported in several stores, but others had Negroes only in the lowest level occupations. In other cities the study reported Negroes employed mostly in "minor occupational categories" such as counter girls, attendants, bus boys, and maids.

Urban League efforts to increase Negro employment and "break the resistance of department store management" took place in cities such as Flint, Michigan and Akron, Ohio as well as in Chicago, Newark, and New York City. The report stressed that "in no instance has it been reported by department store officials that they have lost sales or customers because of the integration of Negroes in the sales and clerical staffs." [19]

The decade of the 1940's also saw eastern state fair employment practice commissions look into minority employment in retail trade. Several investigations into charges of discrimination involved department stores. For example, a Boston store allegedly refused to offer an experienced Negro woman a sales position, asking her to work as an elevator operator instead, although it was hiring saleswomen at the time. The investigation launched by the state commission revealed a lack of Negro salespeople in this department store. By the time the case was finally

---

17. Confidential study in the author's possession.

18. National Urban League, "Integration of Negroes in Department Stores," New York, July 1946, mimeo.

19. *Ibid.*, p. 6.

closed, things were very different: 14 Negro women and 2 Negro men were reported to hold sales jobs.[20]

The New Jersey fair employment agency, also active in the late 1940's in expanding Negro opportunities in sales positions, held conferences with businessmen aimed at persuading them to improve retail trade employment of Negroes. One participant hired three more Negroes after such a conference, and was reported to be willing to employ Negro saleswomen if other stores did so as well.[21]

NEGRO EMPLOYMENT GAINS, 1940 TO 1960

Table 10 gives the best figures available on Negro employment in 1940, 1950, and 1960. Unlike those for eleven cities in Table 9, the numbers and proportions shown for 1940, as well as the latter two years, are for Negro rather than all nonwhite employment. A definite increase in Negro employment between 1940 and 1950 can be seen, although it is not possible to distinguish trends among occupational groups. Negro female employment showed the greatest increase, up almost five times in 1950 over 1940 to 20,890, 2.7 percent of the female work force, while overall Negro employment rose from 2.2 to 3.7 percent.

For the selected cities, improvement for Negro workers was also quite evident. Data in Table 11 (which are only generally comparable since they compare nonwhite in 1940 with Negro employment in 1950 and include San Francisco data in the latter years) show a gain from 3.1 to 5.4 percent in total representation, and Negro female employment up to 4.5 percent. These can be considered very real gains since, if anything, inclusion of San Francisco with its relatively low Negro population in 1950 would tend to lower the averages in the absence of gains in other cities.

The Shift to Female Employment

Between 1940 and 1950 the composition of general merchandise store employment changed drastically. Before World War II, women had held just 60 percent of all jobs and Negroes had barely been represented, particularly among women workers.

---

20. Unpublished files of the Massachusetts fair employment commission, 1948.

21. Unpublished files of the New Jersey fair employment comission, 1948.

TABLE 10. *General Merchandise Industry Including Department Stores Employment by Race and Sex United States, 1940, 1950, and 1960*

	All Employees			Male			Female		
	Total	Negro	Percent Negro	Total	Negro	Percent Negro	Total	Negro	Percent Negro
1940	802,640	17,472	2.2	318,173	12,988	4.1	484,467	4,484	0.9
1950	1,138,775	41,908	3.7	370,775	21,018	5.7	768,000	20,890	2.7
1960	1,581,797	78,411	5.0	498,061	34,885	7.0	1,083,756	43,526	4.0

Source: *U.S. Census of Population:*

1940: Vol. III, *The Labor Force,* Part 1, United States Summary, Table 76.

1950: Vol. II, *Characteristics of the Population,* Part 1, United States Summary, Table 133.

1960: PC(1) 1D, *United States Summary, Detailed Characteristics,* Table 213.

TABLE 11. General Merchandise Industry Including Department Stores
Employment by Race and Sex
Twelve Cities, 1940, 1950, and 1960

Year	All Employees			Male			Female		
	Total	Negro[a]	Percent Negro	Total	Negro[a]	Percent Negro	Total	Negro[a]	Percent Negro
1940[b]	197,675	6,108	3.1	78,162	4,418	5.7	119,513	1,690	1.4
1950	362,817	19,623	5.4	122,736	8,908	7.3	240,081	10,715	4.5
1960	473,267	41,181	8.7	157,785	16,141	10.2	315,482	25,040	7.9

Source: *U.S. Census of Population:*

1940: Vol. III, *The Labor Force*, Parts 2-5, Selected States, Table 17.

1950: Vol. II, *Characteristics of the Population*, State Volumes, Table 83.

1960: PC(1) D, *Detailed Characteristics*, State Volumes, Table 129.

Note: Cities are listed in Table 1. San Francisco omitted in 1940.

[a] Nonwhite in 1940.

[b] Does not include limited price variety stores.

Women gained over 280,000 department store jobs in the country as a whole during the war years, while male employment remained nearly stable, so by 1950 there were over twice as many women as men in the industry (Table 10).

Negro employment, particularly among women, grew faster than white employment, and as a result Negro women's share of female employment increased to 2.7 percent. The census figures *from 1940 – 1960* in Table 10, although not broken down by occupation, must reflect to some degree the efforts to gain sales positions for Negro women which accompanied the fair employment laws enacted by northeastern states during the latter half of the 1940's.

The heavy and increasing reliance on women can be attributed to basic labor market conditions and wage developments during the period which weakened the competitive position of low wage general merchandise stores. The dramatic change in the ratio of Negro female to Negro male employees since 1940 is not so easily explained. The relatively low level of Negro and other nonwhite female employment in general merchandise stores in 1940 may be traced to the following forces: (1) exclusion of Negroes from some predominantly female white collar jobs; (2) preference for males in most nonclerical jobs; and (3) access to an adequate supply of nonwhite male labor, in part due to the existence of racial discrimination elsewhere in the labor market and particularly in high wage industries and jobs.

Whereas in 1940 Negro males held far more jobs in the industry than Negro females, their proportions were about equal in 1950, and the female segment had clearly become dominant by 1960, although the Negro employment still was not nearly so heavily female as was total employment. The shift in the sex structure of Negro employment toward conformity with the sex structure of total employment between 1940 and 1960 may be traced to a weakening of two factors mentioned above: the exclusion of Negroes from female sales positions and the adequacy of the Negro male blue collar labor supply. The very slow rate of this shift, however, indicates that there was no dramatic change in the industry's acceptance of Negro female labor.

Total Employment by 1960

Census data make it possible to assess the position of Negroes in general merchandise stores on the eve of the decade of intensified civil rights and equal employment opportunity activities. Total employment as well as figures on the selected cities and statistics on occupational distributions all show decided improvement in the twenty years from 1940 to 1960. The changes were, however, neither uniformly distributed among occupations and between sexes, nor did they result in bringing Negro employment into parity with white employment by 1960.

As Table 10 shows, Negro employment in the general merchandise industry stood at 5 percent of the total in 1960; in absolute numbers, Negro employment increased almost 350 percent while total employment grew by 97 percent between 1940 and 1960. Although Negro female employment grew more rapidly than that of Negro men, the female segment still lagged behind in 1960, making up only 4.0 percent of the female work force compared to Negro men's 7.0 percent share. By 1960, women made up 68.5 percent of all employment; Negro women only 55.5 percent of all black employment. Clearly, future improvement would require continued changes in the female empolyment sector.

Occupational Distribution

Only a general comparison is possible of the occupational positions of Negro workers in 1960 over 1940. Table 12 is based on total United States data in 1960, while Table 9 showed distributions in eleven cities. Both, however, are based on nonwhite, rather than Negro employment and therefore represent about 10 percent more minority employment than data on Negroes alone would show. It is probable that data on the twelve cities in 1960, if it were available, would reveal even larger changes in occupational representation since these cities had considerably greater Negro employment in general merchandise stores than the country as a whole.

Negroes increased their representation in both white collar and blue collar occupations between 1940 (Table 9) and 1960 (Table 12). Overall white collar employment stood at 3.1 percent by 1960, and blue collar employment was up to 18.5 percent. Both managerial occupations and sales and clerical work had large numbers of nonwhite workers, but the overall proportion remained extremely small, less than 3.0 percent.

Among blue collar occupations Negroes and other nonwhites had the largest gains in the craftsmen and operatives jobs, but they continued to be overrepresented in service work occupations. Concentration in this category, however, declined. In the 1940 data, 66 percent of all Negro employees were service workers; in 1960, this had declined to 31.8 percent. More Negroes and other

TABLE 12. *General Merchandise Industry Including Department Stores Employment by Race, Sex, and Occupational Group United States, 1960*

Occupational Group	All Employees			Male			Female		
	Total	Nonwhite	Percent Nonwhite	Total	Nonwhite	Percent Nonwhite	Total	Nonwhite	Percent Nonwhite
Officials and managers	224,993	2,782	1.2	153,004	1,929	1.3	71 989	853	1.2
Professionals and technicians	20,694	382	1.8	8,315	183	2.2	12 379	199	1.6
Sales workers	797,604	18,044	2.3	142,113	4,411	3.1	655 491	13,633	2.1
Office and clerical	275,540	19,864	7.2	50,598	6,467	12.8	224 942	13,397	0.6
Total white collar	1,318,831	41,072	3.1	354,030	12,990	3.7	964 801	28,082	2.9
Craftsmen	71,212	4,395	6.2	56,032	3,118	5.6	15 180	1,277	8.4
Operatives	60,839	8,154	13.4	27,455	4,247	15.5	33 384	3,907	11.7
Laborers	30,336	5,036	16.8	26,796	3,733	13.9	3 540	1,353	38.2
Service workers	81,670	27,429	33.6	27,987	13,800	49.3	53,683	13,629	25.4
Total blue collar	244,057	45,064	18.5	138,270	24,898	18.0	105 787	20,166	19.1
Total	1,562,888	86,136	5.5	492,300	37,888	7.7	1,070 588	48,248	4.5

Source: *U.S. Census of Population: 1960*, PC(2) 7A, *Occupational Characteristics*, Table 36.

Note: Negroes accounted for about 90 percent of total nonwhites. Data in Table 10 are based on a 25 percent sample in 1960; data in this table on a 5 percent sample.

nonwhite workers held blue collar jobs than white collar jobs, but in 1960 this reversal of the total employment pattern was confined to the male job sector. Slightly over one-quarter of all Negro women held sales jobs, compared to nearly two-thirds of all women workers.

Negro Employment Concentration

A comparison of Tables 10 and 11 indicates that Negro employment in 1950 and 1960 was heavily concentrated in the twelve cities selected for this study. While less than one-third of total employment in general merchandise stores was in these twelve cities in 1950, close to 50 percent of all Negro employment was located there. By 1960, there was an increase in that concentration. In 1960, slightly less than 30 percent of total employment in general merchandise stores was in these twelve cities, as compared with over 50 percent of total Negro employment in the industry. Proportionally, Negro men held 10.2 percent of male jobs in 1960 in the twelve cities, and Negro women, although still behind, held 7.9 percent of jobs among females, as compared with 7.0 and 4.0 percent, respectively, on a national basis.

Negro population shifted during the twenty years following 1940. With the exception of two cities in the South, the urban areas studied experienced something in excess of a doubling of Negro population as a percentage of total population between 1940 and 1960. Thus, while Negro employment in general merchandise stores in the cities studied grew significantly in absolute and relative terms, this growth exceeded only slightly the absolute and relative growth of Negro population in the relevant retail and labor markets and was insufficient to alter dramatically the historical discrepancy between Negro employment as a percentage of total employment and Negro population as a percentage of total population.

It is difficult to determine the exact relationship between expanding Negro employment in urban general merchandise stores and increasing Negro population in urban areas. In all of the firms and divisions studied, managers were very aware of the fact that they had faced an increasingly Negro supply of labor since World War II, particularly in downtown stores. In many of these firms and divisions, managers also expressed an early realization that their clientele was also becoming increasingly Negro. Few of these managers, however, indicated the existence of any clear institutional commitment to this emerging Negro market before 1960. Thus, it seems likely that the absolute and relative growth of Negro employment in the industry was more a reflection of the labor market impact of changing urban residential patterns than of the product market considerations.

Summary of National Trends

Clearly there were significant changes in racial employment patterns over the two decades from 1940 to 1960. In the department store industry, the opening of white collar jobs to Negroes was a two-step process. In virtually all of the firms and divisions studied, Negroes were placed in clerical jobs before they appeared in sales positions. Although the pattern of introduction of Negroes into white collar jobs was remarkably uniform within the sample, there was considerable variation with respect to the timing of the patern. In a few cases, Negroes occupied clerical and sales positions prior to 1940 while in another limited set of cases Negroes had not been granted complete access to white collar jobs by 1960. In general, however, the process of introducing Negroes into white collar jobs began in the late 1940's and was completed in the late 1950's. Most of the firms and divisions studied reported that the first Negro clerical worker had been hired sometime between 1948 and 1955 and the first Negro sales worker between 1955 and 1960.

The breakdown of barriers to the entry of Negroes into clerical jobs in the urban segment of the department store industry appears to have been primarily the result of labor market forces. Generally increasing demand for clerical labor in the cities coupled with the migration of the white middle class to the suburbs weakened the ability of low wage department stores to attract and retain an adequate supply of white clerical workers and, therefore, their ability to ignore the growing supply of Negro labor.

The breakdown of barriers to the entry of Negroes into sales positions was a more complex phenomenon. To some extent, the same labor market forces which were instrumental in the opening of clerical jobs to Negroes also operated in the sales area. There is, however, evidence that product market forces were an important, if not crucial, factor in the acceptance of Negroes in the sales area. In most of the firms and divisions studied, the managers interviewed made reference to earlier problems in rationalizing an all-white sales force given an increasingly Negro clientele and clerical labor force. These problems were sufficient in most cases to induce firms to upgrade some of their more experienced Negro service workers into sales positions. In a surprising number of firms such upgrading decisions were forced and/or facilitated by the installation of automatic elevators and the consequent displacement of long service Negro employees who had considerable customer contact experience.

The importance of fair employment commission activities and civil rights pressures cannot be overlooked in this process. State and local fair employment commissions continued to investigate complaints, initiate reviews, and undertake other efforts to improve Negro department store employment throughout the 1950's.

REGIONAL AND LOCATIONAL VARIATIONS, 1940 TO 1960

Negro employment in northern cities increased at a much faster rate than in other areas during the period between 1940 and 1960. This, of course, coincided with a period of extensive Negro migration to northern cities and white movement to suburban areas. Population trends alone, however, cannot account for the growth in Negro employment, nor did they influence the shifts in occupational distribution of Negro employees in all cities during this period. Employment in these cities by regional group are presented in Table 13.

Northeastern Cities

In general, the firms and divisions studied in New York, Pittsburgh, and Philadelphia reported relatively early use of Negroes in both clerical and sales positions, although there was considerable dispersion among those firms and their divisions. In New York City, some Negroes occupied clerical and sales jobs in a number of firms by 1940, although generally the first introduction of Negroes into these positions came during and after World War II.

Gimbel's reportedly "broke with tradition" when it hired 750 Negroes during the war.[22] Another study of Negro workers in New York at this time reported employment discrimination in department and retail stores, as well as in a number of other

22. H. D. Block, "Discrimination Against the Negro in Employment in New York," *American Journal of Economics and Sociology*, Vol. 24 (October 1965), p. 372.

TABLE 13. General Merchandise Industry Including Department Stores
Employment by Race, Sex, and Region
Twelve Cities, 1940, 1950, and 1960

Region		All Employees			Male			Female		
		Total	Negro[a]	Percent Negro	Total	Negro[a]	Percent Negro	Total	Negro[a]	Percent Negro
Northeast	1940[b]	88,402	2,132	2.4	37,171	1,645	4.4	51,231	487	1.0
	1950	143,981	7,958	5.5	52,762	3,752	7.1	91,219	4,206	4.6
	1960	172,350	16,239	9.4	60,020	6,807	11.3	112,330	9,432	8.4
Border	1940[b]	25,045	1,792	7.2	9,395	1,353	14.4	15,650	439	2.8
	1950	43,339	3,987	9.2	13,389	1,995	14.9	29,950	1,992	6.7
	1960	50,377	5,974	11.9	14,373	2,583	18.0	36,004	3,391	9.4
South	1940[b]	6,511	644	9.9	2,325	492	21.2	4,185	152	3.6
	1950	16,484	1,440	8.7	5,270	853	16.2	11,214	587	5.2
	1960	27,177	3,150	11.6	9,444	1,773	18.8	17,733	1,377	7.8
Midwest	1940[b]	63,747	1,091	1.7	24,297	607	2.5	39,450	484	1.2
	1950	97,585	4,636	4.8	32,498	1,529	4.7	65,087	3,107	4.8
	1960	128,369	12,222	9.5	44,153	3,482	7.9	84,703	8,740	10.3
West	1940[b]	13,970	449	3.2	4,974	321	6.5	8,996	128	1.4
	1950	61,428	1,602	2.6	18,817	779	4.1	42,611	823	1.9
	1960	94,494	3,596	3.8	29,785	1,496	5.0	64,709	2,100	3.2

Source: *U.S. Census of Population:*
1940: Vol. III, *The Labor Force,* Parts 2-5, Selected States, Table 17.
1950: Vol. II, *Characteristics of the Population,* State Volumes, Table 83.
1960: PC(1)-D, *Detailed Characteristics,* State Volumes, Table 129.

[a] Nonwhite in 1940.

[b] Does not include limited price variety stores.

industries, but noted that "a few of the large [department and retail stores] have recently begun employing Negroes as stock and sales persons." [23] An Urban League report in 1946, following up on its efforts to increase department store hiring of Negroes, found Negro sales workers in 9 of 17 New York City and Brooklyn department and apparel stores and Negro clerical workers in 10.[24]

The early and continuing work of the New York State Commission Against Discrimination (later the Commission for Human Rights) in investigating complaints against and studying the status of Negroes in department stores in New York City deserves special attention. Although industry representatives deny that the work of these commissions had any real impact on minority group employment policies or practices over the 1940-1960 period, their activities hardly went unnoticed. While investigating 81 verified complaints against New York City department stores between 1945 and 1963, the commission made inquiries into broad employment policies and practices to assess possible discriminatory activities. These, together with the conduct of a full-scale study of Negro employment in the industry in the 1950's, may have played an important role in the following changes in the range of numbers of Negroes in sales positions in Manhattan department stores: [25]

1945-1950 period	5-12
Early 1950's	7-40
Late 1950's	9-100
1963	10-200

Firms in Philadelphia reported that Negroes were holding sales and clerical positions by 1950 and those in Pittsburgh indicated that this same development occurred there in the mid-1950's. In most of the firms and divisions studied, management indicated that once historical barriers were broken the combination of civil rights climate and changing residential patterns produced a substantial inflow of Negroes into white collar jobs. By 1960, Negro representation in clerical and sales positions in

---

23. Warren M. Banner, "Profiles: New York" in "The Negro in the North During Wartime," *Journal of Educational Sociology*, Vol. 17 (January 1944), p. 273

24. National Urban League, "Integration of Negroes in Department Stores," New York, July 1946, mimeo, pp. 1-3.

25. Confidential study in the author's possession.

urban department stores in the Northeast probably exceeded the industry average by a significant margin. This differential, however, did not extend to managerial positions in white collar areas as none of the firms and divisions studied reported Negroes in such positions prior to 1960.

The migration of Negroes into the northeastern cities coupled with the movement of department stores to the suburbs of these cities fostered relatively rapid change in Negro representation in blue collar and service jobs. In the cities, Negro employment in these occupational categories increased with increasing Negro employment, while in the suburbs these jobs were filled primarily by whites. On balance, the concentration of craftsman, operative, and laborer jobs in downtown stores and central city warehouse operations produced a net increase in Negro representation in such jobs, while the greater dispersion of service jobs produced stability or decline in Negro representation in these occupations.

Border Cities

Baltimore, St. Louis, and Washington, D.C. showed a higher relative level of Negro employment in general merchandise stores in both 1940 and 1960 than did all cities combined but a lower rate of growth in absolute or relative Negro employment over the period than the average for all cities. The difference in level of total Negro employment correlates with the generally higher percentage of Negro population in these cities as compared with all but the southern cities. The rate of growth in absolute and relative Negro employment, however, cannot be traced to a slower rate of growth in Negro population percentage in these cities than in all twelve cities. Over the 1940-1960 period, all of the border cities experienced an approximate doubling of Negro population as a percentage of total population. This is about equal to the change in Negro employment as a percentage of total employment in general merchandise stores.

The pattern of overall Negro employment growth in general merchandise stores in the border cities suggests the existence of some restrictions on Negro employment opportunities. According to Mrs. Green's study of Washington, D.C., the largest downtown retail businesses did not undertake even token hiring of Negroes until 1957. This event followed a one-day boycott organized by a volunteer Committee for Equal Employment Opportunities.[26]

In most of the firms and divisions studied in the three border cities, Negroes first appeared in clerical jobs after 1955 and in sales positions between 1958 and 1960. Thus, it appears that in these cities Negro employment remained heavily concentrated in blue collar and service jobs throughout the 1940-1960 period. These developments are clearly consistent with the cultural context in which the firms operated as indicated by the existence of racially segregated restrooms and employee cafeterias in some department stores in these cities as late as 1960.

Southern Cities

The level of Negro employment in general merchandise stores over the 1940-1960 period in Atlanta and Houston was closely correlated with the relative size of the Negro population in those cities, as was the case in the border cities. In both 1940 and 1960, a comparatively large percentage of all employees in general merchandise stores in the two cities was Negro, but the rate of increase in this percentage over the period was comparatively low. This pattern conforms almost perfectly with the pattern of Negro population as a percentage of total population in these cities, although the absolute level of the two percentages were markedly different.

It is also interesting that the southern cities were the only ones to show a majority of males among total Negro employment in 1960. This phenomenon could well have been a reflection of some basic difference between the southern cities and the other cities in the occupational and/or industrial structure of Negro employment opportunities. There is, however, strong evidence from the firms and divisions studied that it is also, at least in part, a reflection of barriers to the entry of Negroes into primarily female white collar jobs. None of these firms or divisions reported that their first Negro clerical or sales worker had assumed such a position before 1960. Thus, it is clear that Negro employment in department stores in the southern cities, as in the border cities, remained concentrated in relatively low skill blue collar jobs throughout the 1940-1960 period. Cultural forces and customer and employee attitudes dictated or facilitated the

26. Constance McLaughlin Green, *The Secret City* (Princeton: Princeton University Press, 1967), p. 315.

emergence and preservation of this pattern of Negro employment.

Midwestern Cities

In general, both the level and the pattern of Negro employment in general merchandise and department stores over the 1940-1960 period in the midwestern cities, Chicago and Detroit, developed along much the same lines as they did in the north-eastern cities. In both cases, Negro employment in general merchandise stores grew in absolute and relative terms faster than the average for all cities and faster than the rate of growth of Negro population as a percentage of total population within the individual cities over the 1940-1960 period, although in neither case did such growth result in proportional Negro representation by 1960. In the midwestern cities, as in the northeastern cities, Negroes had been accepted into both clerical and sales positions in most department stores by the mid-1950's and were relatively well represented in all but managerial positions by 1960.

Females have consistently accounted for a relatively high percentage of total Negro employment in the midwestern cities in comparison to the other regional combinations of cities, and by 1960 Negro women accounted for a higher percentage of total Negro employment than the female proportion in the total general merchandise store work force. One possible basis for this phenomenon is Negro male access to high wage job opportunities in manufacturing plants during much or all of this period. This hypothesis receives some implicit support from the fact that Detroit showed an earlier majority of women among Negro employees than did Chicago. This suggests that labor market forces may have played a somewhat more important role in Negro employment progress in this region than was the case in the northeastern cities. At the same time, however, there is also evidence that some of the firms in these two cities were sensitive and responsive to the growing market potential of the Negro industrial worker prior to 1960.

Western Cities

The two western cities, Los Angeles and San Francisco, provide a third distinct pattern in the growth of Negro employment in general merchandise stores. Census and/or interview data for the two western cities indicate that Negroes were already well represented in most occupational categories in general merchandise stores, in relation to their representation in the total population, in 1940 and had been placed in both clerical and sales jobs in most department stores before 1950. Since 1940, Negro employment in general merchandise stores has grown in both absolute and relative terms, but this growth has not kept pace with the growth of Negro population in either of the two cities between 1940 and 1960. Information gained in interviews suggests that much of the overall growth in Negro employment in department stores over the 1940-1960 period was accounted for by an expansion in the number and percentage of Negroes in blue collar jobs, rather than in white collar occupations as found in the midwestern and northeastern cities.

The early proportional representation of Negroes and acceptance of Negroes in white collar jobs in department stores in the western cities may be attributed to a complex set of economic, social, and institutional forces. Both cities were characterized by tight labor markets during the 1940's. The pressure generated by such a market appears to have been sufficient to overcome any discriminatory tendencies. In part, this was possible because discriminatory tendencies were neither particularly strong nor deeply entrenched in these cities for the following reasons: (1) Negroes were not the only or the largest minority group; and (2) some of the larger department stores in these cities were new and affiliated with firms and divisions elsewhere which had already accepted Negroes into white collar positions.

The subsequent rate and pattern of growth of Negro employment in general merchandise and department stores in these cities was heavily influenced by demographic factors. The rapid and continuing influx of population created a large supply of both white and Negro labor seeking temporary or transitory employment. At the same time, the increasing geographic dispersion of population coupled with the relatively complete dominance of private transportation in these cities served to limit Negro access to employment opportunities in department stores. This access limitation was more pronounced in the western cities than in the northeastern or midwestern cities because fewer of the department store firms operating in the western cities had opened neighborhood stores prior to the influx of Negro population into the cities.

INSTITUTIONAL VARIABLES

Throughout the analysis of national and regional Negro employment patterns, reference consistently has been made to variations among the firms and divisions studied. Two institutional variables have been suggested as possible bases for such variations: the scope and structure of the firm and the market position and image of the operating division. There is some evidence that both of these institutional factors were related to the establishment and evolution of racial employment policies in urban department stores over the 1940-1960 period, although the nature of this relationship was far more complex than originally anticipated.

Impact of Corporate Scope and Structure

The major department store chain companies, operating stores across the country under a company name, did not lead the industry in the employment and upgrading of Negro employees, as might have been expected on the basis of their size and geographic scope. Furthermore, there is little evidence of the uniformity among chain store units in different cities with respect to Negro employment patterns or practices over the 1940-1960 period which might have been expected given the comparatively centralized management structure of these firms.

The failure of the national chains to lead the industry in the adoption of nondiscriminatory employment policies or to enforce rigorously or encourage adherence to those policies at the unit level, once they were adopted, can be traced to the visibility and dispersion of these firms. In combination, these factors appear to have led corporate management to conclude that a strong stand in the civil rights area would have a strong and immediate adverse impact on total sales. This perception was based, at least in part, on the heavy concentration of chain store units and sales —including catalogue sales—outside major urban centers.

The companies which operated as national federations generally preceded the major chains in the adoption and enforcement of nondiscriminatory employment policies. Considerable regional variation did exist among divisions of federations with respect to the timing of the introduction of Negroes into clerical and sales positions—as would be expected given the managerial structure of these firms—but, in most of the cities studied, divisions of national federations tended to lead other firms in the introduction of Negroes into sales positions.

The willingness of the national federations to take a relatively early positive stand on minority group employment can be traced to two basic differences between federations and chains. First, unlike the chains, the headquarters and/or major divisions of many federations were located in New York or San Francisco where social, political, and economic forces had early forced or induced the introduction of Negroes into white collar positions. Second, the decentralized structure of these firms coupled with their reliance on locally known trade names reduced their visibility and, thereby, the geographic extent of any expected market repercussions of changes in racial employment policies. These locational and/or anonymity variables, of course, differed among the various federations and tended to "explain" variations among them in the extent of positive corporate pressure for change in racial employment policies and practices at the divisional level. Differences among divisions of the same federation and among divisions of different federations in the same region regarding the timing of major changes in Negro employment practices can also be attributed to the relative strength of the locational and visibility factors.

The racial employment policies and practices of independent local firms displayed the expected sensitivity to community mores and attitudes. In the northern cities, the emergence of nondiscriminatory employment policies and the introduction of Negroes into white collar and particularly sales positions tended to lead slightly or to coincide with similar action by divisional units of federations. In other areas, changes in Negro employment policies and practices in local firms tended to lag slightly or coincide with action by federation divisions.

Impact of Market Position and Image

Among local firms, carriage trade stores generally appear to have employed fewer Negroes in both 1940 and 1960 and to have been slower to place Negroes in clerical and particularly sales positions than the regional averages for all local firms. To a slightly lesser extent, the same was true for carriage trade divisions of federations relative to other divisions of the same and similar firms.

This pattern may have been a function of either labor market or product market forces. Many of the managers of carriage trade stores indicated a historical "deficiency" in the number of Negro job applicants in their units which they attributed to the fact that Negroes did not or could not shop in their stores. A few of the managers of carriage trade stores attributed low Negro employment to fear of an adverse customer reaction. Many more suggested that this fear had been a major concern in the decision to place the first Negro in a sales position. They generally indicated that great care has been taken in the selection of both the individual and the sales department for the "breakthrough," and that top management had been "surprised" at the relatively limited customer reaction to this move. Overall, it appears that the real and imagined biases of customers and the self image of carriage trade stores made such stores unwilling to assume any leadership role in the area of Negro employment, while their ability to attract white labor and/or inability to attract Negro labor on the basis of market image prevented them from being forced into such a role.

In most of the cities studied, a moderate price store, either a local company or division of a national federation, was the first to introduce Negroes into sales positions. Such stores were the only ones to have Negro sales personnel in a significant range of sales departments by 1960. This pattern was a direct reflection of the fact that it was this type of store which experienced the greatest reduction in market scope and the greatest change in labor supply structure as the white middle class moved to the suburbs. In the moderate price stores studied, there was substantial explicit and implicit evidence that Negro employment policies and practices were regarded as important variables in market strategy in the central city and that racial policies were liberalized to the point of active recruiting and remedial training in the hope of attracting a large Negro clientele.

Budget stores might have been expected to have been the first to utilize large numbers of Negroes in a wide range of positions on the basis of both product market and labor market forces. In fact, they did not occupy this position and displayed Negro employment patterns which suggest greater discriminatory barriers than existed in carriage trade stores, particularly with respect to sales positions. Budget stores, including units of the major chains, employed large numbers of Negroes in blue collar positions in 1940 and showed no significant lag in introducing them into clerical jobs in most of the cities studied. In chain stores and particularly in local budget stores, however, the movement of Negroes into sales positions came well after second line stores had taken this step and, in some cities, only after carriage stores also had taken this step.

This pattern is a reflection of a complex set of economic and sociological forces. Economically, budget stores did not experience as great a decline in white clientele or supply of labor as did second line stores due to the concentration of their clientele in the lower middle class and upper lower class groups not much a part of the early flight to the suburbs. Sociologically, the "white working class" population from which these stores drew their customers and workers was felt to be and, in some cases, was proved to be extremely hostile to Negroes. This perceived or real hostility appears to have been a sufficiently strong factor in managerial decision making to have counterbalanced or outweighed the rapidly increasing sales potential of the Negro market. This is not surprising, however, in light of the fact that budget stores could expect an increasing Negro market regardless of their employment policies, by virtue of their relative prices and/or greater number of neighborhood stores.

CHAPTER IV

Negro Employment in the 1960's

Two basic forces shaped Negro employment policies and patterns in general merchandise and department stores in the 1960's —the civil rights revolution and the changing locational structure of industry employment within urban areas. Civil rights activity and legislation directly and/or indirectly influenced employment policies in this highly visible and volume oriented segment of retail trade. The increasing concentration of industry employment outside the boundaries of the major cities, however, tended to limit the overall impact of policy changes stemming from economic, political, or legal pressures for equal opportunity or equal employment on Negro employment patterns.

During the first half of the 1960's, both civil rights pressure and locational structure were strong forces, but civil rights pressure was dominant. The net result was a slight acceleration in the basic historical trends in growth of Negro employment in the industry through the mid-1960's, despite the emergence of an increasingly sharp dichotomy between the urban and suburban segments of the industry with respect to Negro employment. Later in the decade, both forces intensified, but locational change became dominant. The enhanced civil rights pressures generated by the Civil Rights Act of 1964 and the riots of 1965-1968 coupled with tight labor market conditions resulted in a further acceleration of the established trend toward liberalization of industry Negro employment policies. At the same time, however, the continued decline in central city retail activity and shift of industry sales to the suburbs coupled with greater reliance on part-time labor in the suburbs resulted in an absolute decline in industry employment in major cities and a further dichotomization of the industry. The net result by the end of the decade was a retardation in the rate of growth in Negro employment coincident with increasing Negro representation in higher level positions.

GENERAL MERCHANDISE EMPLOYMENT, 1966, 1967, AND 1969

Table 14 presents employment data from the Equal Employment Opportunity Commission for the United States and for twelve selected metropolitan areas for the middle and late 1960's. These data, from general merchandise companies with 100 or more employees, cover all but the smallest independent local firms in the industry. Although some sampling variations from year to year affect comparability, it is felt that these data give a fairly accurate picture of total and Negro employment in general merchandise stores during this period.

Employment Growth and Decline

Only a general comparison with census data for earlier years is possible, since census data cover a much larger group of workers than EEOC data. Such a comparison indicates that Negroes had experienced both absolute and relative growth in general merchandise store employment by the mid-1960's, during a period of increasing total employment. Negro employment in 1960 stood at 5.0 percent according to the census; by 1966 the EEOC data revealed 7.4 percent Negro employment for the United States as a whole among larger employers. In the twelve cities, where Negro employment was consistently higher than United States averages in 1940, 1950, and 1960, Negroes made up 12.3 percent of the work force in 1966.

Total and Negro employment grew between 1966 and 1967 in both the United States as a whole and in the twelve cities, with Negro employment growing at a more rapid rate. By 1967, Negro men comprised 9.7 percent of the male work force in the United States, 13.8 percent in the twelve metropolitan areas; and Negro women held 6.9 percent of total female jobs, 12.5 percent of jobs in the twelve metropolitan areas.

Between 1967 and 1969, employment in the industry began to decline. Negro employment generally kept pace with the decline, rather than being disproportionately affected. In the twelve-city group, however, Negro females experienced a greater than average drop in employment, while Negro males did not lose as many jobs as white males and actually increased their proportion by 0.1 percentage point. The vital importance of Negro female employment is evident, since the net result of these opposite trends

TABLE 14. *General Merchandise Industry Including Department Stores Employment by Race and Sex United States and Twelve Metropolitan Areas, 1966, 1967, and 1969*

Year	All Employees			Male			Female		
	Total	Negro	Percent Negro	Total	Negro	Percent Negro	Total	Negro	Percent Negro
United States									
1966	1,456,624	108,024	7.4	484,856	45,939	9.5	971,768	62,085	6.4
1967	1,319,729	126,653	7.8	539,709	52,115	9.7	1,080,020	74,538	6.9
1969	1,553,610	121,381	7.8	521,843	50,540	9.7	1,031,767	70,841	6.9
Twelve Metropolitan Areas									
1966[a]	487,538	59,774	12.3	n.a.	n.a.	n.a.	n.a.	n.a.	n.a.
1967	562,699	72,868	12.9	193,471	26,755	13.8	369,228	46,113	12.5
1969	505,344	62,806	12.4	173,069	24,011	13.9	332,275	38,795	11.7

Source: Appendix Tables A-1—A-6.

Note: Cities are listed in Table 1.

[a] Including Pittsburgh and San Francisco-Oakland. See note, Appendix Table A-4.

was a drop in total Negro employment proportion in these cities from a 1967 high of 12.9 percent to 12.4 percent in 1969.

Occupational Change

Negro workers in general merchandise stores experienced the same occupational restrictions in the late 1960's as had characterized their employment in the 1940's and 1950's. As Table 15 shows, fully 79 percent of all employees were in white collar jobs, while the black work force was almost equally distributed between white and blue collar occupations. Negro women's occupational status was far closer to the norm than that of their male counterparts, but still only 66.7 percent were in white collar occupations compared to 87.1 percent of all female workers. The occupational distribution of Negro males was almost the exact opposite of that of the whole male work force: 27.5 percent

TABLE 15. *General Merchandise Industry Including*
Department Stores
Percent Distribution of Employment by Race, Sex, and
Occupational Group
United States, 1969

Occupational Group	All Employees		Male		Female	
	Total	Negro	Total	Negro	Total	Negro
Officials and managers	11.7	3.6	23.2	5.5	5.9	2.3
Professionals	0.9	0.3	1.7	0.5	0.5	0.2
Technicians	0.7	0.5	1.6	0.8	0.3	0.2
Sales workers	46.5	27.9	29.6	13.4	55.0	38.2
Office and clerical	19.2	18.1	6.9	7.3	25.4	25.8
Total white collar	79.0	50.4	63.0	27.5	87.1	66.7
Craftsmen	3.1	2.5	7.7	4.3	0.8	1.3
Operatives	5.4	10.2	10.4	17.0	2.8	5.4
Laborers	3.9	10.4	7.8	16.3	1.9	6.1
Service workers	8.6	26.5	11.1	34.9	7.4	20.5
Total blue collar	21.0	49.6	37.0	72.5	12.9	33.3
Total	100.0	100.0	100.0	100.0	100.0	100.0

Source: Computed from Appendix Table A-3.

white collar and 72.5 percent blue collar, compared to 63.0 percent and 37.0 percent, respectively, for all men in the industry.

On a national basis, there is surprisingly little evidence of any significant increase in Negro representation in the more skilled white collar or blue collar jobs. Although a relatively high 5.5 percent of Negro men were in official and managerial positions, the occupation with the heaviest concentration continued to be service work, followed by operative and laborer occupations. Negro women were most concentrated in sales (38.2 percent), clerical (25.8 percent), and service (20.5 percent) occupations.

Table 16 presents the percentage Negro employment situation in all large general merchandise companies for 1966, 1967, and 1969. Table 17 shows the similar pattern occurring at higher levels of employment for the twelve selected metropolitan areas.

Overall, the general merchandise data for 1966, 1967, and 1969 indicate a heavy, though decreasing, overrepresentation of Negroes in blue collar jobs similar to that found in earlier years. They also show some significant increases in Negro white collar employment during this period.

Except among office and clerical workers, Negro employment proportions increased in each white collar occupational group both in the country as a whole and in the twelve selected cities between 1966 and 1969. Negro female officials and managers in the twelve cities had reached 4.8 percent of this category by the end of the decade, an unusually high proportion in any industry. Their only losses were among office and clerical workers, where they declined to 13.3 percent from a 1966 high of 15.6 percent in cities (Table 17). Negro women lost blue collar positions, proportionately, in all occupations except laborers both in the twelve cities and in the country as a whole. Negro men increased their employment proportions in general merchandise store occupations in every group except service workers in the nation as a whole (Table 16) and in every group except laborers and service workers in the twelve cities studied (Table 17).

DEPARTMENT STORE SAMPLE, 1966 TO 1968

Survey data on the department stores studied in twelve cities, presented in Table 18, reveal a slightly lower total Negro percentage representation in department stores than in all general

TABLE 16. *General Merchandise Industry Including Department Stores*
Percent Negro Employment by Sex and Occupational Group
United States, 1966, 1967, and 1969

Occupational Group	All Employees			Male			Female		
	1966	1967	1969	1966	1967	1969	1966	1967	1969
Officials and managers	1.4	1.7	2.4	1.3	1.6	2.3	1.5	1.8	2.7
Professionals	1.5	1.9	2.6	1.6	2.0	2.6	1.3	1.9	2.7
Technicians	3.0	3.5	5.1	2.7	3.5	5.1	3.5	3.5	5.2
Sales workers	3.3	3.6	4.7	2.8	3.3	4.4	3.4	3.6	4.8
Office and clerical	7.4	8.2	7.4	8.8	9.9	10.3	7.3	8.0	7.0
Total white collar	4.0	4.5	5.0	2.9	3.4	4.2	4.4	4.8	5.3
Craftsmen	5.6	5.7	6.3	4.3	4.7	5.4	12.1	10.6	10.4
Operatives	14.8	16.1	14.9	14.5	15.3	15.8	15.3	17.6	13.2
Laborers	19.1	21.2	21.0	18.8	20.1	20.3	19.7	23.1	22.3
Service workers	26.2	25.2	24.1	34.5	32.8	30.4	19.9	19.7	19.2
Total blue collar	19.1	19.4	18.5	19.6	19.5	19.0	18.4	19.3	17.8
Total	7.4	7.8	7.8	9.5	9.7	9.7	6.4	6.9	6.9

Source: Appendix Tables A-1—A-3.

TABLE 17. *General Merchandise Industry Including Department Stores*
Percent Negro Employment by Sex and Occupational Group
Twelve Metropolitan Areas, 1966, 1967, and 1969

Occupational Group	All Employees			Male			Female		
	1966a	1967	1969	1966	1967	1969	1966	1967	1969
Officials and managers	2.4	2.8	4.2	2.1	2.7	3.9	2.9	2.9	4.8
Professionals	1.2	2.1	3.2	1.2	2.3	3.0	1.1	1.7	3.5
Technicians	3.9	4.4	8.2	3.3	4.6	8.0	5.2	3.9	8.6
Sales workers	5.8	6.1	7.6	4.8	5.5	6.7	6.1	6.3	7.9
Office and clerical	15.1	15.2	13.6	12.0	13.3	15.3	15.6	15.5	13.3
Total white collar	7.7	8.3	8.7	4.8	5.5	6.9	9.3	9.4	9.4
Craftsmen	9.3	8.6	8.7	7.4	7.0	8.2	8.8	15.2	11.2
Operatives	22.8	23.7	21.2	20.2	21.5	21.4	26.6	27.6	20.8
Laborers	28.3	23.3	29.1	28.3	26.4	26.7	28.4	30.8	32.8
Service workers	36.2	34.1	33.0	43.5	39.8	40.2	30.1	29.3	27.1
Total blue collar	26.1	26.8	25.8	26.7	25.5	25.7	28.2	28.6	26.1
Total	12.3	12.9	12.4	14.1	13.8	13.9	12.4	12.5	11.7

Source: Appendix Tables A-4—A-6.

a Twelve metropolitan areas used in total white collar, blue collar, and total. Individual occupational groups based on ten metropolitan areas, excluding Pittsburgh and San Francisco. Cities are listed in Table 1.

TABLE 18. *Department Store Industry*
Employment by Race and Sex
Sample Companies
Twelve Metropolitan Areas, 1966, 1967, 1968

Year	All Employees			Male				Female		
	Total	Negro	Percent Negro	Total	Negro	Percent Negro	Total	Negro	Percent Negro
1966	316,417	37,972	12.0	111,690	15,163	13.6	204,727	22,809	11.1
1967	310,272	36,861	11.9	108,523	14,950	13.8	201,749	21,911	10.9
1968	293,333	36,191	12.3	102,255	14,839	14.5	191,078	21,352	11.2

Source: Data in author's possession.

Note: Employment totals vary in part because of lack of comparability in sample groups over the three years. See Tables 25 and 26 for 1967-1968 matched samples. Cities are listed in Table 1.

merchandise stores, which could be traced to a lower percentage representation of Negro females in these stores. This pattern appears to reflect two forces: (1) department stores generally attracted a larger supply of white female labor than did the other major types of general merchandise stores—limited price variety stores and discount houses—by virtue of their better market image and greater concentration outside the city; and (2) department stores were more "selective" and "appearance conscious" in hiring than were other general merchandise stores due to their greater service orientation and concern for customer relations.

Employment Decline

Between 1966 and 1968, total employment in the department stores studied declined from over 315,000 to about 300,000. Over the same period, total Negro employment in those stores also declined in absolute numbers but grew slightly in relative terms. Coincident with these overall changes in total employment were some equally significant changes in the sex structure of employment. In general, there was a more than proportionate drop in total male employment in the stores studied, as would be expected given the low wage status of department stores and the relatively tight labor market conditions prevailing in the major cities over this period. In Negro employment, however, the opposite was the case. Although both total Negro male and total Negro female employment decreased in absolute terms between 1966 and 1968, total Negro male employment decreased much less, down only 2.1 percent compared to 6.4 percent decrease in Negro female employment.

Occupational Distribution, 1968

Occupational data for total and Negro employment in the twelve city department store sample are presented in Table 19. A comparison of the twelve city sample with Negro occupational data on general merchandise stores in these cities reveals white collar employment somewhat below general merchandise averages in 1967 and 1969 and blue collar employment somewhat above that in all general merchandise stores. The latter seems to be due to considerably higher Negro female representation in laborer and service worker occupational groups in department stores—35.7 and 32.9 percent, respectively.

TABLE 19. *Department Store Industry*
Employment by Race, Sex, and Occupational Group
Sample Companies
Twelve Metropolitan Areas, 1968

Occupational Group	All Employees			Male			Female		
	Total	Negro	Percent Negro	Total	Negro	Percent Negro	Total	Negro	Percent Negro
Officials and managers	30,057	746	2.5	18,490	451	2.4	11,567	295	2.6
Professionals	2,074	57	2.7	919	37	4.0	1,155	20	1.7
Technicians	2,405	177	7.4	1,576	117	7.4	829	60	7.2
Sales workers	126,399	8,695	6.9	28,025	1,701	6.1	98,374	6,994	7.1
Office and clerical	62,648	7,633	12.2	8,294	1,070	12.9	54,354	6,563	12.1
Total white collar	223,583	17,308	7.7	57,304	3,376	5.9	166,279	13,932	8.4
Craftsmen	11,066	655	5.9	9,705	560	5.8	1,361	95	7.0
Operatives	18,152	3,910	21.5	13,436	2,921	21.7	4,716	989	21.0
Laborers	15,731	4,993	31.7	9,619	2,809	29.2	6,112	2,184	35.7
Service workers	24,801	9,325	37.6	12,191	5,173	42.4	12,610	4,152	32.9
Total blue collar	69,750	18,883	27.1	44,951	11,463	25.5	24,799	7,420	29.9
Total	293,333	36,191	12.3	102,255	14,839	14.5	191,078	21,352	11.2

Source: Data in author's possession.

Note: Cities are listed in Table 1.

TABLE 20. *Department Store Industry*
Percent Distribution of Employment by Race, Sex,
and Occupational Group
Sample Companies
Twelve Metropolitan Areas, 1968

Occupational Group	All Employees		Male		Female	
	Total	Negro	Total	Negro	Total	Negro
Officials and managers	10.2	2.1	18.1	3.0	6.1	1.4
Professionals	0.7	0.1	0.9	0.3	0.6	0.1
Technicians	0.8	0.5	1.5	0.8	0.4	0.3
Sales workers	43.1	24.0	27.4	11.5	51.5	32.8
Office and clerical	21.4	21.1	8.1	7.2	28.4	30.7
Total white collar	76.2	47.8	56.0	22.8	87.0	65.3
Craftsmen	3.8	1.8	9.5	3.8	0.7	0.4
Operatives	6.2	10.8	13.2	19.7	2.5	4.6
Laborers	5.4	13.8	9.4	18.9	3.2	10.2
Service workers	8.4	25.8	11.9	34.8	6.6	19.5
Total blue collar	23.8	52.2	44.0	77.2	13.0	34.7
Total	100.0	100.0	100.0	100.0	100.0	100.0

Source: Computed from Table 19.

A comparison of percentage distributions of the total and Negro work forces in the department store sample in 1968 (Table 20) with general merchandise stores in 1969 for the United States (Table 15) shows that the department store sample had a slightly lower overall proportion of white collar workers than all general merchandise—76.2 percent compared to 79.0 percent. Given the heavier overall blue collar employment in the department store sample, the Negro work force occupational distribution was almost exactly the same as in general merchandise stores in 1969. Negro workers were slightly more heavily concentrated in clerical (21.1 percent), operative (10.8 percent), and laborer (13.8 percent) positions in the department stores studied than in general merchandise stores as a whole.

LARGE DEPARTMENT STORE COMPANIES, 1969

The most recent and most complete data on Negro department store employment are those from the EEOC for the year 1969. They represent all large department store employers, that is, those with over 100 employees in the company as a whole. These data are presented in Table 21.

Comparison with EEOC general merchandise data the twelve city department store sample indicates very similar patterns of Negro employment in the all department store group. The proportions of Negro employment in each occupational category, however, are somewhat lower than those revealed in earlier data. As Table 21 shows, overall Negro employment stood at 8.1 percent of the total in 1969; by occupations, 5.2 percent of white collar and 19.2 percent of blue collar work.

The lower overall participation rates shown in EEOC data for 1969 are affected by population factors as well as company size factors, since they are based on the entire country including cities with very low Negro populations. A comparison of the 1969 industrywide data with those for selected cities in 1968 indicates that the Negro proportion of upper level white collar occupations and of craftsmen jobs was fairly similar throughout the country, while other occupations were less heavily Negro outside the selected cities. Nationwide, Negroes held quite low proportions of sales and clerical jobs compared to their representation in the 1968 sample stores. Only 4.6 percent of the sales group and 8.2 percent of the clerical group were Negroes in the industry as a whole, while these occupations were 6.9 and 12.2 percent Negro, respectively, in the twelve cities in

TABLE 21. *Department Store Industry*
Employment by Race, Sex, and Occupational Group
3,705 Establishments
United States, 1969

Occupational Group	All Employees			Male			Female		
	Total	Negro	Percent Negro	Total	Negro	Percent Negro	Total	Negro	Percent Negro
Officials and managers	128,079	3,110	2.4	83,924	1,947	2.3	44,155	1,163	2.6
Professionals	12,774	325	2.5	7,779	194	2.5	4,995	129	2.6
Technicians	9,994	516	5.2	7,102	369	5.2	2,892	147	5.1
Sales workers	533,775	24,701	4.6	118,564	5,325	4.5	415,211	19,376	4.7
Office and clerical	234,903	19,254	8.2	28,450	3,126	11.0	206,453	16,128	7.8
Total white collar	919,525	47,904	5.2	245,819	10,961	4.5	673,706	36,943	5.5
Craftsmen	38,508	1,983	5.1	31,805	1,538	4.8	6,703	445	6.6
Operatives	65,446	10,111	15.4	40,767	6,894	16.9	24,379	3,217	13.0
Laborers	45,542	9,855	21.6	30,202	5,973	19.8	15,340	3,882	25.4
Service workers	91,567	24,332	26.5	42,237	13,923	33.0	49,430	10,409	21.1
Total blue collar	241,163	46,281	19.2	145,011	28,328	19.5	96,152	17,953	18.7
Total	1,160,688	94,185	8.1	390,830	39,289	10.1	769,858	54,896	7.1

Source: U.S. Equal Employment Opportunity Commission, 1969.

Note: Companies with 100 or more employees.

1968. This trend was even more pronounced in lower level blue collar occupations, where Negroes trailed from 6.1 to 11.1 percentage points behind in operative, laborer, and service worker representation in the industry nationwide.

The total industry work force was slightly more heavily white collar than the work force in the twelve selected cities. Percentage distributions are presented in Table 22 for comparison with those in Table 20. In the industry as a whole, the male work force was 21.5 percent managerial and 30.3 percent sales, accounting for a significantly greater overall white collar proportion—62.9 percent. Although Negro men were underrepresented in these groups, their proportions were somewhat higher in the industrywide data. In fact, fully 5.0 percent of the male Negro work force was in managerial positions in 1969 (Table 22).

The Negro female work force had a relatively better occupational distribution, more nearly parallel to that of all women workers than was the case among men. Whereas only 27.9 percent of Negro men were in white collar occupations industrywide, 67.3 percent of Negro women held such positions, 35.3 percent in sales work. This would seem to indicate that occupational barriers to Negro women have been greatly reduced in department store work, even though overall they held only 7.1 percent of all female jobs by 1969. Since women dominate the white collar occupations and are much less significant among blue collar jobs, the high proportion of laborer and service worker jobs Negro women held in 1969 did not result in the relatively high overall proportion of jobs which was found among Negro men, who made up 33.0 percent of the 42,237 service workers in 1969 (Table 21).

OCCUPATIONS: THE WHITE COLLAR FRONTIER

Both department store and general merchandise data indicate that the differential rate of Negro movement into the various white collar occupational groups, noted for the 1940-1960 period, continued in the 1960's. During this decade, however, Negroes began to reach the highest levels of employment in the department store industry.

Officials and Managers

Most of the firms studied had Negroes in some first line supervisory positions in predominantly Negro blue collar and serv-

TABLE 22. *Department Store Industry*
Percent Distribution of Employment by Race, Sex,
and Occupational Group
3,705 Establishments
United States, 1969

Occupational Group	All Employees		Male		Female	
	Total	Negro	Total	Negro	Total	Negro
Officials and managers	11.0	3.3	21.5	5.0	5.7	2.1
Professionals	1.1	0.3	2.0	0.5	0.7	0.2
Technicians	0.9	0.6	1.8	0.9	0.4	0.3
Sales workers	46.0	26.2	30.3	13.5	53.9	35.3
Office and clerical	20.2	20.5	7.3	8.0	26.8	29.4
Total white collar	79.2	50.9	62.9	27.9	87.5	67.3
Craftsmen	3.3	2.1	8.2	3.9	0.9	0.8
Operatives	5.7	10.7	10.4	17.6	3.2	5.8
Laborers	3.9	10.5	7.7	15.2	2.0	7.1
Service workers	7.9	25.8	10.8	35.4	6.4	19.0
Total blue collar	20.8	49.1	37.1	72.1	12.5	32.7
Total	100.0	100.0	100.0	100.0	100.0	100.0

Source: Computed from Table 21.

Note: Companies with 100 or more employees.

ice departments prior to 1960. Few firms, however, had experimented with a Negro in a higher level management position or a first line supervisory position in white collar departments before 1960 and virtually none of the firms reported having Negroes in such positions as of 1960. This pattern changed gradually over the first half of the 1960's and rapidly over the 1966-1968 period.

The basic forces underlying change were increasing civil rights pressure in the employment area and increasing competition for the Negro market in the city. The nature of these forces was clearly reflected in the placement of Negroes in highly visible management positions during the early 1960's, as was the case with sales personnel during the 1950's. To a large extent, this pattern persisted after 1965, but was extended to higher level positions and to management positions in all stores.

Despite the "numbers game" aspect of the initial movement of Negroes into managerial ranks, considerable real progress was made during the 1960's. Experience with Negro managers convinced most firms that minority groups represented a potentially valuable pool of managerial talent, particularly in light of the increasing difficulty experienced by many department stores in recruiting and retaining an adequate supply of white management trainees.

Buyers

In the most part, there were no Negro buyers in the department stores studied prior to 1960, although one firm did report having a Negro buyer in the mid-1950's who failed to perform largely because of "rejection" by the market. A majority of the firms studied indicated having their first Negro buyer sometime during the 1960-1965 period. In most cases, the first Negro buyer, like the first Negro sales worker, was in a "bargain basement department," as would be expected given the fact that a perceived knowledge of consumer tastes and merchandise lines gained through experience is a job prerequisite.

There was no significant increase in the total number or departmental spread of Negro buyers in the stores studied following their initial appearance in such jobs. While a few stores reported several Negro buyers, including some in the most prestigious departments, as of 1968, many had none at all or only a few, generally located in lower quality merchandise areas. This phenomenon is not solely a function of management disinterest. The buyer position is a crucial one in the operating success of a store and requires both substantial entrepreneurial ability and long experience. The top managements interviewed were not willing to relax their requirements in this area given the amounts of corporate funds expended by buyers, and were generally of the opinion that existing Negro employees lacked either the ability or experience to quality. In many firms, top management indicated that they had identified one or more Negroes with strong buyer potential, but also indicated a doubt that they could retain those individuals long enough to give them the requisite experience. Several managers cited Negro impatience as one basis for this retention problem and many cited the very active market for Negro buyers which has arisen from widespread efforts to hire established Negro buyers as a long run alternative or short run supplement to internal development efforts.

Sales Workers

By the mid-1960's, Negro sales personnel had been introduced into all sales departments except those with very high service or recurrent sales characteristics, such as home furnishings and high fashion clothing in most urban stores; they were also present in some "selected" departments in suburban stores. This pattern was accentuated in those stores which early decided to bid actively for the Negro market through positive recruitment and placement of Negro sales personnel as part of a larger sales campaign. In some cases this also included advertising in Negro papers and use of Negro manikins in window displays. In most firms, these trends accelerated after the riots of 1965 and this acceleration was reflected in the widespread establishment of internal reporting requirements on Negro employment by unit and department and the emergence of stronger corporate or divisional pressure on unit and department managers to show "adequate" Negro employment representation and to justify any decline in the level of such representation.

Big Ticket Sales

In most firms or divisions, the "big ticket" departments were the last to be integrated and continued to show a relatively low level of Negro employment in the late 1960's. This phenomenon can be traced to the fact that all the forces which had historically limited Negro access to sales positions were at work and were strongest in these departments. The late integration of "big ticket" departments was a direct reflection of a particularly strong top management fear of and aversion to adverse customer reaction. The fear stemmed from stereotypes such as that Negroes do not have a sense of style or fashion and that Negroes are not mechanically inclined; the aversion stemmed directly from the fact that "big ticket" departments were the most profitable.

The slow growth of Negro employment in "big ticket" sales after initial integration did not necessarily result from a continuing lack of top management interest in seeing Negroes in sales positions in these departments. In many firms, it was quite the opposite—a reflection of resistance at the departmental level. One course of action open to top management in its efforts to increase the number of Negro "big ticket" sales personnel was the addition of Negroes to existing sales forces. This was opposed by personnel already in the department who feared a reduction in individual sales, commissions, and income. The alternative was to fill openings created by turnover with Negroes. In general, however, turnover in "big ticket" sales is low, due to high earnings, and departmental managers in these areas are insistent on "proven" personnel in order to insure a consistent level of growth in department sales. Given these constraints, most firms were satisfied with a compromise which involved filling only those openings created by attrition and only with a Negro if he had some sales experience in the area. The inevitable result was a high demand for experienced Negro salesmen and a low rate of expansion of Negro employment in these departments in most department stores.

IMPACT OF LOCATION

Locational data on Negro employment by occupation in the department stores studied for 1968 reveal the expected higher Negro percentage representation in urban stores in all categories. The degree of Negro representation in urban stores is extremely high, not only overall but also in the white collar categories of sales and clerical. Total employment and occupational distributions for urban units are shown in Table 23. Similar data for suburban units are presented in Table 24.

TABLE 23. *Department Store Industry*
Employment by Race, Sex, and Occupational Group
Sample Companies
Urban Units, 1968

Occupational Group	All Employees			Male			Female		
	Total	Negro	Percent Negro	Total	Negro	Percent Negro	Total	Negro	Percent Negro
Officials and managers	16,517	537	3.3	10,339	321	3.1	6,173	216	3.5
Professionals	1,521	50	3.3	677	31	4.6	844	19	2.3
Technicians	1,415	152	10.7	954	98	10.3	461	54	11.7
Sales workers	46,408	5,841	12.6	10,446	1,097	10.5	55,962	4,744	13.2
Office and clerical	39,288	6,446	16.4	4,777	801	16.8	34,511	5,645	16.4
Total white collar	105,149	13,026	12.4	27,193	2,348	8.6	77,953	10,678	13.7
Craftsmen	5,161	367	7.1	4,436	311	7.0	725	56	7.7
Operatives	11,203	3,057	27.3	8,035	2,239	27.9	3,168	818	25.8
Laborers	10,919	4,051	37.1	6,234	2,142	34.4	4,685	1,909	40.7
Service workers	12,439	5,696	45.8	6,175	3,179	51.5	6,264	2,517	40.2
Total blue collar	39,722	13,171	33.2	24,880	7,871	31.6	14,842	5,300	35.7
Total	144,871	26,197	18.1	52,073	10,219	19.6	92,798	15,978	17.2

Source: Data in author's possession.

Note: Represents only those units for which urban/suburban designations were available. Urban and suburban total is about 35,000 less than total 1968 sample shown in Table 19.

TABLE 24. Department Store Industry
Employment by Race, Sex, and Occupational Group
Sample Companies
Suburban Units, 1968

Occupational Group	All Employees			Male			Female		
	Total	Negro	Percent Negro	Total	Negro	Percent Negro	Total	Negro	Percent Negro
Officials and managers	9,965	162	1.6	6,043	103	1.7	3,922	59	1.5
Professionals	316	6	1.9	129	5	3.9	187	1	0.5
Technicians	807	22	2.7	568	17	3.0	239	5	2.1
Sales workers	60,963	2,099	3.4	14,115	459	3.3	46,848	1,640	3.5
Office and clerical	17,158	695	4.1	2,513	172	6.8	14,645	523	3.6
Total white collar	89,209	2,984	3.3	23,368	756	3.2	65,841	2,228	3.4
Craftsmen	5,445	258	4.7	4,873	227	4.7	572	31	5.4
Operatives	6,163	617	10.0	4,833	517	10.7	1,330	100	7.5
Laborers	3,145	586	18.6	2,350	438	18.6	795	148	18.6
Service workers	9,279	2,656	28.6	4,272	1,547	36.2	5,007	1,109	22.1
Total blue collar	24,032	4,117	17.1	16,328	2,729	16.7	7,704	1,388	18.0
Total	113,241	7,101	6.3	39,696	3,485	8.8	73,545	3,616	4.9

Source: Data in author's possession.

Note: Represents only those units for which urban/suburban designations were available. Urban and suburban total is about 35,000 less than total 1968 sample shown in Table 19.

Occupational Distribution

Overall Negro employment in urban units in the 1968 sample was 18.1 percent. Negro representation was greater among blue collar jobs than white collar jobs—33.2 percent and 12.4 percent respectively. The Negro male/female distribution generally followed industry patterns of more females than males employed overall with the male segment concentrated in the blue collar occupations, while females were primarily in white collar jobs. High employment proportions were found in every occupation among both males and females except among officials and managers, professionals, and craftsmen.

Suburban units showed not only lower overall proportions of Negro employees, but some interesting variations from the distributions of all workers. Overall Negro employment stood at 6.3 percent in the 1968 sample, 3.3 percent white collar and 17.1 percent blue collar. Suburban units exhibited a heavier concentration of female workers in white collar jobs than urban units, but the Negro female suburban work force was less concentrated in these groups than in the cities. A similar difference appeared in the male work force, where Negro workers were more concentrated in blue collar jobs than in urban stores. The female white collar proportion was 84.0 percent in urban stores, 89.5 percent in suburban ones, while among Negro women the proportions were 66.8 and 61.6 percent respectively. The male work force was 47.8 percent blue collar in urban units, compared to only 41.1 percent in suburban ones, whereas 77.0 percent of Negro men were in blue collar jobs in the cities and 78.3 percent in the suburbs.

The data on urban concentration of Negro employment by occupation confirm earlier observations regarding the relative impact of civil rights and market pressures on urban and suburban stores. Specifically, the fact that the ratio of Negro percentage representation in all white collar jobs to Negro percentage representation in all blue collar jobs in urban stores is twice what it is for suburban stores suggests quite different approaches to Negro employment in these two sectors of the industry. To some extent, these differences may be a function of differences in the structure of employment opportunities in the two sectors. The relatively greater number of part-time white collar jobs in suburban stores undoubtedly reduces Negro interest in such jobs vis-a-vis full-time blue collar jobs. To a greater extent, however, these differences are a reflection of differences in the structure of labor supply. The preponderance of white secondary wage earners desiring short hour jobs in the suburban supply of labor places the Negro at a severe competitive disadvantage in the sales and clerical area, but makes him a valuable commodity in the blue collar and service areas which have little attraction for the suburban housewife. In this context, the costs of an affirmative action program to upgrade Negroes into white collar jobs are far higher than in urban stores, and at the same time offer no positive short run market gains.

Locational Variations

The overall pattern of employment changes in the department stores studied masks two very different employment trends found within the urban segment of the industry during the latter half of the 1960's. Complete locational data on Negro employment in the sample are available only for 1967 and 1968, but they clearly reveal opposite trends in white and Negro employment in urban stores. Matched samples of urban and suburban units of the same companies for 1967 and 1968 show these trends. The urban sample, broken down by region, is presented in Table 25, the suburban sample in Table 26.

In urban units, total employment declined between 1967 and 1968, while Negro employment grew in both relative and absolute terms, as black workers replaced whites in some jobs. Negro employment grew from 16.6 percent of the total in these stores in 1967 to 18.4 percent of the total, while urban units lost 1,028 workers overall (Table 25). In sum, Negro employment grew 9.8 percent while non-Negro employment declined by 2.9 percent.

In suburban stores, total employment increased more than enough to offset the decrease in city employment, while total Negro employment in these stores increased only slightly in both absolute and relative terms. Total employment grew by 4,201, Negro employment by 440, resulting in a proportional increase of 0.2 percentage points, to 6.1 percent in 1968 (Table 26).

This divergence between Negro and non-Negro urban employment trends was evident in each of the regional groupings of cities. White employment declined between 1967 and 1968 in

TABLE 25. Department Store Industry
Employment by Race, Sex, and Region
Sample Companies
Urban Units, 1967 and 1968

Region		All Employees			Male			Female		
		Total	Negro	Percent Negro	Total	Negro	Percent Negro	Total	Negro	Percent Negro
Northeast	1967	42,212	6,239	14.8	15,447	2,420	15.7	26,765	3,819	14.3
	1968	41,188	6,374	15.5	14,664	2,383	16.3	26,524	3,991	15.0
South	1967	13,803	1,896	13.7	5,758	1,161	20.2	8,045	735	9.1
	1968	14,020	2,192	15.6	5,696	1,211	21.3	8,324	981	11.8
Midwest	1967	35,378	6,888	19.5	13,464	2,700	20.1	21,914	4,188	19.1
	1968	35,221	7,577	21.5	13,373	2,960	22.1	21,848	4,617	21.1
Border	1967	17,512	3,862	22.1	6,670	1,517	22.7	10,842	2,345	21.6
	1968	17,865	4,710	26.4	6,659	1,822	27.4	11,205	2,888	25.8
West	1967	16,039	1,873	11.7	6,007	666	11.1	10,032	1,207	12.0
	1968	15,622	1,941	12.4	5,889	697	11.8	9,733	1,244	12.8
Total	1967	124,944	20,758	16.6	47,346	8,464	17.9	77,598	12,294	15.8
	1968	123,916	22,794	18.4	46,281	9,073	19.6	77,635	13,721	17.7

Source: Data in author's possession.

Note: These figures are based on a matched sample and therefore represent fewer units than those in Table 23.

TABLE 26. Department Store Industry
Employment by Race, Sex, and Region
Sample Companies
Suburban Units, 1967 and 1968

Region	Year	All Employees			Male			Female		
		Total	Negro	Percent Negro	Total	Negro	Percent Negro	Total	Negro	Percent Negro
Northeast	1967	26,425	1,435	5.4	10,007	781	7.8	16,418	654	4.0
	1968	26,199	1,514	5.8	9,747	808	8.3	16,452	706	4.3
South	1967	3,992	382	9.6	1,464	221	15.1	2,528	161	6.4
	1968	4,992	406	8.1	1,742	202	11.6	3,250	204	6.3
Midwest	1967	24,911	1,353	5.4	8,788	594	6.8	16,123	759	4.7
	1968	27,663	1,755	6.3	9,958	770	7.7	17,705	985	5.6
Border	1967	19,607	1,527	7.8	6,563	774	11.8	13,044	753	5.8
	1968	20,288	1,425	7.0	6,586	653	9.9	13,702	772	5.6
West	1967	21,213	943	4.4	8,721	574	6.6	12,492	369	3.0
	1968	21,207	980	4.6	8,777	608	6.9	12,430	372	3.0
Total	1967	96,148	5,640	5.9	35,543	2,944	8.3	60,605	2,696	4.4
	1968	100,349	6,080	6.1	36,810	3,041	8.3	63,539	3,039	4.8

Source: Data in author's possession.

Note: These figures are based on a matched sample and therefore represent fewer units than those in Table 24.

every region, while Negro employment increased. In two, the southern and border cities, female Negro employment grew more than enough to offset male and female non-Negro employment declines, resulting in slight increases in total employment. In other areas, total employment declined despite Negro increases between 1967 and 1968.

Irregular patterns were also exhibited between 1967 and 1968 in suburban units in the southern and border cities. Although total employment grew in both regions, Negro males experienced declines in both relative and absolute numbers, and Negro female employment growth did not keep up with that of all females, resulting in slight decreases in Negro employment proportions for these areas. It should also be noted that the northeastern and western cities experienced slight total employment decreases in suburban stores during this period, despite some Negro employment growth.

There is considerable evidence that the labor market and/or product market forces generated by changes in urban residential and retail patterns were not, in and of themselves, sufficient to produce the observed absolute and relative increases in Negro employment. Specifically, it appears that in most cities overt or covert legal, political, or economic pressure for equal opportunity or equal employment was an important factor in Negro employment gains in department stores. A substantial percentage of the firms and divisions studied indicated that they had been the focus of such pressure at some time during the 1960's in one of the following ways: (1) a direct confrontation with civil rights groups involving the threat or occurrence of picketing; (2) a suggestion from local elected officials regarding the employment of Negroes; or (3) a formal charge of discrimination under local, state, or national law. A number of firms also indicated that they had been "used" by civil rights groups in the efforts of those groups to secure employment concessions elsewhere. In virtually all cases, management was willing to admit a high degree of sensitivity and responsiveness to such pressures and this sensitivity and responsiveness was reflected in the existence of dual hiring standards and/or preferential hiring policies in many stores by 1968.

In this context, it is surprising that total Negro employment in the department stores in the cities studied did not increase more rapidly. The rate of growth of total Negro employment in central city department stores over the 1967-1968 period is

of particular interest in this respect, given the accelerated
abandonment of downtown department stores by the white middle class in most cities after the riots of 1965 and 1966 and the
increasing overrepresentation of Negroes among job applicants
in such stores as the labor market became and remained tight.

Factors in Urban/Suburban Differences

Three possible explanations can be put forward for this apparent discrepancy between real and potential Negro employment gains: (1) Negro job applicants were concentrated in
units in which the demand for labor was low; (2) turnover was
concentrated among Negro employees; and (3) Negro job applicants generally faced greater problems in qualifying for jobs
than did white applicants. To some extent, all three of these
factors do appear to have been at work to reduce Negro employment gains in department stores during most or all of the
1960's.

All of the firms studied reported a clear concentration both of
Negro job applicants and of employment cutbacks in downtown
stores vis-a-vis neighborhood and suburban units. Most firms
also reported a decline in Negro job applicants in suburban
units during the 1966-1968 period, as might be expected with
the expansion in employment opportunities elsewhere in the city
as the labor market tightened. The continually increasing reliance on part-time workers in suburban units may have further
discouraged Negro applicants while it encouraged applications
from white middle class suburban housewives who wanted to work
short hours. In this context, it is not surprising that little evidence could be found of active Negro recruiting by suburban
stores prior to 1968. The only incentive to undertake such recruiting would have been corporate or divisional management
pressure. Although such pressure was not entirely lacking, it
was found to be strong only where a suburban unit showed
either an unreasonably low Negro percentage representation or
a dramatic decline in such representation over a very short
period of time.

All firms and divisions studied also reported that they had a
highly stable core of long service workers in most job categories
in all stores. Few firms had turnover data by race, but most
employment managers expressed the opinion that turnover was
higher among Negroes than whites during the 1967-1968 period.

In general, this is not illogical given the lower age/service distribution of Negro employees in most of the units studied coupled with the low earnings and long distance to work for many
Negro employees and particularly those in suburban units. A
few of the managers interviewed also suggested that lack of
acceptance by fellow workers may have been a factor in higher
turnover rates among Negroes in some departments in urban
units and many suburban stores.

There is also evidence that Negro job applicants faced some
systematic qualification problems in securing jobs in the stores
studied throughout the 1960's, despite the existence of dual
standards and/or informal preferential hiring policies. Ostensi-
bly, at least, these problems did not include race, as all of the
firms and divisions studied had adopted formal nondiscriminatory employment policies before 1964, but were a function of
failure to meet basic performance standards. As cited by management, Negro employment handicaps included the following:
(1) youth (immaturity, inexperience); (2) appearance (dress,
grooming); (3) background (employment history, police record); and (4) achievement (education, test performance).

The subjective nature of some of these factors makes it virtually impossible to assess the extent to which they reflect
rational rather than racial judgments. It is probable, however,
that the application of white middle class standards of dress
and grooming (with a consequent suspicion of beards, mous-
taches, and Afro hair and dress styles) and behavior (with a
consequent rejection of individuals without a high school education or with a police record) by fairly autonomous personnel
interviewers led to the classification of disproportionately large
numbers of Negro job applicants as "high risk" potential employees. In many of the firms studied, civil rights pressure to
ignore such risk was partially or completely offset by real and/
or imagined customer, supervisor, or employee resistance and/or
the weight of historical precedent, corporate conservatism, and
managerial concern for short run profits. This was particularly
apparent in suburban units where the availability of "low risk"
white middle class housewives and the presence of a predominantly white clientele coupled with corporate insistence only on
"some" visible Negro representation made affirmative action
neither necessary nor desirable.

CHAPTER V

Impact of Regional and Institutional Variables

Several different trends within the industry become evident from examination of the employment data when they are broken down by region. In addition, institutional variables, such as market image and corporate form, continued to have an effect on Negro employment patterns in recent years.

THE REGIONS

A comparison of data in the 1960's on Negro employment in all general merchandise stores in the cities studied, grouped by region, shows some narrowing of regional differentials in total Negro employment, but little change in the structure of those differentials. Regional data on total and Negro employment in all general merchandise stores in the cities studied for 1966, 1967, and 1969 are presented in Table 27.

Employment totals in Table 27 indicate that the most accurate comparison of regional change in the 1960's is probably between 1967 and 1969 (except in the Midwest, where reporting errors in Chicago sharply depressed the total in 1969). Data for 1966, when EEOC reporting was first instituted, are included only for general information, since the northeastern and western totals clearly indicate reporting shortages in that year.

Negro employment increased sharply between 1960 and 1967 in all cities except those in the South, Atlanta and Houston, where it apparently grew only slightly. (Compare with Table 13 in Chapter III.) The midwestern cities experienced the greatest increase and led all regions in 1967 in both total and relative Negro employment in that year, an extremely high 17.3 percent. Chicago and Detroit, of course, continued to have substantial Negro in-migration during the 1960's. Border cities followed in 1967 with 15.2 percent Negro employment, and the southern cities trailed with 12.7 percent. General merchandise Negro employment grew slightly in the northeastern cities dur-

TABLE 27. *General Merchandise Industry Including Department Stores Employment by Race, Sex, and Region. Twelve Metropolitan Areas, 1966, 1967, and 1969*

Year	All Employees			Male			Female		
	Total	Negro	Percent Negro	Total	Negro	Percent Negro	Total	Negro	Percent Negro
Northeast									
1966	144,023	18,077	12.6	49,317	6,908	14.0	94,706	11,169	11.8
1967	193,927	21,882	11.3	69,001	8,652	12.5	124,926	13,230	10.6
1969	190,098	23,905	12.6	65,049	9,180	14.1	125,049	14,725	11.8
Border									
1966	56,546	8,287	14.7	18,480	3,433	13.6	38,066	4,854	12.8
1967	73,222	11,164	15.2	24,111	4,369	13.1	49,111	6,795	13.8
1969	71,332	12,263	17.2	24,330	4,573	18.8	47,002	7,690	16.4
South									
1966	35,092	4,228	12.0	12,738	2,309	18.1	22,354	1,919	8.6
1967	39,027	4,946	12.7	14,128	2,594	18.4	24,899	2,352	9.4
1969	34,369	5,008	14.6	12,917	2,304	17.8	21,452	2,704	12.6
Midwest									
1966	145,414	22,096	15.2	51,104	7,076	13.8	94,310	15,020	15.9
1967	161,759	28,046	17.3	54,000	8,484	15.7	107,759	19,562	18.2
1969	128,573	15,944	12.4	44,791	5,817	13.0	83,782	10,127	12.1
West									
1966[a]	58,860	4,411	7.5	20,173	1,710	8.5	38,687	2,701	7.0
1967	94,764	6,830	7.2	32,231	2,656	8.2	62,533	4,174	6.7
1969	80,972	5,686	7.0	25,982	2,137	8.2	54,990	3,549	6.5

Source: Appendix Tables A-7—A-21.
Note: Cities are listed in Table 1.
[a] Los Angeles-Long Beach only.

ing this period, to 11.3 percent, while it jumped to 7.2 percent in the two western metropolitan areas, Los Angeles and San Francisco, by 1967.

The range of employment in 1960 was from a low 3.8 percent in the two western cities to 11.9 percent in the border cities, a spread of 8.1 percentage points (Table 13). In 1967, the range was from 7.2 to 17.3 percent, an even larger spread of 10.1 percentage points. Negro employment no longer represented a continuum, but seemed to fall into three groups: very high employment (the Midwest and Border), moderately high employment (South and Northeast) and fairly low employment (the West).

In the late 1960's, total general merchandise employment apparently declined in all regions. It is extremely significant that Negro employment did not follow this trend but rather grew both absolutely and relatively in three of the five regions (all but the Midwest and West) during this period. Although absolute numbers increased only slightly in the northeastern, border, and southern cities, relative increases of 1.3 to 2.0 percentage points resulted in these areas owing to the declining total employment. Apparently both total and Negro employment declined in the Midwest, but the precipitous drop indicated by the data must be due in part to reporting variations between the two years. In the West, Negro general merchandise employment apparently declined slightly faster than total employment, leading to a slight decline in representation from 7.2 to 7.0 percent by 1969.

Regional data for the department store sample tend to correlate closely with those on all general merchandise stores in the cities studied in the mid-1960's and to correlate similarly with regional differentials in percentage Negro population. Tables for each group of cities, by region, are presented in the following discussion of the 1968 department store sample.

Northeastern Cities

The levels of Negro employment in general merchandise stores in 1967 and in department stores studied in 1968 in the northeastern cities are very similar—11.3 percent for the former and 11.9 percent for the latter. Complete data by sex and occupation for the 1968 sample are presented in Table 28.

TABLE 28. *Department Store Industry*
Employment by Race, Sex, and Occupational Group
Sample Companies
New York, Philadelphia, and Pittsburgh Metropolitan Areas, 1968

Occupational Group	All Employees			Male			Female		
	Total	Negro	Percent Negro	Total	Negro	Percent Negro	Total	Negro	Percent Negro
Officials and managers	8,409	268	3.2	5,195	158	3.0	3,214	110	3.4
Professionals	901	23	2.6	384	14	3.6	517	9	1.7
Technicians	729	42	5.8	475	40	8.4	254	2	0.8
Sales workers	34,977	2,269	6.5	7,548	403	5.3	27,429	1,866	6.8
Office and clerical	18,349	2,301	12.5	2,456	300	12.2	15,893	2,001	12.6
Total white collar	63,365	4,903	7.7	16,058	915	5.7	47,307	3,988	8.4
Craftsmen	3,085	113	3.7	2,689	87	3.2	396	26	6.6
Operatives	3,932	637	16.2	2,831	440	15.5	1,101	197	17.9
Laborers	4,643	1,460	31.4	2,994	658	22.0	1,649	802	48.6
Service workers	7,260	2,691	37.1	3,964	1,806	45.6	3,296	885	26.9
Total blue collar	18,920	4,901	25.9	12,478	2,991	24.0	6,442	1,910	29.6
Total	82,285	9,804	11.9	28,536	3,906	13.7	53,749	5,898	11.0

Source: Data in author's possession.

In 1968, department stores in New York, Philadelphia, and Pittsburgh showed a high ratio of female Negroes to male Negroes, and it was in these cities that interview data most strongly indicated that Negro females had become a preferred commodity to Negro males in department stores. In part, this was a natural outgrowth of sustained efforts to move Negroes into white collar jobs in department stores in these cities. At the same time, however, it also appears to have been a reflection of a change in the age distribution of Negro job applicants as the labor market tightened over the 1965-1968 period. Specifically, as job applicants became younger, the Negro male tended to become a "higher risk" vis-a-vis the Negro female in terms of appearance, honesty, and reliability. In this context, the older Negro female also enjoyed priority over teenage white males in many cases.

One-half all Negro employees in department stores in these cities in 1968 were in white collar jobs, higher than the industry average, while the relative and absolute concentration of Negro sales and clerical workers was very close to industry averages presented in the preceding chapter. Northeastern stores had almost the highest Negro proportion of officials and managers—3.2 percent, and the largest number in relation to all Negroes employed—2.7 percent of the total. These phenomena coupled with information gained in interviews indicate that department stores in the northeastern cities, and particularly in New York City, continued to lead the industry in the upgrading of Negroes. In large part, this leadership reflects the relative strength of legal, political, and social rather than economic pressures for equal opportunity in these cities.

Border Cities

Department stores sampled in Baltimore, St. Louis, and Washington, D.C. led the regions in 1968 with 16.2 percent Negro employment. High employment levels were apparent in all occupational groups, but the most important were officials and managers (3.8 percent), sales (8.9 percent), and office and clerical (17.3 percent), leading to an overall white collar representation of 10.3 percent. Although Negro female occupational distributions approached that of all female workers, the Negro male work force evidenced the heavy blue collar concentration found in all other regions. Almost 60 percent of all male service workers were Negro, and these 909 employees represented over 30 percent of the Negro male work force. Almost two-thirds of all Negro women, however, were white collar employees, and this group accounted for almost 40 percent of the total Negro work force. These data are presented in Table 29.

The level of Negro employment in general merchandise and department stores in these cities is a clear reflection of the racial composition of the population in them. The sustained growth of percentage Negro employment in these cities even after 1966 may also be traced to demographic forces. Specifically, these cities experienced a dramatic abandonment of the central city by whites in terms of both residential location and retail activity, leaving urban general merchandise and department stores with a far more predominantly Negro clientele and supply of labor than is reflected in gross population figures. In this context, it is not surprising that the racial employment effect of geographic dispersion had not yet offset Negro employment gains in center city stores by 1968.

Southern Cities

Total Negro employment in general merchandise stores as a percentage of total employment was comparatively high in 1960 and grew consistently between 1960 and 1969. The rate of this growth, however, was well below that observed in the border cities and in all of the cities combined over the period. Department store figures for 1968 indicate a similar pattern in the South compared to other regions.

The southern cities also show the lowest Negro percentage representation in white collar jobs in department stores in 1968. Only 25.7 percent of all Negro workers were in such positions as compared with approximately 50 percent in the other regions.

Southern department stores had a preponderance of Negro male employees and an exceptionally high percentage representation in the service worker classification, 60.3 percent. Occupational distributions were also sharply different for southern department stores. Only 0.4 percent of the Negro work force was in the officials and managers category as compared with 1.8 percent or above in the other regions. Similarly, 13.0 and 12.1 percent were in sales and clerical occupations, respectively, compared to over 20 percent elsewhere.

TABLE 29.   *Department Store Industry*
Employment by Race, Sex, and Occupational Group
Sample Companies
Baltimore, St. Louis, and Washington, D.C. Metropolitan Areas, 1968

Occupational Group	All Employees			Male			Female		
	Total	Negro	Percent Negro	Total	Negro	Percent Negro	Total	Negro	Percent Negro
Officials and managers	4,763	179	3.8	2,698	101	3.7	2,065	78	3.8
Professionals	253	12	4.7	100	7	7.0	153	5	3.3
Technicians	313	31	9.9	243	31	12.8	70	—	—
Sales workers	22,456	2,001	8.9	5,076	468	9.2	17,380	1,533	8.8
Office and clerical	9,276	1,601	17.3	1,395	213	15.3	7,881	1,388	17.6
Total white collar	37,061	3,824	10.3	9,512	820	8.6	27,549	3,004	10.9
Craftsmen	1,645	174	10.6	1,252	134	10.7	393	40	10.2
Operatives	2,913	961	33.0	2,034	726	35.7	879	235	26.7
Laborers	1,444	682	47.2	881	408	46.3	563	274	48.7
Service workers	3,680	1,928	52.4	1,541	909	59.0	2,139	1,019	47.6
Total blue collar	9,682	3,745	38.7	5,708	2,177	38.1	3,974	1,568	39.5
Total	46,743	7,569	16.2	15,220	2,997	19.7	31,523	4,572	14.5

Source: Data in author's possession.

TABLE 30. Department Store Industry
Employment by Race, Sex, and Occupational Group
Sample Companies
Atlanta and Houston Metropolitan Areas, 1968

Occupational Group	All Employees			Male			Female		
	Total	Negro	Percent Negro	Total	Negro	Percent Negro	Total	Negro	Percent Negro
Officials and managers	2,606	16	0.6	1,732	13	0.8	874	3	0.3
Professionals	260	1	0.4	109	—	—	151	1	0.7
Technicians	286	8	2.8	215	8	3.7	71	—	—
Sales workers	12,444	512	4.1	2,881	131	4.5	9,563	381	4.0
Office and clerical	6,629	477	7.2	1,002	128	12.8	5,627	349	6.2
Total white collar	22,225	1,014	4.6	5,939	280	4.7	16,286	734	4.5
Craftsmen	995	55	5.5	894	46	5.1	101	9	8.9
Operatives	1,776	551	31.0	1,234	476	38.6	542	75	13.8
Laborers	2,631	843	32.0	1,737	575	33.1	394	268	30.0
Service workers	2,460	1,483	60.3	1,128	634	56.2	1,332	849	63.7
Total blue collar	7,862	2,932	37.3	4,993	1,731	34.7	2,869	1,201	41.9
Total	30,087	3,946	13.1	10,932	2,011	18.4	19,155	1,935	10.1

Source: Data in author's possession.

In the southern cities, the introduction of Negroes into sales positions did not come until well into the 1960's and then only as a direct result of civil rights agitation in the form of lunch counter sit-ins. Since that time, some significant progress has been made in the sales area largely through the upgrading of long service Negro workers rather than an expansion in total Negro employment. In 1968, however, the proportion of Negro sales workers among all sales workers was only 4.1 percent, lower than in any other region.

Midwestern Cities

Department stores in Chicago and Detroit in 1968 had a Negro employment level somewhat lower than the exceptionally high level recorded for all general merchandise stores in the previous year—14.5 percent compared to 17.3 percent, but this was among the highest in the sample. Complete employment data by occupation for 1968 are presented in Table 31.

As in the northeastern and border cities, over 45 percent of all Negro workers were in sales and clerical positions, but the proportion in the managerial category was below 2 percent. In all, slightly less than one-half of the Negro work force was in white collar jobs.

Despite its high overall Negro employment, Negro blue collar proportions were lower than both the border and southern cities and only slightly above those of the Northeast. This was largely because Negroes made up only 33.4 percent of the service worker group in the Midwest, slightly below that in the Northeast and substantially below proportions in border and southern cities.

In part, the percentage level of Negro employment in the industry in these cities can be explained by the relatively high level and rate of growth of Negro population in Chicago and Detroit over this period, but it may also reflect structural factors in the labor market. Specifically, it may be a reflection of the following: (1) the concentration of large chain store warehouse and distribution facilities in these cities which resulted in a comparatively large number of clerical and laborer jobs in urban units in this region; and (2) the existence of large numbers of high wage job opportunities in manufacturing in and around these cities which limited the supply of white male labor to low wage department stores. These two factors would partially explain both relatively high percentage representation of Negroes in the industry and the relatively high percentage of

TABLE 31. *Department Store Industry*
Employment by Race, Sex, and Occupational Group
Sample Companies
Chicago and Detroit Metropolitan Areas, 1968

Occupational Group	All Employees			Male			Female		
	Total	Negro	Percent Negro	Total	Negro	Percent Negro	Total	Negro	Percent Negro
Officials and managers	7,650	186	2.4	4,855	117	2.4	2,795	69	2.5
Professionals	329	17	5.2	170	15	8.8	159	2	1.3
Technicians	626	40	6.4	477	33	6.9	149	7	4.7
Sales workers	27,918	2,442	8.7	5,536	302	5.5	22,382	2,140	9.6
Office and clerical	15,320	2,215	14.5	1,737	274	15.8	13,583	1,941	14.3
Total white collar	51,843	4,900	9.5	12,775	741	5.8	39,068	4,159	10.6
Craftsmen	2,772	161	5.8	2,574	155	6.0	198	6	3.0
Operatives	5,967	1,391	23.3	4,758	1,020	21.4	1,209	371	30.7
Laborers	4,247	1,740	41.0	2,503	1,016	40.6	1,744	724	41.5
Service workers	6,398	2,134	33.4	3,009	1,135	38.7	3,389	969	28.6
Total blue collar	19,384	5,426	28.0	12,844	3,356	26.1	6,540	2,070	31.7
Total	71,227	10,326	14.5	25,619	4,097	16.0	45,308	6,229	13.7

Source: Data in author's possession.

total employment and total Negro employment accounted for by females.

Western Cities

Negroes accounted for a comparatively low percentage of total employment in general merchandise stores in the western cities throughout the 1960's although their proportions grew rapidly. Occupational data for the 1968 sample of department stores in Los Angeles and San Francisco, presented in Table 32, show an identical total Negro proportion—7.2 percent—as was reported for all general merchandise stores in this region in 1967.

Despite low overall Negro employment, the West showed the best occupational distribution of all regions. One-third of all Negro men and three-quarters of all Negro women were in white collar occupations. This was furthered by the fact that the West led in the percentage of the Negro work force in sales positions —32.4 percent.

The reasons for such a high Negro white collar representation are difficult to identify, but it does appear that the existence of an "inferior" minority group—the Mexican-American—in both cities and particularly in the Los Angeles area was an instrumental factor in the ability of Negroes to move into white collar jobs. This movement, which was evident long before the 1960's, accelerated during this period under the impact of national and local civil rights activity. The resultant widening gap between Negroes and Mexican-Americans was perceived by some of the managers interviewed as the basis of a future set of racial employment problems. Only in New York City, with its large Puerto Rican population, was there any evidence of a similar potential problem.

The low level of total Negro employment in these cities can be traced to a combination of relatively low Negro percentage representation in the population, geographical concentration of the Negro population, grossly inadequate public transportation systems, and high geographical dispersion within the industry.

SCOPE AND STRUCTURE OF FIRMS

On a national basis, independent local companies showed the highest total Negro percentage employment in 1968 by a substantial margin over both federations and chains. The federations and the chains showed almost identical total Negro per-

TABLE 32. *Department Store Industry*
Employment by Race, Sex, and Occupational Group
Sample Companies
Los Angeles and San Francisco Metropolitan Areas, 1968

Occupational Group	All Employees			Male			Female		
	Total	Negro	Percent Negro	Total	Negro	Percent Negro	Total	Negro	Percent Negro
Officials and managers	6,629	97	1.5	4,010	62	1.5	2,619	35	1.3
Professionals	531	4	1.2	156	1	0.6	175	3	1.7
Technicians	451	56	12.4	166	5	3.0	285	51	17.9
Sales workers	28,604	1,471	5.1	6,984	397	5.7	21,620	1,074	5.0
Office and clerical	13,074	1,039	7.9	1,704	155	9.1	11,370	884	7.8
Total white collar	49,089	2,667	5.4	13,020	620	4.8	38,069	2,047	5.7
Craftsmen	2,559	152	5.9	2,296	138	6.0	273	14	5.1
Operatives	3,534	370	10.4	2,579	259	10.0	985	111	11.3
Laborers	2,766	268	9.7	1,504	152	10.1	1,262	116	9.2
Service workers	5,003	1,089	21.8	2,549	659	25.9	2,454	430	17.5
Total blue collar	13,902	1,879	13.5	8,928	1,208	13.5	4,974	671	13.5
Total	62,991	4,546	7.2	21,948	1,828	8.3	41,043	2,718	6.6

Source: Data in author's possession.

centage representation on a national basis. National data on total Negro employment by type of firm are presented in Tables 33, 34, and 35.

Data on the occupational representation of Negroes by scope and structure of firm reveals one further potentially significant difference in Negro employment patterns. Local companies led both chains and federations with respect to Negro percentage representation in all white collar jobs and in all blue collar jobs taken together. Among service workers specifically, the chains show the highest Negro percentage representation of all blue collar jobs—44.6 percent. Chain companies also have the highest Negro proportion in the laborer category.

Civil Rights Impact

There is no evidence to suggest that these interfirm differences in the level and occupational structure of Negro percentage employment reflect differences in formal minority group employment policies. There is, however, considerable evidence that there were significant differences in the strength of the impact of formal nondiscrimination policies on local employment practices which were directly related to the scope and structure of the firm. Specifically, the observed differences were a function of the extent to which local civil rights developments resulted in the conversion of equal employment policies into affirmative action programs.

In chain stores, local civil rights pressures generated little pressure on top management for active enforcement of nondiscrimination policies or positive encouragement of affirmative action programs. The scope and scale of these firms appears effectively to have insulated top management from short run economic, political, and social pressures to expand Negro employment in individual cities other than the city in which corporate headquarters were located. At the same time, the impact of such pressures on local management was weakened by the existence of clear corporate hiring procedures and standards which enabled unit managers to "pass the buck" and limited their flexibility in responding to changing local mores and market conditions. The inevitable result was a high rate of rejection of Negro job applicants for white collar jobs and a relatively low Negro percentage representation in such jobs and in total employment. These phenomena do much to explain the basic reluctance of the chains to release data on Negro employment, in

TABLE 33. *Department Store Industry*
Employment by Race, Sex, and Occupational Group
Sample Local Independent Companies
Twelve Metropolitan Areas, 1968

Occupational Group	All Employees			Male			Female		
	Total	Negro	Percent Negro	Total	Negro	Percent Negro	Total	Negro	Percent Negro
Officials and managers	10,758	367	3.4	5,435	197	3.6	5,303	170	3.2
Professionals	1,189	40	3.4	526	26	4.9	663	14	2.1
Technicians	639	38	5.9	348	35	10.1	291	3	1.0
Sales workers	47,992	4,127	8.6	7,296	480	6.6	40,396	3,647	9.0
Office and clerical	15,273	3,113	20.4	1,751	344	19.6	13,522	2,769	20.5
Total white collar	75,851	7,685	10.1	15,376	1,082	7.0	60,475	6,603	10.9
Craftsmen	2,420	177	7.3	1,987	138	6.9	433	39	9.0
Operatives	2,467	519	21.0	1,444	340	23.5	1,023	179	17.5
Laborers	5,902	1,970	33.4	3,864	1,216	31.5	2,038	754	37.0
Service workers	10,997	4,310	39.2	5,208	2,119	40.7	5,789	2,191	37.8
Total blue collar	21,786	6,976	32.0	12,503	3,813	30.5	9,283	3,163	34.1
Total	97,637	14,661	15.0	27,879	4,895	17.6	69,758	9,766	14.0

Source: Data in author's possession.

Note: Cities are listed in Table 1.

TABLE 34. Department Store Industry
Employment by Race, Sex, and Occupational Group
Sample Federated Companies
Twelve Metropolitan Areas, 1968

Occupational Group	All Employees			Male			Female		
	Total	Negro	Percent Negro	Total	Negro	Percent Negro	Total	Negro	Percent Negro
Officials and managers	8,784	199	2.3	4,521	113	2.5	4,263	86	2.0
Professionals	821	14	1.7	374	9	2.4	447	5	1.1
Technicians	617	60	9.7	258	10	3.9	359	50	13.9
Sales workers	40,044	2,053	5.1	6,256	301	4.8	33,788	1,752	5.2
Office and clerical	14,418	1,877	13.0	1,449	206	14.2	12,969	1,671	12.9
Total white collar	64,684	4,203	6.5	12,858	639	5.0	51,826	3,564	6.9
Craftsmen	2,285	144	6.3	1,634	104	6.4	651	40	6.1
Operatives	4,907	1,072	21.8	2,640	627	23.8	2,267	445	19.6
Laborers	3,088	686	22.2	2,139	481	22.5	949	205	21.6
Service workers	9,421	3,061	32.5	4,165	1,629	39.1	5,256	1,432	27.2
Total blue collar	19,701	4,963	25.2	10,578	2,841	26.9	9,123	2,122	23.3
Total	84,385	9,166	10.9	23,436	3,480	14.8	60,949	5,686	9.3

Source: Data in author's possession.

Note: Cities are listed in Table 1.

TABLE 35. *Department Store Industry*
Employment by Race, Sex, and Occupational Group
Sample Chain Companies
Twelve Metropolitan Areas, 1968

Occupational Group	All Employees			Male			Female		
	Total	Negro	Percent Negro	Total	Negro	Percent Negro	Total	Negro	Percent Negro
Officials and managers	10,515	180	1.7	8,514	141	1.7	2,301	39	1.9
Professionals	64	3	4.7	19	2	10.5	45	1	2.2
Technicians	1,149	79	6.9	970	72	7.4	179	7	3.9
Sales workers	38,363	2,515	6.6	14,473	920	6.4	23,390	1,595	6.7
Office and clerical	32,957	2,643	8.0	5,094	520	10.2	27,363	2,123	7.6
Total white collar	83,048	5,420	6.5	29,070	1,655	5.7	53,978	3,765	7.0
Craftsmen	6,361	334	5.3	6,084	318	5.2	277	16	5.8
Operatives	10,778	2,319	21.5	9,352	1,954	20.9	1,426	365	25.6
Laborers	6,741	2,337	34.7	3,616	1,112	30.8	3,125	1,225	39.2
Service workers	4,383	1,954	44.6	2,818	1,425	50.6	1,565	529	33.8
Total blue collar	28,263	6,944	24.6	21,870	4,809	22.0	6,393	2,135	33.4
Total	111,311	12,364	11.1	50,940	6,464	12.7	60,371	5,900	9.8

Source: Data in author's possession.

Note: Professionals and technicians are understated because one firm did not separate these employees from officials and managers. Cities are listed in Table 1.

marked contrast to their willingness to discuss Negro employment policies in general terms.

At the other end of the continuum, independent firms continued to show the greatest sensitivity to local mores and responsiveness to local civil rights pressure in the 1960's, as they had over the 1940-1960 period. In this respect, both the national pattern and the "deviant" pattern in the southern cities are significant. This sensitivity and responsiveness is not difficult to explain, given the dependence of local firms on a single market for their survival. It was undoubtedly enhanced by the existence of large downtown units which were increasingly dependent on the Negro community for both workers and customers. Both of these factors differentiated local firms from the chains which were not heavily dependent on a single urban market or on a single unit within such a market, given the dispersion of urban chain stores throughout most cities. The impact of the locational factor should not be underestimated as the concentration of urban employment in local firms in a single large downtown unit both fostered affirmative action and facilitated top management scrutiny and control of such programs. To some extent, the same phenomenon was observed in the chains with respect to large central service and distribution facilities in all cities and particularly in regional and national headquarters cities.

The federations provide interesting contrasts to both the chains and the local firms. Although the scope of these firms parallels the chains, this factor did not generate the same degree of insensitivity to pressures for affirmative action. There are two possible explanations for this difference: (1) federations are more dependent on major city markets than are the chains; and (2) constituent division managements are highly sensitive to local mores and exercise greater influence in corporate policy than do unit or regional managers in the chains. The managerial structure of the federations and the locational structure of their divisions coupled with use of local trade names make those divisions very similar to local firms, but this did not result in identical or similar Negro employment patterns. In part, these phenomena may be statistical rather than real, as divisions of federations were not uniformly represented in all regions and were concentrated in the carriage trade category. Despite these factors, there is suggestive evidence that, even in the face of comparatively strong central management support for affirmative action with respect to Negro employment, local mores coupled with divisional profit accountability effectively restrained the scope of affirmative action and focused it on the upgrading of Negro employees in center city units rather than on the expansion of the total percentage and geographical range of Negro employees. In this respect, it is important to note that the divisions of the major federations showed the greatest declines in urban employment over the 1966-1968 period and gave evidence of the highest managerially imposed elasticity of demand for labor of the three types of firms in the sample.

MARKET POSITION OF INDEPENDENT AND FEDERATED COMPANIES

Data on 1968 Negro employment in the department stores studied, grouped by market position or self-image of the firm or division, also reveal some interesting and potentially significant differences. Overall, carriage trade stores showed the lowest Negro percentage representation, which may explain the refusal of a relatively large number of these stores to participate in the study. Moderate price stores showed the highest overall percentage level of Negro employment. National data on total Negro employment in nonchain store units studied, by market position of firm or division are presented in Tables 36-38.

Data on the occupational percentage representation of Negro employees in the department stores studied, grouped by market position, provide some further insight into the bases of the differentials in total Negro representation. Overall, moderate price stores show a significantly higher Negro percentage representation in white collar jobs which can be traced directly to Negro representation in sales positions, but which is partially offset by a lower Negro representation in service jobs. Budget stores, however, show a comparatively high Negro representation in blue collar jobs, particularly service occupations, which partially offsets a relatively low level of Negro representation in sales positions. Carriage trade stores are distinguished by having the lowest Negro percentage representation in sales in contrast to the high Negro percentage representation in managerial and clerical positions.

The observed differences in the level and occupational structure of Negro employment between firms based on market position and self-image do not conform to simple product market and labor market models which predict increasingly Negro clientele

TABLE 36. *Department Store Industry*
Employment by Race, Sex, and Occupational Group
Carriage Trade Stores, Sample Companies
Twelve Metropolitan Areas, 1968

Occupational Group	All Employees			Male			Female		
	Total	Negro	Percent Negro	Total	Negro	Percent Negro	Total	Negro	Percent Negro
Officials and managers	4,595	145	3.2	1,959	72	3.7	2,636	73	2.8
Professionals	514	10	1.9	253	6	2.4	261	4	1.5
Technicians	356	20	5.6	158	15	9.5	198	5	2.5
Sales workers	20,265	1,101	5.4	2,662	140	5.3	17,603	961	5.5
Office and clerical	7,477	1,303	17.4	785	133	16.9	6,692	1,170	17.5
Total white collar	33,207	2,579	7.8	5,817	366	6.3	27,390	2,213	8.1
Craftsmen	1,178	54	4.6	786	45	5.7	392	9	2.3
Operatives	1,800	439	24.4	660	205	31.1	1,140	234	20.5
Laborers	2,014	551	27.4	1,225	281	22.9	789	270	34.2
Service workers	4,172	1,490	35.7	1,712	702	41.0	2,460	788	32.0
Total blue collar	9,164	2,534	27.7	4,383	1,233	28.1	4,781	1,301	27.2
Total	42,371	5,113	12.1	10,200	1,599	15.7	32,171	3,514	10.9

Source: Data in author's possession.

Note: Independent and federated companies only. Cities are listed in Table 1.

TABLE 37. Department Store Industry
Employment by Race, Sex, and Occupational Group
Moderate Price Stores, Sample Companies
Twelve Metropolitan Areas, 1968

Occupational Group	All Employees			Male			Female		
	Total	Negro	Percent Negro	Total	Negro	Percent Negro	Total	Negro	Percent Negro
Officials and managers	11,622	320	2.8	6,383	180	2.8	5,239	140	2.7
Professionals	1,300	33	2.5	545	18	3.3	755	15	2.0
Technicians	807	75	9.3	372	27	7.3	435	48	11.0
Sales workers	53,854	4,128	7.7	9,061	524	5.8	44,793	3,604	8.0
Office and clerical	18,017	3,056	17.0	1,932	343	17.8	16,085	2,713	16.9
Total white collar	85,600	7,612	8.9	18,293	1,092	6.0	67,307	6,520	9.7
Craftsmen	2,982	222	7.4	2,348	158	6.7	634	64	10.1
Operatives	4,773	1,002	21.0	3,080	695	22.6	1,693	307	18.1
Laborers	4,658	1,398	30.0	3,214	925	28.8	1,444	473	32.8
Service workers	14,414	5,020	34.8	6,822	2,572	37.7	7,592	2,448	32.2
Total blue collar	26,827	7,642	28.5	15,464	4,350	28.1	11,363	3,292	29.0
Total	112,427	15,254	13.6	33,757	5,442	16.1	78,670	9,812	12.5

Source: Data in author's possession.

Note: Independent and federated companies only. Cities are listed in Table 1.

TABLE 38. *Department Store Industry*
Employment by Race, Sex, and Occupational Group
Budget Stores, Sample Companies
Twelve Metropolitan Areas, 1968

Occupational Group	All Employees			Male			Female		
	Total	Negro	Percent Negro	Total	Negro	Percent Negro	Total	Negro	Percent Negro
Officials and managers	3,325	101	3.0	1,634	58	3.5	1,691	43	2.5
Professionals	196	11	5.6	102	11	10.8	94	—	—
Technicians	93	3	3.2	76	3	3.9	17	—	—
Sales workers	13,917	951	6.8	1,829	117	6.4	12,088	834	6.9
Office and clerical	4,197	631	15.0	483	74	15.4	3,714	557	15.0
Total white collar	21,728	1,697	7.8	4,124	263	6.4	17,604	1,434	8.1
Craftsmen	545	45	8.3	487	39	8.0	58	6	10.3
Operatives	801	150	18.7	344	67	19.5	457	83	18.2
Laborers	2,318	707	30.5	1,564	491	31.4	754	216	28.6
Service workers	1,832	861	47.0	839	474	56.5	993	387	39.0
Total blue collar	5,496	1,763	32.1	3,234	1,071	33.1	2,262	692	30.6
Total	27,224	3,460	12.7	7,358	1,334	18.1	19,866	2,126	10.7

Source: Data in author's possession.

Note: Independent and federated companies only. Cities are listed in Table 1.

and supply of labor with movement from carriage trade to budget stores. There was considerable evidence in the stores studied that the models and particularly the product market model were a reasonable approximation of reality. In this context, the observed differences in Negro employment patterns can be attributed primarily to institutional forces on the demand side of the labor market. Specifically, the differences were a function of managerial commitment to the Negro market.

Carriage Trade Stores

Stores selling high price, first line merchandise generally reported lower Negro percentage representation among their clientele and supply of labor than did other stores. Management in these stores generally suggested a causal relationship between these two phenomena, but one which had clientele as the causal factor and supply of labor as the effect. This view coupled with the limited Negro carriage trade market generally led top management in these firms to see little potential for short run market gains as a result of expanded Negro employment until late in the 1960's—if at all. At the same time, management in these firms anticipated a strong adverse customer reaction to the placement of Negroes in sales positions. There was no clear or consistent rationale for this phenomenon and very little evidence that the anticipated reaction did materialize when Negroes were placed in sales positions.

The absence of strong customer reaction is perhaps not surprising, given the relatively weak status threat of the Negro to carriage trade clientele, but this did not induce management to abandon its traditionally conservative approach to minority group employment in sales positions. In the absence of product market pressure to place Negroes in sales positions, the only pressure to change traditional practices in this area had to come from the labor market. This pressure was sufficiently strong to move Negroes into clerical jobs, but not sufficiently strong to move any large numbers of Negroes into sales positions past the basic barriers of management conservatism and insistence on "outstanding" appearance qualifications.

Moderate Price Stores

The level and pattern of Negro employment in moderate price stores can be traced to widespread management commitment to the Negro retail market in this type of firm. Moderate price stores generally were the first to feel the impact of changing residential and retail patterns and the ones to suffer the most as those changes continued and accelerated. In a large number of cases, the management response was concerted effort to woo the Negro consumer, in part through strong affirmative action in Negro employment. The result was a marked expansion in Negro recruiting activities, development of special hiring and training programs for Negroes, and the placement of Negroes in a wide range of sales positions on the assumption that there could and would be a cause and effect relationship between employment and patronage.

Budget Stores

The level and pattern of Negro employment in budget stores reflect the impact of a complex set of sociological and economic considerations on management policy. Budget stores experienced the greatest increases in both Negro clientele and Negro supply of labor in the cities as the racial composition of the population changed. The impact of these increases in the employment area, however, was largely confined to service and other blue collar jobs and did not extend to sales positions. There appear to have been three reasons for this: (1) budget stores did not have to court the Negro consumer; (2) budget store management anticipated an adverse reaction from their white lower and lower middle class clientele to upgrading of Negroes into sales positions based on the larger status threat of the Negro to this socioeconomic group; and (3) budget store management was faced with a sales force composed primarily of lower middle class whites who were expected to be highly resistant to integration of work groups.

Although differences in managerial commitment to improving Negro employment tended to correlate with the sales position of the firms, there was evidence of efforts in this direction among a variety of firms. Activities prompted by such commitment, and some of their early results, are the subject of the following chapter.

CHAPTER VI

Factors Affecting Negro Employment

In the late 1960's, the urban segment of the department store industry continued to be characterized by decreasing center city sales and employment and increasing suburban sales and employment, with much of this expansion in employment accounted for by part-time or contingent personnel. At the same time, urban department stores continued to face both a very tight labor market and a highly competitive product market, with Negroes assuming an increasingly important role in both markets.

These economic forces were necessary conditions for the observed changes in Negro employment trends, but were not, however, sufficient to explain completely those changes. Such an explanation must include the changing nature and extent of legal, political, and social pressures to expand minority group employment opportunities.

THE EMPLOYMENT PROCESS

Various factors in the employment process differentially affect Negro job applicants and employees. These factors help to account for disproportionately large Negro representation in some occupations, underrepresentation in others, and differential rates of change in racial employment patterns among the various occupational groups.

Recruitment

At the managerial level, the breakdown of traditional reliance on internal upward mobility and the source of management personnel has and will continue to limit the access of Negroes to these positions. The fact that management personnel now come almost exclusively from the ranks of specially recruited and selected management trainees, rather than from among existing personnel, has tended to limit the impact of generally increasing Negro employment on Negro representation in managerial jobs.

The primary source of management trainees for the industry has shifted over the postwar period from major colleges and universities to smaller colleges, to junior colleges, and in some cases, to high schools. This shift has tended to favor the Negro and other minority groups, but the impact of the shift on actual Negro employment has been slight. There are two reasons for this limited impact. One is that retail sales, in general, and department stores, in particular, do not have a favorable image within the black community with respect to equal employment opportunity. A second reason is that qualified black candidates for management training programs in the industry may find it more attractive to seek and accept employment in industries where starting salaries are higher and where the prospects for rapid advancement are better.

Most of the firms studied were acutely aware of these two problems, often as the result of their experience in recruiting at predominately black colleges and junior colleges during the late 1960's. Some firms have undertaken efforts to change their image with these colleges and their students, but none is overly optimistic about the impact of such efforts given low starting salaries and slow advancement which are seen as permanent problems in recruiting Negro management trainees.

The recent shift of some firms to top high school students as a source of management trainees may have a real impact in future Negro representation in management jobs in the industry. To date, however, only a few firms have been forced to take this step and virtually none have undertaken intensive programs to identify and recruit management trainees from among existing employees. It is the latter type of program which holds the greatest prospect for Negroes, given the progress they have made over the 1960's in penetrating both sales and clerical work forces in department stores.

The basic recruitment pattern for sales workers—walk-ins, employee referrals, and internal store advertising—historically has not encouraged large numbers of Negro applicants for the cities. The lack of active external recruiting coupled with the image of the industry in the black community has weakened the link between changing population and employment. In the suburbs, these two factors have tended to limit the labor market geographically. In short, recruiting practices have tended to reinforce other more basic barriers to Negro entry into sales positions over the postwar period and are at least partially responsible for low Negro representation in sales positions and, thereby, for the surprisingly low level of overall Negro representation in the industry in the major cities.

The turnover pattern among sales workers also has not worked to benefit Negroes. The fact that turnover has been concentrated among part-time and contingent sales personnel, rather than among full-time, high earnings sales personnel, must have limited the attractiveness of available job opportunities in the sales area and did inhibit the efforts of some firms to alter racial employment patterns in the sales force.

The clerical work force provides an interesting contrast to the sales force in terms of the impact of recruitment and turnover on Negro employment. In general, department stores have experienced high clerical turnover and have been required to undertake active recruiting for clerical workers. As a result, there has been a relatively rapid rate of change in the level of Negro representation in these positions once the Negro gained acceptance.

At the blue collar level, the combination of high turnover and active recruiting has created a consistently friendly environment for the Negro. To some extent, the image of the industry coupled with the existence of real and/or perceived employment barriers in other industries tended to enhance the attractiveness of this industry, particularly as manufacturing operations moved out of the cities. The industry's initial approach to and early experience with hardcore employment programs is consistent with this more basic phenomenon.

Selection Standards and Testing

Both management trainees and sales workers are hired at the unit level and are assigned to departments in consultation with and/or on the approval of the department manager. These two factors have tended to weaken the impact of formal equal employment opportunity policies on actual employment patterns in managerial and sales jobs throughout most of the postwar period.

Most of the firms studied relied on a combination of sight screening, written tests, and interviews in the selection of management trainees and sales workers. Sight screening and interviews were used to evaluate such subjective factors as dress, grooming, poise and speech which are regarded as crucial in good customer relations. White interviewers with the reaction of white customers in mind may be more critical of Negro candidates on such factors. A wide variety of written tests are used in the industry, but most prevalent are ones designed to measure arithmetic ability. Basic intelligence tests such as the Wonderlic have been and continue to be used, but on a diminishing scale and with lessening importance. Minimum performance standards for such tests are generally set on a divisional basis.

The primary emphasis in selection of clerical workers is on a minimum level of technical proficiency. Appearance factors, which are important in the selection of sales workers, are distinctly secondary. In this respect, it is interesting to note that most stores are far more willing to employ young people in clerical jobs than in sales positions. Generally, this preference creates no real problems in the assignment of applicants, as younger workers often prefer the regular hours of clerical jobs to the evening and weekend work in sales.

Selection standards for semiskilled and unskilled labor are minimal, but considerable attention is paid to an applicant's socioeconomic background and to the presence or absence of a police record. Stores are very concerned about the temptation of valuable merchandise to someone from a deprived background who may have a police record. Losses from "inventory shrinkage," often the result of employee theft, have grown to the extent that they can spell the difference between profit and loss for a unit. Thus, these jobs, which otherwise would be an important source of Negro employment, may tend to be available on a much more limited basis because of relatively stringent employment standards.

CIVIL RIGHTS PRESSURES

From the mid-1960's on, retail businesses felt the increasing tempo and pressure of various civil rights organizations and other community groups which chose to make the highly visible jobs in these industries targets for increased Negro employment and Negro occupational upgrading. Retail companies also found themselves under pressure, both covert and overt, for other types of contributions to Negro groups in some cities, such as support for Black Panther breakfast programs.

There were only isolated instances, during the period, of protests specifically against department stores, but in some cities department stores were included in general boycott or picketing activities aimed at the white business community. Even where entirely different retail groups were singled out, such as Operation Breadbasket's early activities against supermarkets,[27] department store management could not ignore the implications for the broader range of retail firms.

Department stores have been picketed in such cities as Richmond, Virginia, where the NAACP chose to picket and boycott a number of merchants who failed to denounce a Ku Klux Klan rally in 1965.[28] The Emporium, in San Francisco, discharged two of its own employees in 1968 who picketed the store and made charges that it was racist.[29] A 1969 Negro boycott in Baton Rouge, Louisiana, succeeded in reducing sales volume at a J. C. Penney store there to 5 percent of its normal volume.[30]

A series of destructive fires occurred at the stores of seven New York and Chicago department store firms in the spring of 1968.[31] Although these were of unknown origin, the lesson that department stores are highly vulnerable to extremists' actions could not be overlooked.

AFFIRMATIVE ACTION

Few of the firms or divisions studied held government contracts which would have made them subject to a formal affirmative action test of minority group employment. Despite the absence of widespread contractual obligations to undertake affirmative action, there is considerable evidence that affirmative action was widely practiced in the firms studied by 1970. In a limited number of cases, the roots of an affirmative action program could be traced back to Plans for Progress. In most cases, however, affirmative action evolved gradually after the passage of the Civil Rights Act and became a formal corporate policy or program during the 1968-1970 period. The chains are an exception to this pattern, as affirmative action programs tended to emerge "full-blown" in these firms between 1968 and 1970.

---

27. See the supermarket study in this series for a detailed discussion of Operation Breadbasket.

28. "Court Upholds Picket Rights," *New Pittsburgh Courier*, June 17, 1967.

29. The Emporium, 192 NLRB No. 19, *Daily Labor Report*, No. 207, October 24, 1969, pp. A-9—A-11; and No. 143, July 26, 1971, pp. D-1—D-6. The NLRB ruled that the company had a right to discharge these employees.

30. U.S. Equal Employment Opportunity Commission, *Hearings*, Houston, Texas, 1969.

31. "Fires at Big New York and Chicago Stores . . .," *Wall Street Journal*, April 1, 1968.

The basis for these voluntary affirmative action programs generally rested on individual managerial concern in the civil rights area at or near the top of the organization—often in the staff functions of personnel or public relations. The conversion of this concern into action was generally encouraged by the increasing marginal significance of the Negro consumer market and facilitated by the prolonged tight labor market in most urban areas. These two essentially economic variables explain the timing of the emergence of affirmative action programs in various types of stores, just as they explain differences in the evolution of Negro employment patterns in various types of stores prior to 1968.

The affirmative action programs at work in the stores studied during the latter part of the 1960's generally were based on close and continual scrutiny of minority group employment data on a unit-by-unit basis. In many cases, this scrutiny was the task of a special minority group employment coordinator at the divisional or corporate level who also served as an internal "devil's advocate" with respect to overall employment policies and practices. These individuals generally operated with strong implicit top management support, but without clearly stated formal authority. In the largest national firms, however, the authority of minority group employment coordinators was, by 1970, supported by formal minority group employment goals for individual units in the managerial and sales areas.

Early Response and Results

Corporate and/or divisional pressure for affirmative action and visible employment results has not been universally well accepted by unit managers who must devise and implement action programs, and the results of such pressure generally have not been entirely satisfactory from the viewpoint of those corporate or divisional staff members responsible for minority group employment. Despite considerable variability of response within organizations, the overall impact of pressures for affirmative action appears to have been significant in the 1968-1970 period. At a minimum, it produced some major changes in recruiting efforts in the direction of greater reliance on Negro colleges, high schools, newspapers, civil rights leaders, and clergymen as labor market intermediaries. There is little clear evidence that affirmative action alone involved any significant lowering of selection standards or increase in training effort, but there is some evidence that it did involve change in placement decisions. The result of these changes has been an acceleration in the rate of growth of overall Negro percentage representation in managerial and sales positions and a marked increase in the number of Negroes in such positions in suburban stores.

Within this overall industry framework, there is relatively little evidence that affirmative action has narrowed historical regional differences in Negro employment patterns within the industry or, with the possible exception of chain stores, altered traditional institutionally based differences in such patterns. The cultural and economic forces which generated differential Negro employment patterns prior to 1968 tended to generate parallel differences in the nature and extent of commitment to affirmative action at all managerial levels. To the extent that chain stores are an exception to this pattern, it is a reflection of the imposition of specific employment goals and of the effectiveness of management by results rather than by exhortation in the area of minority group employment. There is, however, reason to question the extent to which the gains made in the chains under management by results would have come about had such a policy been widely adopted in the industry or could be sustained without some lowering of selection standards should the rest of the industry move toward such a policy. The same question can be raised for the entire industry relative to the rest of the labor market.

Nieman-Marcus Purchasing Policies

In the context of a discussion of affirmative action programs in the department store industry, mention should be made of the decision of Nieman-Marcus to purchase only from firms which could demonstrate good records in the minority group employment area, in addition to implementing a fair hiring policy of its own.[32] To date, this decision stands alone in the industry and there was no evidence that similar policies were being considered seriously in any of the firms studied. Given the importance of style and price factors in this highly competitive industry, only a firm with the market position of Nieman-Marcus could afford to risk cutting itself off from any number or range

---

32. "Texas Store Takes Crack at Job Bias," *New Pittsburgh Courier,* January 20, 1968.

of potential suppliers on the basis of the racial employment issue. At the same time, it would take an equally prestigious or much larger firm successfully to exert economic pressure on suppliers to change their racial employment policies.

For the most part, only chain stores have both sufficient size and sufficiently centralized buying functions to meet the size test, although both consolidation and cooperation within the industry are changing the buying structure of the industry. The national chains and, to a lesser extent, cooperative buying syndicates have used their market power to influence production specifications as well as price in the private brand area. In theory, they could extend this influence into the area of racial employment policies, but the potential economic costs of such action are high and likely to remain so barring a major change in the structure of retail trade.

HARDCORE EMPLOYMENT

Programs to hire the hardcore were not entirely unknown in the department store industry prior to the emergence of the Job Opportunities in the Business Sector—National Alliance of Businessmen programs in this area. Several of the moderate price stores studied had instituted programs for high school dropouts during the late 1950's or early 1960's. Two of the more widely publicized of these programs were those instituted by Carson Pirie Scott and Company in Chicago and the Bamberger's division of R. H. Macy and Company in Newark.

Programs for High School Dropouts

Carson Pirie Scott, whose commitment to hire Negroes in nontraditional jobs dates from 1950, initially focused on hiring only fully qualified Negroes who otherwise would not have applied because of a belief that they would not be hired. Its early program included special recruitment efforts and careful supervision of new employees, as well as special efforts to make the management decision understood by all employees, but did not involve revising selection standards or instituting special training programs.[33] In the early 1960's, while continuing its earlier efforts, Carson's instituted an "Education and Employment" program to

---

33. Stephen Habbe, *Company Experience with Negro Employment,* Personnel Policy Study No. 201 (New York: National Industrial Conference Board, 1966), Vol. I, pp. 94-103.

help motivate potential high school dropouts to finish their education.[34] Slightly more than one-half of those enrolled in the pilot program were Negro. The program called for the students to go to school two days a week in company-provided classrooms and to work three days a week under the guidance of specially appointed counselors. The training program was geared to the work experience and gave high school credit for time spent in school.

Bamberger's early training program also was aimed at high school dropouts and potential dropouts.[35] The company's eight New Jersey stores offered evening jobs as store clerks or messengers to juniors and seniors who agreed to stay in school. The employment manager of each store coordinated the program, called the D Squad, keeping in touch with each student's school and work performance. Although initially only potentially college bound students were considered, this criterion was later changed to require only the potential for high school graduation. Both the Carson and Bamberger early programs working with dropouts were considered quite successful in their goals of encouraging high school graduation, but they had little impact on department store work forces since they were not primarily intended to make these employees permanent, full-time workers.

In general, these early employment programs appear to have been either an integral part or a logical extension of campaigns to enhance the market position and image of these firms in the Negro community. Although such programs were widely publicized and praised, their employment results were mixed and their market impact uncertain. Managers in directly competing stores often expressed the opinion that these programs had not justified their cost and would have been abandoned had they not been so widely publicized and praised at their inception. This "white elephant" view receives some support from the fact that such programs did not maintain their size, much less expand, over time within these firms and clearly explains the failure of such programs to spread within the industry.

---

34. C. Virgil Martin, "Utilizing the Dropout," in Herbert R. Northrup and Richard L. Rowan (eds.), *The Negro and Employment Opportunity* (Ann Arbor: Bureau of Industrial Relations, University of Michigan, 1965), pp. 331-341.

35. Charles W. Garrison, "A Program for High School Dropouts in Bamberger's, New Jersey," in Northrup and Rowan, *op. cit.*, pp. 343-347.

JOBS Programs

The emergence of the Job Opportunities in the Business Sector program and the National Alliance of Businessmen organization to administer that program produced a dramatic change in the status of hardcore employment programs in the department store industry. The size, location, and visibility of department stores made them a logical focus for pressure to hire the hardcore. In the context of a highly publicized national campaign to aid the hardcore, department stores could not easily resist such pressure, as resistance could result in essentially the same type of unfavorable publicity and adverse customer reaction as had been anticipated in earlier years from any dramatic deviations from the status quo in minority group employment. Any incentive to risk such publicity and customer reaction was weakened by the very tight labor market which had left many downtown department stores with a supply of job applicants which was at best only marginally superior to the hardcore.

Hardcore Hiring Decisions

Many companies had begun hardcore programs by 1968 and virtually all of the firms and divisions studied had made some commitment to hire the hardcore by 1970, but there were significant differences among the three types of firms with respect to the timing and form of commitment. In most cities, local firms made the first and most formal commitment to hire the hardcore. Divisions of the federations generally followed the action of local firms after a relatively short time lag. Chain stores were the last to make formal commitments in this area. This same ordering was observed with respect to willingness to make commitments on specific numbers.

Given the local focus of the JOBS program and the highly decentralized structure of the NAB, pressure to make formal commitments in the hardcore employment area was more effective in local firms and federation divisions than in chain store units, by virtue of the greater degree of local control of employment policies in the former types of stores. In the case of federation divisions, profit accountability to a distant higher authority produced some hesitancy to exercise this control quickly and/or completely in response to new developments and accounted for the slower response of these stores and their greater reluctance to make a commitment on specific numbers. The highly centralized nature of the chains meant that local action had to wait not only on corporate tolerance of increased personnel costs, as in the federations, but on corporate authorization and development of hardcore employment programs. The structure of these firms prevented the effective transmission of local pressure to top management to a greater extent than did the structure of the federations.

Within this overall framework, there was further diversity in the response to pressure to hire the hardcore. Among both local firms and divisions of federations, there was some tendency for budget stores to lag behind other stores in making any commitment to hire the hardcore and for carriage trade and budget stores to make less specific commitments on numbers. Within the chains, there was some significant intercity variation in early hardcore employment activity with the greatest activity concentrated in those cities in which corporate and regional headquarters were located.

These patterns appear to reflect differences in the balance between institutional pressure for positive action and economic pressures against such action. In general, the extent of moral pressure exerted on a department store varied directly with visibility which was, in turn, a function of market position. The extent of labor market and product market pressure to hire the hardcore followed the same complex pattern as was observed in the area of Negro employment. The net result was the "polarization" of moderate price and budget stores with carriage trade stores occupying a compromise position between them—just as was the case for Negro employment. The same logic can be applied to the chain stores as the observed pattern clearly suggests that, given a common organizational and/or economic environment, the response to local pressure to employ the hardcore was a function of the extent to which that pressure had a direct impact at those levels of management which had substantial control over employment policies.

Initial Hardcore Activities

In general, most of the firms and divisions studied took a fairly narrow view of the meaning of a commitment to hire the hardcore. Few of the stores studied perceived either an active recruitment campaign or a significant modification of traditional selection standards as an integral part of their commitment to hire the hardcore and most initially did little more than await the appearance of hardcore job applicants with the intention of selecting only the best qualified. This approach was a logical outgrowth of the fact that society generally anticipated a flood of hardcore job seekers once a promise of jobs existed.

When the expected flood of hardcore job seekers did not materialize, the public relations benefits of results forced most firms to abandon a strictly passive approach. For the most part, the firms and divisions studied continued to be highly reluctant to lower selection standards and tended to confine their positive action to the recruiting area. A number of firms which had developed effective recruiting channels in the Negro community as part of a program of affirmative action in the area of minority group employment were both willing and able to adapt such channels to recruiting hardcore. The cost of adapting or developing such channels, however, deterred a majority of the stores studied and induced them to turn to existing and emerging labor market intermediaries such as state employment services and the Urban League. The result was the emergence of a strong competition for the "soft" hardcore and a high demand for pre-employment trained hardcore workers.

In most cities, intensified recruiting efforts produced an adequate supply of "soft" hardcore to permit most stores to hire some hardcore by the end of 1968. In most cases, these hardcore employees were predominantly female and in many cases some significant number had been hired as walk-ins and then referred to the employment service for certification as "hardcore." These two characteristics of early hardcore employees tend to confirm a general feeling in the industry that the central location of department stores and their ability to utilize female labor in large quantities can give them a competitive advantage in the hardcore labor market. Such an advantage was valued highly in most firms both for public relations reasons and because it promised to generate an expansion in the supply of labor to the industry despite increasingly noncompetitive wages.

The competitive disadvantage of the department store industry should not be overestimated. The low wage character of the industry has made it difficult to hire or retain the hardcore. In part, this reflects competition within the labor market, but it also reflects the inability of the industry to compete with welfare. The costs of going to work in a department store—transportation, clothes, babysitters—have proven to more than offset the difference between entry level earnings and welfare in a number of cases. To date, only a limited number of department stores have been willing to subsidize these costs of going to work out of corporate resources as part of their commitment to hire the hardcore.

Provisions for Training

Considerable variation was observed among the firms and divisions studied with respect to training of the hardcore at the outset of hardcore employment programs. Some firms did little more than augment normal training with close supervision and/ or a "buddy system." A majority of the firms, however, created one or more special staff positions to handle hardcore training. At a minimum, these firms hired an employment counselor— usually a Negro—to handle the psychological and social problems of absorbing the hardcore into the organization. At a maximum, these firms also hired a director of hardcore training —usually a Negro school teacher—to develop and administer basic education and/or job training programs.

Over time, the degree of diversity in hardcore training programs in the industry has decreased and the form of such programs has changed. Experience has shown that some extra training for the hardcore is highly desirable, if not absolutely necessary. At the same time, experience has also shown that basic education for the hardcore is an expensive and complex undertaking which may be better done by other specialized organizations. The result of these two types of experience has been widespread acceptance of the need for a hardcore employment counselor or coordinator and reduced emphasis on internal basic education programs.

The availability of government subsidies for hardcore employment programs has also influenced the degree of diversity in and the form of such programs within the department store industry. This force has become increasingly important as managerial units have become linked together, through substitution of a local consortium for individual firm action or of a federation program for divisional programs, in order to meet scale and other subsidy requirements.

Entry Level Jobs

In general, the range of jobs open to the hardcore has been and will continue to be limited in department stores. Initial placement in most of the stores studied was in a low skill or service department in the downtown store or central warehouse facility. These departments were selected primarily on the basis of management's assessment of the ability of the department supervisor to work with hardcore employees—an assessment in which race often appeared to have been an important factor. Promotional opportunities from these jobs have been severely limited with promotion heavily dependent on distinguished performance and superior potential.

There is relatively little reason to assume that a hardcore employee could not display distinguished performance with experience. There is, however, reason to question the ability of such an employee to develop potential with experience. This type of development generally depends on education and training and none of the firms and divisions studied had even considered the establishment of upgrading programs for their hardcore employees.

Impact of the Programs

Regardless of the nature of management commitment to hardcore employment programs in the department store industry, it is clear that such programs have brought some individuals into the industry who would have been excluded in the absence of such programs. In most cities, the overwhelming majority of these individuals were Negroes who were attracted to the industry through the enhanced recruiting efforts in the urban ghetto associated with the emergence of hardcore programs and admitted to it under selection standards which were only slightly lower than would have prevailed in the absence of such programs. Thus, on balance, it appears that hardcore programs have had a marginal impact on Negro employment in department stores in the major cities in the form of facilitating and/or accelerating the "substitution" of Negro for white labor in central city department stores already dictated by basic labor market forces. There is no evidence to suggest that these programs have had any significant impact on Negro employment in suburban stores or in the higher occupational categories.

The performance record of the hardcore in the department stores studied did not appear to differ significantly from the performance record of other recently hired employees. This comparability can be traced to the minimal change in selection standards required or undertaken in conjunction with hardcore employment programs. In short, many of the hardcore hired under formal programs in downtown and neighborhood stores might well have been hired in the absence of such programs and some of the very early hardcore hired in the industry were clearly superior to the average walk-in in terms of job skills.

Despite the comparability in performance between hardcore and nonhardcore new hires, the rate of return to individual firms from hardcore programs has been limited and far below initial expectations. This has been clearly reflected in growing interest in government subsidies for hardcore employment programs in the industry despite a strong early aversion to getting involved in governmental "red tape." Turnover among hardcore employees is substantial, although not significantly above normal for recent new hires. This turnover has tended to be concentrated among the "best" hardcore workers who leave to take higher paying jobs and the "poorest" employees who must be fired for deviant behavior including, but not limited to, stealing. Thus, the long run employment returns to firms from hardcore programs is low and has declined as the supply of "soft" hardcore has been exhausted. These returns do not appear to have been augmented to any significant extent by tangible sales increases.

The long run tolerance of most firms in the industry for a low return on investment is clearly limited by their low profit margins. This is the case even in the most profitable national federations and chains. This basic economic limitation on commitment to hardcore employment programs is supported by a strong explicit dissatisfaction within the industry with the quality of the current external supply of labor and an equally strong implicit desire to raise selection standards when labor market conditions become more favorable. In this context, there is reason to question the viability of formal hardcore employment programs in department stores in the face of a decline in corporate profits and/or a loosening in urban labor markets. The former development would exert strong pressure on most firms to abandon all but directly job related training for the hardcore and could result in a return to the pre-1968 employment situation. The latter development would permit complete abandonment of hardcore employment and could easily result in a return to the pre-1965 employment situation.

LOCATIONAL DECISIONS

One of the factors which restricted Negro employment opportunities in the urban segment of the department store industry throughout the 1960 decade to 1968 was the continuing decline in the relative importance of the central city in terms of retail trade. This was responsible for an absolute decline in central city department store employment in the cities studied over the 1966-1968 period. There is some evidence, however, that central city department store employment in the cities studied has stabilized since 1968 and may have grown slightly in some cases. To some extent, this undoubtedly reflects greater stability and growth in central city sales with continued prosperity, once the impact of the riots during the mid-1960's had run its course. There is also evidence to suggest, however, that this phenomenon may be a reflection of more than a short run response to changes in sales activity. Specifically, there is evidence that recent stability in central city employment may reflect, in some small measure, a corporate or divisional response to economic, social, and political pressures to reassess the long run market potential of the cities. This reassessment has had an impact on decisions regarding the short run fate of existing units and may have an impact on future unit development decisions and locational employment trends, with a potentially significant beneficial impact on the number and nature of job opportunities accessible to Negroes.

Unit Closings

In recent years, the continued decline in central city retail activity has forced a number of department store firms seriously to consider closing some city units. Such decisions have arisen on a larger scale and in a broader range of firms recently than was the case over the 1960 to 1968 period. Historically, these unit closing decisions arose first and on the largest scale in the chains simply because they operated the largest number of neighborhood stores which were most susceptible to changes in residential patterns. In recent years, however, unit closing decisions have arisen in a number of local firms and federation divisions which operate neighborhood stores and/or stores in predominantly Negro satellite cities such as Camden, Newark, and Oakland. There is also a definite prospect that many firms of all types will eventually have to face such a decision with respect to center city units should existing trends continue.

In general, unit closings within cities have been strongly opposed by local governments and civil rights groups. For the most part, the firms involved have been responsive to such opposition and have agreed to reconsider their decisions. In most cases, such reconsideration has led to abandonment of plans to close the units in question and affirmation of corporate concern for the economic future of the city, in general, and for the economic problems of the Negro in the city, in particular.

There is little reason to doubt the social dimensions of these corporate decisions and the commitment to the city which they entailed. There is, however, reason to question the strength or durability of that commitment. While few existing units were actually closed, firms have done little to refit and refurbish either the units they once considered closing or other neighborhood units, despite suggestions that they do so from the same sources which urged them to reconsider unit closing decisions. The short run incremental costs of refitting such units is high, since most are relatively old, and the long run return on investment in such units has not yet been perceived as sufficient to justify those costs. By comparison the costs of keeping existing city units in operation is low and can be justified in terms of the much larger overall investment of department store firms in the cities. Any substantial increase in these costs due to decreasing sales volume or increasing variable costs such as wages, taxes, theft, and vandalism could easily change this calculus, given low profit margins in the industry. Thus, it may be that some unit closing decisions have been temporarily deferred rather than permanently abandoned.

Nonstore Facilities

An interesting special case of the unit closing problem has arisen in several firms with respect to central service and warehouse facilities. In general, these facilities closely approximate manufacturing plants in operating requirements and have been subject to the same economic pressures to move out of the city, particularly as the balance of firm activity has shifted to the suburbs. Where firms have contemplated such movement, they have generally been urged to remain and some have been asked to relocate into ghetto areas rather than into the suburbs.

The cost calculus for decisions regarding the locations of non-store facilities is somewhat more complex than is the case for retail outlets and somewhat more favorable to location in the city. The availability of a large supply of skilled and semi-skilled labor in the city is a significant positive factor, given the low wage status of the industry, and has served to offset partially the economic disadvantages of central city location. This has been sufficient to forestall or prevent movement to the suburbs in a large number of cases and particularly in the case of the chains which often operate large labor intensive catalogue distribution centers in conjunction with central service facilities for retail units in the major cities. It has clearly not been sufficient, however, to induce movement into ghetto areas where all the basic costs of urban operation are likely to be highest and are augmented by a higher risk of theft, vandalism, and destruction.

In summary, there is evidence that the department store industry has made a conscious positive contribution to the level of Negro employment opportunities in major cities in recent years through locational decisions. To date, the major share of this contribution has been made by the national chains, who were best able and most willing to make it by virtue of their greater existing total investment in central city facilities and their larger total profits. So far this effort has been confined to the preservation of existing jobs, as opposed to an expansion of total employment opportunity. In this respect, it is important to note the existence of a few exceptions to the job maintenance rule in the actions of the national chains such as the decision of one chain to expand, refit, and restock a ghetto unit and the decision of another chain to build a new service facility in a ghetto area.

The long run willingness and ability of department stores to maintain or expand central city job opportunities is uncertain. A continuing decline in sales volumes in existing downtown and neighborhood department store units would undoubtedly exert strong economic pressure for change in locational structure in the industry. Past experience indicates that such pressure would result in an acceleration of the rate of suburban unit additions and city unit abandonment. It is possible, however, that the established trend could be reversed and that such pressure could result in the addition of new city units. Such a development would seem to depend on corporate commitment to salvaging the cities, but may, in fact, be a logical outgrowth of "saturation" of existing large scale suburban markets which may enhance the relative economic attractiveness of unexploited urban markets. There is some preliminary evidence of department store saturation of the suburban market in some areas in the decisions of firms to concentrate on expansion through the addition of small, limited line suburban units in order to penetrate currently untapped low density, geographically isolated markets. This same strategy might become profitable in urban areas at some future date, particularly if it is accepted on a large scale in suburban areas within the industry. This possibility does not appear to have been seriously contemplated in the industry, except by those individuals who are most directly involved in and concerned with the narrow employment and broad economic problems of Negroes.

UNION IMPACT

We noted in Chapter II that unions have not played a significant role in department store racial policies. In New York City, the Retail, Wholesale and Department Store Workers has often issued statements condemning race discrimination and encouraging minority employment. Other than to avoid putting a bar on managerial affirmative action, however, the net effect of such activity is not likely to be measurable. The Retail Clerks' union has been less given to verbalizing, but it too has welcomed members without discrimination while taking no strong active role in racial employment policies.

In general, managers interviewed in the field study made few unsolicited comments on the impact of any unions on divisional or unit personnel policies and practices. Direct questions regarding the role and impact of unions normally confirmed our findings by eliciting the response that the unions had done little to influence and/or constrain management policies with respect to recruiting, selection, training, placement, transfer, or promotion. In this context, therefore, it is not surprising that managers generally asserted that unions had created no obstacles to change in racial employment policies and practices. At the same time, most managers also stated that unions had made little or no positive contribution to any improvement in the employment status of Negroes.

This management view is consistent with the findings of several other, but more limited studies. Thus, studies of minority employment in retail stores in Baltimore and Philadelphia by human relations commissions make little or no reference to unions.[36] Even more striking is the 1966 City of New York Commission on Human Rights analysis which was based on an extensive sample of general merchandise retail stores.[37] This study is of particular interest in this respect because of the prevalence of unionization in retail trade in that city and because it reports that retail unions did not challenge the prevailing management view of union impact in the staffing area. Specifically, the study concluded:

Employers reported that unions have had little or no effect in the retail employment picture generally, including the employment of Negroes, with the exception of one union. Unions reported the same thing. Both believe that retail unions can do little to change the employment status of Negroes.[38]

---

36. *Survey of Retail Stores: Baltimore, Maryland* (Baltimore: Baltimore Community Relations Commission, 1966); and *Retail Stores Employment Study* (Philadelphia: Commission on Human Relations, City of Philadelphia, 1967).

37. Don O. Watkins and David McKinney, *A Study of Employment Patterns in the General Merchandise Group Retail Stores in New York City* (New York: City of New York Commission on Human Rights, 1966).

38. *Ibid.*, p. 3.

CHAPTER VII

Determinants of Negro Employment

The nature and extent of the changes in Negro employment patterns in the department store industry over the 1940-1970 period suggest that a complex set of forces have shaped most patterns and the policies which underlie them. In general, the foundation for the observed changes in Negro employment patterns can be found in the changing residential and retail patterns in urban areas which characterized the period. The two sets of patterns, however, are imperfectly correlated; other forces or factors conditioned the impact of demographic change on change in the level and structure of Negro employment. Three such intervening variables can be identified—market orientation, labor market position, and civil rights activity. The first of these acted to weaken the link between population change and employment change in both the short and long run. The latter two served to strengthen that link—labor market position in the long run and civil rights activity in the short run. Variations in the strength of these forces over time and between firms explain reasonably well both the evolution of the industry pattern of Negro employment and individual deviations from that pattern.

MARKET ORIENTATION

Department store managements generally have been highly sensitive and responsive to the real and/or imagined biases of their clientele in the employment area. This sensitivity and responsiveness can be traced to the basic service orientation and volume requirement of the institution coupled with the highly competitive nature of the industry. The service orientation of department stores increased contact and, thereby, the possibility of offending customers through "poor" personnel selection or placement. The volume requirement of department stores made customer dissatisfaction potentially costly, while competition virtually assured that such dissatisfaction would be reflected in a loss of sales.

Characteristics of Customers

The department store industry historically has catered to a predominantly white, primarily middle class consumer group. The commitment of the industry to this clientele has been only slightly weakened or modified by changing urban residential and retail patterns and emerging large scale urban Negro retail markets, as is evident in unit location decisions. This relatively unchanging market orientation has severely limited the impact of increases in Negro clientele on the perceptions and values of management and left the attitudes of the white middle class as the basic determinant of policy and practice in a broad range of operational areas. In this context, it is hardly surprising that department store management has been highly reluctant to change traditional standards of dress, grooming, speech, and personality in screening potential sales workers.

Customer Attitudes

The attitudes of the white middle class toward the Negro undoubtedly have not been and are not now either simple or stable. In general, it may be asserted that such attitudes have been, at any point in time, normally distributed across some negative-positive scale. To some extent, this appears to have been the case with respect to customer reaction to change in Negro employment policies and practices in department stores. Most firms reported no large scale customer reaction of any type to the introduction of Negroes into sales positions, but did report some limited customer praise and support for this step and some strong negative reaction in the form of oral and/or written complaints and cancelled charge accounts from a few customers.

The diversity of white middle class attitudes toward the Negro coupled with social pressures to disguise such attitudes made it extremely difficult for department store management to predict the market consequences of changes in Negro employment policies and practices. In the face of this uncertainty, managements most often made very conservative estimates of the tolerance of customers for change in order to minimize the probability of adverse reaction among their traditional clientele. This risk avoidance strategy was clearly viable in the absence of any social or economic pressure to change their narrow market orientation. It resulted in a prolonged perpetuation of the status quo and slower rate of change in Negro employment policies and practices in the industry than would have been suggested by modal middle class values or Negro representation in department store clientele.

In this framework, the history of Negro employment in the department store industry is better related to gradual change in managerial perceptions of the range and focus of white middle class attitudes toward Negroes than to the far more rapid emergence of the Negro as an important factor in retail trade in the city. Given slow but accelerating change in middle class attitudes from an even moderately negative position in 1940 to a moderately positive position in 1970 and a conservative management perception of such change, one can account for: (1) the almost complete absence of Negro white collar workers in 1940; (2) the continuing absence of Negro sales personnel in 1950 and Negro managerial personnel in 1960; (3) the timing and tentative nature of the introduction of Negroes into both sales and managerial positions; and (4) the continuing underrepresentation of Negroes in both sales and managerial positions in 1970.

Company Variations

The same analytical framework can be applied to variations in Negro employment patterns within the industry. The basis for this application is the assumption that firms or divisions or units differ with respect to the basic distribution of the attitudes of their white middle class clientele toward Negroes. This assumption seems well supported by the historical and contemporary regional differences in Negro employment patterns, by the early heavy concentration of Negro white collar employment in city units, and by the low representation of Negroes in white collar occupations in carriage trade and budget stores. In this respect, it is important to note that these differences tended to override common ownership and/or common operating management.

There are some apparent exceptions to this basic market orientation/customer attitude model of intraindustry variation. Specifically, the relatively greater progress of the Negro in white collar employment in department stores in the midwestern and border cities and in moderate price department stores over carriage trade and budget stores is not clearly consistent with the basic model. Further analysis of these exceptions indicates that they may be attributed to a change in the relative importance of the white middle class to the department stores in question. The midwestern and border cities experienced the most dramatic increases in Negro population over the 1940-1965 period, while moderate price stores in all cities were most adversely affected by the migration of the white middle class to the suburbs. Thus, it was stores in these regions and in this market position which were subjected to the greatest economic pressure to modify or abandon the traditional narrow market orientation, at least in the city. In this respect, it is significant that there was little or no evidence of any relatively early or particularly rapid change in Negro employment patterns in suburban units in these regions or types of stores.

LABOR MARKET POSITION

There is considerable evidence that labor market forces and changing labor market conditions have had an impact on racial employment policies and practices in the department store industry. In general, basic labor market forces during the 1940-1970 period encouraged expansion in Negro employment in all but managerial jobs in the city, but discouraged similar expansion in the suburbs. Short run tightness in the labor market accentuated pressures to employ and upgrade Negroes in the city, but had only a minor impact on Negro employment policies, practices, and patterns in suburban units.

The department store industry traditionally has been a low wage industry which competed for labor primarily on the basis of job availability and accessibility and drew heavily on a "residual" labor force composed largely of secondary wage earners (women) and marginal labor force participants (the young and the old). The competitive position of the industry in the labor market has tended to worsen over the postwar period as industry wages have failed to keep pace with wages in the economy generally, increasing primarily in response to changes in the legal minimum wage. This long run deterioration in the competitive position of the industry has been accentuated by increasing reliance, since 1960, on short hours personnel which has served further to limit short run earnings and discourage nonmarginal workers. The net result of these forces has been a long run reduction in the geographical scope of the labor market, and a narrowing of the quality range of the labor supply.

The localization and limitation of labor supply in the department store industry have magnified the impact of changing residential patterns on the racial composition of the supply of labor to individual units. In most downtown stores and many neighborhood stores, Negroes have been increasingly overrepresented among walk-ins in relation to their overall representation in the population of the city or the standard metropolitan statistical area, while the opposite was the case in suburban stores. In this context, some change in basic racial employment policies, practices, and patterns was inevitable in city units, but hardly necessary in suburban stores. Thus, the labor market position of department stores has been an important counterforce to market orientation In the translation of changing residential and retail patterns into changing racial employment patterns In the cities, but has reinforced market orientation in limiting Negro employment opportunities in the suburbs.

The impact of labor market position on racial employment policies, practices, and patterns has not been uniform across occupational categories. In general, the ability of department stores to recruit and retain white labor has increased with movement up the occupational hierarchy, thereby supporting the operation of market orientation in the determination of the structure of Negro employment.

The relative inability of department stores to recruit and retain white labor for blue collar jobs and, to a lesser extent, for clerical positions can be traced to the fact that wage differentials tend to be greatest in these areas because department stores compete directly with high wage industries for full-time employees. The existence of gross wage differentials coupled with real or imagined racial discrimination in high wage industries has left department stores with a predominantly Negro supply of labor for these jobs in both city and suburban units.

The superior ability of department stores to recruit and retain white managerial and particularly sales employees can be traced to the large and growing supply of white female labor force participants, many of whom are secondary wage earners. Wages are somewhat less important in relation to such nonwage factors as status, location, hours, and employee discounts in the operational decisions of these workers than in the decisions of Negroes. The latter are likely to be required by economic circumstances to maximize money income rather than net advantage and therefore voluntarily to seek or accept the higher short run earnings of blue collar or clerical jobs in preference to the higher status sales and entry level management positions in the industry.

Within this framework, two other sources of variation in the nature and extent of the impact of labor market position on

Negro employment policies and practices can be identified—region and market image. In the southern and border cities, there is evidence to suggest that the existence of comparatively strong discriminatory barriers elsewhere in the labor market provided department stores with an unusually abundant supply of Negro labor, in general, and Negro male labor, in particular, to be used to fill blue collar and service jobs. Conversely, the situation in midwestern cities provides some insight into the impact of the availability of relatively high paying jobs in manufacturing for Negroes on the racial composition and sex structure of blue collar and service employment in department stores. There is also strong evidence that the market image of carriage trade stores greatly enhanced their ability to recruit and retain white female employees in virtually all occupational categories, but particularly in the sales area, thereby permitting them the greatest labor market latitude to indulge their relatively strong market orientation incentive to perpetuate the status quo in Negro white collar employment.

LOCATION

From the 1940's to the mid-1960's, industry location was favorable to increasing Negro employment, as demand for labor remained high in areas where the labor force was becoming increasingly black—the central cities. The construction of new stores in the suburbs, however, was also well under way by this time. By the end of the 1960's, central city department store employment was declining, as stores closed down in response to changing economic and residential patterns.[39] The general decline of urban business districts has accompanied the movement of whites to the suburbs and rising crime rates in cities. Even where stores have not closed entirely, rising crime in the cities has deterred nighttime shoppers, even during the Christmas rush.[40] The consequent loss of employment has fallen heavily in areas that otherwise would have led to increased jobs for Negroes.

---

39. Manhattan, for example, lost ten major stores in the 1960's. See Isadore Barmash, "Suburbs Gaining on Manhattan," *New York Times*, June 21, 1971, pp. 41-42.

40. Isadore Barmash, "New York's Angry Retailers," *New York Times*, November 29, 1970, Section 3, pp. 1, 8.

The long run decline in central city employment could be sufficient to more than offset Negro gains in all areas. Given continuing concentration of Negro population in the city coupled with the increasing isolation of the suburban department store from the urban Negro due to a combination of poor and expensive transportation and short hours and low wages, this development would result in a sharp reduction in total Negro employment. The only counterforce is affirmative action within the industry with respect to both employment and unit location. There is some recent evidence of such action, but it is not clear that it will persist in the face of either a continuing decline in the relative profitability of central city units or a sudden decline in central city unit sales volumes such as occurred after the riots of 1965-1966 and can be expected in a recession.

CIVIL RIGHTS ACTIVITY

The visibility and accessibility of department stores has made them a logical and successful focus for civil rights pressure in the employment area. Most of the firms and divisions studied reported having been party to an overt or covert civil rights confrontation during the 1950's or 1960's which resulted in change in racial employment policies and practices. In many of these cases, the employment policies of the store were at issue, but in a surprising number of cases, the issue was broader and extended to employment policies elsewhere in the community.

Department stores are extremely vulnerable to picketing and boycotting and they have found themselves the subject of both formal individual and informal group charges of discrimination. A recent NLRB decision may somewhat reduce the use of these tactics, at least by a store's own employees [41] but they may well continue to find themselves used by civil rights groups to exert pressure on such less visible and accessible industries as construction and manufacturing. One example of the latter tactic occurred in New Rochelle, New York, where a Macy's store under

---

41. The NLRB affirmed the Trial Examiner's decision that an employer could dismiss employees who went outside of regular union-management procedures to protest alleged discriminatory activities. Two employees of The Emporium, in San Francisco, picketed the store on two occasions and distributed accusatory pamphlets without union endorsement after walking out of an adjustment board meeting intended to settle such matters. 192 NLRB No. 19, reported in *Daily Labor Report* No. 143 (July 26, 1971), pp. A-1—A-3, D-1—D-6.

construction was picketed by civil rights activists over the issue of the lack of Negroes in the unions then working at the construction site.[42] In addition, department stores have been widely called upon by local government officials to provide some of the employment concessions necessary to ease large scale racial tension.

The overall impact of these varied civil rights pressures on Negro employment policies, practices, and patterns in the industry has been significant and has generally served to supplement labor market forces in breaking down employment barriers in the city and to substitute for those forces in breaking down similar barriers in the suburbs. Historically, civil rights pressures were an important factor in the introduction of Negroes into sales positions in many cities and were the crucial factor in this respect in the South. Civil rights pressures were more important in the expansion of the range of sales positions open to Negroes and were a crucial factor in the very recent increase in Negro sales personnel in suburban stores. Finally, civil rights pressures are directly responsible for the current emphasis in the industry on balanced Negro representation in the management ranks and the emergence of informal and formal quota systems.

As civil rights pressure has dictated acceleration in the movement of Negroes into higher level white collar positions, the labor market position of department stores has become an increasingly significant restraining factor and a major source of problems under quota systems. Department stores generally have not been able to attract and/or retain the most qualified Negroes, in terms of education, experience, and appearance, and suburban stores have been at a particular disadvantage in this respect. In recent years, this problem has been accentuated by increased competition for the better educated Negro, continued tight labor market conditions, and enhanced black consciousness as manifested in the emergence of black styles of dress and grooming. In this context, external and internal pressures for equal employment have exerted strong pressures on traditional selection, training, and promotion policies in department stores, and have resulted in some changes in those policies above and beyond those dictated by basic labor market conditions. To date, these changes have involved the lowering of educational and experience stand-

---

42. Ralph Blumenthal, "Jobs Go Begging in New Rochelle," *New York Times*, August 12, 1967.

ards for Negroes and the emergence of "inverse discrimination" at lower levels and "preferential hiring and promotion" at higher levels. Appearance standards have not yet been significantly changed in order to accommodate black styles of dress and grooming and are not likely to be so changed until a large scale market exists for Afro styles which department stores find it advantageous to exploit. Similarly, training and development programs have not been greatly expanded and promotion continues to be dependent on experience and individual initiative, thereby perpetuating the problem of retaining the best and/or most highly motivated Negro white collar workers and compounding the problem of meeting quotas for Negro managers.

There is considerable evidence of variations within the industry in the timing of civil rights pressure in the employment area and in the nature and extent of the response to such pressure which are related to the visibility and importance of the firms, divisions, and units involved. In general, civil rights activity had its first and strongest impact on Negro employment policies in the Northeast and last and least impact in the South where other civil rights issues took precedence over employment. In most cities, the initial employment impact of civil rights activity was confined to downtown and neighborhood stores and did not extend to suburban units, where both product and labor market forces were unconducive to expansion in the number and occupational range of Negro employees. Within this framework, carriage trade stores, by virtue of their stature in the community, were often the initial target of civil rights activity, and budget stores the last to be subjected to pressure for equal opportunity and equal employment. This difference in timing was an important factor in the observed variations between carriage trade and budget stores in Negro representation in white collar positions as recently as 1968, although these differences were also consistent with the anticipation of extremely adverse reaction to changes in Negro employment policies from long term employees and customers. The impact of civil rights activity, per se, on moderate price stores in most cities outside the South appears to have been minimal in relation to the impact of market forces.

There is also evidence to suggest that the differences in the level and structure of Negro employment among the three basic types of firms in the industry—chains, federations, and local firms—are related to differential sensitivity and responsiveness to civil rights activity. In general, local firms and federation divisions were more visible and accessible to civil rights activists and/or local government agencies, by virtue of their operation of a large downtown store which housed "top management," than were the chains with their neighborhood units and distant "top management." Complete budgetary autonomy and control over employment policies and practices gave the management of local firms the greatest freedom to respond to civil rights pressures, while federation divisions were constrained by profit accountability and chain store units both by budgetary controls and by corporate hiring standards and staffing procedures. In combination, these coincident differences in managerial sensitivity and responsiveness to civil rights pressures are sufficient to account for the overall ranking of the types of firms in Negro employment and the differences between them in the nature and extent of participation in formal hardcore employment programs and practice of affirmative action.

THE FUTURE OF THE NEGRO IN THE DEPARTMENT STORE INDUSTRY

The Negro has made significant employment progress in the department store industry over the past thirty years. To a considerable extent he has moved from the position of an inferior commodity to the point of being a preferred commodity. It is, of course, highly doubtful that the Negro will retain a preferred status in the long run, but it is equally doubtful that he will again be relegated to an inferior status simply on the basis of race. Thus, it seems appropriate to assume that equal opportunity will be approximated in the industry, and to speculate as to the implications of it for the economic future of the Negro. Such speculation requires both a projection of the industry demand for labor and an assessment of the competitive status of the Negro in meeting that demand.

The department store industry historically has been and, barring a significant change in the relative labor market position and/or the basic service orientation of the industry, should continue to be characterized by a high and growing demand for comparatively low skill labor. It appears that most of this demand, however, will be for part-time workers and will be concentrated in suburban areas. Thus, there is little reason to expect that the Negro will be much benefitted by replacement and growth demand for labor in the department store industry unless there are dramatic changes in the basic residential patterns and transportation systems in urban areas. Such structural changes are only a necessary condition to provide Negroes with access to jobs in the industry and are not sufficient to insure that they will secure such jobs in competition with white middle class housewives as long as dress, grooming, and speech continue to be economically important selection criteria. The growing cultural gap between Negro and white society simply compounds this competitive disadvantage for the Negro.

The one factor which would alter this pessimistic view of the future of the Negro in the department store industry is the emergence of a large scale, profitable Negro retail market within the cities. Such a development could induce department stores to alter or segment their basic market orientation and restructure their operations. Specifically, it could lead to a reversal of migration of the industry to the suburbs and to the emergence of a demand for special managerial and sales personnel who "understand" the Negro consumer. This possibility seems remote at this time and is not enhanced by the relocation of department stores in the suburbs in pursuit of the white middle class. Thus, it is quite possible that the greatest long run contribution of the industry to the economic status of the Negro can be made through short run decisions regarding unit location and/or renovation. Such a contribution, however, is dependent on a modification of traditional market orientation and sacrifice of current profits— both of which are difficult, if not impossible, in this conservative, low profit industry.

Appendix

BASIC STATISTICAL TABLES, 1966, 1967, AND 1969

TABLE A-1. General Merchandise Industry Including Department Stores Employment by Race, Sex, and Occupational Group
4,704 Establishments United States, 1966

Occupational Group	All Employees			Male			Female		
	Total	Negro	Percent Negro	Total	Negro	Percent Negro	Total	Negro	Percent Negro
Officials and managers	161,511	2,211	1.4	110,055	1,421	1.3	51,456	790	1.5
Professionals	11,542	171	1.5	6,867	110	1.6	4,675	61	1.3
Technicians	8,880	268	3.0	5,509	150	2.7	3,371	118	3.5
Sales workers	667,844	22,043	3.3	137,616	3,904	2.8	530,228	18,139	3.4
Office and clerical	280,414	20,874	7.4	34,879	3,067	8.8	245,535	17,807	7.3
Total white collar	1,130,191	45,567	4.0	294,926	8,652	2.9	835,265	36,915	4.4
Craftsmen	45,299	2,525	5.6	37,960	1,639	4.3	7,339	886	12.1
Operatives	77,602	11,511	14.8	47,855	6,948	14.5	29,747	4,563	15.3
Laborers	68,532	13,073	19.1	46,108	8,661	18.8	22,424	4,412	19.7
Service workers	135,000	35,348	26.2	58,007	20,039	34.5	76,993	15,309	19.9
Total blue collar	326,433	62,457	19.1	189,930	37,287	19.6	136,503	25,170	18.4
Total	1,456,624	108,024	7.4	484,856	45,939	9.5	971,768	62,085	6.4

Source: U.S. Equal Employment Opportunity Commission, Job Patterns for Minorities and Women in Private Industry, 1966, Report No. 1 (Washington: The Commission, 1968), Part II.

Note: Companies with 100 or more employees.

TABLE A-2. *General Merchandise Industry Including Department Stores*
Employment by Race, Sex, and Occupational Group
6,011 Establishments
United States, 1967

Occupational Group	All Employees			Male			Female		
	Total	Negro	Percent Negro	Total	Negro	Percent Negro	Total	Negro	Percent Negro
Officials and managers	182,402	3,054	1.7	123,980	2,016	1.6	58,422	1,038	1.8
Professionals	13,196	255	1.9	7,716	151	2.0	5,480	104	1.9
Technicians	10,697	375	3.5	7,318	258	3.5	3,379	117	3.5
Sales workers	731,703	26,047	3.6	153,685	5,148	3.3	578,018	20,899	3.6
Office and clerical	317,108	26,125	8.2	37,340	3,690	9.9	279,768	22,435	8.0
Total white collar	1,255,106	55,856	4.5	330,039	11,263	3.4	925,067	44,593	4.8
Craftsmen	51,128	2,939	5.7	41,768	1,951	4.7	9,360	988	10.6
Operatives	87,552	14,080	16.1	56,336	8,599	15.3	31,216	5,481	17.6
Laborers	78,090	16,564	21.2	49,555	9,971	20.1	28,535	6,593	23.1
Service workers	147,853	37,214	25.2	62,011	20,331	32.8	85,842	16,883	19.7
Total blue collar	364,623	70,797	19.4	209,670	40,852	19.5	154,953	29,945	19.3
Total	1,619,729	126,653	7.8	539,709	52,115	9.7	1,080,020	74,538	6.9

Source: U.S. Equal Employment Opportunity Commission, *Job Patterns for Minorities and Women in Private Industry, 1967*, Report No. 2 (Washington: The Commission, 1970), Vol. 1.

Note: Companies with 100 or more employees.

TABLE A-3. *General Merchandise Industry Including Department Stores Employment by Race, Sex, and Occupational Group 6,762 Establishments United States, 1969*

Occupational Group	All Employees			Male			Female		
	Total	Negro	Percent Negro	Total	Negro	Percent Negro	Total	Negro	Percent Negro
Officials and managers	182,089	4,405	2.4	121,253	2,788	2.3	60,836	1,617	2.7
Professionals	14,294	377	2.6	8,836	227	2.6	5,458	150	2.7
Technicians	11,630	596	5.1	8,233	419	5.1	3,397	177	5.2
Sales workers	722,062	33,809	4.7	154,581	6,780	4.4	567,481	27,029	4.8
Office and clerical	298,489	21,974	7.4	35,702	3,685	10.3	261,787	18,289	7.0
Total white collar	1,227,564	61,161	5.0	328,605	13,899	4.2	898,959	47,262	5.3
Craftsmen	49,092	3,069	6.3	40,540	2,182	5.4	8,552	887	10.4
Operatives	83,351	12,413	14.9	54,153	8,559	15.8	29,198	3,854	13.2
Laborers	60,018	12,582	21.0	40,580	8,252	20.3	19,438	4,330	22.3
Service workers	133,585	32,156	24.1	57,965	17,648	30.4	75,620	14,508	19.2
Total blue collar	326,046	60,220	18.5	193,238	36,641	19.0	132,808	23,579	17.8
Total	1,553,610	121,381	7.8	521,843	50,540	9.7	1,031,767	70,841	6.9

Source: U.S. Equal Employment Opportunity Commission, 1969.

Note: Companies with 100 or more employees.

TABLE A-4. *General Merchandise Industry Including Department Stores Employment by Race, Sex, and Occupational Group Ten Metropolitan Areas, 1966*

Occupational Group	All Employees			Male			Female		
	Total	Negro	Percent Negro	Total	Negro	Percent Negro	Total	Negro	Percent Negro
Officials and managers	45,739	1,081	2.4	31,135	661	2.1	14,604	420	2.9
Professionals	5,862	71	1.2	3,856	48	1.2	2,006	23	1.1
Technicians	3,957	154	3.9	2,770	92	3.3	1,187	62	5.2
Sales workers	171,112	9,962	5.8	35,403	1,686	4.8	135,709	8,276	6.1
Office and clerical	102,040	15,452	15.1	13,790	1,660	12.0	88,250	13,792	15.6
Total white collar	328,710	26,720	8.1	86,954	4,147	4.8	241,756	22,573	9.3
12 metropolitan areas	366,172	28,053	7.7						
Craftsmen	14,269	1,332	9.3	11,859	879	7.4	2,410	453	18.8
Operatives	27,741	6,323	22.8	16,401	3,314	20.2	11,340	3,014	26.6
Laborers	29,544	8,361	28.3	18,523	5,235	28.3	11,021	3,126	28.4
Service workers	39,671	14,358	36.2	18,075	7,861	43.5	21,596	6,497	30.1
Total blue collar	111,225	30,379	27.3	64,858	17,289	26.7	46,367	13,090	28.2
12 metropolitan areas	121,366	31,716	26.1						
Total	439,935	57,099	13.0	151,812	21,436	14.1	288,123	35,663	12.4
12 metropolitan areas	487,538	59,774	12.3						

Source: U.S. Equal Employment Opportunity Commission, *Job Patterns for Minorities and Women in Private Industry, 1966*, Report No. 1 (Washington: The Commission, 1968), Parts I and III.

Note: Atlanta, Baltimore, Chicago, Detroit, Houston, Los Angeles-Long Beach, New York, Philadelphia, St. Louis, and Washington, D.C. The second set of figures under white collar, blue collar, and total include data for Pittsburgh and San Francisco-Oakland. Complete occupational data were not provided for these metropolitan areas in 1966.

TABLE A-5. *General Merchandise Industry Including Department Stores Employment by Race, Sex, and Occupational Group Twelve Metropolitan Areas, 1967*

Occupational Group	All Employees			Male			Female		
	Total	Negro	Percent Negro	Total	Negro	Percent Negro	Total	Negro	Percent Negro
Officials and managers	60,352	1,660	2.8	39,935	1,076	2.7	20,417	584	2.9
Professionals	7,073	148	2.1	4,565	105	2.3	2,508	43	1.7
Technicians	5,052	223	4.4	3,641	168	4.6	1,411	55	3.9
Sales workers	221,252	13,584	6.1	47,989	2,643	5.5	173,263	10,941	6.3
Office and clerical	128,072	19,501	15.2	16,508	2,188	13.3	111,564	17,313	15.5
Total white collar	421,801	35,116	8.3	112,638	6,180	5.5	309,163	28,936	9.4
Craftsmen	17,646	1,517	8.6	14,273	1,004	7.0	3,373	513	15.2
Operatives	33,334	7,912	23.7	20,922	4,489	21.5	12,412	3,423	27.6
Laborers	40,401	11,441	28.3	22,997	6,077	26.4	17,404	5,364	30.8
Service workers	49,517	16,882	34.1	22,641	9,005	39.8	26,876	7,877	29.3
Total blue collar	140,898	37,752	26.8	80,833	20,575	25.5	60,065	17,177	28.6
Total	562,699	72,868	12.9	193,471	26,755	13.8	369,228	46,113	12.5

Source: U.S. Equal Employment Opportunity Commission, *Job Patterns for Minorities and Women in Private Industry, 1967*, Report No. 2 (Washington: The Commission, 1970), Vol. 2.

Note: Cities are listed in Table A-4.

TABLE A-6. *General Merchandise Industry Including Department Stores Employment by Race, Sex, and Occupational Group Twelve Metropolitan Areas, 1969*

Occupational Group	All Employees			Male			Female		
	Total	Negro	Percent Negro	Total	Negro	Percent Negro	Total	Negro	Percent Negro
Officials and managers	56,202	2,360	4.2	36,913	1,433	3.9	19,289	927	4.8
Professionals	7,440	235	3.2	4,950	148	3.0	2,490	87	3.5
Technicians	4,795	393	8.2	3,379	271	8.0	1,416	122	8.6
Sales workers	216,783	16,507	7.6	47,879	3,231	6.7	168,904	13,276	7.9
Office and clerical	110,784	15,052	13.6	15,428	2,364	15.3	95,356	12,688	13.3
Total white collar	396,004	34,547	8.7	108,549	7,447	6.9	287,455	27,100	9.4
Craftsmen	14,701	1,275	8.7	12,202	995	8.2	2,499	280	11.2
Operatives	27,532	5,828	21.2	17,976	3,843	21.4	9,556	1,985	20.8
Laborers	24,941	7,249	29.1	15,378	4,108	26.7	9,563	3,141	32.8
Service workers	42,166	13,907	33.0	18,964	7,618	40.2	23,202	6,289	27.1
Total blue collar	109,340	28,259	25.8	64,520	16,564	25.7	44,820	11,695	26.1
Total	505,344	62,806	12.4	173,069	24,011	13.9	332,275	38,795	11.7

Source: U.S. Equal Employment Opportunity Commission, 1969.

Note: Cities are listed in Table A-4.

TABLE A-7. *General Merchandise Industry Including Department Stores Employment by Race, Sex, and Occupational Group 177 Establishments New York and Philadelphia Metropolitan Areas, 1966*

Occupational Group	All Employees			Male			Female		
	Total	Negro	Percent Negro	Total	Negro	Percent Negro	Total	Negro	Percent Negro
Officials and managers	17,457	537	3.1	12,174	325	2.7	5,283	212	4.0
Professionals	1,941	39	2.0	1,221	24	2.0	720	15	2.1
Technicians	1,303	60	4.6	863	47	5.4	440	13	3.0
Sales workers	56,708	3,893	6.9	10,174	664	6.5	46,534	3,229	6.9
Office and clerical	34,097	5,083	14.9	5,593	798	14.3	28,504	4,285	15.0
Total white collar	111,506	9,612	8.6	30,025	1,858	6.2	81,481	7,754	9.5
Craftsmen	3,620	203	5.6	3,146	155	4.9	474	48	10.1
Operatives	5,311	1,086	20.4	3,230	605	18.7	2,081	481	23.1
Laborers	10,375	2,798	27.0	6,195	1,446	23.3	4,180	1,352	32.3
Service workers	13,211	4,378	33.1	6,721	2,844	42.3	6,490	1,534	23.6
Total blue collar	32,517	8,465	26.0	19,292	5,050	26.2	13,225	3,415	25.8
Total	144,023	18,077	12.6	49,317	6,908	14.0	94,706	11,169	11.8

Source: U.S. Equal Employment Opportunity Commission, *Job Patterns for Minorities and Women in Private Industry, 1966*, Report No. 1 (Washington: The Commission, 1968), Part III.

TABLE A-8. *General Merchandise Industry Including Department Stores Employment by Race, Sex, and Occupational Group*
328 Establishments
New York, Philadelphia, and Pittsburgh Metropolitan Areas, 1967

Occupational Group	All Employees			Male			Female		
	Total	Negro	Percent Negro	Total	Negro	Percent Negro	Total	Negro	Percent Negro
Officials and managers	22,490	709	3.2	15,302	457	3.0	7,188	252	3.5
Professionals	2,680	68	2.5	1,652	44	2.7	1,028	24	2.3
Technicians	1,584	74	4.7	1,082	60	5.5	502	14	2.8
Sales workers	74,599	4,598	6.2	16,108	1,012	6.3	58,491	3,586	6.1
Office and clerical	44,025	6,075	13.8	6,016	861	14.3	38,009	5,214	13.7
Total white collar	145,378	11,524	7.9	40,160	2,434	6.1	105,218	9,090	8.6
Craftsmen	5,939	254	4.3	4,878	178	3.6	1,061	76	7.2
Operatives	7,896	1,448	18.3	4,523	704	15.6	3,373	744	22.1
Laborers	16,834	3,413	20.3	9,838	1,806	18.4	6,996	1,607	23.0
Service workers	17,880	5,243	29.3	9,602	3,550	36.8	8,278	1,713	20.7
Total blue collar	48,549	10,358	21.3	28,841	6,218	21.6	19,708	4,140	21.0
Total	193,927	21,882	11.3	69,001	8,652	12.5	124,926	13,230	10.6

Source: U.S. Equal Employment Opportunity Commission, *Job Patterns for Minorities and Women in Private Industry, 1967*, Report No. 2 (Washington: The Commission, 1970), Vol. 2.

TABLE A-9.　*General Merchandise Industry Including Department Stores Employment by Race, Sex, and Occupational Group*
335 Establishments
New York, Philadelphia, and Pittsburgh Metropolitan Areas, 1969

Occupational Group	All Employees			Male			Female		
	Total	Negro	Percent Negro	Total	Negro	Percent Negro	Total	Negro	Percent Negro
Officials and managers	22,758	1,153	5.1	15,277	690	4.5	7,481	463	6.2
Professionals	3,152	110	3.5	1,833	63	3.4	1,319	47	3.6
Technicians	1,888	123	6.5	1,329	101	7.6	559	22	3.9
Sales workers	79,022	6,247	7.9	16,702	1,218	7.3	62,320	5,029	8.1
Office and clerical	43,963	6,738	15.3	7,054	1,211	17.2	36,909	5,527	15.0
Total white collar	150,783	14,371	9.5	42,195	3,283	7.8	108,588	11,088	10.2
Craftsmen	4,678	304	6.5	3,955	239	6.0	723	65	9.0
Operatives	7,021	1,148	16.4	4,097	589	14.4	2,924	559	19.1
Laborers	11,303	2,927	25.9	6,698	1,589	23.7	4,605	1,338	29.1
Service workers	16,313	5,155	31.6	8,104	3,480	42.9	8,209	1,675	20.4
Total blue collar	39,315	9,534	24.3	22,854	5,897	25.8	16,461	3,637	22.1
Total	190,098	23,905	12.6	65,049	9,180	14.1	125,049	14,725	11.8

Source:　U.S. Equal Employment Opportunity Commission, 1969.

TABLE A-10. *General Merchandise Industry Including Department Stores Employment by Race, Sex, and Occupational Group*
95 Establishments
Baltimore, St. Louis, and Washington, D. C. Metropolitan Areas, 1966

Occupational Group	All Employees			Male			Female		
	Total	Negro	Percent Negro	Total	Negro	Percent Negro	Total	Negro	Percent Negro
Officials and managers	6,017	214	3.6	3,613	113	3.1	2,404	101	4.2
Professionals	420	6	1.4	221	5	2.3	199	1	0.5
Technicians	302	9	3.0	183	4	2.2	119	5	4.2
Sales workers	25,177	1,698	6.7	5,271	316	6.0	19,906	1,382	6.9
Office and clerical	10,153	927	9.1	1,388	214	15.4	8,745	713	8.2
Total white collar	42,049	2,854	6.8	10,676	652	6.1	31,373	2,202	7.0
Craftsmen	1,993	221	11.1	1,485	161	10.8	508	60	11.8
Operatives	3,711	919	24.8	2,346	615	26.2	1,365	304	22.3
Laborers	2,073	808	39.0	1,428	558	39.1	645	250	38.8
Service workers	6,720	3,485	51.9	2,545	1,447	56.9	4,175	2,038	48.8
Total blue collar	14,497	5,433	37.5	7,804	2,781	35.6	6,693	2,652	39.6
Total	56,546	8,287	14.7	18,480	3,433	18.6	38,066	4,854	12.8

Source: U.S. Equal Employment Opportunity Commission, *Job Patterns for Minorities and Women in Private Industry, 1966,* Report No. 1 (Washington: The Commission, 1968), Part III.

TABLE A-11. General Merchandise Industry Including Department Stores
Employment by Race, Sex, and Occupational Group
170 Establishments
Baltimore, St. Louis, and Washington, D. C. Metropolitan Areas, 1967

Occupational Group	All Employees			Male			Female		
	Total	Negro	Percent Negro	Total	Negro	Percent Negro	Total	Negro	Percent Negro
Officials and managers	8,084	320	4.0	4,878	196	4.0	3,206	124	3.9
Professionals	503	15	3.0	265	11	4.2	238	4	1.7
Technicians	323	24	7.4	194	16	8.2	129	8	6.2
Sales workers	32,779	2,439	7.4	7,299	467	6.4	25,480	1,972	7.7
Office and clerical	14,129	1,890	13.4	1,982	291	14.7	12,147	1,599	13.2
Total white collar	55,818	4,688	8.4	14,618	981	6.7	41,200	3,707	9.0
Craftsmen	2,475	315	12.7	1,821	223	12.2	654	92	14.1
Operatives	4,480	1,323	29.5	3,145	969	30.8	1,335	354	26.5
Laborers	2,521	908	36.0	1,604	646	40.3	917	262	28.6
Service workers	7,928	3,930	49.6	2,923	1,550	53.0	5,005	2,380	47.6
Total blue collar	17,404	6,476	37.2	9,493	3,388	35.7	7,911	3,088	39.0
Total	73,222	11,164	15.2	24,111	4,369	18.1	49,111	6,795	13.8

Source: U.S. Equal Employment Opportunity Commission, *Job Patterns for Minorities and Women in Private Industry, 1967*, Report No. 2 (Washington: The Commission, 1970), Vol. 2.

TABLE A-12. *General Merchandise Industry Including Department Stores Employment by Race, Sex, and Occupational Group*
181 Establishments
Baltimore, St. Louis, and Washington, D. C. Metropolitan Areas, 1969

Occupational Group	All Employees			Male			Female		
	Total	Negro	Percent Negro	Total	Negro	Percent Negro	Total	Negro	Percent Negro
Officials and managers	7,970	441	5.5	4,781	257	5.4	3,189	184	5.8
Professionals	382	36	9.4	209	26	12.4	173	10	5.8
Technicians	565	52	9.2	455	43	9.5	110	9	8.2
Sales workers	33,571	3,395	10.1	8,313	693	8.3	25,258	2,702	10.7
Office and clerical	13,003	2,286	17.6	1,852	329	17.8	11,151	1,957	17.5
Total white collar	55,491	6,210	11.2	15,610	1,348	8.6	39,881	4,862	12.2
Craftsmen	2,401	393	16.4	1,786	295	16.5	615	98	15.9
Operatives	4,087	1,347	33.0	2,800	972	34.7	1,287	375	29.1
Laborers	2,531	972	38.4	1,562	601	38.5	969	371	38.3
Service workers	6,822	3,341	49.0	2,572	1,357	52.8	4,250	1,984	46.7
Total blue collar	15,841	6,053	38.2	8,720	3,225	37.0	7,121	2,828	39.7
Total	71,332	12,263	17.2	24,330	4,573	18.8	47,002	7,690	16.4

Source: U.S. Equal Employment Opportunity Commission, 1969.

TABLE A-13. *General Merchandise Industry Including Department Stores Employment by Race, Sex, and Occupational Group*
62 Establishments
Atlanta and Houston Metropolitan Areas, 1966

Occupational Group	All Employees			Male			Female		
	Total	Negro	Percent Negro	Total	Negro	Percent Negro	Total	Negro	Percent Negro
Officials and managers	3,373	22	0.7	2,452	20	0.8	921	2	0.2
Professionals	301	—	—	106	—	—	195	—	—
Technicians	178	—	—	113	—	—	65	—	—
Sales workers	14,744	480	3.3	3,292	83	2.5	11,452	397	3.5
Office and clerical	7,226	356	4.9	1,060	117	11.0	6,166	239	3.9
Total white collar	25,822	858	3.3	7,023	220	3.1	18,799	638	3.4
Craftsmen	1,136	94	8.3	995	55	5.5	141	39	27.7
Operatives	1,693	388	22.9	1,222	339	27.7	471	49	10.4
Laborers	3,335	955	28.6	2,100	728	34.7	1,235	227	18.4
Service workers	3,106	1,933	62.2	1,398	967	69.2	1,708	966	56.6
Total blue collar	9,270	3,370	36.4	5,715	2,089	36.6	3,555	1,281	36.0
Total	35,092	4,228	12.0	12,738	2,309	18.1	22,354	1,919	8.6

Source: U.S. Equal Employment Opportunity Commission, *Job Patterns for Minorities and Women in Private Industry, 1966*, Report No. 1 (Washington: The Commission, 1968), Part III.

TABLE A-14. *General Merchandise Industry Including Department Stores Employment by Race, Sex, and Occupational Group*
86 Establishments
Atlanta and Houston Metropolitan Areas, 1967

Occupational Group	All Employees			Male			Female		
	Total	Negro	Percent Negro	Total	Negro	Percent Negro	Total	Negro	Percent Negro
Officials and managers	3,964	30	0.8	2,706	24	0.9	1,258	6	0.5
Professionals	252	3	1.2	119	2	1.7	133	1	0.8
Technicians	196	6	3.1	125	5	4.0	71	1	1.4
Sales workers	16,774	613	3.7	3,864	121	3.1	12,910	492	3.8
Office and clerical	8,234	471	5.7	1,268	162	12.8	7,016	309	4.4
Total white collar	29,470	1,123	3.8	8,082	314	3.9	21,388	809	3.8
Craftsmen	1,322	87	6.6	1,076	64	5.9	246	23	9.3
Operatives	2,001	640	32.0	1,481	575	38.3	520	65	12.5
Laborers	2,847	992	34.8	1,976	717	36.3	871	275	31.6
Service workers	3,387	2,104	62.1	1,513	924	61.1	1,874	1,180	63.0
Total blue collar	9,557	3,823	40.0	6,046	2,280	37.7	3,511	1,543	43.9
Total	39,027	4,946	12.7	14,128	2,594	18.4	24,899	2,352	9.4

Source: U.S. Equal Employment Opportunity Commission, *Job Patterns for Minorities and Women in Private Industry, 1967,* Report No. 2 (Washington: The Commission, 1970), Vol. 2.

TABLE A-15. General Merchandise Industry Including Department Stores
Employment by Race, Sex, and Occupational Group
102 Establishments
Atlanta and Houston Metropolitan Areas, 1969

Occupational Group	All Employees			Male			Female		
	Total	Negro	Percent Negro	Total	Negro	Percent Negro	Total	Negro	Percent Negro
Officials and managers	3,739	92	2.5	2,761	64	2.3	978	28	2.9
Professionals	129	2	1.6	67	2	3.0	62	—	—
Technicians	173	8	4.6	125	8	6.4	48	—	—
Sales workers	13,589	1,046	7.7	3,491	231	6.6	10,098	815	8.1
Office and clerical	8,145	706	8.7	1,138	134	11.8	7,007	572	8.2
Total white collar	25,775	1,854	7.2	7,582	439	5.8	18,193	1,415	7.8
Craftsmen	1,279	138	10.8	1,093	103	9.4	186	35	18.8
Operatives	2,029	662	32.6	1,469	547	37.2	560	115	20.5
Laborers	2,174	886	40.8	1,475	581	39.4	699	305	43.6
Service workers	3,112	1,468	47.2	1,298	634	48.8	1,814	834	46.0
Total blue collar	8,594	3,154	36.7	5,335	1,865	35.0	3,259	1,289	39.6
Total	34,369	5,008	14.6	12,917	2,304	17.8	21,452	2,704	12.6

Source: U.S. Equal Employment Opportunity Commission, 1969.

TABLE A-16. *General Merchandise Industry Including Department Stores*
Employment by Race, Sex, and Occupational Group
129 Establishments
Chicago and Detroit Metropolitan Areas, 1966

Occupational Group	All Employees			Male			Female		
	Total	Negro	Percent Negro	Total	Negro	Percent Negro	Total	Negro	Percent Negro
Officials and managers	12,803	218	1.7	9,036	142	1.6	3,767	76	2.0
Professionals	2,823	23	0.8	2,140	18	0.8	683	5	0.7
Technicians	1,826	35	1.9	1,398	17	1.2	428	18	4.2
Sales workers	47,723	2,581	5.4	10,032	323	3.2	37,691	2,258	6.0
Office and clerical	38,509	8,147	21.2	4,087	414	10.1	34,422	7,733	22.5
Total white collar	103,684	11,004	10.6	26,693	914	3.4	76,991	10,090	13.1
Craftsmen	5,201	684	13.2	4,318	412	9.5	883	272	30.8
Operatives	13,702	3,452	25.2	7,470	1,501	20.1	6,232	1,951	31.3
Laborers	10,218	3,425	33.5	6,867	2,271	33.1	3,351	1,154	34.4
Service workers	12,609	3,531	28.0	5,756	1,578	34.4	6,853	1,553	22.7
Total blue collar	41,730	11,092	26.6	24,411	6,162	25.2	17,319	4,930	28.5
Total	145,414	22,096	15.2	51,104	7,076	13.8	94,310	15,020	15.9

Source: U.S. Equal Employment Opportunity Commission, *Job Patterns for Minorities and Women in Private Industry, 1966*, Report No. 1 (Washington: The Commission, 1968), Part III.

TABLE A-17. General Merchandise Industry Including Department Stores
Employment by Race, Sex, and Occupational Group
181 Establishments
Chicago and Detroit Metropolitan Areas, 1967

Occupational Group	All Employees			Male			Female		
	Total	Negro	Percent Negro	Total	Negro	Percent Negro	Total	Negro	Percent Negro
Officials and managers	15,266	421	2.8	10,539	281	2.7	4,727	140	3.0
Professionals	2,988	57	1.9	2,240	46	2.1	748	11	1.5
Technicians	2,113	85	4.0	1,592	62	3.9	521	23	4.4
Sales workers	55,502	3,856	6.9	10,722	534	5.0	44,780	3,322	7.4
Office and clerical	41,654	9,531	22.9	4,766	668	14.0	36,888	8,863	24.0
Total white collar	117,523	13,950	11.9	29,859	1,591	5.3	87,664	12,359	14.1
Craftsmen	4,723	679	14.4	3,840	389	10.1	883	290	32.8
Operatives	13,241	3,835	29.0	7,974	1,829	22.9	5,267	2,006	38.1
Laborers	13,039	5,517	42.3	6,668	2,582	38.7	6,371	2,935	46.1
Service workers	13,233	4,065	30.7	5,659	2,093	37.0	7,574	1,972	26.0
Total blue collar	44,236	14,096	31.9	24,141	6,893	28.6	20,095	7,203	35.8
Total	161,759	28,046	17.3	54,000	8,484	15.7	107,759	19,562	18.2

Source: U.S. Equal Employment Opportunity Commission, Job Patterns for Minorities and Women in Private Industry, 1967, Report No. 2 (Washington: The Commission, 1970), Vol. 2.

TABLE A-18. *General Merchandise Industry Including Department Stores*
Employment by Race, Sex, and Occupational Group
184 Establishments
Chicago and Detroit Metropolitan Areas, 1969

Occupational Group	All Employees			Male			Female		
	Total	Negro	Percent Negro	Total	Negro	Percent Negro	Total	Negro	Percent Negro
Officials and managers	12,820	466	3.6	8,903	297	3.3	3,917	169	4.3
Professionals	3,130	73	2.3	2,518	53	2.1	612	20	3.3
Technicians	1,705	143	8.4	1,187	104	8.8	518	39	7.5
Sales workers	51,240	3,844	7.5	10,537	648	6.1	40,703	3,196	7.9
Office and clerical	29,509	4,160	14.1	3,189	522	16.4	23,320	3,638	13.8
Total white collar	98,404	8,686	8.8	26,334	1,624	6.2	72,070	7,062	9.8
Craftsmen	3,672	275	7.5	3,183	224	7.0	489	51	10.4
Operatives	10,492	2,236	21.3	7,007	1,490	21.3	3,485	746	21.4
Laborers	6,078	1,931	31.8	3,745	1,001	26.7	2,333	930	39.9
Service workers	9,927	2,816	28.4	4,522	1,478	32.7	5,405	1,338	24.8
Total blue collar	30,169	7,258	24.1	18,457	4,193	22.7	11,712	3,065	26.2
Total	128,573	15,944	12.4	44,791	5,817	13.0	83,782	10,127	12.1

Source: U.S. Equal Employment Opportunity Commission, 1969.

TABLE A-19. *General Merchandise Industry Including Department Stores Employment by Race, Sex, and Occupational Group*
76 Establishments
Los Angeles-Long Beach Metropolitan Area, 1966

Occupational Group	All Employees			Male			Female		
	Total	Negro	Percent Negro	Total	Negro	Percent Negro	Total	Negro	Percent Negro
Officials and managers	6,089	90	1.5	3,860	61	1.6	2,229	29	1.3
Professionals	377	3	0.8	168	1	0.6	209	2	1.0
Technicians	348	50	14.4	213	24	11.3	135	26	19.3
Sales workers	26,760	1,310	4.9	6,634	300	4.5	20,126	1,010	5.0
Office and clerical	12,075	939	7.8	1,662	117	7.0	10,413	822	7.9
Total white collar	45,649	2,392	5.2	12,537	503	4.0	33,112	1,889	5.7
Craftsmen	2,319	130	5.6	1,915	96	5.0	404	34	8.4
Operatives	3,324	483	14.5	2,133	254	11.9	1,191	229	19.2
Laborers	3,543	375	10.6	1,933	232	12.0	1,610	143	8.9
Service workers	4,025	1,031	25.6	1,655	625	37.8	2,370	406	17.1
Total blue collar	13,211	2,019	15.3	7,636	1,207	15.8	5,575	812	14.6
Total	58,860	4,411	7.5	20,173	1,710	8.5	38,687	2,701	7.0

Source: U.S. Equal Employment Opportunity Commission, *Job Patterns for Minorities and Women in Private Industry, 1966*, Report No. 1 (Washington: The Commission, 1968), Part III.

Note: Occupational breakdowns by race not available for San Francisco-Oakland in 1966.

TABLE A-20. *General Merchandise Industry Including Department Stores*
Employment by Race, Sex, and Occupational Group
174 Establishments
Los Angeles-Long Beach and San Francisco-Oakland Metropolitan Areas, 1967

Occupational Group	All Employees			Male			Female		
	Total	Negro	Percent Negro	Total	Negro	Percent Negro	Total	Negro	Percent Negro
Officials and managers	10,548	180	1.7	6,510	118	1.8	4,038	62	1.5
Professionals	650	5	0.8	289	2	0.7	331	3	0.8
Technicians	836	34	4.1	648	25	3.9	188	9	4.8
Sales workers	41,598	2,078	5.0	9,996	509	5.1	31,602	1,569	5.0
Office and clerical	19,980	1,534	7.7	2,476	206	8.3	17,504	1,328	7.6
Total white collar	73,612	3,831	5.2	19,919	860	4.3	53,693	2,971	5.5
Craftsmen	3,187	182	5.7	2,658	150	5.6	529	32	6.0
Operatives	5,716	666	11.7	3,799	412	10.8	1,917	254	13.2
Laborers	5,160	611	11.8	2,911	326	11.2	2,249	285	12.7
Service workers	7,089	1,540	21.7	2,944	908	30.8	4,145	632	15.2
Total blue collar	21,152	2,999	14.2	12,312	1,796	14.6	8,840	1,203	13.6
Total	94,764	6,830	7.2	32,231	2,656	8.2	62,533	4,174	6.7

Source: U.S. Equal Employment Opportunity Commission, *Job Patterns for Minorities and Women in Private Industry, 1967*, Report No. 2 (Washington: The Commission, 1970), Vol. 2.

TABLE A-21. *General Merchandise Industry Including Department Stores Employment by Race, Sex, and Occupational Group*
136 Establishments
Los Angeles-Long Beach and San Francisco-Oakland Metropolitan Areas, 1969

Occupational Group	All Employees			Male			Female		
	Total	Negro	Percent Negro	Total	Negro	Percent Negro	Total	Negro	Percent Negro
Officials and managers	8,915	208	2.3	5,191	125	2.4	3,724	83	2.2
Professionals	647	14	2.2	323	4	1.2	324	10	3.1
Technicians	464	67	14.4	283	15	5.3	181	52	28.7
Sales workers	39,361	1,975	5.0	8,836	441	5.0	30,525	1,534	5.0
Office and clerical	16,164	1,162	7.2	2,195	168	7.7	13,969	994	7.1
Total white collar	65,551	3,426	5.2	16,828	753	4.5	48,723	2,673	5.5
Craftsmen	2,671	165	6.2	2,185	134	6.1	486	31	6.4
Operatives	3,903	435	11.1	2,603	245	9.4	1,300	190	14.6
Laborers	2,855	533	18.7	1,898	336	17.7	957	197	20.6
Service workers	5,992	1,127	18.8	2,468	669	27.1	3,524	458	13.0
Total blue collar	15,421	2,260	14.7	9,154	1,384	15.1	6,267	876	14.0
Total	80,972	5,686	7.0	25,982	2,137	8.2	54,990	3,549	6.5

Source: U.S. Equal Employment Opportunity Commission, 1969.

Index

PART THREE

THE NEGRO
IN THE DRUGSTORE INDUSTRY

by

F. MARION FLETCHER

with the assistance of
MARIE R. KEENEY

TABLE OF CONTENTS

LIST OF TABLES

CHAPTER I

Introduction

The retail drug industry, the final link of the health care delivery system for noninstitutionalized persons, is an essential element of retail trade. Indeed, the lives of hundreds of thousands depend on the prescriptions they regularly purchase in drugstores. Because of its basic nature, it is to be found in every city, town, and hamlet—a distinguishing feature even in retailing, and in strong contrast to manufacturing industries, where one often finds distinct geographic concentrations.

The complete dispersion of drugstores would make the industry important for a study of Negro employment even in the absence of large sales and employment figures. The industry, however, is also important by these measures, since it provided jobs for about 442,100 people and enjoyed sales of nearly $12 billion in 1970.[1]

The purposes of this study are (1) to examine the historical and current levels of Negro employment in drugstores, (2) to determine the reasons for the employment patterns, (3) to assess the prospects for greater Negro employment in higher status jobs, and (4) to analyze the effects of industry employment policies on the past, present, and future employment of Negroes at all occupational levels. An effort will be made to distinguish those policies controllable by employers from those dictated by such external factors as the labor market, geography, public attitudes, and the inherent characteristics of the industry.

SOURCES OF INFORMATION

The results of the study are based on interviews, basic governmental data, three questionnaires, books and periodicals per-

---

1. *Employment and Earnings*, Vol. 17 (March 1971), Table B-2; and U.S. Department of Commerce, *U.S. Industrial Outlook, 1971* (Washington: Government Printing Office, 1971), p. 426, Table 2.

taining to the industry, and previous research by the writer.[2] Personal interviews were the primary source of information about chain drugstore organizations. A total of thirty-four interviews were held with the major drugstore chains in all geographic regions. Only one large midwestern and one large southern chain refused to grant interviews. Included in the thirty-four interviews are some smaller chain organizations chosen according to their geographical location. Additional personal, telephone, and correspondence interviews were held with trade associations, professional groups, and Negro pharmacy educators.

Information from independent drugstores was elicited via a questionnaire sent to 1,000 such drugstores. Appendix A gives the distribution of responses to this questionnaire. A questionnaire was also sent to the 73 accredited [3] colleges of pharmacy. Of these colleges, four are predominantly Negro and are located in the South.[4] The third questionnaire was sent to 49 state pharmaceutical associations and the District of Columbia. (It was not necessary to send a questionnaire to the Mississippi Association since an article in a trade paper noted that the association had just accepted its first Negro member.)[5]

PLAN OF THE STUDY

The substance of this report begins with an explanation of the retail drug industry, with emphasis on those facets having particular significance for Negro employment. Succeeding chapters explore Negro employment and the factors that have affected its development. The final chapter summarizes the major determinants of Negro employment and assesses the future for Negroes in the retail drug industry.

---

2. See F. Marion Fletcher, *Market Restraints in the Retail Drug Industry*, Industrial Research Unit Study No. 43 (Philadelphia: University of Pennsylvania Press, 1967).

3. The accrediting body is the American Council on Pharmaceutical Education.

4. They are Howard University College of Pharmacy, Washington, D. C. (private); Florida Agricultural and Mechanical University School of Pharmacy, Tallahassee, Florida; Xavier University of Louisiana College of Pharmacy, New Orleans, Louisiana (private); and Texas Southern University College of Pharmacy, Houston, Texas.

5. "Aaron Henry is First Negro in Mississippi Association," *Drug Topics*, July 22, 1968, p. 8. Mr. Henry is president of the Mississippi branch of the Nattional Association for the Advancement of Colored People.

CHAPTER II

The Drugstore Industry

In earlier times drugstores were manufacturers as well as retailers of drugs. Most of the medicinal agents were imported from England and the Continent, even though some of the raw materials used in making drugs were indigenous to the United States. Pharmacists purchased their supplies from drug importing firms and then transformed the basic ingredients into medicines by compounding them into an assortment of pills, lotions, and ointments. Some recipes were developed by pharmacists themselves and others were set forth in reference books and the prescriptions of physicians.

During the Civil War, because of disrupted supplies and wartime demand, a domestic drug manufacturing industry emerged and secured an accepted place in the market. Upon cessation of hostilities, the United States no longer was dependent upon foreign suppliers.

As time passed, it became clear both to manufacturers and drugstore owners that it would be advantageous to adopt the mass production techniques employed in other industries. Gradually drug processors took on the compounding and formulating functions. At the same time some pharmacists began processing their own raw materials so that they, in time, became manufacturers rather than retailers. The compounding function of manufacturers was fairly well established by the 1920's and has become more entrenched with each passing year until, today, only about 2 percent of all prescriptions are compounded at the drugstore.[6]

INDUSTRY STRUCTURE

The retail drug industry is divided into two groups along several lines of analysis. These are independently owned stores and chain stores.

---

6. Drug manufacturing racial policies are covered in another of the author's studies in The Racial Policies of American Industry series, Report No. 21.

Independent versus Chain Drugstores

The traditional concept of the corner drugstore has been the one-man or family operation, closely held, devoted to careful personal service, with little outside help. Negro employment in these operations has generally been limited to the lowest jobs of delivery/porter work and soda fountain/lunchcounter waitress, largely because there was no need for other employees and the extremely low pay did not attract whites to these jobs.

On the other hand are chain drugstore companies, some having hundreds of stores, plus extensive headquarters and warehouse facilities. Chain companies enjoyed phenomenal growth between 1920 and 1930 and continued to increase at an accelerating rate through the 1960's. Table 1 shows relative changes in the number of independent and chain drugstores from 1948 to 1969. Although independents still vastly outnumber chain drugstores, the trend is definitely toward chain operations. From 1948 to 1969 independents declined from 93 percent of all stores to 86 percent. By another indicator, sales, chains grew faster than independents in the 1960's, as their sales increased by 14 percent per year between 1965 and 1970, compared to 4 percent per year for other drugstores. As a result, chains held 34.3 percent of drugstore sales in 1970.[7]

Chain drugstores are significant in the analysis of Negro employment because of the increasing share of the industry which they are obtaining. Racial employment patterns in chains, rather than independents, will be the dominant industry force in the future. Chains are already the major force in the metropolitan areas of Washington, D. C., Dayton, Ohio, New Orleans, San Francisco-Oakland, Los Angeles-Long Beach, and Tampa-St. Petersburg.[8] Since these are also areas of high Negro population, it is extremely important to examine Negro employment in chain drugstores.

Statistics on sales and income for the fifteen largest chain retail drug companies are shown in Table 2. Walgreen dominated the chain sector with 557 stores and $578 million in sales. Drugstore companies are generally smaller than other retail

---

7. U.S. Department of Commerce, *U. S. Industrial Outlook, 1971* (Washington: Government Printing Office, 1971), p. 426, Table 2. Chains are defined as companies with 11 or more retail stores.

8. "1970 Annual Report of the Chain Drug Industry," *Chain Store Age*, Vol. 46 (April 1970), p. 114.

TABLE 1. *Drugstore Industry*
Change in Total Number of Stores by Industry Sector
1948-1969

Year	All Drugstores		Independent Drugstores		Chain Drugstores	
	Number of Stores	Average Change per Year	Number of Stores	Average Change per Year	Number of Stores	Average Change per Year
1948	46,955		43,553		3,402	
1958	51,458	450.3	47,707	415.4	3,751	34.9
1963	50,318	−228.0	45,853	−370.8	4,465	142.8
1969	50,674	59.3	43,583	−378.3	7,091	437.7
Twenty-one Year Average		177.1		1.4		175.7

Source: Table 4 and Robert A. Liebson, "What Happens to the Rx Dollars," *Drug Topics*, March 16, 1970, p. 4.

Note: Figures are for stores operating at the end of the year. Chains are defined as having four or more establishments per company.

industry companies; only Walgreen's made the *Fortune* retail list in 1971.[9] Several drug companies, such as Osco and SupeRx, are units of gigantic retailers such as Jewel Tea and Kroger.

Types of Drugstores

Independent and chain stores also differ in their sales emphasis and location, each having particular implications for Negro employment in the industry. The store traditionally characteristic of drug chains has been the metropolitan drugstore, a high-volume store located in the built-up area of a city. Such stores typically have about 5,000 square feet of selling area and depend on the traffic generated by location for the bulk of sales. In the past, a sizeable proportion of the volume has been derived from fountain sales, the proximity of office buildings inducing a brisk lunch and coffee-break business in addition to drug sundry business. The prescription drug sales are relatively unimportant, unless there are a lot of physicians practicing nearby.

The metropolitan drugstore was traditionally a relatively substantial employer of Negro women. Such stores, especially in the Northeast, have used Negro women extensively as waitresses and short order cooks. Few Negroes have, in the past, been employed in other drugstore occupations. This situation is beginning to change and the change is heralded by new employment patterns in metropolitan drugstores. These stores are, however, experiencing a decline along with the general decay of the downtown areas.

Partially the cause and partially the result of the decline in downtown shopping has been the development of shopping centers and the suburban (or shopping center) drugstore. Shopping centers are also dominated by the chain companies. The stores range from 10,000 to 25,000 square feet in selling area and have very high sales volume: sales of $1 million annually are not uncommon. These stores generally have well-developed specialty departments such as cosmetics, cameras, and small appliances. They do a considerable prescription business, but the proportion to total sales is small—usually about 10 percent of sales.

Chains are able to secure the prime shopping center locations because of their financial strength, well-known names, and aggressive merchandising. Independents are also in shopping

9. *Fortune,* Vol. LXXXIII (May 1971), pp. 196-197.

TABLE 2. *The Fifteen Largest Chain Drugstore Companies, 1970 Statistics*

Company	Headquarters	Drugstores	Sales ($000)	Corporate Earnings ($000)	Earnings as a Percent of Sales
Walgreen	Chicago	554	630,000	9,402	1.5
Thrifty	Los Angeles	346	328,807	7,460	2.3
Skaggs Cos.	Salt Lake City	168	281,355	3,538	1.3
SupeRx	Cincinnati	431	276,592	n.a.	n.a.
Peoples	Washington, D. C.	248	185,100	1,870	1.0
Osco	Franklin Park, Ill.	181	208,971	n.a.	n.a.
Sav-On	Marina Del Rey, Calif.	64	170,114	4,353	2.6
Longs	Oakland	54	168,721	n.a.	n.a.
Jack Ekerd	Clearwater, Fla.	225	143,500	8,288	5.8
Revco	Cleveland	254	132,500	3,509	2.6
Drug Fair	Alexandria, Va.	120	125,940	2,729	2.2
Skaggs Pay Less	Oakland	32	116,532	2,661	2.3
Eckerd	Charlotte, N. C.	113	92,114	2,789	3.0
Cunningham	Detroit	209	91,594	(833)	....
Gray	Cleveland	160	91,000	3,747	4.1

Source: "1971 Annual Report of the Chain Drug Industry," *Chain Store Age*, Vol. 47 (April 1971), p. 112.

centers, usually the smaller centers that chains have turned down or where there is less emphasis on generating heavy traffic.

By their very nature, suburban drugstores have had limited Negro employment. Just the fact of location shuts off the potential source of Negro employees. Moreover, many new drugstores do not contain a lunch counter and hence no demand exists for waitresses or short order cooks, jobs which have traditionally been filled by Negroes.

The most common type of independent store is the neighborhood drugstore. Such stores are located on the fringes of commercial areas or residential districts and are dependent on the local neighborhood for their business. They are quite small (about 2,000 square feet) and receive about one-third of their revenue from prescriptions while their nondrug lines are relatively limited and higher priced than chain stores. The stores owe their prosperity to the personal relationships and loyalty of patrons and to the special services which they provide.

The neighborhood drugstore, also known as a community pharmacy, may participate in some sort of arrangement that permits a measure of competition with the larger drugstores. On the East Coast, there are a few buying cooperatives. Nationally, there are about 12,000 to 15,000 Rexall and Walgreen "agency stores" that enjoy some buying and advertising advantages such as the annual Rexall one cent sale.

Neighborhood drugstores have not been very favorable sources of employment for Negroes for several reasons. First, each drugstore employs few people. Second, the owner is apt to use his wife and children in lieu of employees wherever possible. Third, most of the stores are in white neighborhoods, where few Negroes dwell, and where a sufficient local labor supply exists. The owner may—even if he has no personal objection— be reluctant to employ Negroes because he is fearful of adverse customer reaction. Unlike a chain, his income depends on the neighborhood.

The only other major type of independent drugstore is the apothecary or professional pharmacy. As defined by the retail drug trade, this is a retail outlet in which at least 60 percent of annual sales are in health items such as prescriptions and surgical appliances. In practice, professional pharmacies sell very little general merchandise.

Apothecaries are not as concerned about sales volume as community pharmacies and chain drugstores, and there is less emphasis on self-service. For these reasons, very few professional pharmacies are found in residential areas or shopping centers. For the most part, they are concentrated near medical complexes, office buildings where many physicians are congregated, and dense population centers such as large apartment building areas where there is a sufficient amount of exclusively drug trade to justify their presence.

The pharmaceutical center is a new type of retail drug outlet growing in favor with pharmacists. The concept was introduced by Foremost-McKesson in 1965 and represents an extension of the idea underlying the professional pharmacy. Much of the discussion of the apothecary applies to the pharmaceutical center; the main difference being the store configuration. The customer enters an attractively appointed waiting room with paneled walls and a number of what appear to be bank teller windows. He takes his prescription to one of the windows and is invited to be seated while his order is being readied. While waiting, he may read a magazine, listen to soft music, or examine the pictures on the walls. When the order is ready, he is paged, receives his merchandise, and pays the receptionist.

Since pharmaceutical centers and apothecaries are both primarily staffed by professionals, Negro employment is largely limited by the small number of black pharmacists. The prospects for increasing the Negro percentage of this professional group will be discussed in a later chapter.

INDUSTRY LOCATION

The retail drug industry is one of the most well distributed of all retail operations. Even the most remote location is likely to have a drugstore of some description. In rural Mississippi, 20 percent of the communities with less than 500 people and 69.4 percent of towns with 500-999 people have a pharmacy.[10] In cities, most neighborhoods have a corner drugstore, and no suburban shopping center seems complete without a huge self-service outlet of one of the major drug chains.

---

10. Mickey C. Smith, "Independent Pharmacy Practice in the Rural Community," *Journal of the American Pharmaceutical Association*, Vol. NS10 (April 1970), p. 200.

Drugstores are, however, closing or moving out of the urban inner-city neighborhoods which have been the scenes of racial disturbances and are subject to high crime rates. Some of these traditionally white-owned and operated stores are becoming a source of increased Negro employment as they are taken over by businessmen from the black community. The potential for black entrepreneurs in the retail drug industry will be discussed in Chapter VI.

Huge new drugstores with greatly increased and diversified product ranges are opening in suburban communities around the major metropolitan areas. These stores lose the neighborhood flavor of the corner drugstore, located as they are amid modern shopping complexes to which most customers drive quite a distance to reach. They have less personal service and larger work forces, allowing lower visibility for Negro employees who might have seemed alien in the one-man neighborhood store.

SALES

Drugstore sales have almost quadrupled since 1947, rising from $3.7 billion to over $12 billion in 1968 (Table 3). During this period, drugstores have faced strong competition from food stores, discounters, and other retailers and have actually lost market share of such typically drugstore items as prescription drugs, health products, toiletries, and candy and tobacco.

The inventory and sales emphasis of drugstores are reflected in the shift in the distribution of sales within drugstores, also shown in Table 3. The importance of prescription drug sales has grown from 13.5 percent of sales in 1947 to 33.3 percent in 1968, while other product groups have assumed more evenly divided shares of sales. The most dramatic shift since the 1940's, which indicates the changing nature of the industry itself, is the disappearance of the soda fountain. In 1947, fountains accounted for 18.0 percent of total drugstore sales; by 1968 they were down to only 3.4 percent. This decline, accompanied by a decline in food service employment, has had a major impact on Negro employment owing to the occupational distribution of black workers, as the discussion on manpower will show.

There has been a major change in the concept of the drugstore in recent years. The tradition of selling service has been replaced by the idea of selling products, partly as a result of the increased labor costs arising from minimum wage legisla-

TABLE 3. Drugstore Industry
Sales by Product Group
United States, 1947 and 1968

Product Group	1947				1968			
	Total Sales ($000)	Drugstore Sales	Drugstore Percent of Product Sales	Distribution of Drugstore Sales	Total Sales ($000)	Sales Drugstore	Drugstore Percent of Product Sales	Distribution of Drugstore Sales
Prescription drugs	504,344	493,966	97.9	13.5	4,405,080	4,024,350	91.3	33.3
Nonprescription drugs	837,195	495,079	59.1	13.5	2,095,370	1,273,250	60.8	10.5
Other health items	690,426	322,544	45.7	8.8	1,736,560	754,960	43.5	6.3
Toiletries	1,505,473	492,949	32.7	13.4	5,960,280	1,533,650	25.7	12.7
Candy and tobacco	5,638,409	603,489	10.7	16.4	11,573,160	1,108,790	9.6	9.2
Photographic	312,966	76,058	24.3	2.1	2,443,750	801,580	32.8	6.6
Fountain/luncheonette	....	662,279	....	18.0	2,928,890	407,820	13.9	3.4
Sundries	....	57,226	....	1.5	4,084,570	411,900	10.1	3.4
Magazines/newspapers	1,380,009	120,146	8.7	3.3	2,223,670	380,820	17.1	3.2
Stationery	598,743	79,626	13.3	2.2	1,748,340	285,760	16.3	2.4
Alcoholic beverages	9,640,000	86,718	0.9	2.4	14,585,450	170,710	1.2	1.4
All other products	....	179,386	....	4.9	....	911,330	....	7.6
Total		3,669,466		100.0		12,065,000		100.0

Source: *Drug Topics*, Annual Consumer Expenditures Study, 1947 and 1968.

tion. The result has been the adoption of the self-service operation typical of supermarkets and variety stores.

The change is evident from the rapid rate of sales increase as compared to the moderate increase in employment. Drugstores are selling more, but not hiring very many more people in order to do it. Under this arrangement, sales can be expanded considerably without having to employ more people. Negro employment is held down because cashier becomes the typical occupation and some employers still seem unwilling to place Negroes in this position as freely as in others. In addition, lower educational attainments of Negroes are detrimental to their employment in money handling jobs.

MANPOWER

Drugstore employment has not increased as rapidly as sales. The U.S. Census of Business for 1948 and 1967 indicate that total employment increased only about 58 percent compared to a sales jump of nearly 200 percent in that period (Table 4).

Such a phenomenon hampers the flow of Negro employees into the industry. If the overall demand for labor is growing at a slower rate than sales, the Negro portion will be growing at a correspondingly slower rate, in the absence of other factors. United States Bureau of Labor Statistics data, in Table 5, confirm the employment growth through 1970, although the data were computed differently and are not directly comparable to census figures.

The number of employees per store has risen during the past twenty years. Calculating from data in Table 4 shows that store size rose from an average 5.5 employees per store to 7.6 between 1948 and 1967.

Considering only the fact of the continuing trend toward higher employment per store, Negroes might find their employment opportunities slightly improved since the larger concerns seem more likely to employ minorities in order to satisfy their manpower needs. Moreover, to the extent that more employees per store reflects the growth of chains, Negroes should benefit. As mentioned previously, the chains need a great deal of manpower, and are more visible to government civil rights employment agencies, and are therefore more willing to employ Negroes in nontraditional jobs.

TABLE 4. Drugstore Industry

Number of Stores, Sales, and Employment by Number of Employees per Store
United States, 1948 and 1967

Employees Per Store	1948						1967					
	Stores	Percent of Total	Sales ($000)	Percent of Total	Employees	Percent of Total	Stores	Percent of Total	Sales ($000)	Percent of Total	Employees [a]	Percent of Total
0	5,763	12.3	125,995	3.4	....	....	6,117	11.4	390,834	3.6	....	....
1	5,258	11.2	152,913	4.2	5,258	2.0	4,430	8.3	185,540	1.7	4,480	1.1
2	6,178	13.2	247,363	6.7	12,356	4.8	4,630	8.7	300,728	2.8	9,320	2.3
3	6,043	12.9	307,356	8.3	18,129	7.0	4,894	9.1	427,638	3.9	14,682	3.6
4 or 5	8,959	19.1	603,891	16.4	40,002	15.4	8,029	14.9	974,335	8.9	35,940	8.8
6 or 7	5,700	12.1	504,983	13.7	36,660	14.1	6,342	11.8	1,038,247	9.5	40,975	10.0
8 or 9	2,504	5.3	274,554	7.5	21,011	8.1	4,726	8.8	955,578	8.7	39,882	9.8
10 to 14 [b]	4,572	9.7	720,037	19.6	50,333	23.3	6,277	11.7	1,739,910	15.9	73,388	17.9
15 to 19	1,749	3.7	551,926	15.0	28,930	18.9	2,880	5.4	1,124,412	10.3	48,048	11.7
20 to 49	206	0.4	149,452	4.1	13,105	5.1	3,695	6.9	2,673,215	24.5	103,211	25.2
50 to 99	23	0.1	39,993	1.1	3,445	1.3	354	0.6	678,091	6.2	21,296	5.2
100 or more	n.a.	n.a.	n.a.	n.a.	n.a.	n.a.	28	0.1	110,747	1.0	3,491	0.9
New stores [c]	n.a.	n.a.	n.a.	n.a.	n.a.	n.a.	1,260	2.3	330,981	3.0	14,496	3.5
Total	46,955	100.0	3,678,463	100.0	259,234	100.0	53,722	100.0	10,930,256	100.0	409,209	100.0

Source: U.S. Census of Business: 1948: *Retail Trade: General Statistics,* Vol. I, pp. 4.02-4.07.
1967: *Retail Trade: Employment Size,* BC67-RS3. Vol. I, Table 1.

[a] For week of March 12, 1967.

[b] For group of stores having 10 to 19 employees in 1948.

[c] Stores opened during year and in business at end of year.

Occupational Distribution

According to the Bureau of Labor Statistics, the entire drug-store industry employed 442,100 workers in 1970 (Table 5). Just over 100,000 of these were pharmacists, about one-quarter of the work force, and most of the rest were in either sales or service occupations.

TABLE 5. *Drugstore Industry*
Total, Female, and Pharmacist Employment
United States, 1960-1970

Year	All Employees	Female Employees	Percent Female	Pharmacists [a]	Percent Pharmacists
1960	367,800	211,200	57.4	104,256	28.3
1966	416,000	242,600	58.3	104,693	25.2
1969	432,600	261,500	60.4	105,203	24.3
1970	442,100	268,100	60.6	n.a.	n.a.

Source: U. S. Bureau of Labor Statistics, *Employment and Earnings Statistics for the United States, 1909-68*, Bulletin No. 1312-6, August 1960, pp. 788-790; *Employment and Earnings*, March 1970 and 1971, Tables B-2 and B-3; and National Association of Boards of Pharmacy, *Proceedings of the Annual Convention, 1960*, Chart 5, p. 64; *1966*, Chart 5, p. 163, *1969*, Table 2, p. 194.

[a] From data on licensed pharmacists in retail stores collected by the NABP.

The pharmacist's position in the operation of drugstores is regulated and protected by state laws—in some states, a drug-store cannot even be opened unless a pharmacist is on duty. It is the presence of these highly paid and highly skilled professionals that primarily distinguishes drugstores from other neighborhood retail operations. About one-half of all pharmacists in retail drugstores are owners or partners in their own businesses, and the rest are salaried employees.[11] This occupation, and the shortage of Negroes in it, will be examined more fully in Chapter V.

The sales worker group in drugstores is made up of sales clerks, sales specialists, and cashiers. The medium-sized and

11. U.S. Bureau of Labor Statistics, *Occupational Outlook Handbook, 1966-1967*, Bulletin No. 1450 (Washington: Government Printing Office, 1965), p. 113.

larger drugstores are self-service and therefor do not employ
clerks to any great extent, except those that are large enough
to include sizable camera departments and other specialized departments. There may be one clerk employed, perhaps on a
part-time basis, to keep shelf stock complete and in good order.

Drugstores employ saleswomen trained as cosmetic specialists
to promote the sale of these high markup items to their female
customers. Negro jobs in this area tend to be limited to stores
in Negro neighborhoods because the salesperson herself is usually
the model for the products she sells. Larger stores frequently
have camera departments, in which case someone may be specially trained for this job. There are no reasons for racial
distinctions among these personnel.

Cashiers are used fairly extensively. Most stores have at least
two, one for prescriptions and one for other purchases in the
store. Many also have two or three general checkout cashiers
and additional cashiers for the tobacco department and the
liquor department, if the store sells alcoholic beverages.

Most blue collar jobs fall into the service work category in
the drugstore industry. Both chain and independents have a
stockboy or porter who is responsible for stocking shelves, keeping the store neat, and sometimes delivering orders. The larger
group is food service personnel: soda jerks, short order cooks,
lunch counter waitresses. These traditionally have been low paid
jobs. Until the 1966 amendments, food service workers were
exempt under the Fair Labor Standards Act, but were subject
to state minimum wage laws in some states.

The food service area has been the scene of some of the major
changes in drugstores since 1940. Drugstore renovations have
increasingly removed food service facilities in order to devote
floor space to the more profitable product lines such as cosmetics
and photographic supplies and equipment. The shift in sales
proportion was shown in Table 4. Minimum wage legislation
has also been a factor in the change, as will be explained below.
In retail drugstores, Negroes have been disproportionately affected by the decline of food service.

Data for the chain company segment of the industry for 1969
are shown in Table 6. Managers and professionals together accounted for 17.2 percent of the total work force: these were
pharmacists and company executives primarily, plus a few departmental managers, such as the heads of lunch counter operations. Almost one-half of all employees and 59.2 percent of the

TABLE 6. *Drugstore Industry*

Total Employment and Percent Distribution by Occupational Group, Chain Companies
United States, 1969

Occupational Group	All Employees		Male		Female	
	Total	Percent Distribution	Total	Percent Distribution	Total	Percent Distribution
Officials and managers	7,176	11.7	6,431	25.2	745	2.1
Professionals	3,387	5.5	3,010	11.8	377	1.0
Technicians	158	0.3	88	0.4	70	0.2
Sales workers	29,106	47.3	7,743	30.4	21,363	59.2
Office and clerical	4,587	7.4	1,587	6.2	3,000	8.3
Total white collar	44,414	72.2	18,859	74.0	25,555	70.8
Craftsmen	276	0.4	241	0.9	35	0.1
Operatives	853	1.4	581	2.3	272	0.8
Laborers	1,387	2.2	1,170	4.6	217	0.6
Service workers	14,625	23.8	4,636	18.2	9,989	27.7
Total blue collar	17,141	27.8	6,628	26.0	10,513	29.2
Total	61,555	100.0	25,487	100.0	36,068	100.0

Source: U.S. Equal Employment Opportunity Commission.

female work force were in sales; just under one-fourth were service workers. Jobs in this latter category, including janitors, porters, delivery boys, and fountain/lunch counter employees, make up most of the blue collar group. These proportions vary, of course, with the type of store, as outlined in a preceding section. A closer look at these occupational distributions in later chapters will show, however, that the Negro sector of the work force is strongly concentrated in the lowest of these three categories.

Female Employment

The retail drug industry is a major retail employer of women workers because of the numerous low paying white collar sales positions available. The percentage of female employees has increased steadily to over 60 percent of the work force (Table 5), much higher than the average for retail trade, which is about 46 percent female.[12] In chain companies, women held a slightly lower proportion of the jobs, partly because of the concentration of males in executive positions (Table 6). Although about two-thirds of all women are sales workers, most Negro women in this industry are blue collar workers, largely food service workers at lunch counters and soda fountains. The position of women will be examined in greater detail in Chapter IV.

Earnings and the Effect of Minimum Wage Laws

For nonprofessionals, the retail drug industry yields relatively low wages. Table 7 shows the 1970 average weekly and hourly earnings for nonsupervisory workers to be less than the average for all retail trade. Drugstore workers earned $74.41 a week or about $2.34 an hour during 1970. This, of course, is related to both the black/white and male/female employment proportions in the industry, since larger proportions of Negroes and females are usually found in lower paying industries.

Minimum wage legislation has recently had a strong impact in one particular area of retail drugstore employment—that of soda fountain and lunch counter workers. Prior to 1966, food service workers in retail enterprises were exempted from minimum wage legislation. The 1966 amendments, however, extended this coverage to the category which includes most drugstore soda fountain and lunch counter employees. This legislation

---

12. *Employment and Earnings*, Vol. 17 (March 1971), Table B-3.

TABLE 7. *Drugstore Industry and All Retail Trade*
Average Earnings of Nonsupervisory Workers
United States, 1970

	Average Weekly Earnings	Average Hourly Earnings	Average Weekly Hours
All retail trade (SIC 52-59)	$82.47	$2.44	33.8
Drugstores and pharmacies (SIC 591)	74.41	2.34	31.8

Source: *Employment and Earnings,* Vol. 17 (March 1971), Table C-2.

went into effect on February 1, 1967 and the Department of
Labor noted that "covered retail stores recorded a 12 percent
decline in the number of workers employed in food service occupations between June 1966 and May 1967." [13]

Fountains and luncheonettes are visibly absent from many
new drugstores. In addition, they are being replaced in many
older stores by high profit departments such as cameras and
cosmetics. Walgreen's, which once operated 17 lunch counters in
midtown Manhattan, now has only one—in the Port Authority
Bus Terminal—which generates enough traffic in the face of
high rent and labor costs to remain profitable. [14]

Most of the field research for this report was conducted shortly
before and after the February 1968 minimum wage increase and
interviewees were asked how their companies would counteract
the higher hourly wages. Most planned to use some combination
of price increases, reduction of store hours, and reduction in
full-time personnel to reduce the impact of the higher minimums.
The store hours cutback reduces the need for part-time employees
as well as the overtime pay for full-time employees. A similar
reaction will probably be forthcoming with every minimum wage
increase, since most drugstore employees are at or very near
the federal minimums. To the extent that Negroes constitute
marginal full-time and regular part-time employees, they undergo
employment declines with extensions and increases in federal
(and state) minimum wage laws.

13. U. S. Department of Labor, *Minimum Wage and Maximum Hour Stand-*
ards under the Fair Labor Standards Act, January 1968, p. 11.

14. Richard Phalon, "Drugstore Lunch Counters Fading Out," *New York*
Times, December 12, 1970.

Unionization

Drugstores are not highly unionized except in New York City and California. In the former, retail drug employees have been unionized by Local 1199, Retail, Wholesale and Department Store Union. This union has recently been making considerable news by unionizing hospital employees and now has many more of the latter than retail drug workers.

Local 1199 has a long history of militant unionism and support of leftwing and liberal causes. Its hospital organizing campaigns have featured close coordination with and support by civil rights organizations and personalities, including the widow of the late Rev. Martin Luther King, Jr. Negroes are not as active in its retail drug decisions as in its hospital activities.

Far larger is the Retail Clerks International Association, whose locals include the drug chain employees in large California cities and elsewhere where unionized. Both RCIA and the Retail, Wholesale and Department Store Union are AFL-CIO affiliates. RCIA was affiliated with the American Federation of Labor before the AFL-CIO merger, its rival with the Congress of Industrial Organizations. Both organizations admit pharmacists as well as lesser skilled employees.

Most of the unionized stores are chains, with the unions often using boycotts and harrassments to force recognition or to extend recognition after unionizing one or more stores. The number of employees per location is small, however, so that the cost of organizing, even in this manner, is relatively high.

RCIA is more conservative and at least less overtly interested in Negro employment than Local 1199. In neither case, however, has unionization been a significant factor in racial policy and therefore it will not be extensively considered in this study.

CHAPTER III

Negro Employment, 1920 to 1960

Drugstore industry jobs were largely unavailable to Negro workers until very recent years. The historically low level of employment was attributable largely to the industry's employment structure, tied as it has been to the entrepreneurial efforts of pharmacists.

PRE-WORLD WAR II EMPLOYMENT

The vast majority of drugstores were one-man or family operations before World War II, with few employees hired from the general labor force. Since there were not many black pharmacists, Negro family members were also excluded from the industry. In addition, as many studies have shown, the general practice in retail trade was to exclude black workers from sales positions even in larger establishments. Thus the few Negroes who were employed held the low level, service occupations.

Table 8 shows census data from 1920 to 1960 for total and Negro employment. Although the data are not strictly comparable between the earliest two decades and later years, it is clear that Negroes held very few drugstore jobs in 1920 and 1930, not more than 2 percent of the total. Negro women did have proportionately more of the female jobs than Negro men had of male jobs, since the use of Negroes in retail trade during this period was largely confined to menial work, except in stores serving black communities exclusively. A United States Women's Bureau study of Negro employment in 15 states during the 1920's found only four Negro women in "sales" positions in 61 retail stores they examined. These four women were soda fountain attendants,[15] quite probably in drugstores.

Negro pharmacists were not totally lacking during this period, and they tended to operate their own drugstores with all-

---

15. U.S. Women's Bureau, *Negro Women in Industry in 15 States*, Bulletin No. 70 (Washington: Government Printing Office, 1929), p. 26.

TABLE 8. *Drugstore Industry Employment by Race and Sex United States, 1920-1960*

	All Employees			Male			Female		
	Total	Negro	Percent Negro	Total	Negro	Percent Negro	Total	Negro	Percent Negro
1920 a	80,157	910	1.1	76,995	837	1.1	3,162	73	2.3
1930 a	104,727	1,482	1.4	100,123	1,314	1.3	4,604	168	3.6
1940	224,697	16,709	7.4	170,798	15,587	9.1	53,899	1,122	2.1
1950	290,580	19,860	6.8	164,910	14,070	8.5	125,670	5,790	4.6
1960	380,392	23,578	6.2	192,136	15,159	7.9	188,256	8,419	4.5

Source: *U.S. Census of Population:*

1920: Vol. IV, *Occupations*, Table 5.

1930: Vol. IV, *Occupations*, Table 13.

1940: Vol. III, *The Labor Force*, Part 1, U.S. Summary, Table 76.

1950: Vol. IV, *Industrial Characteristics*, Table 2.

1960: PC(2) 7F, *Industrial Characteristics*, Table 3.

Note: Census data are computed differently from U.S. Bureau of Labor Statistics data, so the 1960 figures above do not match those in Table 5.

a Probably underestimates lower-level workers.

black work forces. Wendell Dabney's study of the Negro community in Cincinnati during the 1920's listed four Negro-owned drugstores [16] and 21 pharmacists, 12 of whom had passed the Ohio state board examination.[17] One remarkable woman, Mrs. Richard Kyles Smith, had obtained a PhC degree from Meharry Medical School in 1916, and after working in Richmond, Virginia, Tulsa, Oklahoma, and Louisville, Kentucky drugstores, came to work for a black-owned pharmacy in Cincinnati. Mrs. Smith was put in charge of a branch operation in the mid-1920's.[18] Mrs. Anna Beckwith, another leading member of Cincinnati's Negro community in the 1920's had been educated at Berea (Kentucky) College and was the pharmacist-owner of the Peerless Pharmacy.[19]

In Harlem in the 1930's, "most of the drug stores owned by whites employed whites or Spanish pharmacists. The Negro drug store owners were usually their own pharmacists." [20] The Pharmacists' Union of Greater New York listed two black registered pharmacists among its 1,550 members, and had plans to recruit other black pharmacists and place them in Harlem area drugstores.[21] This union later became Local 1199 of the Retail, Wholesale and Department Store Union. As noted earlier, it is now the largest union of hospital employees. Its drugstore membership remains largely confined to New York City. There is no evidence that its activities have significantly altered the employment pattern of Negroes in drugstores.

The Depression Years

Census data for 1940 indicate a large increase in male Negro drugstore employment during the Depression years. Although only 16,709 black workers were reported in the drugstore industry in 1940, this represented an increase from 1.4 to 7.4

---

16. Wendell P. Dabney, *Cincinnati's Colored Citizens* (Cincinnati: The Dabney Publishing Company, 1926), reprinted by Johnson Reprint Corporation, 1970, The Basic Afro-American Reprint Library, p. 403.

17. *Ibid.*, p. 408.

18. *Ibid.*, p. 255.

19. *Ibid.*, p. 255-256.

20. Charles Lionel Franklin, *The Negro Labor Unionist of New York*, Columbia University Studies in History, Economics, and Public Law, No. 420 (New York: Columbia University Press, 1936), p. 392.

21. *Ibid.*, pp. 180, 393.

percent of all employment (Table 8). This jump may in part be due to changes in the categorization of workers, but Negro men certainly did not lose drugstore jobs during the 1930's. They held a relatively high proportion of male jobs—9.1 percent of the total—while Negro women's employment dropped to 2.1 percent of the female work force.

The presence of so many men in the work force indicates the nature of the industry and the economic conditions in 1940 and, simultaneously, suggests the reasons for the low level of Negro employment.[22] The national economy in 1940 had not fully recovered from the Depression. The scarcity of jobs caused more men to seek employment in this low wage industry than would ordinarily be the case. Employers preferred men to women and the work force reflected that preference. Negroes continued to be generally unable to find sales positions in white-owned stores, and the number of black pharmacists was extremely small, as Table 9 shows.

Practically all of the stores in 1940 were still small independents and many were one-man stores in which the owner was the pharmacist/manager/sales clerk. If he had any assistants they were members of his family (this no doubt accounts for much of the female employment recorded in 1940) or a relief pharmacist or a delivery boy. In the South especially, the delivery boy might well be a Negro who was also employed as janitor and general odd-jobs man.

Because so many of the stores were so small in 1940, there were few employment opportunities for nonpharmacists except in some metropolitan areas where chains were becoming established. This effectively shut Negroes out of the job market because there were less than 850 Negro pharmacists, only about one percent of the total (Table 9).

The lack of Negro pharmacists had a double effect, as mentioned above. Not only did this greatly restrict the opportunities for a Negro man, the possibility of his wife or other relative minding the till for him in the drugstore was foreclosed. The level of Negro female employment in 1940 is probably a fairly accurate reflection of Negro entrepreneurship in the drugstore business, because it is evident from the employment level of Negro women for 1940 that Negro females were not gen-

---

22. Low in comparison to the proportion of Negroes in the population. Compared to some other industries, notably banking and insurance, Negro employment in the retail drug industry was high.

TABLE 9. *Drugstore Industry and Other Industries*
Pharmacist Employment by Race and Sex
United States, 1940-1960

	All Pharmacists			Male			Female		
	Total	Negro	Percent Negro	Total	Negro	Percent Negro	Total	Negro	Percent Negro
1940	79,347	843	1.1	76,131	769	1.0	3,216	74[a]	2.3[a]
1950	84,480	1,370	1.6	77,130	1,100	1.4	7,350	270	3.7
1960	92,233	1,685	1.8	84,803	1,543	1.8	7,430	142	1.9

Source: *U.S. Census of Population:*

1940: Vol. III, *The Labor Force*, Part 1, U.S. Summary, Tables 58 and 62.

1950: Vol. IV, *Occupational Characteristics*, Table 3.

1960: PC(2) 7A, *Occupational Characteristics*, Table 3.

Note: Includes pharmacists in hospitals and industries such as drug manufacturing as well as in retail drugstores. See Table 5 for drugstore industry pharmacists in the 1960's.

[a] Estimated. There was no breakdown for Negro female pharmacists given in 1940, so the percentage of Negroes among all unspecified professional women was applied to the total female pharmacists figure to estimate the number of Negroes.

erally used as sales clerks or fountain help in white-owned drug-stores.

The South

Segregated facilities such as lunch counters in the South co-incided with restricted Negro employment. Few black workers had jobs above the janitor-porter-service worker level. During the 1930's, Washington, D. C. experienced "sit downs" at soda fountains and 15 months of picketing in an unsuccessful effort to move Peoples Drug Stores to hire Negro clerks.[20] Nonwhite clerical and sales workers made up just 3.7 percent of drugstore clerical workers in Alabama in 1940, but comprised 51.7 percent of the men and 12.9 percent of the women service workers.[24] Since there were 28 nonwhite professionals and proprietors in the Alabama drugstore industry, it is possible that most of the nonwhite sales workers were confined to Negro drugstores.

EMPLOYMENT DECLINES AFTER WORLD WAR II

Although both total and Negro employment increased between 1940 and 1950, the Negro proportion of jobs declined from 7.4 to 6.8 percent (Table 8). During this decade, men moved out of the drugstore industry to better paying jobs in the expanding economy. In 1940, men had held over three-quarters of the jobs; by 1950, their proportion was nearer 50 percent. Negro male employment declined at a slightly faster rate than white male employment, shown in the drop from 9.1 to 8.5 percent of the Negro male segment of the work force. It is likely that white women took over some of the jobs previously held by black men, particularly at lunch counters. Certainly white women obtained the bulk of the expanding employment in the industry.

Female employment more than doubled during the decade, while Negro female employment quadrupled, raising their pro-portion of the female work force to 4.6 percent. This was not enough, however, to offset Negro male losses.

The sizeable loss of Negro men on an industry basis com-pared to their small loss among all male employees points to the great influx of women during the decade. This had a defi-nite impact on Negro employment. As the job opportunities for

23. Constance McLaughlin Green, *The Secret City* (Princeton: Princeton University Press, 1967), p. 230.

24. *U.S. Census of Population: 1940*, Vol. III, The Labor Force, Part 2, Table 20.

men improved during and after World War II, they moved out of (or did not go into) the retail drug industry and employers therefore turned increasingly to women, more and more of whom desired jobs outside the home. The movement of men to better jobs and the resulting job opportunities for women in drugstores was coupled with the beginnings of changes in the industry that required more employees. The small one-man stores began to decline and larger stores requiring sales clerks on a large-scale basis began to emerge.

Negro women did not benefit from these changes as much as they might have because, except for a few stores in eastern areas, Negro women were excluded from sales clerk and cashier jobs. Their gains were largely limited to the waitress/dishwasher jobs available at the lunch counters in the drugstores.

Negro men declined disproportionately because practically all of them could improve their incomes by taking jobs in other industries as they became available. Many white men, however, were pharmacists and hence had a much stronger economic attachment to the drugstore industry. The number of Negro pharmacists increased to only 1,370 during this decade (Table 9). To the extent that these new pharmacists became independent businessmen, this increase probably accounted for some of the new Negro women employed during this period.

Suburban Movement

Another factor which tended to reduce opportunities for black employees was the movement of the industry to the suburbs following World War II. Particularly, the chains began to concentrate their new, large stores in the suburban shopping centers, in areas where few Negroes dwelled. In addition, new independent stores opened in white suburban areas as the center cities began their postwar decline. Jobs in the suburbs usually went to the suburban dwellers—and few of these were black.

Federal and State Fair Employment Commissions

Federal concern over racial employment, through the Roosevelt and Truman Executive Orders,[25] had little direct effect on retail employment patterns since war related industries and gov-

---

25. Executive Orders 8802, June 25, 1945; 9346, May 27, 1943, and 9664, December 20, 1945. President's Committee on Fair Employment Practice, *Final Report* (Washington: Government Printing Office, 1947), Appendix A, pp. 98-101.

ernment employment were the subjects of the presidential non-discrimination directives. In reviewing postwar employment opportunities for black workers, the President's Commission on Fair Employment Practice did point out that Negroes in wholesale and retail trade were confined to low skill positions.[26]

A factor which had a favorable impact on Negro employment in the late forties and fifties was the passage of state fair employment practice legislation. Retail establishments as well as manufacturing industries became the subject of complaint investigations and surveys of racial employment in such states as New York, New Jersey, and Massachusetts. Although drugstores escaped much of the direct inquiries which larger retail establishments such as department stores experienced, the larger chain and independent drugstores in the North did begin employing Negroes in greater numbers, particularly as sales clerks. Yet the overall changes wrought were small, as industry location and lack of black pharmacists weighed heavily against black employment.

In the South, integration of facilities, and with it, jobs, generally awaited the civil rights activities of the 1960's. Washington, D.C., however, was subject to the organized efforts of civil rights groups much earlier: drugstore lunchrooms in the downtown area were opened to Negroes in 1952, after years of demonstrations and legal battles. The largest downtown stores did not begin token hiring of Negroes, however, until 1957.[27]

The Negro Chamber of Commerce in Chattanooga, Tennessee, listed two black-owned drugstores in the early 1950's. These probably provided the only opportunities for blacks to hold sales positions in drugstores, since, according to a National Planning Association study, they did not occupy "administrative, office-clerical, and sales positions in White-operated stores, with minor exceptions," in Chattanooga at the time.[28]

Negro Employment in 1960

The Negro proportion of drugstore employment had declined still further by 1960, down to only 6.2 percent of the total, al-

---

26. *Ibid.*, p. 90.

27. Green, *op. cit.*, pp. 297 and 315.

28. NPA Committee of the South, *Selected Studies of Negro Employment in the South*, Report No. 6 (Washington: National Planning Association, 1955), pp. 443 and 444.

though both Negro men and women gained in absolute numbers of jobs as total employment increased. Two-thirds of the 90,000 new workers, however, were white females.

In contrast to the previous decade men (both white and Negro) increased in numbers, but continued to decline in proportion to women. In 1940 they had been 76 percent of the work force, by 1960 they were barely 50 percent. Negro men shared in the absolute increase in male employment, but more slowly than white men, declining from 8.5 to 7.9 percent of all male employees between 1950 and 1960.

Negro pharmacist employment had increased to almost 2 percent in 1960, but their total number was only 1,685 (Table 9). Since nearly one-fifth of all drugstore jobs were in the professional category, the Negro occupational distribution continued to be concentrated in the lower categories.

Based on historical trends, the future employment outlook for Negroes looked bleak in 1960. Stores were getting larger and sales were increasing handsomely, but employment was growing slowly, largely because of the encroachment of the self-service concept in retailing. The new jobs that were available seemed to be reserved, for the most part, for pharmacists (of whom well over 95 percent were white males) and white female sales clerks.

Direct efforts to improve black employment opportunities had met with only limited success in a very few areas. In the South, facilities such as drugstore lunch counters remained segregated, although they sometimes employed black service workers. But the 1960's brought vastly increased governmental and community pressure for equal employment in general in American industry. The following chapter will examine what happened in the drugstore industry during this period.

CHAPTER IV

Negro Drugstore Industry Employment in the 1960's

In the 1960's, several new factors began to influence Negro employment in predominately white industries and a few events had special implications for the retail drug industry in particular. The civil rights movement sit-ins at segregated lunch counters occurred at a time when these were still focal points in southern drugstores. Also in the early 1960's, Negro boycotts of products and businesses which maintained discriminatory employment practices were initiated.[29] Independent drugstore owners, reliant on community goodwill and dealing in name-brand products, could not overlook their own vulnerability in the face of such tactics.

Chain drugstores could more easily withstand local black boycotts and other civil rights activity, perhaps, but their size made their employment practices accountable to the federal government pursuant to the Civil Rights Act of 1964. In addition, few chains wish to risk alienating a potential customer group.

THE 1968 FIELD SAMPLES

This chapter utilizes data compiled by the author, divided into the two industry sectors—independents and chain companies. Although independents employ the majority of the industry's work force,[30] the chain segment is important both because of its past and predicted growth and because major shifts in an area such as racial employment policy are likely to emanate from

29. These were not entirely new tactics, as the Washington protests mentioned in the previous chapter demonstrate.

30. An estimate of independent-to-chain employment can be derived from a comparison of total employment as reported by the Bureau of Labor Statistics with that reported by the EEOC. The latter reflect only the larger employers in the industry, almost entirely chains. For 1969, approximately 24 percent of all employment was in chains by this measure. (Compare Table 5, Chapter II with Table 23, *infra*.)

the industry leaders and large employers. Furthermore, it is possible that factors such as location or store type, which may be more characteristic of one segment of the industry or the other, may affect Negro employment.

The 1968 chain field sample is drawn from small, medium, and large chain companies and is, we believe, a fair representation of employment in that sector of the drugstore industry. The sample data on independents, however, should be viewed with more caution. Although various regions, locations, and sizes are represented, the actual sample is only a tiny fraction of total independent drugstore employment. Furthermore, since it is based on voluntary responses to the author's questionnaire, self-selection which could seriously bias results may have occurred. For example, responders may be only those who feel particularly proud of their racial employment record; a larger percentage of independents with very low Negro employment may simply have failed to respond.

Since earlier racial employment data were collected by the U.S. Census on an industry wide basis by individuals' responding to census enumerators, it is not possible to say whether differences noted in the 1968 sample reflect true changes in employment patterns, or simply differences among the groups surveyed. Therefore, it is difficult to make comparisons between 1960 and 1968 data.

A summary of the 1968 sample appears in Table 10. It shows that Negroes held about 10 percent of all jobs in both independent and chain drugstores, with a slightly higher percentage among chains than among independents. The difference between independents and chains may be much greater, depending on the accuracy of the small independent sample, but the lead of chains is not unexpected by reason of their structure and location as described in Chapter II.

Women and Other Minorities

Women outnumbered men in the retail drug industry in 1968 both among chains and in the industry in general. (See Table 10 and Table 5, Chapter II.) Although specific data by sex were not available for independent stores, there is nothing to indicate that proportions and employment distribution varied significantly from those in chain companies. Female employment was almost entirely concentrated in the sales worker category, as will be discussed in a later section.

TABLE 10. *Drugstore Industry*
Employment by Race, Sex, and Industry Sector
Independent Stores and Chain Companies
United States, 1968

Industry Sector	All Employees			Male			Female		
	Total	Negro	Percent Negro	Total	Negro	Percent Negro	Total	Negro	Percent Negro
Independent drugstores	1,555	152	9.8	n.a.	n.a.	n.a.	n.a.	n.a.	n.a.
Chain companies Drugstores only	56,377	5,915	10.5	22,532	2,951	13.1	33,845	2,964	8.9
Headquarters and warehouses	5,178	555	10.7	2,955	359	12.1	2,223	196	8.8
Total company	61,555	6,470	10.5	25,487	3,310	13.0	36,068	3,160	8.8

Source: Data in author's possession.

The survey of independent stores did yield statistics on employment of other minority groups in the drugstore industry. White, Negro, Spanish-American, and Oriental employment are compared in Table 11. The regional variations show that in areas where there are few Negroes, such as the Rocky Mountain region, other minority group members are hired, lending support to the idea that there are some jobs that whites simply leave to minority people.

Regional Variations

Although store chain and independent work forces have similar Negro percentages for the United States as a whole, there are large differences between the two sectors in most regions, as Table 12 indicates. In the South, however, each segment has about 16 percent Negro employment—considerably above the national average, but more in line with Negro population distribution. The continued utilization of Negroes in menial work in stores and the smaller number of self-service operations may be factors in the strong representation of Negroes in southern drugstores.

Store Employment in Chains

In the Midwest, 12.5 percent of the chain employment in stores is Negro, somewhat above expectations. The Midwest figures are without doubt the result of a large concentration of chains—there are more chain stores in the Midwest than in the other sections of the country, based on proportion of total stores in the region. The large number of stores and the resulting competition for pharmacy manpower creates better employment conditions for Negro pharmacists than would ordinarily obtain. Nearly all the black employment in this region is concentrated in such large cities as Chicago, Cleveland, Detroit, and St. Louis.

The major drug chains in the Midwest have long recruited at schools of pharmacy in the East and South and several now include the Negro colleges of pharmacy in their recruiting tours. Walgreen's, headquartered in Chicago, has been recruiting at Howard University since the late 1950's.

The low black employment in the Rocky Mountain area is, of course, a population mix phenomonon. In the West Coast region, Negro employment is heavily concentrated in the Los Angeles and San Francisco-Oakland areas where the bulk of blacks on the West Coast dwell.

TABLE 11. *Drugstore Industry*
White, Negro, Spanish-American, and Oriental Employment
Independent Stores
United States and Regions, 1968

Racial/Ethnic Group	Northeast		South		Midwest		Rocky Mountain		Far West		United States	
	Number	Percent of Total	Number	Percent of Total	Number	Percent of Total	Number	Percent of Total	Number	Percent of Total	Number	Percent of Total
White	325	87.1	451	83.8	445	92.9	119	93.0	28	75.7	1,368	87.9
Negro	39	10.5	86	16.0	25	5.2	—	—	2	5.4	152	9.8
Spanish-American	8	2.1	1	0.2	6	1.3	9	7.0	5	13.5	29	1.9
Oriental	1	0.3	—	—	3	0.6	—	—	2	5.4	6	0.4
All employees	373	100.0	538	100.0	479	100.0	128	100.0	37	100.0	1,555	100.0

Source: Data in author's possession.

Note: For regional definitions, see Appendix Table A-1.

TABLE 12. *Drugstore Industry*
Total and Negro Employment
Independent and Chain Company Stores
United States and Regions, 1968

Region	Independent Drugstore			Chain Drugstores		
	Total	Negro	Percent Negro	Total	Negro	Percent Negro
Northeast	373	39	10.5	6,242	175	2.8
South	538	86	16.0	19,883	3,097	15.6
Midwest	479	25	5.2	19,335	2,409	12.5
Rocky Mountain	128	—	—	5,631	97	1.7
Far West	37	2	5.4	5,286	137	2.6
United States	1,555	152	9.8	56,377	5,915	10.5

Source: Data in author's possession and Appendix Tables B-7—B-12.

Note: For regional definitions, see Appendix Table A-1.

The low employment of Negroes in the Northeast by chains (2.8 percent of the work force) compared to independents, is a result of locational factors. Most chain stores in the Northeast are situated in suburban shopping areas, far from the heavy concentrations of Negro population in northeastern cities. The importance of location will be shown in the following section.

LOCATIONAL FACTORS

Both chain and independent drugstores generally draw their nonprofessional employees from the neighborhoods in which the stores are located. The long, irregular hours make commuting to work impractical, especially for the largely female work force, and the low skill requirements make it unnecessary to actively recruit beyond most neighborhoods. Drugstores located in especially high income neighborhoods do, of course, employ workers from outside the immediate area, and the professional and managerial level employees do not necessarily reside in the neighborhood and may indeed have been recruited from outside the area.

Negro employment in chain companies including headquarters and warehouses, by location, is shown in Table 13. Metropolitan areas with large minority populations are divided into central city and suburban locations and compared with small town and rural locations. About 42 percent of all chain employment was concentrated in these selected central city locations in 1968, compared with 52 percent of Negro employment. Only 5 percent of Negro employment was in nonmetropolitan locations, where 12 percent of all employees worked. (Compare with Table 16.)

Core City Locations

Negro employment is concentrated in central city drugstores among both chains and independents (Tables 13 and 14). Every region had a higher Negro percentage of the work force in cities than in the region as a whole in 1968. The difference is particularly striking in the Northeast, where the chain work force is 7.0 percent Negro in the core cities, 2.0 percent in the suburbs, and 0.2 percent in the small towns and rural areas. In the Midwest as well, the suburban black percentage was about one-third that of the urban work force. In the Rocky Mountain region, all Negro employment was in chain companies in cities, and in the Far West, Negro employment was almost entirely in the cities for both chain and independent stores.

The overwhelming fact is that Negroes are concentrated in the cities. Employers typically—and small retail establishments almost universally—draw their employees from the nearest source of labor available. The drugstore employment data reflect the realities of the local labor market.

In addition, the chain stores are concentrated in the major business areas within a city, in keeping with their high volume, rapid turnover merchandising philosophy. Such situations create an aura of impersonality between the business and its patrons, lacking the friendly corner drugstore image that an independent owner seeks to foster. This minimization of genuine person-to-person contact is reinforced by the self-service emphasis and the net result is that there is not likely to be the same concern about unfavorable customer reaction if the chain employs Negroes that the neighborhood store manager may feel.

In the business areas that serve exclusively Negro neighborhoods there is, of course, an even more compelling reason to hire Negroes. Here the sales volume depends on Negro customers and the chain can hire Negroes without having qualms about customer acceptance. In fact, the reverse may well be true. The same conditions, of course, affect independent operators in Negro neighborhoods.

TABLE 13. *Drugstore Industry*
Employment by Race and Selected Location
Chain Companies
United States and Regions, 1968

| Region | Selected Metropolitan Areas [a] | | | | | | Nonmetropolitan Areas | | |
| | Core City Locations | | | Suburban Locations | | | | | |
	Total	Negro	Percent Negro	Total	Negro	Percent Negro	Total	Negro	Percent Negro
Northeast	2,236	156	7.0	1,580	32	2.0	1,304	2	0.2
South	8,539	1,529	17.9	3,094	549	17.7	3,208	242	7.5
Midwest	11,080	1,572	14.2	2,839	161	5.7	1,272	47	3.7
Rocky Mountain	2,014	50	2.5	216	—	—	208	—	—
Far West	1,717	89	5.2	1,430	31	2.2	1,394	4	0.3
United States	25,586	3,396	13.3	9,159	773	8.4	7,386	295	4.0

Source: Appendix Tables B-14—B-29.

Note: For regional definitions, see Appendix Table A-1.

[a] Excluding metropolitan areas with less than 10 percent Negro populations.

TABLE 14. Drugstore Industry
Employment by Race and Location
Independent Stores
United States and Regions, 1968

| Region | All Metropolitan Areas [a] | | | | | | Nonmetropolitan Areas | | |
| | Core City Locations | | | Suburban Locations | | | | | |
	Total	Negro	Percent Negro	Total	Negro	Percent Negro	Total	Negro	Percent Negro
Northeast	238	38	16.0	131	1	0.8	4	—	—
South	204	55	27.0	329	31	9.4	5	—	—
Midwest	247	22	8.9	221	3	1.4	11	—	—
Rocky Mountain	70	—	—	53	—	—	5	—	—
Far West	27	2	7.4	10	—	—	—	—	—
Total	786	117	14.9	744	35	4.7	25	—	—

Source: Data in author's possession.

Note: For regional definitions, see Appendix Table A-1.

[a] Includes all metropolitan areas, regardless of Negro population.

One problem in store operations also causes chains to employ any worker obtainable, white or black. The chains experience an incredible turnover rate, particularly in periods of high employment. One chain claimed to have a complete turnover among nonprofessional store employees every three months. This indicates that drugstore employment is frequently among marginal groups. A perennial shortage of labor traditionally results in increased black employment.

It is not altogether inaccurate, then, to say that chains operating in the major core cities cannot afford to adopt discriminatory hiring practices, even if laws did not forbid discrimination. This is not to say that discrimination is totally absent. Much depends on the individual store manager, whose attitudes and staffing problems are more important than any other single factor. Nevertheless, one need but note the racial composition of center city drugstore staffs to see that black employees are heavily represented.

Suburban Areas

Percent Negro employment in the suburbs is lower than that for their counterpart cities by a large margin, except among chain companies in the South (Tables 13 and 14). Comparing the suburban employment regional averages (Table 12) yields a similar conclusion although there is less disparity than between the figures for the cities and suburbs.

These patterns prevail, in general, for all occupations, as shown in Table 15. Among blue collar occupations, Negroes are particularly lacking in the suburban Northeast and Midwest. Hence, although Negroes find few white collar jobs in the suburbs, they find even fewer blue collar jobs there.

The South does not show the same variation by location found among other regions of the country. Suburban Negro employment is within 0.2 percentage point of that in southern cities in chain companies, although it is much lower in suburban independents. Among chains, Negro employment is higher in the cities in white collar occupations, but higher in the suburbs in blue collar occupations.

Outside the South, the generally lower Negro employment in the suburbs seems to be compounded from the same elements that produce higher city Negro employment. First, there are not many Negroes in the suburbs and drugstores typically draw their nonpharmacist employment from the surrounding neigh-

TABLE 15. *Drugstore Industry*

Percent Negro Employment by Occupational Group and Location

Chain Companies

Five Regions, 1968

Occupational Group	City Locations					Suburban Locations				
	Northeast	South	Midwest	Rocky Mountain	Far West	Northeast	South	Midwest	Rocky Mountain	Far West
Officials and managers	0.9	3.3	5.6	—	0.4	0.4	12.1	1.5	—	1.1
Professionals	1.1	3.3	3.5	—	3.4	6.2	9.9	0.7	—	2.7
Technicians	—	14.3	—	—	—	100.0	14.3	—	—	—
Sales workers	4.8	8.3	10.8	1.1	4.3	1.1	4.7	1.3	—	1.6
Office and clerical	4.3	13.6	6.5	2.1	3.3	—	4.1	4.0	—	3.6
Total white collar	3.8	8.1	8.3	1.0	3.3	1.2	6.4	1.4	—	1.8
Craftsmen	—	—	1.4	—	—	—	14.3	—	—	—
Operatives	46.7	38.8	14.6	—	—	—	51.0	—	—	7.7
Laborers	23.0	47.7	22.0	—	—	—	60.6	9.4	—	—
Service workers	14.4	38.3	29.2	5.5	22.0	3.9	46.3	17.7	—	4.5
Total blue collar	16.6	38.7	25.9	5.5	18.8	3.9	47.6	15.8	—	4.5
Total	7.0	17.9	14.2	2.5	5.2	2.0	17.7	5.7	—	2.2

Source: Appendix Tables B-15—B-19 and B-21—B-24.

Note: For regional definitions, see Appendix Table A-1.

borhood. Second, customer/employee interaction is not quite as impersonal as in the city, and thus there may be reluctance to hire Negroes. Third, the hiring problem is not as severe as in the cities, because there are a number of residential neighborhoods from which drugstores (and other retail establishments) can draw their personnel. Finally, the chain stores in the suburbs are heavily located in shopping centers, which cannot be reached except by automobile. This effectively cuts off employment opportunities for center city Negroes. Moreover, even if transportation is available, the jobs do not often pay enough to justify commuting costs.

In the South, the situation is somewhat different, but is changing toward the northern pattern. Housing traditionally has not been nearly so segregated in the South, where black servants lived near white employers. New suburbs, however, are segregated and fear of busing school children is likely to accelerate the trend toward segregated communities. Nevertheless, blacks in the South, although today heavily a city population, are found in all sections and work in drugstores continues to be a traditional source of employment. The shopping center and segregated suburban development threaten this pattern, but employment of Negroes remains at a substantially higher ratio in southern non-city areas than anywhere in the country.

Small Towns and Rural Areas

As shown in Tables 13 and 14, Negro employment in nonmetropolitan areas is very low. The national average among chain company stores was only 4.0 in 1968; the independent sample showed no Negro employment at all. If only the total for each region is considered, some credence might be given to the demographic fact that few Negroes reside in small towns and rural areas except in the South. The individual occupational and the blue and white collar distributions (Appendix Tables B-25—B-29), however, make it clear that the low Negro employment rates result from the almost complete absence of Negro females in white collar jobs. This may result from discrimination against Negro women. More significant, probably, is the fact that Negro women are less likely to travel great distances to work than are men, and are likely thus to be unavailable. We found that to be the case in such industries as automobiles and aerospace [31] and it is likely to be even more true when the wages, as in drugstores, are much lower.

It would be possible to conclude that racial attitudes in small towns and rural areas enforce a kind of discrimination not found elsewhere. Although that may be true, it is also a fact that employers there are able to be much more selective in the hiring process. Since whites, more so in rural areas than elsewhere, are likely to have more education and work experience than Negroes, they tend to obtain the white collar jobs.

It stands to reason, of course, that a more personal atmosphere exists outside the big cities and hence a chain store manager may feel impelled to foster this condition in his store by hiring people that the bulk of the customers know. Again, such a person is more likely to be white than black, except in some areas of the South.

Neighborhood Composition

The racial composition of the drugstore's surrounding neighborhood also affects the likelihood of Negro employment. Although such data are not available for chain drugstores, Table 16 shows Negro employment in independent drugstores according to the racial texture of the trade area, and reveals some interesting characteristics of independent stores as well as their racial employment patterns.

In 1968 Negro trade was more than 20 percent in only 33 stores in the sample, but that number represented almost 19 percent of the 175 stores for which data were available. These figures suggest that the Negro trade is more important to independents than indicated by the national proportion of Negro population (11 to 12 percent).[32]

When one reviews by region the number of drugstores where Negroes constituted more than 20 percent of the trade, some odd conditions appear. In the Northeast, an unexpectedly high 31 percent of the stores (13 of 42) were in such neighborhoods. Even more surprising was the Rocky Mountain region, where

31. See Herbert R. Northrup, *et al.*, *Negro Employment in Basic Industry* (Philadelphia: Industrial Research Unit, Wharton School of Finance and Commerce, University of Pennsylvania, 1970), Part Two, pp. 89-91; Part Three, pp. 185-188.

32. This statement, of course, assumes that the responses to the questionnaire are an accurate representation of the randomly sampled population of independent drugstores and that responses themselves are accurate.

TABLE 16. *Drugstore Industry*
Store and Employment Distribution by Race and
Percent Negro Population in Neighborhood
Independent Stores
Five Regions, 1968

Region and Employment	Percent Negro Population in Neighborhood				
	0-5.0	5.1-20.0	20.1-50.0	Over 50.0	Total
Northeast					
Total employment	255	37	46	35	373
Negro employment	15	5	1	18	39
Percent Negro	5.9	13.5	2.2	51.4	10.5
Number of stores	23	6	7	6	42
Midwest [a]					
Total employment	336	97	29	11	473
Negro employment	9	6	1	9	25
Percent Negro	2.7	6.2	3.4	81.8	5.3
Number of stores	39	6	3	2	50
South					
Total employment	109	363	27	39	538
Negro employment	21	36	5	24	86
Percent Negro	19.3	9.9	18.5	61.5	16.0
Number of stores	11	30	4	5	50
Rocky Mountain					
Total employment	96	12	20	—	128
Negro employment	—	—	—	—	—
Percent Negro	—	—	—	—	—
Number of stores	15	4	3	—	22
Far West					
Total employment	19	6	7	5	37
Negro employment	—	—	—	2	2
Percent Negro	—	—	—	40.0	5.4
Number of stores	6	2	2	1	11

Source: Data in author's possession.

Note: For regional definitions, see Appendix Table A-1.

[a] Two stores with six employees did not respond.

13.6 percent (3 of 22) of the stores were in neighborhoods with substantial Negro trade, but no black employment was reported.

This perverse situation was exactly reversed in the South. There, one would expect a considerable proportion of the drugstores to have a sizeable Negro trade, but only 18 percent (9 of 50) reported Negro trade in excess of 20 percent.

Although there are several possible explanations for the differences, the likely reason is bias introduced by nonresponders. It appears that a high proportion of independent drugstores serving primarily white neighborhoods in the Northeast and Rocky Mountain regions as well as those in the South serving mainly black neighborhoods did not respond. It may well be, then, that the conclusions of the preceding section—that total percent Negro employment in chains and independents is about the same and that, occupationally, Negroes were better represented in independent stores—are affected by sample biases and therefore not correct.

In analyzing the way in which Negro employment was distributed in relation to Negro population in the neighborhood or trading area, some unusual features appear. It does not seem unreasonable to expect a rough correspondence between the proportion of Negro population in a neighborhood and the proportion of Negro employees in that neighborhood's drugstore, owing to the common practice of drawing employees from the immediate vicinity. Moreover, even if racial discrimination exists (intentionally or otherwise), the same relationship should occur although the proportion of Negro employment will be lower than otherwise. Hence, the expectation is that observations of several neighborhoods and their drugstores, when arranged into progressively higher proportions of Negro neighborhood population, would exhibit progressively more Negro employment.

Table 16 does not conform to such expectations. The relationship between employment and population was consistent for all regions only in neighborhoods with over 50 percent Negro population, and lowest employment corresponded with smallest Negro population only in the Midwest. The intermediate ranges of Negro neighborhood populations did not progress from low to high employment.

Only the Northeast, Midwest, and South reported any black employment in neighborhoods where Negro population was less than 50 percent. In the two northern regions, Negro employment was higher in neighborhoods with 5.0 to 20.0 percent Negro populations than in the very low or moderately high areas. In the South, however, employment was lowest in this intermediate population neighborhood.

The proportion of Negro population in the neighborhood also seems to be related to the kind of jobs that Negroes are able to obtain. As shown in Table 17, Negroes held the best jobs in independent drugstores where Negro neighborhood population was 5.0 percent or less or 50.0 percent or more. Three reasons can be offered for Negroes holding the better jobs where Negro population is low. First, any Negro who applies for such a job in a white neighborhood has probably traveled a relatively long distance from his own neighborhood. Such an extended job search indicates motivation and perhaps education above that to be found in applicants from the indigenous white population. There is, therefore, a good chance of getting a good job.

TABLE 17. *Drugstore Industry*
Negro Employment by Occupation and
Percent Negro Population in Neighborhood
Independent Stores
United States, 1968

Occupation	Percent Negro Population in Neighborhood				Total	Percent Distribution
	0-5.0	5.1-20.0	20.1-50.0	Over 50.0		
Managers	1	—	—	4	5	3.3
Pharmacists	1	1	—	—	2	1.3
Office workers	—	—	—	—	—	—
Cashiers	—	—	—	3	3	2.0
Sales workers	32	12	2	35	81	53.3
Stockers	1	9	—	5	15	9.9
Delivery boys	6	12	5	5	28	18.4
Warehousers	1	8	—	—	9	5.9
Porters	2	2	—	1	5	3.3
Fountain help	1	3	—	—	4	2.6
Total	45	47	7	53	152	100.0
Distribution of stores	94	48	19	14	175	
Total employment	815	515	129	90	1,549	

Source: Data in author's possession.

A second reason is that stores where Negro trade is practically nil are likely to be located in neighborhoods considerably above the median income level for the entire community. The sales clerk and cashier jobs usually filled by neighborhood housewives will therefore be difficult to fill because most of these particular housewives are not in the job market—at least for those jobs. Negroes will therefore be looked upon more favorably because the preference for hiring locally cannot be fulfilled.

Finally, these higher income neighborhoods (as characterized by few Negro residents in the trade area) usually do not display the magnitude of racial prejudice found in lower income white neighborhoods. The drugstore owner, therefore, has more latitude in deciding whom to hire.

That Negroes obtain good jobs in drugstores where the Negro population exceeds 50 percent is a natural consequence of the usual practice of hiring neighborhood residents. It is also the only sensible course of action from a business standpoint, whether the owner is white or Negro.

One final point is noteworthy in connection with independent stores in predominantly white and predominantly Negro neighborhoods. The average number of employees was considerably higher in neighborhoods where Negro population was low (8.7 employees per store for 0 to 5.0 percent Negro population and 11.7 for 5.1 to 20.0) than where Negro population was high (6.8 per store for 20.1 to 50.0 percent and 6.4 per store for over 50.0 percent). Since larger numbers of employees are indicative of more modern stores, it appears that the older, more inefficient, more likely to go out of business drugstores are located in the very neighborhoods where prospects for Negro employment is best.

OCCUPATIONAL DISTRIBUTIONS

Although data on the occupations which Negroes held and their proportion to total employment is more complete for chains than for independents, it is possible to make some general comparisons. As before, chain company data must be separated to show in-store employment alone, since independent drugstores do not have comparable supporting headquarters executive and clerical staffs or extensive warehouse and distribution facilities. Table 18 shows the occupational distributions of black workers in the independent drugstores sampled and selected chain company drugstores in 1968. Chain data on total company employment of all and Negro workers is included in Table 18 for comparison.

Chain and Independent Variations

Independent drugstore employment of Negroes differs sharply from that in chains when occupational distributions are examined. The vitally important sales category, where 51.4 percent of all chain in-store workers were employed was the primary source of employment for black workers in the sampled inde-

TABLE 18. *Drugstore Industry*
Percent Distribution of Employment by Race, Occupational
Group, and Industry Sector
Independent Stores and Chain Companies
United States, 1968

| | Independent Drugstore | Chain Companies | | | |
| | | Stores Only | | Total Company | |
Occupational Group	Negro Employment	Total	Negro	Total	Negro
Officials and managers	4.6 a	10.8	3.2	11.7	3.1
Professionals		5.5	1.3	5.5	1.3
Technicians		0.1	*	0.3	0.1
Sales workers	55.3	51.4	22.6	47.3	20.7
Office and clerical	—	4.4	3.6	7.4	5.1
Total white collar	59.9	72.2	30.7	72.2	30.3
Craftsmen	—	0.2	0.1	0.4	0.2
Operatives	5.9 b	1.2	2.7	1.4	3.3
Laborers	9.9 c	1.1	2.0	2.2	5.6
Service workers	24.3 d	25.3	64.5	23.8	60.6
Total blue collar	40.1	27.8	69.3	27.8	69.7
Total	100.0	100.0	100.0	100.0	100.0

Source: Calculated from Table 17 and Appendix Tables B-1 and B-7.

* Less than 0.05 percent.

a Professionals and technicians as well as officials and managers.

b Warehousemen.

c Stockers.

d Delivery boys, porters, and fountain help.

pendents in 1968, but employed less than one-quarter of those in chain stores. This would indicate that prospective black employees had a far better opportunity for a sales position in an independent store than in a chain store in 1968. This conclusion is reinforced by the relatively low proportion of black service workers in independent drugstores compared to chains. Once again, however, it must be said that these distributions may be strongly influenced by the sample itself, and that a more complete survey of independent stores might not show such a positive occupational distribution for black workers. Nevertheless, the independent figures are impressive.

Chain Distributions by Race

Managerial and professional, sales, and service occupations occupied almost all employees, both white and black, in chain stores, but the relative proportions were sharply reversed. One-half of all employees, but only one-quarter of black workers, were in sales positions, while 64.5 percent of Negro employees were in the lower paid and lower skilled service work category, compared to 25.3 percent of the total. The black occupational distribution is further lowered by the smaller proportion of black managers and professionals. In these two occupations, where 16.3 percent of all chain drugstore workers were employed in 1968, only 4.5 percent of the black store employees could be found.

CHAIN COMPANY OCCUPATIONAL DISTRIBUTIONS

This section will examine employment in chain companies only, from the 1968 sample, and will separate stores, company headquarters (where most of the nonstore white collar employment is located), and warehouse facilities (where the remainder of the blue collar employment is found). It should be kept in mind that store employment is numerically much more significant than employment in other retail drug chain company operations. Over 90 percent of all white and blue collar jobs were located in the stores in 1968. Appendix Tables B-7 and B-13 show the actual figures for storewide and headquarters/warehouse employment in these companies. Negro employment percentages by occupation are summarized in Table 19.

Pharmacists and Managers

The vast majority of those in the managerial category in stores are pharmacists who both supervise store operations and spend a good deal of their time doing the usual pharmacist work. In addition, professional pharmacists can be found among the top managerial and official rank at the company headquarters level. There are only a few opportunities for nonprofessional managers in the larger stores. Therefore, Negro employment in these two groups will be discussed in combination, although for clarity, they are presented separately in Table 19.

Negroes held very few managerial and professional positions in drugstore companies in 1968. They averaged 2.9 percent of the store employees in these positions and only 1.9 percent of those at headquarters locations. This is in line with the previously mentioned low overall proportion of black workers in these occupations. Increased black entry into this occupational level, which is both numerically and economically important, is strictly tied to pharmacy school enrollment, to be discussed in the next chapter.

Sales Workers

The chain store sales force in 1968 was only 4.6 percent Negro (Table 19). This was an extremely important occupation in the drugstore industry, especially among female workers, 63 percent of whom were in sales occupations. (See Appendix Table B-7 for total employment.) As described in Chapter II, sales work in cosmetics departments might be limited to whites in white neighborhoods, but otherwise neither educational requirements nor location should limit Negro employment in such jobs as cashier and general sales clerk. Yet very few black workers held sales positions in chain stores. Negro men held disproportionately more sales jobs than Negro women, even though, overall, men were employed in only about one-third of the sales jobs. Improvement in the black female proportion of the sales work force would have a significant impact on store-wide racial compositions in chains.

Office and Clerical

Secretarial and clerical workers, in the traditional sense, are not very important in drugstores; such workers are almost entirely absent in independent operations, and are found mainly

TABLE 19. *Drugstore Industry*
Percent Negro Employment by Occupational Group and Industry Sector
Chain Companies
United States, 1968

Occupational Group	All Employees			Male			Female		
	Stores Only	Headquarters and Warehouses	Total Company	Stores Only	Headquarters and Warehouses	Total Company	Stores Only	Headquarters and Warehouses	Total Company
Officials and managers	3.1	1.7	2.9	2.2	1.2	2.0	10.6	6.6	10.1
Professionals	2.5	2.5	2.5	2.2	1.8	2.1	5.3	5.1	5.3
Technicians	3.3	3.1	3.2	8.3	3.1	4.5	—	2.9	1.4
Sales workers	4.6	3.6	4.6	6.4	1.1	6.3	4.0	8.3	4.0
Office and clerical	8.7	5.4	7.2	15.8	7.1	13.3	2.7	4.9	3.9
Total white collar	4.5	3.9	4.4	5.0	2.8	4.8	4.1	5.1	4.2
Craftsmen	2.2	4.3	3.3	2.9	4.3	3.7	—	—	—
Operatives	24.1	29.7	25.3	34.0	31.3	33.2	8.2	12.5	8.5
Laborers	19.4	31.4	26.0	20.6	30.7	25.8	5.8	33.9	27.2
Service workers	26.7	29.3	26.8	41.7	29.5	41.1	20.0	29.0	20.2
Total blue collar	26.1	28.1	26.3	38.2	27.4	36.4	19.6	30.7	19.9
Total	10.5	10.7	10.5	13.1	12.1	13.0	8.8	8.8	8.8

Source: Appendix Tables B-1, B-7, and B-13.

in the headquarters offices of chains. The Negro proportion of headquarters clerical positions was 7.1 percent among men and 4.9 percent among women. The large proportion of black male clericals does not represent very many workers, although they outnumbered black female clericals in stores. Most male clericals were probably stock clerks and other low level white collar employees. Besides being numerically insignificant, this occupation where Negroes were relatively well represented is also generally unimportant in terms of job upgrading.

Craftsmen, Operatives, and Laborers

Together, the three upper level blue collar occupations comprised only 2.5 percent of chain in-store work forces in 1968 (Table 18) and were primarily filled by men. Negro workers were more heavily concentrated in the lower two occupations making up 34.0 percent of the store operatives and 20.6 percent of the laborers—but only 2.2 percent of the craftsmen (Table 19). While it would be desirable to have a larger percentage of black craftsmen, change in this direction would have very little impact on overall black employment in the drugstore industry.

Service Workers

If it were not for the large numbers of black workers in service occupations in chain store operations, Negro representation in chain companies would be extremely low, instead of the relatively high 10.5 percent. As Tables 18 and 19 show, 26.7 percent of all store service workers were black in 1968, and these workers made up 64.5 percent of all black drugstore employment. On the other hand, of the non-service work occupations in 1968, in store operations, Negroes comprised only 5 percent of total employment. Breaking down male and female employment separately, Negro men, who comprised 41.7 percent of all male service workers, would drop from 13.1 to 6.1 percent of the male store employment if service work were not available. The black female proportion without service work would drop from 8.8 to 4.1 percent.

These are very discouraging figures, both because they indicate the extent to which black workers were concentrated in the lowest level of employment in 1968, and also because of the changing nature of the industry. As was pointed out in Chapter II, drugstore lunch counters are becoming a thing of the past, largely being replaced by other, more profitable departments.

Other types of service work, such as janitors, will only increase slowly as the number of drugstores expands. Thus the high 10.5 percent Negro employment in 1968 cannot possibly be maintained in the 1970's unless more employment in other occupations, particularly sales work, becomes available to black workers.

Female Employment

The high employment of Negro women managers (10.6 percent) in chain drugstores compared to Negro men (3.1 percent) strongly reflects employment patterns in the South. Of 68 Negro female managers, 52 were in southern stores of chain companies, as Table 20 shows. These women were mainly employed in the Washington, D.C. and Baltimore areas, where Negro employment in all occupations—but especially white collar—is much higher on a percent basis than in other parts of the South.

The Negro women employed in these areas as managers are not in charge of drugstores. Rather, they manage the sizeable lunch counters found in the chain operations in these metropolitan areas. They are managers in the sense that they supervise food service employees, but they do not in any sense enjoy the salary and status ordinarily associated with higher managerial positions.

It is likely that the proportion of store managers, rather than department supervisors, who are Negro, including both men and women, does not exceed 2 percent. Given that there are about 50,000 drugstores in the United States and that about 15 percent of these are chain drugstores, the 2 percent figure means that only about 150 chain drugstores in the country are managed by Negroes. The vast majority of these Negro managers are employed by Thrifty Drug Stores (Los Angeles), Walgreen Drugstores (Chicago), Peoples Drug Stores (Washington, D. C.), and Drug Fair (Washington, D. C.).[33]

Headquarters and Warehouses

Nearly all employment in the chain warehouses and headquarters is in four employment categories: managers, office and clerical workers, laborers, and service workers. The managers are concentrated in the headquarters unit; the office and clerical group is split, with the secretaries and file clerks working in the headquarters unit and the shipping and receiving clerks in

---

33. Data in the author's possession.

TABLE 20. Drugstore Industry
Female Employment by Race and Occupational Group
Chain Stores
United States and South Region, 1968

Occupational Group	United States			South Region		
	Total	Negro	Percent Negro	Total	Negro	Percent Negro
Officials and managers	639	68	10.6	320	52	16.2
Professionals	318	17	5.3	126	7	5.6
Technicians	36	—	—	1	—	—
Sales workers	21,315	847	4.0	7,080	340	4.8
Office and clerical	1,350	36	2.7	634	13	2.1
Total white collar	23,658	968	4.1	8,161	412	5.0
Craftsmen	35	—	—	15	—	—
Operatives	256	21	8.2	115	—	—
Laborers	52	3	5.8	15	1	6.7
Service workers	9,844	1,972	20.0	4,128	1,138	27.6
Total blue collar	10,187	1,996	19.6	4,273	1,139	26.7
Total	33,845	2,964	8.8	12,434	1,551	12.5

Source: Appendix Tables B-7 and B-9.

Note: For regional definitions, see Appendix Table A-1.

the warehouses; and the laborers and service workers are in the warehouses.

The headquarters and warehouse operations in chain organizations may be combined at the same site, but the racial texture of the two operations is completely different. There are not, to the writer's knowledge, more than two or three Negroes occupying important positions in the corporate hierarchy of the drug chains. Since 1965, the number of Negro clerical and secretarial workers in the corporate headquarters has increased, but overall the total is not large. The Negroes shown in Table 19 as occupying white collar jobs were heavily in the warehouse acting as shipping and receiving clerks or supervising loading crews. In many locations, the warehouse work force is almost all black. The combining of practically black and practically white warehouses, and including the truck drivers (mainly white) as warehouse workers contributes substantially to the distributions shown in Table 19.

To summarize Negro employment in chain drugstore companies, as indicated by the 1968 data, the only place where Negroes are employed to any great extent is in the service worker category in stores. Such jobs are the least desirable in the store, being primarily waitresses and short order cooks, along with some janitors. This concentration according to race does not, however, conform to the skill requirements in the drugstore. If a person can add up a check and present it to a customer, he can just as easily perform the functions of a clerk or cashier.

Thus, although there may be few or no barriers to Negro entry into the drugstore industry at low levels, Negroes obviously meet barriers to upgrading or high level entry positions. Drugstore executives have indicated that these problems are ones of education and training of the applicants, rather than discrimination by the management. Recruitment, training, and other hiring policies will be discussed in Chapter VI.

NEGRO EMPLOYMENT IN SELECTED DRUG CHAINS

It might be supposed that all drug chains have approximately equivalent Negro employment rates, but quite the opposite is true: drug chains show marked differences in Negro employment rates. Tables 21 and 22 show 1968 total and Negro employment figures for four drug chains with very low and four drug chains with very high Negro employment.

TABLE 21. *Drugstore Industry*
Employment by Race, Sex, and Occupational Group
4 Chain Companies with Low Negro Employment, 1968

Occupational Group	All Employees			Male			Female		
	Total	Negro	Percent Negro	Total	Negro	Percent Negro	Total	Negro	Percent Negro
Officials and managers	349	1	0.3	338	1	0.3	11	—	—
Professionals	289	—	—	274	—	—	15	—	—
Technicians	16	—	—	16	—	—	—	—	—
Sales workers	1,856	2	0.1	653	2	0.3	1,203	—	—
Office and clerical	238	3	1.3	81	2	2.5	157	1	0.6
Total white collar	2,748	6	0.2	1,362	5	0.4	1,386	1	0.1
Craftsmen	14	—	—	14	—	—	—	—	—
Operatives	28	1	3.6	20	1	5.0	8	—	—
Laborers	74	—	—	53	—	—	21	—	—
Service workers	46	1	2.2	9	1	11.1	37	—	—
Total blue collar	162	2	1.2	96	2	2.1	66	—	—
Total	2,910	8	0.3	1,458	7	0.5	1,452	1	0.1

Source: Data in author's possession.

TABLE 22. Drugstore Industry
Employment by Race, Sex, and Occupational Group
4 Chain Companies with High Negro Employment, 1968

Occupational Group	All Employees			Male			Female		
	Total	Negro	Percent Negro	Total	Negro	Percent Negro	Total	Negro	Percent Negro
Officials and managers	717	73	10.2	496	8	1.6	221	65	29.4
Professionals	425	29	6.8	390	22	5.6	35	7	20.0
Technicians	12	1	8.3	11	1	9.1	1	—	—
Sales workers	3,225	277	8.6	926	80	8.6	2,299	197	8.6
Office and clerical	307	34	11.1	48	4	8.3	259	30	11.6
Total white collar	4,686	414	8.8	1,871	115	6.1	2,815	299	10.6
Craftsmen	35	5	14.3	35	5	14.3	—	—	—
Operatives	138	85	61.6	134	83	61.9	4	2	50.0
Laborers	261	144	55.2	201	113	56.2	60	31	51.7
Service workers	2,038	1,149	56.4	576	397	68.9	1,462	752	51.4
Total blue collar	2,472	1,383	55.9	946	598	63.2	1,526	785	51.4
Total	7,158	1,797	25.1	2,817	713	25.3	4,341	1,084	25.0

Source: Data in author's possession.

The tables show that the chains with high Negro employment were larger, averaging almost 1,800 employees, than those with very low Negro employment. This fact lends support to the idea that manpower problems increase with the size of a chain, leading larger companies to be less selective in terms of employing Negroes. But this idea should not be given too much emphasis, because all the chains with high Negro employment have their major operations in large metropolitan areas with correspondingly large Negro populations, which itself makes it easier to employ Negroes while some of the smaller chains operate in areas with low Negro populations.

It is significant, however, that the high Negro employment chains do not relegate Negroes exclusively to the less desirable jobs. These chains employed Negroes in 1968 in managerial (10.2 percent) and professional (6.8 percent) jobs at a rate considerably above the national average. Since many other chains also operate in large metropolitan areas, it seems that some factors other than just large city location are at work.

The chains with high Negro employment do not show a single concentration by region, though none of the four is headquartered in the West. Three of the four chains, however, have stores on either the East or West coast.[34] The chains with low Negro employment show a different geographic dispersion. One of the chains operates in the Northeast in an area where the Negro population is less than 5 percent of the total. Another is in the South and operates primarily in a medium-sized city (250-500 thousand) in which Negro population is about 20 percent of the total. Of the other two chains, one is in the Midwest and the other is on the West Coast, and both have access to a Negro population far above the proportion they employ.

DRUGSTORE INDUSTRY EMPLOYMENT, 1969

Data for the retail drug industry (SIC 591) are available from the Equal Employment Opportunity Commission for 1969 and are set forth in Tables 23 and 24. This is the first time that EEOC has made drugstore company data available separate from other retail establishments in SIC 59. Although the EEOC data do not segregate chains and independents, it appears safe to conclude that they reflect chain store employment almost

---

34. Data in the author's possession.

TABLE 23. *Drugstore Industry*
Employment by Race, Sex, and Occupational Group
Companies with 100 or More Employees
United States, 1969

Occupational Group	All Employees			Male			Female		
	Total	Negro	Percent Negro	Total	Negro	Percent Negro	Total	Negro	Percent Negro
Officials and managers	11,456	424	3.7	10,460	328	3.1	996	96	9.6
Professionals	6,030	324	5.4	5,262	250	4.8	768	74	9.6
Technicians	416	31	7.5	240	11	4.6	176	20	11.4
Sales workers	51,930	3,202	6.2	14,979	1,106	7.4	36,951	2,096	5.7
Office and clerical	7,023	609	8.7	1,672	203	12.1	5,356	406	7.6
Total white collar	76,860	4,590	6.0	32,613	1,898	5.8	44,247	2,692	6.1
Craftsmen	896	22	2.5	843	12	1.4	53	10	18.9
Operatives	1,722	392	22.8	1,184	289	24.4	538	103	19.1
Laborers	3,183	743	23.3	2,615	552	21.1	568	191	33.6
Service workers	20,761	5,780	27.8	7,370	2,673	36.3	13,391	3,107	23.2
Total blue collar	26,562	6,937	26.1	12,012	3,526	29.4	14,550	3,411	23.4
Total	103,422	11,527	11.1	44,625	5,424	12.2	58,797	6,103	10.4

Source: U.S. Equal Employment Opportunity Commission.

Note: Since these data exclude employers of less than 100, it is reasonable to conclude that most independent stores are not included.

TABLE 24. *Drugstore Industry*
Percent Distribution of Employment by Race, Sex, and
Occupational Group
Companies with 100 or More Employees
United States, 1969

Occupational Group	All Employees		Male		Female	
	Total	Negro	Total	Negro	Total	Negro
Officials and managers	11.1	3.7	23.4	6.1	1.7	1.6
Professionals	5.8	2.8	11.8	4.6	1.3	1.2
Technicians	0.4	0.2	0.5	0.2	0.3	0.3
Sales workers	50.2	27.8	33.6	20.4	62.8	34.3
Office and clerical	6.8	5.3	3.8	3.7	9.1	6.7
Total white collar	74.3	39.8	73.1	35.0	75.2	44.1
Craftsmen	0.9	0.2	1.9	0.2	0.1	0.2
Operatives	1.6	3.4	2.6	5.3	0.9	1.7
Laborers	3.1	6.5	5.9	10.2	1.0	3.1
Service workers	20.1	50.1	16.5	49.3	22.8	50.9
Total blue collar	25.7	60.2	26.9	65.0	24.8	55.9
Total	100.0	100.0	100.0	100.0	100.0	100.0

Source: Computed from Table 23.

exclusively, since they cover only employers with 100 or more employees. This excludes nearly all independents.

The 1969 data cover a far larger number of companies, and consequently report more than two-thirds more employees than our 1968 chain data. Nevertheless the 1969 data are valuable for comparison because our 1968 sample was, we believe, representative of the same segment of the drugstore industry.

The reversed occupational distributions of black workers compared to all workers in sales and service work are only slightly less evident in 1969 than in 1968. (Compare company total in Table 18 with Table 24.) Just over one-fourth of all employees in chain companies in 1969 held blue collar jobs, while 60 percent of the black employees were so employed.

Comparing the total company columns in Table 19 with Negro percentages in Table 23 shows higher black employment in each white collar group in 1969, although the actual number of Negro white collar workers was still very small. Black employment in each of the blue collar occupations was lower in 1969, except among service workers, where Negroes continued to find the major portion of their employment opportunities. It is interesting to note that the 1969 data, which reflect 68 percent more employment than the 1968 data overall, only show 42 percent more employment in the service worker category. (See Appendix Table B-1.)

The occupational and Negro employment differences between 1968 and 1969 probably do not reflect actual changes in the industry, except perhaps in the service worker category. It is more likely that differences among individual companies which were not included in the 1968 survey account for the variations between the two years. It is important to note, however, that in general the position of black workers in this larger group of companies differed very little from those in the companies included in 1968.

THE DRUG FAIR EXPERIENCE, 1963 and 1970

Washington, D. C. has had a Negro majority throughout the 1960's and was 72 percent black by 1970, according to the census of that year. Drug Fair is one of the leading chain drugstore companies in the Washington metropolitan area. In 1963, Dr. Milton Elsberg, the company's president, presented data on Negro employment at Drug Fair to a congressional committee.[35] He kindly updated those figures in a letter to the Industrial Research Unit for this study.[36] His company was cited in 1963 as having an "exemplary" positive action program regarding Negro employment by the Washington Urban League.[37] In addition, all Drug Fair stores were on the Washington Congress of Racial Equality chapter's "Christmas Selective Buying List" for

---

35. *Equal Employment Opportunity Hearings before the House General Subcommittee on Labor,* 88th Congress (Washington: Government Printing Office, 1963), statement of Milton L. Elsberg, pp. 296-303, 309-311.

36. Letter from Milton L. Elsberg, dated June 11, 1970.

37. *Equal Employment Opportunity Hearing, op. cit.,* letter from Robert L. Taylor, p. 312.

1962, indicating the Negro salespeople were employed at all locations.[38]

Dr. Elsberg estimated in 1963 that 30 to 35 percent of Drug Fair's 2,000 employees in metropolitan Washington were Negro. Table 25 shows total and Negro employment in upper level occupations for Washington stores in 1963 and 1970. Negro proportions in all occupations listed were far above the industry's average in 1963, and had all improved by 1970. Obviously, a concerted effort was made to employ Negroes as sales workers during this period, as their proportion rose from 20.6 to 61.9 percent. The progress made by Drug Fair from an already above industry average ratio for sales workers during the latter part of the 1960's was sharply superior to that of the industry generally. As the 1969 national data in the preceding section show, most companies had made very little progress in this area by the end of the decade.

The percentage of Negro pharmacists at Drug Fair, although unusually high, did not increase very much by 1970, but the number nearly doubled. The very small supply of available black pharmacists, as will be explained in the following chapter, is a truly inhibiting factor even though Drug Fair has the advantage of being located in one of the four cities with predominantly Negro colleges of pharmacy. The particularly high proportions of Negroes in the fountain work area verify our earlier observation that black workers are able to move up to more responsible positions within this "Negro job" area.

Drug Fair's distribution center is located in Alexandria, Virginia, where the Negro population is about 10 percent of the total. Dr. Elsberg has supplied racial breakdowns of warehouse jobs for 1963 and 1970, shown in Table 26. Although Negro employment slipped somewhat between 1963 and 1970, the overall proportion, 62.9 percent, was still extremely good, and the inclusion of one Negro among three general management personnel is encouraging. It has already been shown that warehouse laborer positions are generally areas of high Negro employment; hence the Drug Fair figures are not so startling. The high percentages of black truck drivers and clerks are important and uncommon; that blacks hold larger proportions of the lower

---

38. *Ibid.*, Washington Congress of Racial Equality, "Christmas Selective Buying List, 1962," p. 179. Peoples, Standard, and Rexall were also on the 1962 list.

TABLE 25. *Drugstore Industry*
Total and Negro Drugstore Employment in Selected Occupations
Drug Fair, Inc., Washington, D.C., 1963 and 1970

Occupation	1963			1970		
	Total	Negro	Percent Negro	Total	Negro	Percent Negro
Pharmacist	17	4	23.5	26	7	26.9
Store bookkeeper	1	1	100.0	4	4	100.0
Sales worker	97	20	20.6	139	86	61.9
Fountain manager	10	6	60.0	12	9	75.0
Fountain supervisor	3	2	66.7	3	2	66.7
Other selected occupations	205	166	81.0	225	204	90.7
Total	333	199	59.8	409	312	76.3

Source: *Equal Employment Opportunity Hearings before the House General Subcommittee on Labor*, 88th Congress (Washington: Government Printing Office, 1963), Drug Fair District of Columbia area survey; p. 310, and correspondence from Dr. Milton L. Elsberg, June 1970.

TABLE 26. *Drugstore Industry*

Total and Negro Warehouse Employment by Occupation

Drug Fair, Inc., Alexandria, Virginia, 1963 and 1970

Occupation	1963			1970		
	Total	Negro	Percent Negro	Total	Negro	Percent Negro
Truck driver	15	14	93.3	18	15	83.3
Truck helper [a]	8	8	100.0			
Receiving worker	12	10	83.3	17	13	76.5
Shipping worker	6	5	83.3	22	12	54.5
Returns department	2	1	50.0	8	5	62.5
Lift operator	5	5	100.0	15	10	66.7
Order fillers	39	32	82.1	94	64	68.1
Stock clerk [b]	9	6	66.7			
Pricing clerk	5	5	100.0	16	6	37.5
Mechanic	2	—	—	2	—	—
Guard	2	—	—	3	—	—
Inventory controller	4	3	75.0	4	1	25.0
General management	3	—	—	3	1	33.3
Total	112	89	79.5	202	127	62.9

Source: *Equal Employment Opportunity Hearings before the House General Subcommittee on Labor,* 88th Congress (Washington: Government Printing Office, 1963), Drug Fair distribution center survey, p. 311; and correspondence from Dr. Milton L. Elsberg, June 1970.

Note: Does not include office staff.

[a] Job classification eliminated in 1970.

[b] Combined with order fillers in 1970.

level warehouse jobs is in line with practice in the industry generally.

The very high employment of black pharmacists and sales-people at Drug Fair is an exception in the industry generally, while black employment in fountain work management exemplifies earlier conclusions about the nature of Negro female managerial group in the industry. At Drug Fair, as in the industry generally, the major factor in Negro professional and managerial employment is the supply of Negro pharmacists. The prospects for growth in this sector will be examined in the following chapter, after which other determinants of Negro employment will be reviewed.

CHAPTER V

The Negro Pharmacist

The degree to which Negro pharmacists are accepted by drugstore employers is probably the most reliable indication of prospects for all Negro employment in the retail drug industry. The purpose of this chapter is to assess the employment situation for Negro pharmacists and to analyze the labor market conditions that have produced it.

THE LABOR MARKET FOR PHARMACISTS

The professional segment of drugstore employment consists exclusively of registered pharmacists. A person who becomes a pharmacist is the product of a highly technical five-year (six in California) college degree program composed primarily of chemistry and properties-of-drugs courses. Many states require, in addition, six months to one year of practical experience in filling prescriptions. Besides on-the-job training and academic credentials, each person must score satisfactorily on the state's registration examination, which tests candidates on college work and prescription-filling procedures.

The pharmacist is the crucial employee in a drugstore. No one can substitute for him, because state laws prohibit the filling of a prescription by anyone except a registered pharmacist, and in many states a drugstore cannot even be opened for business unless a pharmacist is on duty. A pharmacist, therefore, is essential more than in the usual sense.

As described in Chapter III, the profession of pharmacy has long been the preserve of white males. The number of black pharmacists constituted only 1.6 percent of the total in 1950 and 1.8 percent in 1960. The 1950 decade, however, saw a relative decline of women pharmacist employment as their total only increased by about 80 while the male total increased by more than 7,000. Negro women experienced an absolute decline from 270 to 142 pharmacists (Table 9, Chapter III).

The statistics collected annually by the National Association of Boards of Pharmacy (NABP)[39] and by Professor Chauncey I. Cooper, Dean of the College of Pharmacy, Howard University,[40] as well as statistics collected by a special Health, Education and Welfare task force investigating the advisibility of adding out-patient prescriptions to Medicare Plan B,[41] suggest that the census figures understate total pharmacist employment and the proportion of Negroes in the total. Based on the HEW study, it is estimated that 4.8 percent of all pharmacists were Negroes in 1968. This represents a correction of census figures rather than a portrayal of a dramatic increase in Negro pharmacists. The proportion of Negro pharmacists in the total population of pharmacists probably has risen by about one percent each decade from 1940 and the proportion is likely to stand at 5 percent as of 1970. The different forces at work in the latter part of the 1960 decade will no doubt alter the pattern for subsequent decades.

THE SHORTAGE OF PHARMACISTS

For the past several years, there has been an exceptionally short supply of pharmacists. This means that chains have had to engage in college recruiting or expand college recruiting efforts to areas where pharmacists are more plentiful. These activities have reflected on the independents by restricting the supply of graduating pharmacists who would normally be returning to their home towns to look for jobs. The independents seemingly have had to offer additional inducements in order to attract pharmacists. One indication is the number of pharmacists who are partners in or the owners of drugstores. Owner and partner status of practicing retail pharmacists rose from 43.6 to 45.8 percent [42] between 1962 and 1967 in the face of a general decline of independents and a corresponding increase in

---

39. These statistics are published annually in the *Proceedings of the National Association of Boards of Pharmacy*. In 1960, for example, the *Proceedings* counted 117,776 pharmacists engaged in practice as compared to 92,233 tallied by the Bureau of Census.

40. Professor Cooper has been collecting and reporting national statistics on the number of Negro pharmacy students since 1927.

41. *Weekly Pharmacy Reports*, July 8, 1968.

42. "Nearly 46% of Retail Pharmacists are Either Owners or Partners," *American Druggist*, February 26, 1968, p. 28.

the number of chain drugstores. It is likely that the pharmacist shortage has contributed to the owner/partner increase because of the need to entice pharmacists away from chains and other career choices.

The demand for pharmacists, however, is not limited to drugstores, and the shortage has been felt in other areas as well. There are several factors that cause shortages to exist in some geographic regions and in particular vocations chosen by pharmacists.

Changes in Degree Requirements

The recent restructuring of pharmacy degree programs has had a substantial impact on the annual incremental increase in registered pharmacists. In 1961, pharmacy degree requirements were lengthened to a five-year program. This meant that there were virtually no new pharmacists available for 1965. In addition to not supplying pharmacists for the annual attrition, the one-year interruption of supply did not meet the new pharmacist requirement imposed by growth of the industry.

The extra year of school also at first reduced the number of students entering pharmacy school so that in 1966 and later years, the number of graduates was lower than would have been the case with a continuation of the four-year program. These conditions have been intensified in California, where a pharmacy degree requires six years of academic study.

Also adding to the lead time is the intership requirement. The states are more and more requiring a six or twelve month period of practical experience prior to registration. This adds even more to the lead time if the student has not fulfilled the experience requirement by summer work or if the state requires some or all of the practical work to be performed after graduation.

By active recruiting, improved high school guidance, and college scholarships, colleges and drug organizations (source of a large amount of scholarship money) have been able to overcome the students' reluctance to commit themselves to a program longer than that for most vocations. The shortage has also been ameliorated by the slow growth rate of the number of drugstores.

Despite the efforts of the colleges of pharmacy and chain drugstores, the shortage still exists (for drugstores if not in other career choices) and seems to have even intensified. An indication is the statement by an official of Drug Fair that the company is being forced to open fewer new drugstores than it desires.[43] This is the first acknowledgement that expansion plans have been hampered by the shortage of pharmacists.

Mobility Problems

Those whose job is to recruit pharmacists say that pharmacists are an odd breed of college graduate in that they very strongly prefer to return to their home towns to work at their chosen profession. A town within a couple of hours' drive from home is usually acceptable, but practically all refuse to go beyond that distance. In New York City, the graduates native to that city are even more obstinate, exhibiting a strong reluctance to accept a job outside the New York metropolitan area. This situation persisted even when there was a surplus of pharmacists in New York City and severe shortages (and therefore very attractive salaries) in upstate New York. The reluctance to relocate to adjacent cities and more distant points has created the peculiar situation of a nationwide shortage with islands of adequacy and even some surplus.

If the natural barrier to geographic mobility were not enough, three states have created an artificial wall by not entering into reciprocal licensing arrangements with other states. California, Florida, and New York apparently felt that they would be flooded with pharmacists from other states if they agreed to register out-of-state pharmacists holding a license in some other states. New York began reciprocal licensing a few years ago, but it appears that the migration has been away from rather than toward New York. Often students get around the artificial barrier by taking the California and Florida examinations about the same time as they take one in the state where they are attending college. This is particularly true for Oregon students, most of whom seem to want to work in California.

Career Choices

Even after surviving the rigorous study and long time period required to obtain registration and even if the pharmacist is willing and able to live and work in a distant state, there is no guarantee that he will enter the retail drug industry, because there are several alternate career choices available to pharma-

---

43. *Wall Street Journal,* June 3, 1969, p. 1.

cists which are clearly gaining favor. In 1961, retail pharmacy accounted for 88.6 percent of all practicing pharmacists. Hospital pharmacy was the occupation of an additional 3.6 percent, and 7.8 percent were in industry and other activities. By 1966, pharmacists in retail pharmacy had declined to 82.5 percent and in hospital pharmacy had risen to 8.0 percent, while 3.9 percent were in manufacturing and wholesaling activities, and 5.6 percent were in teaching, government, and other occupations.[44]

The relative decline of retail and hospital pharmacy in only five years is marked, as is the upsurge of postbaccalaureate degree holders implicit in manufacturing and education jobs. The shift also indicates that a large proportion of the total increased supply of pharmacists has been diverted into nonretailing jobs, thus heightening the effect of other elements on the retail drug industry.

The shortage has produced several reactions as the dynamic point of demand/supply equilibrium has shifted. As salaries have risen sharply, most drug manufacturers have dropped out of competition for pharmacists to some extent by adopting the policy of hiring and training nonpharmacists to serve as drug salesmen. At the same time, salary increases have reinforced the recruiting campaigns of pharmacy schools. Finally, higher salaries have induced pharmacist drugstore owners to give up their businesses and become employees—particularly in view of increasing competition by chains and the chains' success at attracting young pharmacists.

The success in recruiting students combined with demand adjustments and modification in the retail drug industry structure seem to have greatly reduced the slack in enrollments in colleges of pharmacy and the inefficient deployment of pharmacists in drugstores. Even so, the persistently short supply of pharmacists, plus civil rights pressures, have forced many employers in the retail drug industry to recruit and hire Negro pharmacists for the first time. The good experience with these men, both as employees and in their acceptance by drugstore patrons, has reinforced the decision to seek Negro pharmacists.

---

44. U. S. Department of Health, Education and Welfare, National Center for Health Statistics, Series 14, No. 2, *Pharmacy Manpower, United States—1966*, Table K, p. 11.

THE SUPPLY OF NEGRO PHARMACISTS

Data were gathered from 66 of the 69 predominantly white colleges of pharmacy and each of the four Negro schools in order to determine several characteristics of Negro enrollment and the future supply of Negro pharmacists. Table 27 gives the data for total and Negro enrollment during the 1967-1968 school year in 47 of the predominantly white colleges for which complete data were available. Table 28 shows Negro enrollment for all 66 predominantly white and the four Negro colleges.

The vast majority of Negro pharmacists are educated by the four Negro schools, all located in the South. These four enrolled 621 black students during 1967-1968, while 66 white schools enrolled only 245. (No data were available for three other predominantly white colleges, one in the Northeast, one in the South, and one in the Rocky Mountain Region.) Only 1.2 percent of all students at 47 schools for which total and Negro enrollment were available were Negro—just 169 students. A similar study conducted by *American Druggist* in 1969 showed the 69 predominantly white schools to have a black proportion of 1.7 percent of their 14,352 students.[45]

At the 47 predominantly white schools, in no region were Negroes as much as 2 percent of the student body; in the South they numbered just 17 of 3,077 students, 0.6 percent of the total, in contrast to 1.9 percent in the Far West. This, of course, is completely out of line with Negro population distributions, and may say something about educational disadvantages for black students before they reach college in the South. Since several schools indicated that intensive recruiting efforts had taken place, some of the lack of Negro pharmacy students must be attributable to disinterest or reluctance on the part of young Negroes themselves to enter this field.

Nine schools had no Negro enrollment in 1967-1968, but only four were in very low Negro population areas. Of the schools reporting total enrollment, only eight had over 2 percent Negro students, and only one of these—Wayne State in Detroit—had more than 5 percent. At Wayne State, 10.4 percent of the students were black—23 of 221 in 1967-1968.[46]

---

45. "Untapped Reservoir," *American Druggist*, Vol. 159 (February 24, 1969), p. 13.

46. Data in author's possession.

TABLE 27. *Predominantly White Colleges of Pharmacy*
Total and Negro Enrollment by Region
47 Colleges
United States, 1967-1968 Academic Year

Region	Predominantly White Colleges			
	Distribution	Total Enrollment	Negro Enrollment	Percent Negro
Northeast	12	4,467	56	1.3
South	10	3,077	17	0.6
Midwest	16	4,357	73	1.7
Rocky Mountain	6	1,243	7	0.6
Far West	3	824	16	1.9
Total a	47	13,968	169	1.2

Source: Data in author's possession.

Note: All but seven colleges reported totals for five-year course, plus
          graduate students. The remainder did not report first and second
          year students.

a See Table 28 for total Negro enrollment in 66 predominantly white colleges
and 4 Negro colleges in 1967-1968.

There were potentially only 112 Negro pharmacy graduates in
1968, 26 of whom attended predominantly white schools. Comments from the schools indicated that the number who actually
graduated was closer to 100. In 1969, the predominantly white
schools graduated about 36 Negro pharmacists and the Negro
colleges graduated about 107. These facts point out the recruiting problems involved for those chains and independents who
wish to hire Negro pharmacists. First, not many are available.
Second, it is frequently necessary (given population and drug
chain headquarters locations) to travel great distances to get to
the supply, not to mention the competition among employers during the job interview period.

Thus, the geographic dispersion of the Negro graduates who
go into retailing is much less than one would expect. In the case
of Howard University for example, most graduates remaining
in the Washington area upon graduation work for Dart, Drug
Fair, Peoples, and black and white independents. Some later return to their home towns, provided the home town is in the

TABLE 28. *All Colleges of Pharmacy*
Negro Enrollment and Percent Change by Region
United States, 1967-1968 and 1968-1969 Academic Years

Region	Distribution of Colleges	Negro Enrollment		Percent Change
		1967-1968	1968-1969	
Predominantly White colleges				
Northeast	14	75	118	+57.3
South	19	34	49	+44.1
Midwest	21	110	104	— 5.5
Rocky Mountain	6	7	6	—14.3
Far West	6	19	15	—21.1
Total	66	245	292	+19.2
Predominantly Negro colleges	4	621	703	+13.2
All Colleges [a]	70	866	995	+14.9

Source: Data in author's possession.

[a] No data available for three predominantly white colleges.

North. Those from the South (which amounted to about 41 percent of the 1968 graduates who were United States residents—and not counting the District of Columbia as a part of the South in the calculation) are very slow to return,[47] an indication that the South to North "brain drain" continues.[48] At Texas Southern University, graduates are being interviewed and hired by California companies and by chains in the Houston area.[49]

Changes in Negro enrollment between 1967 and 1968 are shown in Table 28 for all 66 of the 69 predominantly white colleges and the 4 predominantly Negro colleges. The number of black students actually declined in the Midwest, Rocky Mountain, and Far West regions; although the totals were not very high the

47. Letter from Professor Chauncey I. Cooper, dated September 20, 1968.

48. An excellent analysis of the South's manpower problems is presented in James G. Maddox *et al.*, *The Advancing South: Manpower Prospects and Problems* (New York: The Twentieth Century Fund, 1967).

49. Telephone conversation with the Dean of the College of Pharmacy, Texas Southern University.

previous year, the decline is discouraging. The large jump in Negro students in the Northeast and South accounts for an overall increase of black enrollment of 19.2 percent among white colleges. These increases were concentrated in just a few schools; 89 per cent of the 66 colleges still had less than 10 black students in 1968-1969, although total enrollment averaged about 300. The four Negro colleges increased their enrollment by about 13 percent, from 621 to 703 students.

To gauge the future supply of Negro pharmacists in the years beyond those reflected in current enrollments, the deans of the predominantly white colleges of pharmacy were asked (1) how growth in Negro enrollment compared with the growth in total enrollment and (2) how Negroes compare academically with average students enrolled in the college of pharmacy. The responses to these questions are tabulated in Table 29.

Of the 56 responses, 21 did not specifically indicate relative Negro/white growth in enrollment. Of the remaining 35 responses, 16 said relative enrollment increases are about the same, 11 said Negro enrollment is growing slower than white enrollment, and 8 said Negro enrollment is growing faster. From these, it can be inferred that Negro enrollment gains at predominantly white colleges is at best keeping pace with white enrollment and may in fact be lagging behind.

Moreover, the Negro students who are enrolled are, in the eyes of some of the deans, slightly below the average student in academic success. Fourteen of the 56 responders did not reply to the question on academic comparison, but 31 replied that Negro students are about average or slightly better academically. Eleven believe Negroes to be poorer students. Many deans referred to grade records to support the "better" or "worse" finding.

Most encouraging is the interest now being shown by the American Pharmaceutical Association, which has recently been considering ways to increase the number of minority group members in pharmacy. An APhA committee has recommended the establishment of a staff position for the recruitment of minority persons.[50] Since the deans of pharmacy schools have indicated their willingness to enroll more Negroes if they would only apply, a concerted effort at recruitment could have a dramatic impact on the number of black pharmacists in another five or six

---

50. Conversation with Dr. Richard Penna, American Pharmaceutical Association, April 9, 1970.

TABLE 29. *Negro Pharmacy Students and Graduates*
Selected Characteristics
United States and Regions, 1968

	Enrollment Growth Rate Compared to Overall Enrollment		
	Slower	Same	Faster
Northeast	2	5	5
South	5	—	—
Midwest	1	11	—
Rocky Mountain	3	—	—
Far West	—	—	3
Total	11	16	8

	Comparison Academically with Other Students		
	Poorer	Same	Better
Northeast	3	8	—
South	2	4	2
Midwest	4	9	1
Rocky Mountain	—	3	2
Far West	2	2	—
Total	11	26	5

	Difficulties in Obtaining Jobs			
	1963		1968	
	None	Some or Much	None	Some or Much
Northeast	7	2	11	—
South	4	2	5	1
Midwest	10	2	14	—
Rocky Mountain	4	—	4	—
Far West	1	1	—	1
Total	26	7	34	2

	Differences in Career Choice		Concentration in Certain Localities	
	No	Yes	No	Yes
Northeast	8	3	7	4
South	1	3	2	—
Midwest	13	1	8	5
Rocky Mountain	3	—	4	—
Far West	—	—	—	1
Total	25	7	21	10

Source: Data in author's possession.

years. Furthermore, enrollment at the four Negro colleges of pharmacy is growing substantially and so is the number of graduates. At present, these schools are graduating enough students to maintain the present proportion of Negro pharmacists (about 5 percent) and will, within two or three years, expand sufficiently to eventually raise the proportion. They will be aided in this effort by the handful of predominantly white pharmacy schools that are vigorously recruiting Negro students at present.

THE DEMAND FOR NEGRO PHARMACISTS

As an aid in assessing the demand for Negro pharmacists, the deans of the predominantly white colleges of pharmacy were asked the extent to which Negro pharmacy graduates experienced difficulty in locating jobs now and five years ago. Their responses are also shown in Table 29.

Unfortunately, the responses reveal more about the deans than about the nature of the demand in the labor market for Negro pharmacists. Only seven deans recognize (or will so state) that Negro pharmacists had any trouble finding jobs as recently as five years ago. Of those, one said there had been a great deal of difficulty five years ago, and three stated that there had been a little difficulty. The retailers themselves, both chains and independents, acknowledge that they were not overly interested in hiring Negro pharmacists until quite recently. The deans, therefore, exhibit a lack of information which they themselves conceded, prefacing their remarks by saying that they do not conduct any follow-up on graduates. Being out of touch with the job situation in the recent past, however, casts doubt upon the feeling that the deans have for the current job market. Only two profess to see any job market difficulties for Negro pharmacy graduates at present.

Negro pharmacy college deans, as well as independents, chains, individual pharmacists, and a few knowledgeable pharmacy association leaders see the demand for Negro pharmacists in a somewhat different and more realistic light. Most agree that there is a strong demand for Negro pharmacists (one Negro dean reported six job offers per student), but most also agree that the demand is selective in the sense that a Negro pharmacist is not, in the economist's terminology, prefectly substitutable for a white pharmacist.[51]

---

51. If there is an exception to this, it is in Washington, D. C.

First of all, independent drugstore owners (who are over-whelmingly white) do not hire Negro pharmacists except in rare instances. The independents for the most part operate neighbor-hood-type drugstores in all-white neighborhoods. (Those who do operate in the ghettoes are very small and do very little hiring and are being squeezed out anyway.) Discriminatory practices by independents do not violate the Civil Rights Act of 1964, since employers with less than 25 employees are exempted. Where state laws or municipal ordinances exist, however, such practices would be a violation.

An analogous situation exists in the chain organizations, al-though in the case of the chains the practice of not placing Negro pharmacists in stores with all-white clientele does not result in discrimination as defined by law. Five or six years ago, most chains would not have placed a Negro pharmacist in a drugstore that had any white business to speak of. The tight labor market, however, combined with expansion plans compelled the chains to risk placing Negro pharmacists in stores with 50 to 70 percent Negro trade. When the feared reaction was not forthcoming, the chains became bolder and bolder until now one can observe Negro pharmacists working in metropolitan drugstores where Negro trade is only about 20 percent of the total and in neighborhood or shopping center situations where Negroes account for 30 to 40 percent of the trade.

At first the chains were very sensitive to complaints from white customers as they ventured into the unknown and would yank a Negro pharmacist from the store upon receiving a com-plaint. They soon learned, however, to watch prescription re-ceipts rather than reacting to one or two complaints.

The experimentation with its many false starts has given sev-eral of the larger chains a surprisingly sophisticated knowledge of the attitudes of the various income and social groups in their geographic areas of operation. One would think that attitudes would be firmly attached according to income, social position, geographic region or city, but that is not the case.

Negro pharmacists may be well accepted by high income whites in one part of a town and not in another. In like manner, firm conclusions cannot be stated by geographic region. Each store seemingly has a group of customers with its own, unknown at-titudes, despite the general observation that high income groups (except in the Southwest) and low income groups (except in the Midwest) are usually receptive (i.e., do not withhold patronage) to Negro pharmacists while middle income groups vary within the same city. The problem, of course, derives from the fact that most stores have a sizeable group of middle income customers so there is very little chance to predict customer reaction.

At any rate, the larger chains are very anxious to employ more Negro pharmacists and hence cannot be accused of discrimination in employment. They do appear to shift their pharmacists around to place Negro pharmacists in stores where they will be well accepted and, to repeat a frequently heard emphasis, where they will be most comfortable.

CHAPTER VI

Factors Affecting Negro Employment

It is obvious from data in preceding chapters that Negro workers have found most of their employment opportunities in the drugstore industry in the lower level blue collar occupations. Yet in drugstores, as in most retail industries, employment in sales occupations offers the most numerous opportunities and provides the source of candidates for upgrading to managerial ranks. This chapter will attempt to examine employment policies and other factors which affect both the representation and the occupational placement of Negroes in both chain and independent drugstores.

RECRUITMENT AND SELECTION

The executives of chain drugstore companies have emphasized the difficulty of finding minority group members who are qualified for sales work. Even those in metropolitan areas with large black populations have indicated that hiring procedures must include high school and college recruiting as well as close work with Negro organizations in order to yield satisfactory numbers of potential black recruits for white collar jobs.[52] This type of recruitment, however, is lacking in a large segment of the industry among both chains and independents.

Independent drugstores do not use aggressive recruitment techniques to fill job openings; they generally let applicants come to them. The lack of intensive recruiting is no doubt a manifestation of the absence of a need to recruit. One implication is that turnover is low, in contrast to that in chain drugstores. Another is that some independents do not have employees outside the family. A third implication is that vacancies are mentioned in a casual way to friends or neighbors who might indicate in-

---

52. *Equal Employment Opportunity Hearings before the General Subcommittee on Labor*, 88th Congress (Washington: Government Printing Office, 1963), statements of Milton L. Elsberg and William Pannill, pp. 296, 299-301, 337.

terest in a job. An independent might not consider this latter a recruitment method.

Recruitment Procedures

Newspaper ads, walk-ins, the state employment service, personal recommendations, and signs in the window are the methods independents most frequently use to fill job openings.[53] None of these are particularly likely to produce Negro candidates, although newspaper ads and state employment services should be as useful to Negro job seekers as to whites. The popularity of the use of walk-ins, despite its advantages to the employer, puts Negroes at a disadvantage. Most drugstores are not near Negro neighborhoods and going from place to place to find out whether job openings exist is not an efficient job search technique.

Personal recommendation as a recruitment method is used with less frequency than the other three methods, but its results are much superior according to the independents. One-third of those responding consider personal recommendations to be the source of the best job candidates.

The problem with this recruitment technique is that it perpetuates the current proportion of minority employment. The employer's friends are mostly of his own race. The same is true of employees. Hence, if the owner is white and has few Negro employees, that employment mix will continue because most of those recommended by the employer's friends and employees will also be white.

The two recruitment techniques which chains have indicated are useful in finding Negro employees, i.e., recruitment through schools and colleges, and through Negro organizations, are used only rarely by independents. If the labor market should become tight, independents might begin to recruit more intensively and get into areas which would yield more Negro applicants. At present, however, independent drugstore operators have not had difficulty filling openings with their traditional, low key methods, and this will tend to perpetuate the existing racial balance in most stores.

---

53. Data in this and the following sections are from the survey questionnaire of independent drugstore operators, on file in the Industrial Research Unit library.

Employment Standards

In contrast to recruiting methods, there is a clear consensus among independents regarding the qualifications an applicant needs in order to obtain a job. Equally as clear is the relative abundance of qualified labor. There are very few instances of a forced lowering of standards because of a short supply of qualified applicants.

A high school diploma is not mandatory; in fact, the only qualification which is almost universally imposed is neat appearance. This should not necessarily disqualify applicants on the basis of race, but chain organizations have noted that more Negro than white applicants fail to meet this requirement.

The other important qualifications are (1) history of stable employment, (2) no criminal record, (3) stable family life, and (4) residence near the job. It is unlikely, however, that all of these qualifications are rigorously applied. For example, the absence of criminal record is an understandable criterion, but difficult to enforce uniformly. It is not easy to learn such facts about a person beyond what he says, unless an investigative agency is employed. It is doubtful that independent drugstore owners go to such lengths, but instead, as do many employers, suspect the worst when there is a poorly explained gap in the employment history of an applicant. This could be disadvantageous to Negroes if they more frequently have gaps in their employment history.

The other important qualifications seem to be a reflection of the desire of an employer to assure himself that an applicant, if hired, will be with the drugstore a reasonable length of time. If an applicant has shown a tendency to change jobs every few months in the past, he is likely to do the same in the future. If an applicant, male or female, is married, he is apt to stay with the job because he has responsibilities beyond his own personal needs. Similarly, if he lives nearby, he is apt to keep the job because it is convenient.

These qualifications may serve some useful purpose, but at the same time they foreclose job opportunities to young, single individuals who live some distance away. The young black worker is likely to be least able to meet these qualifications, since he is most likely to live in an all-black, inner city neighborhood with a high crime rate. Whether he can afford the costs of transportation is, of course, often doubtful.

Education through high school is evidently not very important, only one-fourth of the independents calling it a requirement. This would seem to aid young Negro job seekers who drop out of school before graduation, but in practice, other more important requirements exclude them. Chain organizations also say that a diploma is not necessary for most jobs, although the higher level sales jobs, in which Negroes are not well represented, probably are open primarily to high school graduates.

Training and Upgrading

The supply of candidates for nonmanagerial jobs in drugstores is, by and large, quite adequate. Most of the clerical and cashier jobs are held by women and there is a large complement of part-time employment because of the traditionally long hours in drugstores. Most independents indicated that the labor market situation has not become so difficult as to induce a lowering of employment qualifications. In addition entry level drugstore jobs have low skill requirements. Given these factors, independent owners expressed disinterest in establishing either industry-sponsored or government-supported training programs in the 1968 survey. There is more recent evidence, however, to indicate that stores are beginning to participate in such programs, as the following section will show.

The high percentage of Negroes in blue collar jobs in a primarily white collar industry is evidence enough that few efforts are currently being made to upgrade black employees. The sole "line of progression" generally open to Negroes is in the food service area, where Negro women can become managers of this department or supervisors of several fountain operations in chain companies. The trend toward declining fountain sales, employment, and facilities, however, may cut off even this avenue of upward mobility for black drugstore employees.

Special Efforts to Increase Minority Employment

Recruitment and training aimed at the "hardcore" unemployed group who need special instruction and guidance in order to succeed in jobs have begun to be undertaken by drugstore owners and other retailers. One example is the training program run by Tanco, Inc., a Newark, New Jersey organization of drug retailers and manufacturers.[54] In conjunction with the National

54. Conversation with Mr. Matthew Waters, May 27, 1971.

Association of Businessmen JOBS program, Tanco had a federal grant under the Manpower Development and Training Act to train minority workers for both store employment and manufacturing jobs. The nine-month program gives on-the-job training and provides a variety of additional help such as job-related education, counseling, medical care, and underwriting the costs of day care for children of working mothers.

The trainees in drugstores are learning to become "pharmacy helpers," an occupation which will combine general sales work with specifically drugstore related duties such as assisting the pharmacist with paperwork. According to the project director, Mr. Matthew Waters, this will be a skilled white collar occupation in the drugstores.

The Newark drugstore owners hope to reduce their very high turnover by developing such a specially trained work force. The extension of such programs could significantly improve the occupational level of black drugstore employees.

JOB PERFORMANCE

Only 41 percent of 135 responders to the independent retailer questionnaire reported any Negro employment at all. Of these, however, 35, or more than 85 percent, compared the job performance of their Negro employees favorably with that of other workers. These stores had both high percentages of black workers and generally high skill distributions among them—Negroes were not concentrated in the service worker category as they tend to be in most chain and independent drugstores.

DISCRIMINATION

Hiring and upgrading practices in the retail drug industry are, of course, subject to the possibility of racial discrimination. Employment policy could be affected by prejudice on the part of the employer, and by the employer's responses to perceptions of customers' racial attitudes.

Drugstore Owners' Attitudes

Independent drugstore owners were asked for their opinions about Title VII of the Civil Rights Act of 1964, Negro unemployment rates, lack of Negro employment as retail clerks, and the nature of retail work in an effort to determine the extent of dis-

criminatory attitudes about Negroes which might affect hiring
and upgrading policies. Their responses to these questions were
quite mixed, but some trends can be distinguished.

Respondents generally favored Title VII of the Civil Rights Act
with some reservations, such as the bureaucratic controls it imposed. This issue is rather impersonal, however, since most independents have considerably fewer than the 25 employees necessary to come under the law's jurisdiction. On the other hand,
state civil rights laws, which exist in most states outside of the
South, do cover small establishments.

Drugstore owners' attitudes about Negro unemployment were
also solicited. About three-quarters thought that lack of education was the primary reason, but a majority also responded that
Negroes do not want to work and have poor employment records.
This is in contrast to those with black employees who rated their
job performance well.

When asked more specifically why Negroes are not employed
as sales clerks, a more viable issue with a drugstore manager in
need of such personnel, only about one-third of the responders
cited lack of education or experience. Almost 20 percent acknowl-
edged that prejudice was a factor and more than 10 percent
listed fearing loss of business. Since these responders also over-
whelmingly said that the nature of retail work itself has not been
a hindrance to Negro employment, it seems fairly clear that
discriminatory attitudes have influenced Negro employment
levels in independent drugstores. Such attitudes are not necessarily lacking in chain companies, but they might be mitigated
by the scale of operations and the more depersonalized hiring
procedures found in chains, and the greater propensity of government to investigate labor policies of large, as compared to
small, concerns.

Impact of Customer Attitudes

Independent and chain stores are differentially affected by outside pressures. Chain organizations all come under the Civil
Rights Act of 1964 because of the size of their work forces. At
the same time, they can afford to discount customer attitudes on
racial matters in order to experiment in one or two stores to see
if the presence of Negro employees really does cause loss of business.

The external force represented by government has much less
impact on the independents. About three out of four felt that

government laws prohibiting discrimination in employment have had no effect on Negro employment in the industry and only 10.6 percent believe that the laws have affected Negro employment in the industry. The influence of the other external force—customers and potential customers—is an entirely different matter. Not even a majority of the independents disagreed with the proposition that some retail stores would lose business if Negroes were hired as sales clerks, although there was considerable variation by region and by urban/suburban location. Both the urban and suburban components of the Northeast had majorities who thought sales would not be adversely affected. The same is true for suburban responders in the Midwest. The urban South was a perfect split, whereas the suburban South and the urban Midwest had majorities suggesting that sales would be lost by some stores if Negroes were hired as sales clerks. Overall, urban responders lent less support than their suburban colleagues to the notion. The Northeast, and the Midwest by a bare majority, believed sales would not be lost, but the opposite opinion was held in the other regions.

The independent drugstore is one of the last locations of a strong customer-retailer service relationship. Independents strive to provide special services to their patrons because the drugstore owners prefer it and because, properly used, it is an effective competitive weapon against inroads by chains and discounters. The independent, therefore, offers delivery service, charge accounts, annual statements on drug expenditures for income tax purposes, and close personal attention. Because of the close relationship he is seeking to build, the independent may well conclude that the intimacy he is cultivating will be reduced if his clerks are Negro when most of his clientele is white.

The independents, despite their greater potential flexibility, do not react quickly to changing economic and social trends. They are slow to tap the Negro labor market because such labor has not been widely used in retailing in the past and they are unaware of or do not believe the reports of the movement of Negroes into retailing. Compared to a chain, which can afford to experiment in one store because it has fifty others to offset losses if they occur, independents must be more cautious.

Even where customer attitudes are thought to be favorable, drug retailers are reluctant to employ Negroes except as dictated by economic necessity. Assessment of customer preferences is always subject to error and it is desirable to let one's competitors make the errors. There is a way to resolve the impasse that has a precedent in the retail field: concerted action by the drug retailers or by all the leading retailers in a city. When all take the same step on the same day, the risk of negative customer reaction is shared equally. This method was used quite effectively by southern and border state retailers in the early 1960's in desegregating lunch counters.

CIVIL RIGHTS AND GOVERNMENT PRESSURE

Drugstores have to some extent escaped the most direct civil rights and government activities aimed at improving employment opportunities for minority groups, but these will be increasingly felt in the future. Boycotts of products and businesses, which have generally been directed at other types of retail stores,[55] could be equally effective against both chain and independent drugstores, although it is possible that in some areas their vital importance to health may protect them from complete boycotts, as it did in Greenwood, Mississippi.[56]

Protest Tactics

The lunch counter sit-ins in the 1960's generally proved the strength of protest tactics, although this particular activity may have actually reduced employment opportunities by contributing to the trend toward eliminating drugstore food service. Walgreen's, for example, has put up some resistance to such protests; a company executive reported in 1966 that Walgreen's had "shut down facilities permanently or temporarily in the face of 'sit-ins' and demonstrations that threaten violence." [57] But few drugstore companies would shut down entirely in response to Negro demands.

Civil rights organizers have made it clear to neighborhood retail businesses that Negroes want jobs in the stores as well as the right to spend their money there. The success of consumer boycotts of food chains to force more hiring of Negroes and

55. See the author's analysis of the effects of Operation Breadbasket on the supermarket industry in the supermarket study in this Series.

56. "Negro Boycott Halts Stores in Greenwood, Mississippi," *Philadelphia Bulletin*, April 29, 1968. Banks were also spared.

57. Quoted by Stephen Habbe, *Company Experience with Negro Employment*, Personnel Policy Study No. 201 (New York: National Industrial Conference Board, 1966), p. 88.

faster upgrading of black employees has not been missed by drug retailers.

One important aspect of Negro employment in the retail drug industry is that gains have been made without direct government prodding. So far as is known, EEOC has not paid particular attention to drug retailer employment practices. The industry has been affected, however, by government involvement in community health programs, as the following section will explain.

The Impact of OEO Health Centers

As a part of the poverty program, the Office of Economic Opportunity has been made responsible for the establishment of health centers in low income neighborhoods. The purpose of the centers is to provide health services at nominal or zero costs for the medically indigent [58] who have not heretofore received the quality of medical care available to the general public.

Drugstores are concerned about the OEO activities because as of May 1, 1968, nineteen of twenty-six federally-sponsored centers included a prescription department. Of eighteen other centers, fourteen are scheduled to contain prescription departments.[59] Since the prediction is that an average health center will generate 100,000 prescriptions a year, they will have a substantial impact on the sale of prescription drugs in low income neighborhoods.[60]

The counsel for the Boston Association of Retail Druggists (BARD) claims that the five additional health centers to be opened in Boston will force 50 to 100 drugstores out of business, based on the experience following the opening of an OEO center in the Columbia Point section of the city. According to the BARD attorney, the center drained off virtually all the prescription business of a nearby drugstore within weeks and the drugstore had to go out of business.[61]

A similar decline in prescription volume is said to have occurred in Denver, Colorado, where three drugstores located with-

---

58. A family of three with an annual income of less than $4,500 is medically indigent, so is an individual earning less than $3,000 a year and a family of six with less than $8,000 yearly.

59. *Weekly Pharmacy Reports*, May 6, 1968, pp. 2-3.

60. *Ibid.*

61. "Five New OEO Centers Will Knock out 100 Boston Pharmacies," *American Druggist*, June 5, 1967, p. 31.

in two blocks of a health center each lost one-half of their prescription business shortly after it opened in the spring of 1966.[62] After a second center opened in Denver in June of 1967, the BARD counsel said he had been informed by pharmacists in Denver that 40 to 60 drugstores there had been forced to close due to the centers.[63]

Consultations with individuals and groups representing the health professions in the neighborhood and community, including pharmacists, have taken place, but there has been little successful opposition to the prescription departments. A modified vendor program proposed by neighborhood pharmacists in low-income West Baltimore and endorsed by the Maryland Pharmaceutical Association and the Baltimore City Council was opposed by the Community Action Committee and Provident Hospital, located in West Baltimore and scheduled to establish a health center. The opposers of the vendor program indicated that West Baltimore neighborhood drugstores are not capable of meeting the human relations needs of the health center clients. They produced photographs of local drugstores showing entire storefronts plastered with signs advertising liquor bargains, which convey the impression that the drugstores are more anxious to sell liquor than to fill prescriptions.

The hearing did not raise any racial matters, but an article in *American Druggist* speculated that

the factor of racial antagonism underlies some of the problems which retail pharmacy has thus far encountered in its efforts to achieve a satisfactory working relationship with the health centers. . . . Considering the fact that most OEO-financed programs involve urban ghettoes—and that a large percentage of the people for whom such programs are developed are Negroes—it would not be surprising. . . .[64]

Racial antagonism may be the reason for opposition to retail pharmacies. In terms of employment, however, the loss of neighborhood drugstores will mean the decline of sales and other work for Negro residents. Although OEO centers are scheduled to operate training programs of their own for nonprofessional personnel, these programs probably will not replace Negro drug-

62. "Free Drugs in Denver," *Drug Trade News,* August 1, 1966, p. 8.

63. "Boston Group Plans Move to Ban Health Center Rxs," *Drug News Weekly,* July 3, 1967, p. 8.

64. "Is Racial Antagonism a Factor in OEO-Pharmacy Difficulties?" *American Druggist,* April 8, 1968, pp. 15-16.

store opportunities. On the other hand, the controversy may improve employment opportunities. The independents and chains which hope to compete with OEO prescription departments or which want to make a case for the exclusion of such departments will have to strongly reflect the community's racial mixture in their own work forces.

DRUGSTORE RELATIONS IN URBAN NEGRO RESIDENTIAL AREAS

There are other aspects of the inner city drugstore's relationship with its surrounding population besides health centers which affect Negro employment. Employment opportunities will continue to be strictly tied to the extent and stability of the white pharmacist owned and operated stores.

In this regard, the fact that the number of drugstores per capita is less where Negroes live than in other residential areas and is changing even more is of extreme importance. The historical pattern of drugstores' migration to the suburbs to follow the middle class has been accelerated by the civil disorders in recent years. The number of drugstores in New York state, for example, declined by about 100 from 1963 to 1968 [65] as the result of the number of closings in the New York City urban area being greater than the number of openings in suburban locations. The major Negro residential area in Philadelphia (called North Philadelphia) lost almost one-half its drugstores between 1960 and 1968 according to a survey taken for the Model Cities program. [66] The 1960 total was 102 drugstores as compared to 57 in 1968, a decline of 44 percent.

Part of the decline in inner city drugstores can be attributed to economics, since the Model Cities survey in Philadelphia showed that only 18 of the 57 drugstores were dispensing 50 or more prescriptions per day. Much of the decline, however, is the result of riots and robberies or the fear of one or both. Quite often the "letters to the editor" department in *Drug Topics* contains a letter to the effect that the owner is closing his inner city

---

65. Robert A. Liebson, "What You Need To Know Before You Open Your Drugstore," *Drug Topics*, March 3, 1969, p. 18; and *U. S. Census of Business, 1963, Retail Trade: Sales Size*, BC 63-RS2, Vol. I, p. 4-38.

66. "Philly Ghetto Drugstores Drop 44 Percent in Eight Years," *Drug Topics*, September 15, 1968, p. 6.

store for those reasons. When this happens, opportunities for black employment decline.

Incidence of Robberies and Racial Disorders

Drugstores and other inner city businesses are much more likely to experience criminal acts than suburban stores. A study by the Small Business Administration revealed that there were 97 burglaries and 19 robberies per 100 retail businesses in low income, largely black central city areas in 1967-1968, compared to 38 burglaries and 6 robberies per 100 stores in other central city areas, and only 28 burglaries and 3 robberies in the suburbs.[67]

Added to violence from riots, which are confined to these areas, small businessmen feel strong pressures to sell out or just close their stores. A study of Jewish businessmen in Philadelphia showed that the total number of all businessmen in neighborhoods affected by riots in 1964 had declined by 36 percent by 1969, and that at least 60 percent of the Jewish businessmen in low income, depressed areas desired to sell out.[68]

Drugstores are a prime target of such crime, and are particularly attractive to narcotic addicts. The rising number of armed robberies combined with racial disorders has accelerated the flight of chains to the suburbs and has so terrified white independents that they are simply going out of business. In addition to the small neighborhood pharmacies, the relatively large independents and chain stores located in the "mini-business districts" sprinkled throughout cities have been closing their doors. The situation in Washington deteriorated to the point where the same Peoples Drug Store unit had been robbed four times in two months. The president of the company took the unprecedented step of placing a full page ad in a Washington newspaper imploring the President of the United States for relief. Thereafter, the chain began closing stores in high crime areas.

Analagous situations exist in other areas. A Detroit executive named four stores that would be closed upon expiration of leases. He further stated, "The stores are all profitable despite an astro-

---

67. Small Business Administration, *Crime Against Small Business* (Washington: Government Printing Office, 1969), p. 3.

68. Center for Community Studies of Temple University and Jewish Community Relations Council of Greater Philadelphia, *Survey of Jewish Businessmen Operating in Selected Inner City Areas of Philadelphia* (Philadelphia: The Center, 1970), pp. 16-17.

nomical shoplifting rate and none suffered during the riots. Our employees refuse to work in these stores even with what we refer to as 'hazardous duty pay.' Many live in the neighborhood and still they are afraid to work there." [69]

Negro employment is vitally affected by these losses. Among the independents and chains both, black employment is tied, by the lack of black pharmacists, to the presence of white pharmacists.

Price Discrimination Experienced by Negroes

Negroes themselves have attitudes about the retail drug industry that may affect their interest in and search for drugstore employment. Most drugstores in urban Negro residential areas are owned and operated by whites and many are of the independent neighborhood type employing few outside workers, though the ones they do hire may well be Negroes. Damage inflicted on these drugstores during racial disturbances certainly indicates the level of animosity toward some of these stores, both chains and independents.

One cause of Negro animosity toward drugstores may be the result of price discrimination which they suffer in some areas. A study of 40 drugstores in a midwestern city discovered that a poorly dressed Negro stands a 23 percent chance of paying more for a given prescription than does a well dressed white person. Two *Boston Globe* reporters, one white and one black, conducted an experiment with similar results. The reporters selected at random five drugstores in white neighborhoods and five in the Roxbury section of Boston which has a heavy concentration of Negroes. Each reporter had a prescription for 50 capsules of 10 milligrams Librium filled at each of the ten drugstores. The prices at the stores in the white neighborhoods varied, but the Negro and white reporter were both charged the same price at each store. In the Roxbury stores, however, the Negro reporter paid a higher price than the white reporter in four of the five stores. The average price paid by the Negro reporter in the five stores was $6.00 as compared to a $5.15 average paid by the white reporter. [70]

---

69. Personal interview, January 1968.

70. "Boston Newspaper Says That City's Ghetto Negroes are Overcharged on Prescriptions," *American Druggist*, December 4, 1967, p. 23; and "Boston Druggists Upset by Charge Pricing Bias," *Drug News Weekly*, November 20, 1967, p. 2.

Upon front-page publication of the results of the experiment, the president of the Massachusetts Pharmaceutical Association commented that "The Globe is to be complimented on a public service." [71] The president of the Boston Association of Retail Druggists, however, retorted:

If the Globe felt there was a problem it should have contacted the Board to express its concern rather than to report unwarratned and unsupported sensationalism at the expense of the Profession.[72]

If these two surveys accurately reflect the situation, the Negro residents in the poverty-stricken urban areas have sound economic grounds for their dislike of their neighborhood drugstore owners. This in turn would be likely to affect their choices about job applications, particularly among those with higher skill levels who are more free to exercise discretion in job hunting.

BLACK CAPITALISM

Because white-owned drugstores in black neighborhoods are often resented by the residents and because a drugstore seems to be a good place for a small businessman, it is worthwhile to explore the prospects for black capitalism in the drugstore business. The economics of a drugstore are such that it is ordinarily impractical to own a drugstore unless one is a pharmacist. The owner cannot avoid being the manager, and in order to manage effectively he must be able to exert knowledgeable control over the prescription department. Technical knowledge (training in pharmacy) is essential.

Black capitalism in the retail drug industry, then, is essentially limited by the small number of Negro pharmacists. Other factors are the difficulty of obtaining financing for Negro enterprises and the size limitation on the potential (Negro) market. It is not surprising, therefore, that there are no Negro-owned chains with as many as twenty stores and that there are prob-

---

71. Quoted in *American Druggist*, December 4, 1967, *loc. cit.*

72. Quoted in *Drug News Weekly*, November 20, 1967, *loc. cit.* "Board" refers to the Massachusetts Board of Registration in Pharmacy (called the State Board of Pharmacy in most states) which regulates the retail drug industry in Massachusetts. The Board has no authority in discriminatory pricing and is proscribed from price regulation by state and federal antitrust statutes.

ably less than 1,000 Negro-owned drugstores in the approximately 51,000 nationally, including chains and independents.

The decline of drugstores in black neighborhoods created by the departure of white owners would seem to offer some prospects for an increase in the number of Negro-owned drugstores, especially in view of increasing emphasis by governmental agencies (the Small Business Administration in particular) on encouraging the establishment of more Negro-owned businesses. Black pharmacists, however, are strongly attracted to employment with the large chain companies. This is a rational expression of the economic motive, since chain starting salary levels are approximately $15,000 per year and there are serious risks associated with starting a new drugstore independently. These risks are emphasized in low-income areas where, as noted above, even long-established stores are no longer able to remain in business.

Added to the preferences of black pharmacists is the growing force of chain drugstores in the retail drug industry. The number of chain drugstores increases each year and the number of independents declines. It may well be that the decision of black pharmacists to opt for chain employment is the best choice over the long run as well as the short run. There is, after all, no compelling reason why a black-owned drugstore should prosper in an area where a white-owned one has failed.

In the absence of a black-owned chain, then, black capitalism does not seem destined to play an important role in the retail drug industry because (1) there are relatively few Negro pharmacists, (2) they do not exhibit a strong entrepreneural drive, and (3) chains are making the economic life of independents more precarious, so that whether the independent is white- or black-owned, his potential for success is declining. Thus black ownership cannot be relied on as a significant future source of Negro drugstore employment.

CHAPTER VII

The Future of the Negro in the Drugstore Industry

This chapter will review those factors which have a determining influence on Negro drugstore employment and will assess the probable future direction of black employment. The trend toward declining opportunities for black workers from 1940 to 1960 seems to have been reversed. It is likely that Negro employment will follow separate paths in independent and chain stores in the future.

NATURE OF THE INDUSTRY

Negro employment in independents in general is very low on a per store basis, judging from the questionnaire responses, and will probably remain so, particularly considering the tendency of independents to be small stores and the complete dispersion geographically compared to Negro population concentrations. Since the industry is not dependent on the male work force for most of its labor, white females, particularly as sales workers, will continue to be able to fill the independents' demand for labor.

The exception among independents, of course, is among inner city stores, both of the neighborhood and metropolitan types. Several factors are working to increase Negro employment in these drugstores.

Those white, independent owners who decide to stay in the inner cities despite the threats of crime and racial disorders will place a higher demand on Negro labor for two reasons. First, white female workers will not be available or willing to work in these stores, and second, druggists will have to respond to black community demands in order to avoid boycotts, government intervention in the form of OEO prescription departments, and outright violence. These forces will also affect chain drugstores located in Negro neighborhoods.

Among chain retail drug operations, the trend is more clearly in the direction of increasing Negro employment and improving occupational distributions. The growth of chains has increased the demand for labor, white and Negro. The continuing need for more pharmacists has forced the chains to recruit more intensively in the Negro manpower pool and this has had a spillover effect into other drugstore jobs. Aside from the direct benefits of growth, organizational changes arising from larger organizations are expected to redound favorably to Negroes.

As chains grow larger, they can afford more personnel (and other) specialists. Specialists tend to depersonalize decisions and are inclined to reach decisions based on facts instead of intuition. The specialists are likely to play an important role in reducing fear about negative customer reaction to the employment of more Negroes in suburban locations.

Chain drugstores have now come to the point where Negro pharmacists are placed in stores with an equal proportion of white and black patrons. This move began in 1963 when there was a desperate shortage of pharmacists. The chains acted out of desperation, so credit is largely due to the labor market. The chains must, however, be given credit for following up on what they learned. Negro pharmacy graduates continue to be in high demand. Most Negro pharmacy educators believe that an irreversible process has begun and that in as few as ten years, there will be no limit whatsoever on the stores where a Negro pharmacist can be placed.

STORE LOCATION

Drugstore companies which have either moved their stores or opened new, larger units in suburban shopping centers have altered the job opportunities for Negro workers, who continue to be concentrated in the central cities, except in the South. Transportation difficulties will continue to limit employment opportunities for Negroes in the growing suburban shopping center locations of chain drugstores. Increasing store size and rapid expansion, however, may create a demand strong enough to overcome this to some extent, particularly among the better-paid sales and professional/managerial workers. Chain interest in urban stores and the new shopping centers of the core cities may also have a definite impact on Negro employment, if such developments are sufficiently extensive. Daylin, Inc., an aggressive and fast-growing drug chain, opened five stores in Watts in the late 1960's. According to Amnon Barness, Chairman of the Board, the purpose of the stores is to make a profit despite the realization that profits will not be forthcoming unless business and government are interested in improving the area.[73]

The likely approach for new inner city stores is through the Model Cities program and community-based private ventures such as the new shopping center under development in North Philadelphia, Progress Plaza. Either way, completely new shopping complexes with all the suburban conveniences could be erected to serve these residents. Since black neighborhoods are typically understored in all areas of retailing, including drugstores, these shopping complexes would be likely to replicate the larger suburban shopping centers. Virtually all of the drugstore employees would be Negro, of course, and total Negro drugstore employment should increase. It is too early, however, to assess how extensive such inner city developments will be.

BLACK PHARMACISTS

The number of Negro pharmacy graduates should increase as colleges make greater recruiting efforts and as it becomes more obvious that companies are eager to hire the black pharmacist. The extent of entrepreneural interest of these professionals remains to be seen, but whether they open their own stores or join larger companies, their presence should have a spillover effect in opening sales and nonpharmacist managerial positions to Negro workers. This will have the effect of raising the currently low occupational distribution of the black drugstore work force. Most nonpharmacist employment, both for white and black workers, however, will continue to be tied to the white pharmacists who operate both independent and chain drugstores.

CONCLUDING REMARKS

In sum, then, Negro employment proportions and occupational distribution in the retail drug industry should continue to improve, although national aggregate data may not show dramatic changes. The biggest gains should be among professional workers as the number of Negro pharmacy college graduates increases, and among all levels of black Workers in urban drugstores, if increased efforts are made to employ Negro salespeople. The least amount of change will occur among suburban, small town, and rural independent drugstore operations, where potential black employees are generally not available.

---

73. Letter from Amnon Barness, dated September 17, 1968.

Appendix A

SURVEY OF INDEPENDENT
DRUGSTORE OPERATORS, 1968

TABLE A-1. *Drugstore Industry*
Questionnaire Responders by Region and Location
Independent Stores
United States, 1968

Region	All Responders		Location of Responders		
	Number	Percent of Total	Urban	Suburban	Rural
Northeast	38	28.1	29	7	2
South	34	27.4	20	13	1
Midwest	37	25.2	22	13	3
Rocky Mountain	16	11.9	10	5	1
Far West	10	7.4	8	2	—
United States	135	100.0	88	40	7

Source: Data in author's possession.

Regional definitions:

Northeast   Connecticut, Maine, Massachusetts, New Hampshire, New Jersey, New York, Pennsylvania, Rhode Island, Vermont.

South   Alabama, Arkansas, Delaware, District of Columbia, Florida, Georgia, Louisiana, Maryland, Mississippi, North Carolina, Oklahoma, South Carolina, Tennessee, Texas, Virginia.

Midwest   Illinois, Indiana, Iowa, Kansas, Kentucky, Michigan, Minnesota, Missouri, Nebraska, North Dakota, Ohio, South Dakota, West Virginia, Wisconsin.

Rocky Mountain   Arizona, Colorado, Idaho, Montana, New Mexico, Nevada, Utah, Wyoming.

Far West (Pacific)   Alaska, California, Hawaii, Oregon, Washington.

TABLE A-2. *Drugstore Industry*
Number of Stores Operated by Stores per Company
Independent Stores
United States, 1968

	Responders		Total Stores	
Stores per Company	Number	Percent of Total	Number	Percent of Total
1	112	83.1	112	63.2
2	15	11.1	30	16.9
3	5	3.7	15	8.5
4	1	0.7	4	2.3
7	1	0.7	7	4.0
9	1	0.7	9	5.1
Total	135	100.0	177	100.0

Source: Data in author's possession.

TABLE A-3. *Drugstore Industry*
Urban, Suburban, and Rural Store Location by Region
Independent Stores, United States, 1968

	Urban		Suburban		Rural		Total	
Region	Stores	Percent of Total	Stores	Percent of Total	Stores	Percent of Total	Stores	Percent of Total
Northeast	32	30.0	8	13.1	2	22.2	42	23.7
South	26	26.2	22	36.1	2	22.2	50	28.3
Midwest	28	26.2	21	34.4	3	33.3	52	29.4
Rocky Mountain	12	11.2	8	13.1	2	22.2	22	12.4
Far West	9	8.4	2	3.3	—	—	11	6.2
Total	107	100.0	61	100.0	9	100.0	177	100.0
Percent of total stores		60.5		34.4		5.1		100.0

Source: Data in author's possession.

TABLE A-4. Drugstore Industry
Racial Composition of Neighborhood Served by Region
Independent Stores
United States, 1968

Neighborhood Composition [a]	Northeast		South		Midwest		Rocky Mountain		Far West		United States	
	Number of Stores	Percent of Total	Number of Stores	Percent of Total	Number of Stores	Percent of Total	Number of Stores	Percent of Total	Number of Stores	Percent of Total	Number of Stores	Percent of Total
White/Negro	16	38.1	35	70.0	17	32.8	10	45.4	5	45.4	83	46.9
White	23	54.7	9	18.0	29	55.8	9	41.0	4	36.4	74	41.8
White/Negro/Spanish [b]	2	4.8	3	6.0	2	3.8	3	13.6	2	18.2	12	6.8
Negro	1	2.4	2	4.0	1	1.9	—	—	—	—	4	2.3
White/Oriental	—	—	1	2.0	1	1.9	—	—	—	—	2	1.1
Other	—	—	—	—	2	3.8	—	—	—	—	2	1.1
Total	42	100.0	50	100.0	52	100.0	22	100.0	11	100.0	177	100.0

Source: Data in author's possession.

[a] To be included in one or another category, each group had to exceed 5 percent. Thus, a "White," "Negro," or "Other" is one in which no other group exceeds 5 percent. Similarly, a "White/Negro," "White/Negro/Spanish," or a "White/Oriental" store has over 5 percent of each named group and 5 percent or less of other groups.

[b] Includes one "White/Spanish" store.

Appendix B

BASIC STATISTICAL TABLES, CHAIN COMPANIES, 1968

TABLE B-1. *Drugstore Industry*
Employment by Race, Sex, and Occupational Group
Chain Company Totals United States, 1968

Occupational Group	All Employees			Male			Female		
	Total	Negro	Percent Negro	Total	Negro	Percent Negro	Total	Negro	Percent Negro
Officials and managers	7,176	206	2.9	6,431	131	2.0	745	75	10.1
Professionals	3,387	84	2.5	3,010	64	2.1	377	20	5.3
Technicians	158	5	3.2	88	4	4.5	70	1	1.4
Sales workers	29,106	1,340	4.6	7,743	489	6.3	21,363	851	4.0
Office and clerical	4,587	328	7.2	1,587	211	13.3	3,000	117	3.9
Total white collar	44,414	1,963	4.4	18,859	899	4.8	25,555	1,064	4.2
Craftsmen	276	9	3.3	241	9	3.7	35	—	—
Operatives	853	216	25.3	581	193	33.2	272	23	8.5
Laborers	1,387	361	26.0	1,170	302	25.8	217	59	27.2
Service workers	14,625	3,921	26.8	4,636	1,907	41.1	9,989	2,014	20.2
Total blue collar	17,141	4,507	26.3	6,628	2,411	36.4	10,513	2,096	19.9
Total	61,555	6,470	10.5	25,487	3,310	13.0	36,068	3,160	8.8

Source: Data in author's posssesion.

TABLE B-2. *Drugstore Industry*
Employment by Race, Sex, and Occupational Group
Chain Company Totals
Northeast Region, 1968

Occupational Group	All Employees			Male			Female		
	Total	Negro	Percent Negro	Total	Negro	Percent Negro	Total	Negro	Percent Negro
Officials and managers	971	5	0.5	850	5	0.6	121	—	—
Professionals	308	4	1.3	297	4	1.3	11	—	—
Technicians	4	1	25.0	4	1	25.0	—	—	—
Sales workers	3,738	79	2.1	810	22	2.7	2,928	57	1.9
Office and clerical	370	12	3.2	101	3	3.0	269	9	3.3
Total white collar	5,391	101	1.9	2,062	35	1.7	3,329	66	2.0
Craftsmen	12	1	8.3	12	1	8.3	—	—	—
Operatives	24	7	29.2	24	7	29.2	—	—	—
Laborers	146	23	15.8	119	20	16.8	27	3	11.1
Service workers	1,295	85	6.6	497	72	14.5	798	13	1.6
Total blue collar	1,477	116	7.9	652	100	15.3	825	16	1.9
Total	6,868	217	3.2	2,714	135	5.0	4,154	82	2.0

Source: Data in author's possession.

TABLE B-3. *Drugstore Industry*
Employment by Race, Sex, and Occupational Group
Chain Company Totals
South Region, 1968

Occupational Group	All Employees			Male			Female		
	Total	Negro	Percent Negro	Total	Negro	Percent Negro	Total	Negro	Percent Negro
Officials and managers	2,284	102	4.5	1,924	43	2.2	360	59	16.4
Professionals	979	39	4.0	849	31	3.7	130	8	6.2
Technicians	14	2	14.3	12	2	16.7	2	—	—
Sales workers	9,539	557	5.8	2,425	214	8.8	7,114	343	4.8
Office and clerical	1,439	160	11.1	517	114	22.1	922	46	5.0
Total white collar	14,255	860	6.0	5,727	404	7.1	8,528	456	5.3
Craftsmen	71	6	8.5	56	6	10.7	15	—	—
Operatives	383	153	39.9	264	151	57.2	119	2	1.7
Laborers	377	184	48.8	304	152	50.0	73	32	43.8
Service workers	6,084	2,231	36.7	1,896	1,067	56.3	4,138	1,164	27.8
Total blue collar	6,915	2,574	37.2	2,520	1,376	54.6	4,395	1,198	27.3
Total	21,170	3,434	16.2	8,247	1,780	21.6	12,923	1,654	12.8

Source: Data in author's possession.

TABLE B-4. *Drugstore Industry*
Employment by Race, Sex, and Occupational Group
Chain Company Totals
Midwest Region, 1968

Occupational Group	All Employees			Male			Female		
	Total	Negro	Percent Negro	Total	Negro	Percent Negro	Total	Negro	Percent Negro
Officials and managers	2,591	94	3.6	2,385	79	3.3	206	15	7.3
Professionals	1,080	32	3.0	931	24	2.6	149	8	5.4
Technicians	80	1	1.2	46	—	—	34	1	2.9
Sales workers	9,405	594	6.3	2,197	205	9.3	7,208	389	5.4
Office and clerical	1,876	130	6.9	615	80	13.0	1,261	50	4.0
Total white collar	15,032	851	5.7	6,174	388	6.3	8,858	463	5.2
Craftsmen	170	2	1.2	150	2	1.3	20	—	—
Operatives	417	55	13.2	269	34	12.6	148	21	14.2
Laborers	833	154	18.5	726	130	17.9	107	24	22.4
Service workers	5,632	1,513	26.9	1,637	705	43.1	3,995	808	20.2
Total blue collar	7,052	1,724	24.4	2,782	871	31.3	4,270	853	20.0
Total	22,084	2,575	11.7	8,956	1,259	14.1	13,128	1,316	10.0

Source: Data in author's possession.

TABLE B-5. *Drugstore Industry*
Employment by Race, Sex, and Occupational Group
Chain Company Totals
Rocky Mountain Region, 1968

Occupational Group	All Employees			Male			Female		
	Total	Negro	Percent Negro	Total	Negro	Percent Negro	Total	Negro	Percent Negro
Officials and managers	653	2	0.3	616	2	0.3	37	—	—
Professionals	535	—	—	502	—	—	33	—	—
Technicians	4	—	—	4	—	—	—	—	—
Sales workers	2,935	42	1.4	938	12	1.3	1,997	30	1.5
Office and clerical	466	13	2.8	227	7	3.1	239	6	2.5
Total white collar	4,593	57	1.2	2,287	21	0.9	2,306	36	1.6
Craftsmen	8	—	—	8	—	—	—	—	—
Operatives	6	—	—	6	—	—	—	—	—
Laborers	—	—	—	—	—	—	—	—	—
Service workers	1,248	45	3.6	459	33	7.2	789	12	1.5
Total blue collar	1,262	45	3.6	473	33	7.0	789	12	1.5
Total	5,855	102	1.7	2,760	54	2.0	3,095	48	1.6

Source: Data in author's possession.

TABLE B-6. *Drugstore Industry*
Employment by Race, Sex, and Occupational Group
Chain Company Totals
Far West Region, 1968

Occupational Group	All Employees			Male			Female		
	Total	Negro	Percent Negro	Total	Negro	Percent Negro	Total	Negro	Percent Negro
Officials and managers	677	3	0.4	656	2	0.3	21	1	4.8
Professionals	485	9	1.9	431	5	1.2	54	4	7.4
Technicians	56	1	1.8	22	1	4.5	34	—	—
Sales workers	3,489	68	1.9	1,373	36	2.6	2,116	32	1.5
Office and clerical	436	13	3.0	127	7	5.5	309	6	1.9
Total white collar	5,143	94	1.8	2,609	51	2.0	2,534	43	1.7
Craftsmen	15	—	—	15	—	—	—	—	—
Operatives	23	1	4.3	18	1	5.6	5	—	—
Laborers	31	—	—	21	—	—	10	—	—
Service workers	366	47	12.8	147	30	20.4	219	17	7.8
Total blue collar	435	48	11.0	201	31	15.4	234	17	7.3
Total	5,578	142	2.5	2,810	82	2.9	2,768	60	2.2

Source: Data in author's possession.

TABLE B-7. *Drugstore Industry*
Employment by Race, Sex, and Occupational Group
Chain Stores
United States, 1968

Occupational Group	All Employees			Male			Female		
	Total	Negro	Percent Negro	Total	Negro	Percent Negro	Total	Negro	Percent Negro
Officials and managers	6,070	187	3.1	5,431	119	2.2	639	68	10.6
Professionals	3,107	77	2.5	2,789	60	2.2	318	17	5.3
Technicians	60	2	3.3	24	2	8.3	36	—	—
Sales workers	28,967	1,335	4.6	7,652	488	6.4	21,315	847	4.0
Office and clerical	2,484	215	8.7	1,134	179	15.8	1,350	36	2.7
Total white collar	40,638	1,816	4.5	17,030	848	5.0	23,658	968	4.1
Craftsmen	138	3	2.2	103	3	2.9	35	—	—
Operatives	671	162	24.1	415	141	34.0	256	21	8.2
Laborers	620	120	19.4	568	117	20.6	52	3	5.8
Service workers	14,260	3,814	26.7	4,416	1,842	41.7	9,844	1,972	20.0
Total blue collar	15,689	4,099	26.1	5,502	2,103	38.2	10,187	1,996	19.6
Total	56,377	5,915	10.5	22,532	2,951	13.1	33,845	2,964	8.8

Source: Data in author's possession.

TABLE B-8. *Drugstore Industry*
Employment by Race, Sex, and Occupational Group
Chain Stores
Northeast Region, 1968

Occupational Group	All Employees			Male			Female		
	Total	Negro	Percent Negro	Total	Negro	Percent Negro	Total	Negro	Percent Negro
Officials and managers	819	3	0.4	710	3	0.4	109	—	—
Professionals	306	4	1.3	296	4	1.4	10	—	—
Technicians	3	1	33.3	3	1	33.3	—	—	—
Sales workers	3,730	79	2.1	802	22	2.7	2,928	57	1.9
Office and clerical	114	2	1.8	34	1	2.9	80	1	1.2
Total white collar	4,972	89	1.8	1,845	31	1.7	3,127	58	1.9
Craftsmen	6	1	16.7	6	1	16.7	—	—	—
Operatives	6	—	—	6	—	—	—	—	—
Laborers	16	—	—	16	—	—	—	—	—
Service workers	1,242	85	6.8	445	72	16.2	797	13	1.6
Total blue collar	1,270	86	6.8	473	73	15.4	797	13	1.6
Total	6,242	175	2.8	2,318	104	4.5	3,924	71	1.8

Source: Data in author's possession.

TABLE B-9. *Drugstore Industry*
Employment by Race, Sex, and Occupational Group
Chain Stores
South Region, 1963

Occupational Group	All Employees			Male			Female		
	Total	Negro	Percent Negro	Total	Negro	Percent Negro	Total	Negro	Percent Negro
Officials and managers	2,021	86	4.3	1,701	34	2.0	320	52	16.2
Professionals	960	37	3.9	834	30	3.6	126	7	5.6
Technicians	1	—	—	—	—	—	1	—	—
Sales workers	9,494	554	5.8	2,414	214	8.9	7,080	340	4.8
Office and clerical	1,026	108	10.5	392	95	24.2	634	13	2.1
Total white collar	13,502	785	5.8	5,341	373	7.0	8,161	412	5.0
Craftsmen	36	1	2.8	21	1	4.8	15	—	—
Operatives	235	107	37.5	170	107	62.9	115	—	—
Laborers	75	20	26.7	60	19	31.7	15	1	6.7
Service workers	5,985	2,184	36.5	1,857	1,046	56.3	4,128	1,138	27.6
Total blue collar	6,381	2,312	36.2	2,108	1,173	55.6	4,273	1,139	26.7
Total	19,883	3,097	15.6	7,449	1,546	20.8	12,434	1,551	12.5

Source: Data in author's possession.

TABLE B-10. Drugstore Industry
Employment by Race, Sex, and Occupational Group
Chain Stores
Midwest Region, 1968

Occupational Group	All Employees			Male			Female		
	Total	Negro	Percent Negro	Total	Negro	Percent Negro	Total	Negro	Percent Negro
Officials and managers	2,037	93	4.6	1,878	78	4.2	159	15	9.4
Professionals	846	28	3.3	749	22	2.9	97	6	6.2
Technicians	2	—	—	1	—	—	1	—	—
Sales workers	9,326	592	6.3	2,127	204	9.6	7,199	388	5.4
Office and clerical	735	86	11.7	408	72	17.6	327	14	4.3
Total white collar	12,946	799	6.2	5,163	376	7.3	7,783	423	5.4
Craftsmen	86	1	1.2	66	1	1.5	20	—	—
Operatives	357	54	15.1	218	33	15.1	139	21	15.1
Laborers	507	100	19.7	480	98	20.4	27	2	7.4
Service workers	5,439	1,455	26.8	1,527	663	43.4	3,912	792	20.2
Total blue collar	6,389	1,610	25.2	2,291	795	34.7	4,098	815	19.9
Total	19,335	2,409	12.5	7,454	1,171	15.7	11,881	1,238	10.4

Source: Data in author's possession.

TABLE B-11. *Drugstore Industry*
Employment by Race, Sex, and Occupational Group
Chain Stores
Rocky Mountain Region, 1968

Occupational Group	All Employees			Male			Female		
	Total	Negro	Percent Negro	Total	Negro	Percent Negro	Total	Negro	Percent Negro
Officials and managers	594	2	0.3	557	2	0.4	37	—	—
Professionals	530	—	—	497	—	—	33	—	—
Technicians	1	—	—	1	—	—	—	—	—
Sales workers	2,933	42	1.4	936	12	1.3	1,997	30	1.5
Office and clerical	336	10	3.0	199	4	2.0	137	6	4.4
Total white collar	4,394	54	1.2	2,190	18	0.8	2,204	36	1.6
Craftsmen	2	—	—	2	—	—	—	—	—
Operatives	6	—	—	6	—	—	—	—	—
Laborers	—	—	—	—	—	—	—	—	—
Service workers	1,229	43	3.5	441	31	7.0	788	12	1.5
Total blue collar	1,237	43	3.5	449	31	6.9	788	12	1.5
Total	5,631	97	1.7	2,639	49	1.9	2,992	48	1.6

Source: Data in author's possession.

TABLE B-12. Drugstore Industry
Employment by Race, Sex, and Occupational Group
Chain Stores
Far West Region, 1968

Occupational Group	All Employees			Male			Female		
	Total	Negro	Percent Negro	Total	Negro	Percent Negro	Total	Negro	Percent Negro
Officials and managers	599	3	0.5	585	2	0.3	14	1	7.1
Professionals	465	8	1.7	413	4	1.0	52	4	7.7
Technicians	53	1	1.9	19	1	5.3	34	—	—
Sales workers	3,484	68	2.0	1,373	36	2.6	2,111	32	1.5
Office and clerical	273	9	3.3	101	7	6.9	172	2	1.2
Total white collar	4,874	89	1.8	2,491	50	2.0	2,383	39	1.6
Craftsmen	8	—	—	8	—	—	—	—	—
Operatives	17	1	5.9	15	1	6.7	2	—	—
Laborers	22	—	—	12	—	—	10	—	—
Service workers	365	47	12.9	146	30	20.5	219	17	7.8
Total blue collar	412	48	11.7	181	31	17.1	231	17	7.4
Total	5,286	137	2.6	2,672	81	3.0	2,614	56	2.1

Source: Data in author's possession.

TABLE B-13. *Drugstore Industry*
Employment by Race, Sex, and Occupational Group
Chain Headquarters and Warehouses
United States, 1968

Occupational Group	All Employees			Male			Female		
	Total	Negro	Percent Negro	Total	Negro	Percent Negro	Total	Negro	Percent Negro
Officials and managers	1,106	19	1.7	1,000	12	1.2	106	7	6.6
Professionals	280	7	2.5	221	4	1.8	59	3	5.1
Technicians	98	3	3.1	64	2	3.1	34	1	2.9
Sales workers	139	5	3.6	91	1	1.1	48	4	8.3
Office and clerical	2,103	113	5.4	453	32	7.1	1,350	81	4.9
Total white collar	3,726	147	3.9	1,829	51	2.8	1,397	96	5.1
Craftsmen	138	6	4.3	138	6	4.3	—	—	—
Operatives	182	54	29.7	166	52	31.3	16	2	12.5
Laborers	767	241	31.4	602	185	30.7	165	56	33.9
Service workers	365	107	29.3	220	65	29.5	145	42	29.0
Total blue collar	1,452	408	28.1	1,126	308	27.4	326	100	30.7
Total	5,178	555	10.7	2,955	359	12.1	2,223	196	8.8

Source: Data in author's possession.

TABLE B-14. *Drugstore Industry*
Employment by Race, Sex, and Occupational Group
Chain Company Totals
Core City Locations, United States, 1968

Occupational Group	All Employees			Male			Female		
	Total	Negro	Percent Negro	Total	Negro	Percent Negro	Total	Negro	Percent Negro
Officials and managers	3,212	116	3.6	2,958	96	3.2	254	20	7.9
Professionals	1,167	36	3.1	998	26	2.6	169	10	5.9
Technicians	107	1	0.9	57	1	1.8	50	—	—
Sales workers	10,057	809	8.0	2,842	300	10.6	7,215	509	7.1
Office and clerical	3,202	254	7.9	930	147	15.8	2,272	107	4.7
Total white collar	17,745	1,216	6.9	7,785	570	7.3	9,960	646	6.5
Craftsmen	183	2	1.1	164	2	1.2	19	—	—
Operatives	469	103	22.0	320	82	25.6	149	21	14.1
Laborers	781	214	27.4	643	175	27.2	138	39	28.3
Service workers	6,408	1,861	29.0	2,174	939	43.2	4,234	922	21.8
Total blue collar	7,841	2,180	27.8	3,301	1,198	36.3	4,540	982	21.6
Total	25,586	3,396	13.3	11,086	1,768	15.9	14,500	1,628	11.2

Source: Data in author's possession.

TABLE B-15. *Drugstore Industry*
Employment by Race, Sex, and Occupational Group
Chain Company Totals
Core City Locations, Northeast Region, 1968

Occupational Group	All Employees			Male			Female		
	Total	Negro	Percent Negro	Total	Negro	Percent Negro	Total	Negro	Percent Negro
Officials and managers	336	3	0.9	297	3	1.0	39	—	—
Professionals	88	1	1.1	84	1	1.2	4	—	—
Technicians	—	—	—	—	—	—	—	—	—
Sales workers	995	48	4.8	229	13	7.9	736	30	3.9
Office and clerical	257	11	4.3	69	3	4.3	138	8	4.3
Total white collar	1,676	63	3.8	679	25	3.7	997	38	3.8
Craftsmen	7	—	—	7	—	—	—	—	—
Operatives	15	7	46.7	15	7	46.7	—	—	—
Laborers	100	23	23.0	79	20	25.3	21	3	14.3
Service workers	438	63	14.4	206	52	25.2	232	11	4.7
Total blue collar	560	93	16.6	307	79	25.7	253	14	5.5
Total	2,236	156	7.0	986	104	10.6	1,250	52	4.2

Source: Data in author's possession.

TABLE B-16. Drugstore Industry
Employment by Race, Sex, and Occupational Group
Chain Company Totals
Core City Locations, South Region, 1968

Occupational Group	All Employees			Male			Female		
	Total	Negro	Percent Negro	Total	Negro	Percent Negro	Total	Negro	Percent Negro
Officials and managers	960	32	3.3	864	21	2.4	96	11	11.5
Professionals	292	11	3.8	237	8	3.4	55	3	5.5
Technicians	7	1	14.3	5	1	20.0	2	—	—
Sales workers	3,569	296	8.3	974	108	11.1	2,595	188	7.2
Office and clerical	988	134	13.6	366	93	25.4	622	41	6.6
Total white collar	5,816	474	8.1	2,446	231	9.4	3,370	243	7.2
Craftsmen	14	—	—	13	—	—	1	—	—
Operatives	129	50	38.8	124	50	40.3	5	—	—
Laborers	172	82	47.7	143	64	44.8	29	18	62.1
Service workers	2,408	923	38.3	807	454	56.3	1,601	469	29.3
Total blue collar	2,723	1,055	38.7	1,087	568	52.3	1,636	487	29.8
Total	8,539	1,529	17.9	3,533	799	22.6	5,006	730	14.6

Source: Data in author's possession.

TABLE B-17. *Drugstore Industry*
Employment by Race, Sex, and Occupational Group
Chain Company Totals
Core City Locations, Midwest Region, 1968

Occupational Group	All Employees			Male			Female		
	Total	Negro	Percent Negro	Total	Negro	Percent Negro	Total	Negro	Percent Negro
Officials and managers	1,417	80	5.6	1,316	71	5.4	101	9	8.9
Professionals	541	19	3.5	455	14	3.1	86	5	5.8
Technicians	79	—	—	45	—	—	34	—	—
Sales workers	3,876	420	10.8	1,066	149	14.0	2,810	271	9.6
Office and clerical	1,475	96	6.5	366	45	12.6	1,109	50	4.5
Total white collar	7,388	615	8.3	3,248	280	8.6	4,140	335	8.1
Craftsmen	145	2	1.4	127	2	1.6	18	—	—
Operatives	315	46	14.6	176	25	14.2	139	21	15.1
Laborers	496	109	22.0	408	91	22.3	88	18	20.5
Service workers	2,736	800	29.2	859	384	44.7	1,877	416	22.2
Total blue collar	3,692	957	25.9	1,570	502	32.0	2,122	455	21.4
Total	11,080	1,572	14.2	4,818	782	16.2	6,262	790	12.6

Source: Data in author's possession.

TABLE B-18. Drugstore Industry
Employment by Race, Sex, and Occupational Group
Chain Company Totals
Core City Locations, Rocky Mountain Region, 1968

Occupational Group	All Employees			Male			Female		
	Total	Negro	Percent Negro	Total	Negro	Percent Negro	Total	Negro	Percent Negro
Officials and managers	232	—	—	226	—	—	6	—	—
Professionals	100	—	—	92	—	—	8	—	—
Technicians	3	—	—	3	—	—	—	—	—
Sales workers	784	9	1.1	233	3	1.3	551	6	1.1
Office and clerical	237	5	2.1	82	2	2.4	155	3	1.9
Total white collar	1,356	14	1.0	636	5	0.8	720	9	1.2
Craftsmen	7	—	—	7	—	—	—	—	—
Operatives	2	—	—	2	—	—	—	—	—
Laborers	—	—	—	—	—	—	—	—	—
Service workers	649	36	5.5	230	24	10.4	419	12	2.9
Total blue collar	658	36	5.5	239	24	10.0	419	12	2.9
Total	2,014	50	2.5	875	29	3.3	1,139	21	1.8

Source: Data in author's possession.

TABLE B-19. Drugstore Industry
Employment by Race, Sex, and Occupational Group
Chain Company Totals
Core City Locations, Far West Region, 1968

Occupational Group	All Employees			Male			Female		
	Total	Negro	Percent Negro	Total	Negro	Percent Negro	Total	Negro	Percent Negro
Officials and managers	267	1	0.4	255	1	0.4	12	—	—
Professionals	146	5	3.4	130	3	2.3	16	2	12.5
Technicians	18	—	—	4	—	—	14	—	—
Sales workers	833	36	4.3	340	22	6.5	493	14	2.8
Office and clerical	245	8	3.3	47	3	6.4	198	5	2.5
Total white collar	1,509	50	3.3	776	29	3.7	733	21	2.9
Craftsmen	10	—	—	10	—	—	—	—	—
Operatives	8	—	—	3	—	—	5	—	—
Laborers	13	—	—	13	—	—	—	—	—
Service workers	177	39	22.0	72	25	34.7	105	14	13.3
Total blue collar	208	39	18.8	98	25	25.5	110	14	12.7
Total	1,717	89	5.2	874	54	6.2	843	35	4.2

Source: Data in author's possession.

TABLE B-20. Drugstore Industry
Employment by Race, Sex, and Occupational Group
Chain Company Totals
Suburban Locations, United States, 1968

Occupational Group	All Employees			Male			Female		
	Total	Negro	Percent Negro	Total	Negro	Percent Negro	Total	Negro	Percent Negro
Officials and managers	1,084	53	4.9	910	19	2.1	174	34	19.5
Professionals	516	25	4.8	464	20	4.3	52	5	9.6
Technicians	9	2	22.2	9	2	22.2	—	—	—
Sales workers	4,812	115	2.4	1,381	49	3.5	3,431	66	1.9
Office and clerical	291	11	3.8	71	7	9.9	220	4	1.8
Total white collar	6,712	206	3.1	2,835	97	3.4	3,877	109	2.8
Craftsmen	41	5	12.2	39	5	12.8	2	—	—
Operatives	87	27	31.0	82	25	30.5	5	2	40.0
Laborers	289	99	34.3	247	84	34.0	42	15	35.7
Service workers	2,030	436	21.5	617	190	30.8	1,413	246	17.4
Total blue collar	2,447	567	23.2	985	304	30.9	1,462	263	18.0
Total	9,159	773	8.4	3,820	401	10.5	5,339	372	7.0

Source: Data in author's possession.

Note: Data on the Rocky Mountain region are not presented separately, as no Negroes were reported in suburban stores.

TABLE B-21. *Drugstore Industry*
Employment by Race, Sex, and Occupational Group
Chain Company Totals
Suburban Locations, Northeast Region, 1968

Occupational Group	All Employees			Male			Female		
	Total	Negro	Percent Negro	Total	Negro	Percent Negro	Total	Negro	Percent Negro
Officials and managers	230	1	0.4	191	1	0.5	39	—	—
Professionals	32	2	6.2	32	2	6.2	—	—	—
Technicians	1	1	100.0	1	1	100.0	—	—	—
Sales workers	821	9	1.1	117	4	3.4	704	5	0.7
Office and clerical	9	—	—	8	—	—	1	—	—
Total white collar	1,093	13	1.2	349	8	2.3	744	5	0.7
Craftsmen	—	—	—	—	—	—	—	—	—
Operatives	—	—	—	—	—	—	—	—	—
Laborers	1	—	—	1	—	—	—	—	—
Service workers	486	19	3.9	177	17	9.6	309	2	0.6
Total blue collar	487	19	3.9	178	17	9.6	309	2	0.6
Total	1,580	32	2.0	527	25	4.7	1,053	7	0.7

Source: Data in author's possession.

TABLE B-22. Drugstore Industry
Employment by Race, Sex, and Occupational Group
Chain Company Totals
Suburban Locations, South Region, 1968

Occupational Group	All Employees			Male			Female		
	Total	Negro	Percent Negro	Total	Negro	Percent Negro	Total	Negro	Percent Negro
Officials and managers	380	46	12.1	285	14	4.9	95	32	33.7
Professionals	191	19	9.9	176	16	9.1	15	3	20.0
Technicians	7	1	14.3	7	1	14.3	—	—	—
Sales workers	1,543	73	4.7	589	34	5.8	954	39	4.1
Office and clerical	123	5	4.1	11	1	9.1	112	4	3.6
Total white collar	2,244	144	6.4	1,068	66	6.2	1,176	78	6.6
Craftsmen	35	5	14.3	35	5	14.3	—	—	—
Operatives	51	26	51.0	47	24	51.1	4	2	50.0
Laborers	142	86	60.6	112	72	64.3	30	14	46.7
Service workers	622	288	46.3	208	109	52.4	414	179	43.2
Total blue collar	850	405	47.6	402	210	52.2	448	195	43.5
Total	3,094	549	17.7	1,470	276	18.8	1,624	273	16.8

Source: Data in author's possession.

TABLE B-23. Drugstore Industry
Employment by Race, Sex, and Occupational Group
Chain Company Totals
Suburban Locations, Midwest Region, 1968

Occupational Group	All Employees			Male			Female		
	Total	Negro	Percent Negro	Total	Negro	Percent Negro	Total	Negro	Percent Negro
Officials and managers	275	4	1.5	240	3	1.2	35	1	2.9
Professionals	151	1	0.7	134	1	0.7	17	—	—
Technicians	1	—	—	1	—	—	—	—	—
Sales workers	1,488	19	1.3	315	4	1.3	1,173	15	1.3
Office and clerical	75	3	4.0	17	3	17.6	58	—	—
Total white collar	1,990	27	1.4	707	11	1.6	1,283	16	1.2
Craftsmen	6	—	—	4	—	—	2	—	—
Operatives	22	—	—	21	—	—	1	—	—
Laborers	138	13	9.4	131	12	9.2	7	1	14.3
Service workers	683	121	17.7	153	59	38.6	530	62	11.7
Total blue collar	849	134	15.8	309	71	23.0	540	63	11.7
Total	2,839	161	5.7	1,016	82	8.1	1,823	79	4.3

Source: Data in author's possession.

TABLE B-24. Drugstore Industry
Employment by Race, Sex, and Occupational Group
Chain Company Totals
Suburban Locations, Far West Region, 1968

Occupational Group	All Employees			Male			Female		
	Total	Negro	Percent Negro	Total	Negro	Percent Negro	Total	Negro	Percent Negro
Officials and managers	184	2	1.1	179	1	0.6	5	1	20.0
Professionals	111	3	2.7	92	1	1.1	19	2	10.5
Technicians	—	—	—	—	—	—	—	—	—
Sales workers	853	14	1.6	355	7	2.0	498	7	1.4
Office and clerical	84	3	3.6	35	3	8.6	49	—	—
Total white collar	1,232	22	1.8	661	12	1.8	571	10	1.8
Craftsmen	—	—	—	—	—	—	—	—	—
Operatives	13	1	7.7	13	1	7.7	—	—	—
Laborers	8	—	—	3	—	—	5	—	—
Service workers	177	8	4.5	69	5	7.2	108	3	2.8
Total blue collar	198	9	4.5	85	6	7.1	113	3	2.7
Total	1,430	31	2.2	746	18	2.4	684	13	1.9

Source: Data in author's possession.

TABLE B-25. *Drugstore Industry*
Employment by Race, Sex, and Occupational Group
Chain Company Totals
Small Towns and Rural Locations, United States, 1968

Occupational Group	All Employees			Male			Female		
	Total	Negro	Percent Negro	Total	Negro	Percent Negro	Total	Negro	Percent Negro
Officials and managers	824	—	—	722	—	—	102	—	—
Professionals	495	5	1.0	447	4	0.9	48	1	2.1
Technicians	41	1	2.4	21	1	4.8	20	—	—
Sales workers	4,016	38	0.9	923	20	2.2	3,093	18	0.6
Office and clerical	280	11	3.9	124	10	8.1	156	1	0.6
Total white collar	5,656	55	1.0	2,237	35	1.6	3,419	20	0.6
Craftsmen	6	—	—	6	—	—	—	—	—
Operatives	17	—	—	17	—	—	—	—	—
Laborers	138	17	12.3	123	16	13.0	15	1	6.7
Service workers	1,569	223	14.2	428	134	31.3	1,141	89	7.8
Total blue collar	1,730	240	13.9	574	150	26.1	1,156	90	7.8
Total	7,386	295	4.0	2,811	185	6.6	4,575	110	2.4

Source: Data in author's possession.

Note: Data on the Rocky Mountain region are not presented separately, as no Negroes were reported in small towns and rural stores.

TABLE B-26. *Drugstore Industry*
Employment by Race, Sex, and Occupational Group
Chain Company Totals
Small Towns and Rural Locations, Northeast Region, 1968

Occupational Group	All Employees			Male			Female		
	Total	Negro	Percent Negro	Total	Negro	Percent Negro	Total	Negro	Percent Negro
Officials and managers	166	—	—	128	—	—	38	—	—
Professionals	60	—	—	57	—	—	3	—	—
Technicians	2	—	—	2	—	—	—	—	—
Sales workers	636	—	—	155	—	—	481	—	—
Office and clerical	36	—	—	11	—	—	25	—	—
Total white collar	900	—	—	353	—	—	547	—	—
Craftsmen	—	—	—	—	—	—	—	—	—
Operatives	3	—	—	3	—	—	—	—	—
Laborers	31	—	—	25	—	—	6	—	—
Service workers	370	2	0.5	113	2	1.8	257	—	—
Total blue collar	404	2	0.5	141	2	1.4	263	—	—
Total	1,304	2	0.2	494	2	0.4	810	—	—

Source: Data in author's possession.

TABLE B-27. *Drugstore Industry*
Employment by Race, Sex, and Occupational Group
Chain Company Totals
Small Towns and Rural Locations, South Region, 1963

Occupational Group	All Employees			Male			Female		
	Total	Negro	Percent Negro	Total	Negro	Percent Negro	Total	Negro	Percent Negro
Officials and managers	378	—	—	327	—	—	51	—	—
Professionals	204	4	2.0	180	3	1.7	24	1	4.2
Technicians	—	—	—	—	—	—	—	—	—
Sales workers	1,581	28	1.8	286	12	4.2	1,295	16	1.2
Office and clerical	145	8	5.5	67	8	11.9	78	—	—
Total white collar	2,308	40	1.7	860	23	2.7	1,448	17	1.2
Craftsmen	—	—	—	—	—	—	—	—	—
Operatives	6	—	—	6	—	—	—	—	—
Laborers	38	16	42.1	38	16	42.1	—	—	—
Service workers	856	186	21.7	221	116	52.5	635	70	11.0
Total blue collar	900	202	22.4	265	132	49.8	635	70	11.0
Total	3,208	242	7.5	1,125	155	13.8	2,083	87	4.2

Source: Data in author's possession.

TABLE B-28. Drugstore Industry
Employment by Race, Sex, and Occupational Group
Chain Company Totals
Small Towns and Rural Locations, Midwest Region, 1968

Occupational Group	All Employees			Male			Female		
	Total	Negro	Percent Negro	Total	Negro	Percent Negro	Total	Negro	Percent Negro
Officials and managers	144	—	—	134	—	—	10	—	—
Professionals	83	1	1.2	74	1	1.4	9	—	—
Technicians	—	—	—	—	—	—	—	—	—
Sales workers	649	8	1.2	119	7	5.9	530	1	0.2
Office and clerical	37	2	5.4	27	2	7.4	10	—	—
Total white collar	913	11	1.2	354	10	2.8	559	1	0.2
Craftsmen	1	—	—	1	—	—	—	—	—
Operatives	6	—	—	6	—	—	—	—	—
Laborers	59	1	1.7	55	—	—	4	1	25.0
Service workers	293	35	11.9	77	16	20.8	216	19	8.8
Total blue collar	359	36	10.0	139	16	11.5	220	20	9.1
Total	1,272	47	3.7	493	26	5.3	779	21	2.7

Source: Data in author's possession.

TABLE B-29. Drugstore Industry
Employment by Race, Sex, and Occupational Group
Chain Company Totals
Small Towns and Rural Locations, Far West Region, 1968

Occupational Group	All Employees			Male			Female		
	Total	Negro	Percent Negro	Total	Negro	Percent Negro	Total	Negro	Percent Negro
Officials and managers	114	—	—	111	—	—	3	—	—
Professionals	128	—	—	119	—	—	9	—	—
Technicians	38	1	2.6	18	1	5.6	20	—	—
Sales workers	1,030	2	0.2	332	1	0.3	698	1	0.1
Office and clerical	55	1	1.8	16	—	—	39	1	2.6
Total white collar	1,365	4	0.3	596	2	0.3	769	2	0.3
Craftsmen	5	—	—	5	—	—	—	—	—
Operatives	2	—	—	2	—	—	—	—	—
Laborers	10	—	—	5	—	—	5	—	—
Service workers	12	—	—	6	—	—	6	—	—
Total blue collar	29	—	—	18	—	—	11	—	—
Total	1,394	4	0.3	614	2	0.3	780	2	0.3

Source: Data in author's possession.

Index

PART FOUR

THE NEGRO
IN THE SUPERMARKET INDUSTRY

by

GORDON F. BLOOM

and

F. MARION FLETCHER

TABLE OF CONTENTS

LIST OF TABLES

LIST OF FIGURES

CHAPTER I

Introduction

The supermarket industry is important in the study of the racial employment policies of American industry for five compelling reasons. First is the ubiquitous nature of the industry. Supermarkets abound from Brooklyn to Hattiesburg, from Anchorage to Miami, and from the small town to the megalopolis.

Second is the size of the industry. Food retailing (grocery, meat, and vegetable stores) employed over 1.5 million workers in 1970.[1] Although data are not available as to the number of such workers who were employed in supermarkets, it is significant that supermarkets account for three-fourths of all grocery store sales in the United States.[2]

Third is the relatively low skill requirements of the industry, particularly when compared to high technology industries. Historically, the supermarket industry has served as a major source of employment for youth without previous job training.

Fourth is the high percentage of part-time employment available in this industry—in 1969 over one-half of all store personnel were estimated to be part-timers.[3] Thousands of young Americans each year obtain their first experience in the labor market working part-time in supermarkets.

Fifth is the relatively attractive nature of the employment patterns in the industry. Employment in supermarkets has been growing steadily over the years and since food sales are relatively recession-proof, the industry does not suffer from the problem of cyclical layoff. Furthermore, most jobs are semi-white collar in nature and reasonably well-paid; therefore they would appear to be attractive to new entrants to, or disadvantaged

---

1. *Employment and Earnings*, Vol. 17 (March 1971), Table B-2.

2. *Progressive Grocer*, April 1971, p. 66. This publication defines "supermarket" as a self-service food store with annual sales in excess of $500,000. Subsequent references will be made to statistics compiled by Super Market Institute which uses $1,000,000 annual sales as the minimum requirement for classification as a supermarket. These differences should be noted in comparing data from the two sources.

3. Super Market Institute, *The Super Market Industry Speaks 1970*, Twenty-Second Annual Report (Chicago: The Institute, 1970), p. 26.

members of, the labor force. These five circumstances combine to make the supermarket industry a major source of employment opportunities for relatively low-skilled job-seekers on a broad geographical basis.

OBJECTIVES OF THE STUDY

This study will focus upon racial employment practices in the industry and will attempt to analyze the forces and conditions which have created and shaped those policies. It is therefore necessary to consider the nature of the industry itself, the institutional environments of companies, and the factors which shape management policy. Employment procedures and practices will be reviewed in the light of their impact upon Negro recruitment and employment. Special attention will be given to the problems met by particular companies in their efforts to employ disadvantaged miniority members of the labor force so that a clearer understanding can be gained of the barriers to increased employment of Negroes which may exist in this industry. Finally, suggestions will be made with respect to changes in management policy which would improve the employment situation for Negroes in the industry.

SOURCES OF DATA

The statistics upon which this study is based were derived from two principal sources: (1) a survey conducted by one of the authors in which data were obtained on thirty major food retailing organizations through personal interviews; and (2) governmental compilations, primarily data collected by the U. S. Bureau of the Census and the U. S. Equal Employment Opportunity Commission. Although both sources suffer from certain limitations hereinafter referred to, it is believed that the overall picture presented is a fair approximation to the actual status of Negro employment in the supermarket industry.

Survey Data

The core of the study is based upon data compiled from personal interviews with executives in large food retailing organizations in the United States. As far as data collection is concerned, companies were selected so as to provide a reasonable cross-section of the industry in terms of size of firm and geographic location, subject, however, to the overall limitation that only firms operating 50 or more stores were included in the survey sample. In addition to the firms which supplied statistical data for the sample survey, a number of companies were interviewed to provide supplementary information concerning employment practices and problems. Among this group were firms with less than 50 stores. Comparison of the experience of these firms with the firms included in the sample survey together with an analysis of the EEOC data (which do include firms with less than 50 stores), suggests that the sample data substantially represent the status of the industry as a whole with respect to Negro employment.

In addition to supermarket chains, interviews were also conducted with three chains which specialize in the operation of convenience stores and with three organizations that were created to bargain with unions on behalf of chain operators in a given metropolitan area. Two local retail grocer associations were also interviewed and provided useful information. (The membership of local and state associations is largely composed of independent supermarket operators.) An attempt to conduct a questionnaire survey of independent grocers was abandoned because of lack of response on the part of local grocery associations. In order to obtain a balanced perspective of the problem, key personnel in a number of community-based civil rights organizations were interviewed to elicit different viewpoints as to the nature of the barriers which exist to recruitment and placement of Negroes in the industry.

Government Data

U. S. Bureau of Census data are used to trace the history of Negro employment in the retail food industry prior to 1960. Data from the U. S. Equal Employment Opportunity Commission did not become available until 1966. Statistics of that agency are therefore used to portray the course of Negro employment from 1966 onward.

Neither census data nor EEOC data are restricted solely to the supermarket industry. Census data, which form the statistical basis for the analysis in Chapter III, are heavily weighted by employment in numerous small grocery store operations and by employment in other types of food retailing such as fish and vegetable markets, milk stores, and specialty food shops. Thus, the quantitative data available for years prior to 1960 reflect the trend in the entire food retailing business, rather than in the supermarket industry per se.

Data from the U. S. Equal Employment Opportunity Commission are, with one exception, also based on this broader food category, but it is felt that they more accurately reflect supermarket employment practices since all employers of less than 100 workers are excluded. These statistics are utilized in Chapters IV and V along with data derived from the supermarket sample based on personal interviews. It should be noted that EEOC data include both store and nonstore employment in the reporting companies; occupational patterns vary considerably between retail outlets and the supporting company headquarters, warehouse facilities, and food production units.

Recently EEOC data on the "grocery store" segment of the "retail food" category were made available. Because of the minimum size criterion of not less than 100 employees, supermarket company employment dominates the grocery store category, although some convenience store companies are also included. Aggregate figures for the United States indicate that total employment and occupational distributions of the larger EEOC retail food compilation and the smaller grocery store segment are extremely similar; only about 2.5 percent of the larger category is non-grocery store employment. Thus the larger retail food category, for which more extensive data are available, can be used with confidence to show general trends in supermarket industry employment of Negroes in the late 1960's despite the limitations above referred to and despite certain errors of misclassification which are more fully discussed in Chapters II and IV.

CHAPTER II

The Supermarket Industry

The entire retail food industry is comprised of 208,300 independent, affiliated, and chain grocery stores in the United States, and their headquarters, warehouses, and related operations,[4] plus specialty food stores such as meat and fish markets, bakeries, etc. Together, these make up Standard Industrial Classification No. 54: Retail Trade—Food Stores.[5] This study will focus on Negro employment in the supermarket companies of the industry, as defined below. Background data on the industry and census and other employment statistics which apply to food retailing in general, or to the grocery store segment, including the thousands of small units, will be carefully distinguished when used in this and other chapters.

INDUSTRY DEFINITION

The supermarket industry comprises both chain and independent companies whose primary business is mass food merchandising on the retail level. A chain is defined as a company operating eleven or more stores; smaller companies operating more than one but less than eleven units are called "multistore" companies. The largest supermarket companies have nonsupermarket and even nonfood operations. Chicago-based Jewel Companies, for example, operates Osco drugstores and Turn-Style self-service department stores as well as a variety of food operations including ice cream stores, home service routes, liquor stores, and "convenience" stores in addition to supermarkets.[6] Other well known regional chains are now subsidiaries of national food companies

---

4. *Progressive Grocer*, April 1971, p. 66.

5. U.S. Bureau of the Budget, *Standard Industrial Classification Manual, 1967* (Washington: U.S. Government Printing Office, 1967), pp. 242-243.

6. *Progressive Grocer*, April 1966, pp. 329-332.

such as Kroger, or of other organizations such as Household Finance.[7]

The stores themselves are defined by sales volume. A supermarket is a self-service food store having sales of $500,000 or more per year; a superette is one having $150,000 to $500,000 in sales a year; and a small store is one with less than $150,000.[8] There are also "convenience" stores, with sales up to $200,000 a year, which are distinguished by long business hours, limited range of brands and products, self-service in all departments, and use of prepackaged foods even in the fresh meat and produce departments.[9] These are sometimes run as franchises, such as the White Hen Pantry stores division of the Jewel Companies.[10] Supermarket companies may operate stores in all of these categories.

In terms of employment, supermarkets are the most important units in the food industry, having large numbers of full and part-time employees. The rapidly growing convenience store group, in contrast, averaged less than four employees per store in 1970.[11] Chain supermarket companies will receive particular attention in this study. Their size and widespread location necessarily gives them a major impact on Negro employment and their corporate structures may enable them to be leaders in equal employment opportunity programs which require coordination, planning, and financing frequently beyond the capabilities of independent store owners.

HISTORICAL BACKGROUND

Today's supermarket is built around self-service shopping, name brand products, and prepackaged convenience. The evolution of this form of food retailing will be discussed briefly, after which the nature of the industry today and its effects on Negro employment will be examined.

---

7. Robert A. Wright, "L.A.'s Food Values," *New York Times*, March 21, 1971, Section F, p. 2.

8. *Progressive Grocer*, April 1971, p. 61, but see also the definitions in note 2.

9. *Ibid.*

10. *Progressive Grocer*, April 1966, p. 334.

11. *Progressive Grocer*, April 1971, p. 100.

The Evolution of Food Retailing

The food retailing system as it is known today can be traced to the pre-Civil War era and can be officially dated 1859, the year in which the first A & P opened. Many of the largest retailing companies were organized between that date and 1900, but significant growth did not begin until the twentieth century dawned.[12] Changes in the philosophy of retailing created and ultimately limited the growth of large food chains.

The first major innovation in food retailing, instituted by the Great Atlantic & Pacific Tea Company (A & P) was the economy store. The idea was to eliminate delivery and credit and to have modest store fixtures and the like so that prices could be reduced. It was assumed that the lower prices would generate enough volume to make up for the lower profit margins so that—combined with the cost savings inherent in the reduction of personal services—aggregate profits would be higher. The concept was so well-received by the public that the number of A & P stores in the 1913-1919 period following the opening of the first economy store increased from 500 to 4,200. By 1930, the total was 15,700 stores![13] As might be expected, the other emerging chains were quick to emulate this fantastic growth.

Since similar changes, though of less magnitude, were occurring in other retail organizations, it did not take long for opposition from independent retailers and wholesalers serving them to build to an anguished cry loud enough to be heard by the state legislatures. A variety of laws were enacted intended to halt the growth of the chains, but the few legislative measures which escaped the ban of unconstitutionality were unable to stem the growth of the chains.

The Rise of Supermarkets

Although legislation had little effect on the growth of chains, a new method of retailing arrived that demanded a competitive reaction. The new method combined the strategy of cash-and-carry and low overhead first introduced by A & P with the self-service concept first introduced by Clarence Saunders of Memphis.[14]

---

12. Godfrey M. Lebhar, *Chain Stores in America, 1859-1962* (New York: Chain Store Publishing Corp., 1963), pp. 25-26.

13. *Ibid.*

14. *Ibid.*, p. 34.

The new concept of the self-service supermarket was a response to the needs of the marketplace. The decade of the thirties was a period of severe unemployment and depressed incomes. Innovative independent entrepreneurs sought to find a way to bring food to the masses at lower prices than was possible under then conventional distribution methods.

The first such operations were launched by "King" Cullen in the Jamaica section of New York City and by Joe Weingarten in Houston, Texas. Typical of the early supermarkets, Cullen's "Price Wrecker" business was begun in an abandoned warehouse with an 80,000 square-foot sales area, an unprecedented size for a grocery store.[15] The spectacular success enjoyed by Cullen was soon overshadowed by the efforts of Roy O. Davidson in a former automobile plant in Elizabeth, New Jersey. Whereas Cullen called his operation the "Price Wrecker", the new operation billed itself the "Price Crusher". First year sales were $2,188,000 and profits were $166,000, both of which were unprecedented in the retail food business.[16]

Some chains reacted more quickly to the supermarket threat than others but by 1937 most, including A & P, were emulating the new technique. Their procedure was to open a supermarket and close their several smaller stores in the vicinity. Thus, the A & P of 1937 with 14,700 stores and sales of $899 million was transformed into the A & P of 1962 with 4,000 stores and $5.24 billion in sales.[17]

Although the supermarket in its inception was a low-price mass merchandising institution, as time passed it tended to acquire more elaborate facilities and to take on high cost promotional schemes involving stamps or other give-aways. Trading stamp popularity reached a peak in the early 1960's and then declined through the rest of the decade. From a high of 78 percent, by 1970, only 37 percent of all supermarkets used them.[18] Professor Malcolm McNair aptly called this development "the wheel of retailing" in which new types of retailers usually enter the market as low-status low-margin operators, take on various frills and

---

15. M. Zimmerman, *The Supermarket: A Revolution in Distribution* (New York: McGraw-Hill, 1955), p. 35.

16. *Ibid.*, p. 43.

17. *Ibid.*, p. 35.

18. Super Market Institute, *The Super Market Industry Speaks 1971*, (Chicago: The Institute, 1971), p. 12.

higher operating costs, and ultimately become vulnerable to newer types of outlets.[19]

During the 1960's an increasingly important segment of the supermarket industry turned back to the original concept of high-volume low-margin food retailing and adopted the strategy of discounting, particularly with respect to the dry grocery department. By 1970, over one third of all supermarkets, both chain and independent, had adopted a discounting policy.[20] The effort to gain more volume through a low-price policy put additional pressure on operating margins in what was already a highly competitive industry.

The decade of the sixties was also marked by a steady rise in the number and size of supermarkets. Although the number of food stores in all categories continued to decline—from 260,050 in 1960 to 208,300 in 1970—the number of supermarkets increased from 33,000 in 1960 to 38,300 in 1970.[21] At the time the average supermarket grew in size and took on an increasing variety of items. The number of items carried by the average supermarket increased from about 6,600 in 1962 to about 7,800 in 1970.[22]

With the advent of the seventies, the supermarket industry appeared to be on the threshhold of another major revolution— the emergence of the "super supermarket." Whereas the average supermarket built in 1960 was about 15,000 square feet in size, today's markets are commonly 30,000 to 50,000 square feet. Many markets are being built in combination with discount department stores in huge buildings of 80,000 to 100,000 square feet. New supermarkets constructed in 1970 reported average sales of more than $46,000 per week, according to one recent survey.[23] The highest volume store averaged $240,000 in sales per week while more than 11 percent of the new stores reported weekly sales in

---

19. M. P. McNair, "Significant Trends and Developments in the Postwar Period," in A. B. Smith (ed.), *Competitive Distribution in a Free, High-Level Economy and Its Implications for the University* (Pittsburgh: University of Pittsburgh Press, 1958), pp. 1-25.

20. *Progressive Grocer*, April 1971, p. 59.

21. *Progressive Grocer*, April 1965, p. 59, and April 1971, pp. 66 and 69. The increase in number of supermarkets was actually greater than these statistics indicate because *Progressive Grocer* had changed its definition of a supermarket by 1970. In 1960, the minimum sales requirement was only $375,000 per annum.

22. *Progressive Grocer*, April 1971, p. 65.

23. *Progressive Grocer*, July 1971, p. 112.

excess of $100,000.[24] The emergence of the "super supermarket" has important implications for manpower policy in the industry, since the demands for skills, managerial ability, and other personnel requirements are quite different in a store doing such huge volume from those in the smaller supermarket characteristic of the early sixties.

SALES AND OPERATING MARGINS

Sales in the grocery store industry in 1970 exceeded $88 billion, up 8.1 percent over 1969.[25] These sales were not, of course, all food items. A significant part of the total sales volume, particularly in supermarkets, is attributable to sales of health and beauty aids, housewares, paper goods, toys, and other items familiar to every shopper. These additions to the product mix have increased sales volume and also have generally improved gross margins since they normally are sold at higher mark-ups than grocery items. Gross profit in supermarkets has also been augmented by the increasing use of prepackaged convenience foods and various gourmet lines, both frozen and canned.

The supermarket industry has always been a high-volume low-profit business. Since 1960, however, a combination of factors has tightened operating margins even more. The spread of discounting, the overbuilding of markets in many areas, the pressure of higher costs, and the resistance of consumers to higher prices have resulted in a decline in profits in the industry whether measured as a percentage of sales or as return on equity. Thus profit after taxes earned by retail food chains as a percentage of retail sales fell from 1.32 percent in 1961 to 0.92 percent in 1970. Food chains keep as profit less than a penny out of every dollar of sales rung through the checkouts. During the same period, net profits measured as a percentage of net worth dropped from 11.25 percent to 9.34 percent.[26]

In 1970 there was only one retail food chain on the list of the 100 most profitable companies in the United States compiled by *Forbes Magazine* and that company—Safeway Stores—was No. 100 on the list. In the same year only seven food chains were

---

24. *Ibid.*

25. *Progressive Grocer*, April 1971, p. 59.

26. New York State College of Agriculture, *Operating Results of Food Chains '69-'70*, State University at Cornell University, Ithaca, N.Y., p. 11.

included in the list of the 500 most profitable companies. The sales of these large chains totaled almost 20 billion dollars— more than twice the sales of the giant Sears, Roebuck and Company—but the profit of Sears was almost twice as great as the combined profit of all seven food chains.[27]

It is apparent, therefore, that the supermarket business is a highly competitive business with narrow profit margins which leave little room for inefficiency. Personnel at all levels of companies operating in this industry are under constant pressure to produce at optimum efficiency. High volume can mean large profits if critical ratios are kept in line, but the same high volume can lead to disastrous losses if costs get out of line. For example, for the year ended June 26, 1971, Allied Supermarkets, one of the giants of the industry, had sales of almost one billion dollars but sustained a loss of $12,090,000.[28] During the year 1969, 13 percent of the supermarket companies participating in the figure exchange sponsored by the Super Market Institute reported a net operating loss.[29]

Companies do not approach social problems in a vacuum. The need to earn a profit is an ever-present constraint. It is obvious that a corporation such as International Business Machines, which in 1970 earned a net profit on sales of approximately 13 percent,[30] may approach the problem of hiring hardcore unemployed with an outlook markedly different from the food chain which earns less than one percent on its sales. An understanding of the economics of the supermarket business is therefore essential to an evaluation of the record of this industry in hiring Negro workers.

INDUSTRY STRUCTURE

The supermarket business is relatively easy for an entrepreneur to enter compared to most other large industries in our economy. The best indication of this is the fact that about 4 out of every 10 supermarkets in the United States are independently owned.[31] Chains and independents compete vigorously with one another in practically every marketing area.

---

27. *Forbes*, May 15, 1971, pp. 115-127.

28. *Supermarket News*, August 23, 1971, p. 17.

29. Super Market Institute, *1970, op. cit.*, p. 11.

30. *Forbes*, May 15, 1971, pp. 79 and 115.

31. *Progressive Grocer*, April 1971, p. 66.

Growth of Independents

Self-service and the supermarket concept were both innovations of the independent-operated food stores. Although chains soon adopted the same concepts, independents have continued to be a viable sector of the industry and have adopted many chain operating practices and procedures in order to compete effectively with the chain markets. Altogether, independent stores had sales volume of $46.3 billion in 1970.[32]

After World War II, independents began to band together to overcome the buying advantages which enabled chains to underprice them. Out of this developed the so-called "affiliated-independent." Affiliated independents are operators of retail food stores who are either stockholder-members of cooperative wholesale buying groups or are members of voluntary merchandising groups sponsored by a wholesaler and generally operating under a common name. All other independent operators are classified as "unaffiliated." In 1970, 36 percent of all independent supermarkets and superettes were operated by members of cooperatives, and 39 percent by members of voluntary wholesale organizations.[33]

In the typical cooperative arrangement, the retailers jointly own the wholesale operation and finance its activities. Orders may be transmitted from store to warehouse by mail, telephone, or data transmission system without the need for salesmen. Deliveries are made on a scheduled basis with a view to balancing warehouse efficiency with store needs. The profit from the wholesale operation is returned to members, usually on a year-end basis, except for such amount as may be required to be retained in the centralized operation for working capital. The margin paid by the retailers, then, is only that due to expenses of carrying on the wholesale operations.[34]

Although cooperatives have been in existence since the 1880's, they did not assume a significant role in the retail food business until the development of chain organizations and the supermarket made an association of independent food retailers a competitive necessity. As late as 1910 there were only three retail food

---

32. *Ibid.*, p. 74.

33. *Ibid.*, p. 75.

34. Paul D. Converse, "Twenty-five years of Wholesaling—A Revolution in Food Retailing," *Journal of Marketing*, Vol. 22 (July 1957), p. 47.

cooperatives. By 1970, the number had grown to 231 with sales of $8.1 billion.[35] Today some cooperatives have reached giant size. Members of Certified, on the West Coast, account for over one billion dollars of retail sales annually while Wakefern, a New Jersey firm, has assumed a dominant position in its trading area with its affiliated Shop-Rite Stores.

Another kind of arrangement which has met with considerable acceptance and success in the retail food industry is the voluntary wholesale organization. They have been of singular importance in the independents' fight for survival in a competitive business.

The voluntary wholesale organization is usually established through the initiative of a pre-existing wholesaler. The wholesaler, whose interest in the survival and profitability of the independent retailer is easy to understand, induces a group of independents to buy a substantial portion of their merchandise from him and to operate under a common name with similar merchandising programs. This arrangement, together with the elimination of the need for salesmen to canvas accounts, provides economies for the wholesaler and enables him to operate at a lower mark-up which in turn enables his customers to be more competitive. The wholesaler provides his customers with many of the services commonly furnished by the headquarters or divisional office of large food chains, such as store design and layout, bookkeeping services, operational advice, advertising and layouts, and so forth.

Stores affiliated with wholesalers or corporations operate independently in personnel matters. Their racial policies are likely to reflect their location, and few are found in black neighborhoods.

Growth of Chains

The sales volume of food chains has grown steadily over the years, although the number of stores operated by them has declined. In 1937 there were 49,250 chain food stores (of all categories) with aggregate sales of $2.9 billion. By 1970, the number of stores operated by chains had fallen to 34,200 (due in part to a redefinition), but aggregate sales amounted to $42.1 billion.[36] This trend reflects the effect of management policy in

---

35. *Progressive Grocer*, April 1971, p. 90.

36. *Ibid.*, p. 69.

closing small antiquated stores and opening large supermarkets. A & P, for example, closed 350 units between 1958 and 1971.[37]

Chain volume has grown both from internal expansion involving the construction of new outlets and through acquisition and merger. Between 1949 and 1958, for example, 83 chains acquired 2,238 stores with sales amounting to $1.9 billion.[38] In recent years, however, a series of antitrust rulings have severely limited the ability of large chains to utilize the merger device as a means of growth.

The industry giants are the chain store companies, led by A & P, which had 1970 sales of over $5.6 billion, 120,000 employees, and 4,575 stores. Financial data for the fifteen largest supermarket companies (including nonfood operations, such as discount stores) are shown in Table 1, derived from the *Fortune* list of the 50 largest retail companies in 1970. Together these firms employed more than 622,000 people and had sales of $29.2 billion in 1970. These huge corporations are in a position to be leaders in racial employment policy and practice.

Market Share

The percentage of total food sales accounted for by affiliated independents, unaffiliated independents, and food chains has fluctuated considerably over the past thirty years. Table 2 shows the industry structure by number of stores and retail sales for the years 1937 and 1970. As can be seen from the table, the total number of stores declined in all three categories. More significant, however, is the market share of each group. Whereas sales were quite evenly distributed in 1937, by 1970 unaffiliated independents held only 7.9 percent of sales, affiliated independents accounted for 44.5 percent, and chains 47.6 percent. Thus the major chains can influence, but not dominate, the racial policies of the industry.

Types of Stores

Both chain and independent stores can be separated by sales volume into super, superette, and small stores. As Table 3 shows, chains operate primarily supermarket-size stores, but there are nearly as many independent supermarkets. The vast majority of

---

37. *Business Week*, February 20, 1971, p. 68.

38. Federal Trade Commission, *Economic Inquiry into Food Marketing*, Part I (Washington: Government Printing Office, 1960), p. 128.

TABLE 1. *The Fifteen Largest Supermarket Companies 1970 Statistics*

Company and 1970 Rank Among Retail Companies		Headquarters	Sales	Assets	Net Income	Stock-holders' Equity	Number of Employees	Number of Stores	Net Income as a Percent of	
			($000)						Sales	Equity
Great Atlantic and Pacific Tea	(2)	New York	5,650,000	947,073	53,000	632,321	120,000	4,575	0.9	8.0
Safeway Stores	(3)	Oakland	4,860,167	875,705	68,892	497,048	96,760	2,274	1.4	13.9
Kroger	(5)	Cincinnati	3,735,774	757,777	39,782	332,452	83,810	1,868	1.1	12.0
Food Fair Stores	(10)	Philadelphia	1,762,005	333,472	10,636	131,861	30,000	622	0.6	8.1
Acme Markets	(11)	Philadelphia	1,650,249	336,448	12,530	176,713	35,288	897	0.8	7.1
Jewel Companies	(12)	Melrose Park, Ill.	1,628,496	436,059	23,962	201,858	48,314	639	1.5	11.9
National Tea	(13)	Chicago	1,512,282	235,993	9,888	123,733	31,000	954	0.7	8.0
Lucky Stores	(14)	San Leandro, Cal.	1,488,715	275,234	23,475	101,950	26,000	411	1.6	23.0
Winn-Dixie Stores	(15)	Jacksonville	1,418,916	201,837	27,615	147,424	27,700	794	1.9	18.7
Grand Union	(20)	East Paterson, N.J.	1,200,831	236,781	15,741	145,874	25,000	569	1.3	10.8
Allied Supermarkets	(23)	Detroit	952,142	228,459	(4,852)	44,816	17,000	396		—
Southland	(24)	Dallas	950,721	239,189	14,430	109,039	18,900	4,000	1.5	13.2
Supermarkets General	(28)	Woodbridge, N.J.	807,458	157,503	7,706	53,639	22,000	167	1.0	14.4
Stop & Shop Companies	(30)	Boston	789,950	220,638	5,637	62,150	22,000	216	0.7	9.1
First National Stores	(31)	Somerville, Mass.	770,780	133,478	4,452	80,333	19,000	392	0.6	5.6

Source: *Fortune*, Vol. LXXXIII (May 1971), pp. 196-197; and *Progressive Grocer*, April 1971, p. 82 (number of stores).

TABLE 2.　*Supermarket and Other Grocery Store Industry Sales Volume and Number of Stores by Industry Sector 1937 and 1970*

Industry Sector	1937				1970			
	Stores	Percent of Total	Sales (Millions)	Percent of Total	Stores	Percent of Total	Sales (Millions)	Percent of Total
Chains[a]	49,250	11.2	$2,898	34.7	34,200	16.4	$42,075	47.6
Independents								
Affiliated	110,000	25.0	2,600	31.1	69,400	33.3	39,390	44.5
Unaffiliated	280,750	63.8	2,858	34.2	104,700	50.3	6,950	7.9
Total	440,000	100.0	$8,356	100.0	208,300[b]	100.0	$88,415	100.0

Source: *Progressive Grocer*, April 1971, p. 69.

Note:　The terms "affiliated" and "unaffiliated" are explained in the text.

[a] Of these, 38,300 were supermarket size stores.

[b] Through 1951, chains were considered to be firms operating four or more stores; after 1951, eleven or more stores. Chains operated 20,400 supermarket-size stores in 1970. (See Table 3.)

TABLE 3. *Supermarket and Other Grocery Store Industry Sales and Number of Stores by Store Size and Industry Sector United States, 1970*

Store Size	Number of Stores	Percent of Total	Sales (Millions)	Percent of Total
Supermarkets	38,300	18.4	$66,665	75.4
Chains	20,400	9.8	39,350	44.5
Independent	17,900	8.6	27,315	30.9
Superettes	33,500	16.1	11,380	12.9
Chains	7,300	3.5	1,980	2.3
Independent	26,200	12.6	9,400	10.6
Small Stores	136,500	65.5	10,370	11.7
Chains	6,500	3.1	745	0.8
Independent	130,000	62.4	9,625	10.9
All Stores	208,300	100.0	$88,415	100.0

Source: *Progressive Grocer*, April 1971, p. 66.

small stores are independently operated. Of the more than 200,-000 grocery stores in 1970, 130,000, or 62.4 percent, were small nonchain stores, but these stores accounted for only 10.9 percent of all grocery store sales. Negro employment is likely to be concentrated in the larger stores and the larger companies for reasons that this study will make clear.

MANPOWER

Despite the size and importance of the supermarket industry in the United States, data on employment in supermarkets—as distinguished from food stores *in toto*—is not available on any continuing consistent basis. One of the problems is the very definition of supermarket; as has already been noted, *Progressive Grocer* and Super Market Institute have adopted different definitions which would obviously have a substantial effect upon employment compilation.

The U.S. Bureau of Labor Statistics reports that for the year 1970 there were 1,566,700 grocery store employees (Table 4). No comparable figure is available from government or industry

TABLE 4. *Grocery Store Industry*
Total, Nonsupervisory, and Female Employment
Selected Years, 1951-1970

	All Employees			Nonsupervisory Workers	
	Total	Female	Percent Female	Total	Percent Nonsupervision Workers
	(In thousands)			(In thousands)	
1951	881.0	n.a.	n.a.	829.7	94.2
1955	1,034.2	n.a.	n.a.	971.6	93.9
1960	1,180.5	346.1	29.3	1,105.4	93.6
1965	1,296.1	386.8	29.8	1,201.7	92.7
1966	1,367.0	416.7	30.5	1,268.7	92.8
1967	1,404.8	437.4	31.1	1,300.7	92.6
1968	1,454.4	459.7	31.6	1,347.4	92.6
1969	1,515.7	490.1	32.3	1,412.9	93.2
1970	1,566.7	510.9	32.6	1,455.8	92.9

Source: U.S. Bureau of Labor Statistics, *Employment and Earnings, United States, 1909-70*, Bulletin 1312-7; and *Employment and Earnings*, Vol. 17 (March 1971), Tables B-2 and B-3.

Note: Standard Industrial Classification 541-543: grocery, meat, and vegetable stores.

sources for employment in supermarkets. However, an estimate as to the occupational classification of employment in supermarkets can be derived from food store (SIC 54) data collected by the Equal Employment Opportunity Commission for 1970, as shown in Table 5. These data are derived from returns filed by food store companies with 100 or more employees in the aggregate. This size limitation means that as a practical matter most reporting companies are supermarket chains and multistore companies, although a few unusually large independently operated supermarket stores may be included. A small proportion of the data reflect other types of food store employment.

Although such data undoubtedly cover practically all supermarket chain *companies*, the employment figures are not necessarily restricted to supermarket operations. Some chains still have superettes or small stores and employment in these units would be included in the total figures. Likewise, a chain of con-

TABLE 5. *Supermarket Industry*
Employment by Sex and Occupational Group
Chains and Large Independents, 10,575 Establishments
United States, 1970

Occupational Group	All Employees		Male		Female	
	Total	Percent Distribution	Total	Percent Distribution	Total	Percent Distribution
Officials and Managers	71,617	9.8	67,656	13.9	3,961	1.6
Professionals	3,653	0.5	3,168	0.6	485	0.2
Technicians	2,525	0.3	1,873	0.4	712	0.3
Sales workers	431,095	58.9	265,104	54.4	165,991	67.9
Office and Clerical	46,593	6.4	11,057	2.3	35,536	14.5
Total white collar	555,483	75.9	348,798	71.6	206,685	84.5
Craftsmen	41,591	5.7	39,174	8.1	2,417	1.0
Operatives	57,734	7.9	42,523	8.7	15,211	6.2
Laborers	41,788	5.7	33,809	6.9	7,979	3.3
Service workers	35,269	4.8	23,011	4.7	12,258	5.0
Total blue collar	176,382	24.1	138,517	28.4	37,865	15.5
Total	731,865	100.0	487,315	100.0	244,550	100.0

Source: Appendix Table A-4.

venience stores would qualify under the "100 or more" limitation and would be included. In supermarket companies, of course, the employment figures apply not only to store operations, but also to warehouse, bakery, office, and manufacturing activities. Where a company operates a chain of supermarkets and also operates a chain of units concentrating on some other product line, such as discount department stores, each major category is supposed to be reported separately.

Employment data for members of cooperatives and independents, both affiliated and nonaffiliated, would normally be excluded from EEOC statistics, except where the member is a multistore operator. Although no data are available which would break out employment statistics for chains versus single store operators, it seems likely that the latter employ a smaller proportion of Negroes than the food chains. Food chains seem to be more subject to pressures of government and various community action groups than independent merchants. Furthermore, locational factors may also reinforce this tendency. Personal observation by the writers adds further weight to the hypothesis adopted in this study, namely that the EEOC figures provide a fair indication of the level of Negro employment among chain and multistore operators in the supermarket industry and that the independent retailer is likely to show an even smaller percentage of Negroes on his employment rolls.

There is one further shortcoming of EEOC data which is worthy of mention. There is no breakdown in the EEOC data between full-time and part-time employment. In most industries this may not pose any serious problem but in the supermarket business, where about one-half of employment is part-time, the lack of specific information as to this breakdown limits the conclusions which can be drawn from employment statistics.

An increase in percentage of Negroes employed could be caused by a rise in Negro part-time employment and an actual reduction in the number of Negroes in full-time jobs. This would hardly represent real progress in the movement for stable job security; yet the figures might give such an impression. In appraising statistics in this industry, therefore, one must be wary of playing the "numbers" game. In a very real sense, the quality of employment may be more important than the quantity, but available data do not permit judgments as to this significant circumstance.

Growth Rate

Table 4 indicates that employment in the entire grocery store industry grew at an annual rate of about 4 percent between 1951 and 1970. Comparable figures are not available for employment in supermarkets but it is to be presumed that employment in supermarkets advanced more rapidly than in all food stores. The proportion of nonsupervisory workers has declined slightly since 1951, from 94.2 percent to 92.9 percent of all grocery store employment.

Occupational Characteristics

As would be expected in a retail industry, the majority of supermarket company employees are in sales positions. Table 5 shows this. Other employees are rather evenly divided among the occupations, except for the small proportions of professionals and technicians, and the relatively large number of male officials and managers. The latter proportion—13.9 percent of the male work force—reflects particularly the large numbers of store managerial positions required in an industry of small units, and to a lesser extent, the corporate executives at company headquarters, necessary to the large scale operations on which these data are based. The male and female distributions indicate that women are much more heavily concentrated in sales than are men, but hold few managerial positions.

The category "officials and managers" includes store managers and supervisors, directors of manufacturing, warehousing and other supporting organizations, and headquarters officials. Unfortunately, evidence collected by the authors indicates that there has been some confusion as to the classification of departmental managers in supermarkets. Apparently some concerns have classified department heads—managers of the meat department and the produce department, for example—as officials, while other companies have classified them as sales workers.

The term "sales workers" is intended to cover all store level personnel engaged wholly or primarily in direct or indirect selling. In the typical supermarket this would indicate all clerks in the grocery and produce department and cashiers and bundleboys. Generally, persons working in the meat department are classified as "craftsmen" or "operatives." The relatively high percentage of females employed as blue collar "operatives" is accounted for by the concentration of women in backroom meatwrapping operations.

The major blue collar jobs are warehouseman, truck driver, meat cutter, and meat wrapper. Except for the latter category, these jobs are predominantly held by men. The category of "service workers" is intended to cover janitors, cafeteria workers, elevator operators, porters, etc. Since such positions are relatively uncommon in the supermarket industry, the relatively significant percentage of workers shown in this classification in Table 5 creates the suspicion that some misclassification exists in the compilation and that the figure for service workers is probably inflated as a result of inaccurate submission of data. This conclusion is partially confirmed by the fact that data collected by one of the authors from selected supermarket companies show only 2.1 percent service employment at the store level and only 3.1 percent for company headquarters and warehouses. (See Chapter V, Tables 21 and 23.)

Female Employment

Tables 4 and 5 indicate that women workers make up about one-third of the work force in grocery stores of all types as well as in supermarkets. In the stores, they work primarily as checkout clerks handling the bagging and payment for merchandise at the registers. As has already been mentioned, women are also found in wrapping operations in meat departments. At company headquarters, women primarily fill office and clerical positions.

Women employed as cashiers are frequently only partially attached to the labor force with no long range career goals. Young girls work until marriage, come back sometime later to supplement family income, drop out again to have children, and work intermittently after the children are in school. Some work for extended periods of time and a few never drop out of the labor force. Since cashiers are generally not considered promotable, skill and education requirements for the jobs are not high. Negro women are increasingly being recruited for these jobs.

Part-time Employment

Part-time employment is an essential requirement in the operation of the modern supermarket. Part-timers are found in all departments, but are most frequently utilized at the checkout operation as cashiers, baggers, and carry-out clerks. For the last two decades, part-time employment in the supermarket industry has steadily increased. Figure 1 shows that in 1951 companies surveyed by the Super Market Institute, whose members employ about 790,000 people in stores and supporting activities, used part-time workers as 30 percent of their work force; by 1970 this proportion had grown to 56 percent. Employment figures in the Institute's sample are heavily weighted by the influence of large concerns. The Super Market Institute study found that smaller companies continued to use fewer part-time employees.[39] Therefore, for the supermarket industry as a whole the proportion of part-timers is somewhat less. There is little doubt, however, that part-timers constitute approximately 50 percent of the total labor force of the industry and that their use is increasing. There are several reasons for this trend.

In the first place, the work load in a supermarket varies considerably over the week because of the extreme fluctuations in daily sales. More than 70 percent of weekly dollar sales of supermarkets occur from Thursday to Saturday, with Friday and Saturday usually accounting for more than one-quarter of the total weekly sales. (See Figure 2.) In addition, daily sales are heavily concentrated toward late afternoon. Therefore, the store manager uses part-time help to augment his staff during peak periods and utilizes a small core of full-time people to carry out the routine functions during the week.

The use of part-timers at the busiest hours in the market means a concentration of the least experienced and least attached employees when the most customers are being served. Furthermore, the turnover among part-timers is heavy and considerable cost is involved simply in the recruitment and training process. Thus supermarkets pay a cost for flexibility, but the nature of the business seems to be such that a high proportion of part-timers will continue to be a normal complement of the work force.

A second reason for the increasing use of part-timers has been the structure of wage rates under union contracts. In most union contracts until recently, there was a substantial differential between the rate per hour for a part-time worker and the rate for a full-time worker. This differential could result from the fact that the part-timer did not receive various fringe benefits, or his actual hourly rate might be lower, or the full-timer would have a higher rate because of longevity increases over the years. Furthermore, union contracts commonly provide that supermar-

---

39. Super Market Institute, *1970, op. cit.,* p. 26.

FIGURE 1.   *Supermarket Industry*
Full-time vs. Part-time Store Employees
Super Market Institute Members
1951-1970

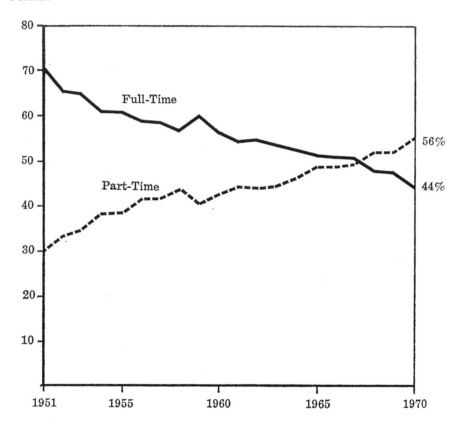

Reprinted from *The Super Market Industry Speaks 1970*, p. 26, by permission
of Super Market Institute, © 1970 by Super Market Institute, Inc.

FIGURE 2. *Supermarket Industry*
Distribution of Sales by Day of the Week
Super Market Institute Members, 1969

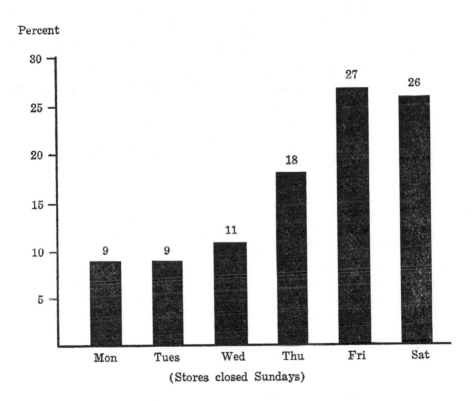

Percent

(Stores closed Sundays)

kets must pay overtime at one and a half times the base rate for hours worked after eight per day, as well as after 40 hours per week. Split shifts for full-time workers (4 hours on, 4 hours off, and 4 hours on) are generally prohibited.[40]

Because of this cost differential and the penalties for overtime work, unionized markets have sought wherever possible to use part-time help. The extent of the stimulus to such use presented by unionization is well illustrated by Super Market Institute's findings that the largest proportion of part-time workers were employed by the larger companies, which, as we shall note below, are the most heavily unionized.

In recent years unions have sought to restrict the freedom of management to utilize part-timers at the expense of full-time employment. One practice which a number of union contracts forbid is the so-called back-to-back hiring practice. Under this practice, supermarkets would employ one part-timer for four hours and then bring in another part-timer for four hours to fill out an eight hour day, rather than utilize a full-time worker. Likewise unions have sought to have the definition of a part-timer restricted so that a man who works, for example, 28 hours a week would be classified as a full-timer and would be entitled to full-time rates and benefits. Other contracts actually limit the ratio of part-timers to full timers permitted in the store complement. The increasing frequency of such provisions in union contracts may tend to reverse the prior relationship which existed between unionization and extent of part-time employment.

The third reason for the increased use of part-time help in supermarkets is the elongation of store hours which has occurred. Many markets are now open until midnight. Night shopping has become a commonplace. In many states supermarkets are open on Sundays. With so many hours to cover it becomes extremely difficult to schedule using only full-time people; part-timers are therefore brought in to fill in the needed hours in excess of normal full-time work loads.

Whether the increased use of part-timers will aid Negro employment is debatable. Large numbers of white students and housewives can work as part-time employees, and thus compete for jobs. Of course, some Negroes are similarly situated, but often locational factors, as we shall note, favor the whites, who

---

40. See Herbert R. Northrup and Gordon R. Storholm, *Restrictive Labor Practices in the Supermarket Industry* (Philadelphia: University of Pennsylvania Press, 1967).

TABLE 6.   *Supermarket Industry*
Turnover Rate among Store Employees by Sales Group
Super Market Institute Members
United States, 1968

Sales Group (In Millions)	Separations per 100 Employees [a]	
	Full-Time	Part-Time
Up to $2	25	79
$2 to $10	19	98
$10 to $25	31	98
$25 to $50	54	141
$50 to $100	37	84
Over $100	29	101
All companies	32	101

Reprinted from *The Super Market Industry Speaks 1969*, p. 26, by permission of the Super Market Institute, © 1969 by Super Market Institute.

Note: Most SMI members operate fewer than ten stores. This report is based on 365 companies operating 7,287 stores in 1968.

[a] Based on average employment in 1968.

are also likely to have superior educational backgrounds. Table 6 shows part-time personnel had extremely high turnover rates, averaging 101 separations per 100 employees, compared to 32 per 100 for full-time workers in 1968. Thus this could be an area where companies could rapidly increase their black employment. If, however, we assume that turnover among part-time black workers is as high as the average, it is unlikely that part-time employment would result in many permanent additions to the supermarket work force.

Unionization

The major chains, except for Winn-Dixie, are highly unionized; the smaller concerns often operate nonunion. The general unionization pattern is for the meat department employees to be unionized by the   Amalgamated Meat Cutters and Butcher Workmen, the balance of the store employees by the Retail Clerks International Association, and the drivers and warehousemen by the International Brotherhood of Teamsters. In some cases, however, either the Retail Clerks or Meat Cutters have "wall to wall" agreements covering all store employees, and in others all employees are represented by the Teamsters. In addition, the Retail, Wholesale and Department Store Union, a former CIO affiliate, represents some supermarket employees in the New York City area, as do some independent unions elsewhere.[41] In mid-1971, the Clerks and Meat Cutters began negotiating a possible merger. Both unions have substantial memberships in other industries, but supermarkets provide more than one-half of the 600,000 members of the clerks and almost that large a proportion of the 600,000 members of the Meat Cutters.[42]

Unionization varies by size of company, location, and department in the supermarket industry. A breakdown of unionization among member companies of the Super Market Institute in 1969 is shown in Figure 3. About 60 percent of these companies were unionized to varying degrees. Smaller companies and those located in New England and the Southeast were less likely to be organized, while nearly all companies having sales over $100 million and/or located in the Pacific region were unionized.

In more than one-half of the companies, all or some of the meat department employees were unionized, and about the same number had at least some unionized workers in other store departments, while 47 percent had some unionized part-time personnel. In over 70 percent of the companies with their own warehouses, nonstore employees worked under union contracts.

Union policies toward Negroes have varied considerably, but for the most part have been passive. Locals of the craft oriented Meat Cutters at one time opposed Negro employment, but more recently this union has aided the training of blacks.[43] The Clerks have generally been unconcerned, and have not opposed or promoted Negro employment. The Teamsters have welcomed Negro employment in warehouses and promoted educational programs for blacks, but have reacted unfavorably to Negro employment as over the road drivers.[44] We shall examine the union impact in more detail in later chapters.

---

41. *Ibid.*, pp. 33-41.

42. Data from union headquarters, 1971.

43. Training programs will be discussed further in Chapter VI.

44. See Herbert R. Northrup, *et al.*, *Negro Employment in Land and Air Transport*, Studies of Negro Employment, Vol. V (Philadelphia: Industrial Research Unit, Wharton School of Finance and Commerce, University of Pennsylvania, 1971), Part Three, pp. 64-67 for a discussion of IBT civil rights activities.

FIGURE 3.   *Supermarket Industry*
Extent of Unionization by Sales Group, Region, and Department
Super Market Institute Members
United States, 1969

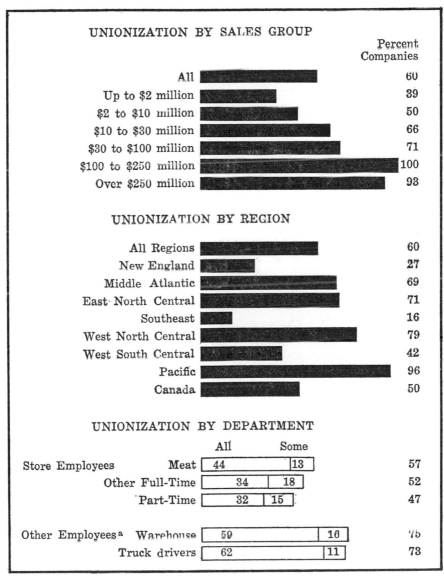

UNIONIZATION BY SALES GROUP

	Percent Companies
All	60
Up to $2 million	39
$2 to $10 million	50
$10 to $30 million	66
$30 to $100 million	71
$100 to $250 million	100
Over $250 million	93

UNIONIZATION BY REGION

All Regions	60
New England	27
Middle Atlantic	69
East North Central	71
Southeast	16
West North Central	79
West South Central	42
Pacific	96
Canada	50

UNIONIZATION BY DEPARTMENT

		All	Some	
Store Employees	Meat	44	13	57
	Other Full-Time	34	18	52
	Part-Time	32	15	47
Other Employees[a]	Warehouse	59	16	75
	Truck drivers	62	11	73

Reprinted from *The Super Market Industry Speaks 1970*, pp. 30-31, by permission of Super Market Institute, © 1970 by Super Market Institute, Inc.

[a] Companies with their own central warehouses.

Wages and Fringe Benefits

There is a wide disparity between wages paid in small grocery establishments and those paid in the large unionized supermarket company sector. Table 7 compares grocery store wage rates with those in other industry in 1960 and 1970. Although the average weekly earnings in 1970, $89.32, were higher than the average for retail industries, earnings are considerably below manufacturing industry wage rates. These data, however, substantially underestimate wages paid by the larger chain companies.

Within the supermarket, wages vary somewhat by department, with meat department employees generally receiving higher rates. Wages in excess of $3.00 per hour are now common for clerks, cashiers, and checkout clerks. In Chicago, contracts negotiated in December 1970 raised top clerks' wages to $186.80 per week. On the East Coast, where the highest rates tend to be paid in Washington, D.C., a contract effective August 22, 1971 called for rates of $179.32 per week for food clerks. The highest rates are paid on the West Coast, where nearly all large supermarket companies are unionized. Members of the RCIA in San Francisco have a contract which will raise clerk's hourly pay from $4.01 in 1970 to $5.26 in 1976.[45]

TABLE 7.   *Grocery Store and Other Industries*
Average Weekly and Hourly Wages and Hours Worked
Production or Nonsupervisory Workers, 1960 and 1970

Industry Group	1960			1970		
	Average Weekly Earnings	Average Hourly Earnings	Average Weekly Hours	Average Weekly Earnings	Average Hourly Earnings	Average Weekly Hours
Grocery stores a	$62.78	$1.72	36.5	$ 89.32	$2.74	32.6
All retail trade	57.76	1.52	38.0	82.47	2.44	33.8
All manufacturing	89.72	2.26	39.7	133.73	3.36	39.8
All industry	80.67	2.09	38.6	120.16	3.23	37.2

Source: U.S. Bureau of Labor Statistics, *Employment and Earnings, United States, 1909-70*, Bulletin 1312-7; and *Employment and Earnings*, Vol. 17 (March 1971), Table C-2.

a SIC 541-543: grocery, meat, and vegetable stores.

---

45. Data from labor relations managers, 1971.

The three major job categories in the meat department—head meat cutter, journeyman meat cutter, and wrapper—all generally are better paid than front end clerical and sales occupations. Meat cutter rates negotiated with the Amalgamated Meat Cutters in Washington, D.C., effective September 1971, call for wages of $241.60 per week for meat managers, $214.24 for journeymen, and $169.97 for wrappers. It should be noted that this latter position is largely a female, unskilled occupation. Meat department employees in Chicago have recently won similarly high rates. The head meat cutters' weekly earnings will jump from $177.00 to $237.00 over an 18 month period, to $12,350 per year. Journeyman meat cutters there will receive $226.00 and wrappers $152.00.[46] All of the wages are, of course, only part of a package which includes substantial fringe benefits.

Supermarket companies are increasingly offering attractive benefits and incentives to their employees. Of those companies in the 1970 Super Market Institute survey, 93 percent offered group health insurance plans and 89 percent had group life insurance. Retirement plans were in effect in 57 percent of these companies.[47] It should be kept in mind, however, that most companies provide these benefits only to full-time workers, so in many stores, less than one-half the workers might actually be covered by these programs.

Substantially more attractive benefits are paid in some regions. In Southern California, for example, health care programs for supermarket employees include psychiatric and dental care, and in other areas, vacations, holidays, retirement and other fringes compare favorably with manufacturing workers. Considering the lack of skill required by most supermarket employees, wages, working conditions, and benefits compare favorably with other industries. Moreover, increases now being generated may well make up for any past lags.

Labor Costs and Operating Profits

Despite many labor saving improvements which have been introduced during the course of evolution of the modern supermarket, the supermarket industry is still a labor intensive business. Labor costs constitute about 50 percent of the total store operating expense and about 80 percent of store variable operat-

---

46. Data from labor relations managers, 1971.

47. Super Market Institute, *1970, op. cit.*, p. 27.

ing costs. The performance of labor at the store level, therefore, is of critical importance in the maintenance of the narrow profit margins that characterize the industry.

The critical role of labor in store level operations is further enhanced by the fact that the supermarket business is a service business. The average customer shops two to three markets from time to time. The proliferation of markets has put a number of supermarkets within convenient range of most shoppers. As a consequence, if the shopper has to wait too long in line at the checkout counter of a particular food store or if the shelves are not properly stocked, she quickly takes her patronage elsewhere. Unlike a manufacturing business, there is no way that a super-market can contract for business for an extended period of time. The performance of its employees is measured every day in the market place and, if found wanting, the impact upon sales and profits is immediate and substantial.

Despite a continuous year-to-year increase in average hourly earnings, which presumably attract more competent employees to the industry, productivity at the store level, as measured by sales per man-hour, has not kept pace with rising wage rates. As a consequence there has been a steady rise in the proportion rep-resented by labor costs to total sales in supermarket operating companies.

From 1960 to 1970, sales per man-hour in supermarkets in-creased from $24.84 to $36.37.[48] When this increase in dollar value is adjusted for the change in retail food prices, it can be seen that productivity as measured by real output per man-hour increased at an average annual rate of only 1.5 percent.

From 1969 to 1970, sales per man-hour rose only about 5 per-cent while prices rose 6 percent so that there was an actual de-cline in physical productivity.[49] This trend is particularly dis-turbing to firms in the industry because the last few years have witnessed a marked change in the magnitude of wage adjust-ments with increases being negotiated in various areas of the country in amounts ranging from 10 percent to 30 percent per annum.

The result of the divergence between productivity, on the one hand, and wage rates, on the other, has been a steady climb in

48. *Ibid.*, p. 12; and *The Super Market Industry Speaks 1971*, **Twenty-**Third Annual Report (Chicago: The Institute, 1971), p. 2.

49. Super Market Institute, *1971*, *op. cit.*, p. 7.

store labor costs. Typical store labor expense in supermarkets increased from 7 percent of sales in 1959 to 8 percent in 1969. From 1969-1970 to 1970-1971 store payroll costs reported by retail food chains increased from 8.02 percent of sales to 8.17 percent.[50]

The retardation in the rate of improvement in productivity together with the continual decline in profit margins has led supermarket officials to put greater emphasis upon employee selection and training. Obviously, such concern for employee productivity can also have important repercussions upon ongoing programs aimed at employment of Negroes and other disadvantaged minorities.

TECHNOLOGICAL CHANGE

The decade of the seventies is likely to witness the introduction of three significant technological innovations in the supermarket industry. The changes in operating procedures and personnel requirements resulting from these innovations could have a significant impact upon opportunities for employment of Negroes in the supermarket industry.

Centralized Meatcutting

An increasing number of companies are establishing meat distribution warehouses for the central processing of meat. One recent survey found that 21 percent of chain organizations had meat distribution centers in operation, 11 percent had begun construction of a center, 42 percent had developed plans for a center, and only 10 percent had no plans for such a facility.[51] Such central facilities will cut, wrap, and ship to the stores either "primals" or so-called "knife-ready" meat, or in some cases retail packages ready for the customer. Obviously meatcutting and wrapping for a group of stores can be conducted more efficiently in one central facility permitting volume production and the use of mechanized equipment than in the back rooms of numerous stores. The spread of this development will, as a consequence, reduce the total number of meatcutting jobs in the industry—a

---

50. Super Market Institute, *1970, op. cit.*, p. 13; and New York State College of Agriculture and Life Sciences, *Operating Results of Food Chains, 1970-71* (Ithaca: Cornell University, 1972), p. 20.

51. K. V. Flood, "Meat Distribution Center Developments," *The National Provisioner*, February 6, 1971.

fact which is apparent to the Amalgamated Meat Cutters Union which is seeking to retard or control the rate of introduction of such facilities. Agreements concluded by some companies with this union provide for transferance by store level meat cutters to jobs at the central facility. The prospect of curtailment of jobs at the store level together with strict seniority provisions with respect to transfer to meat warehouse jobs will limit opportunities for new entrants—whether black or white—in the meat departments of supermarkets.

Automatic Warehouses

New equipment, which is now commercially available, promises to make possible major improvements in warehouse productivity. Automation is being applied primarily to the replenishment function, through the use of stacker cranes, and the selection process, through the use of picking platforms or sophisticated computer-controlled automatic release devices. Application of these innovations will be slow because in general they cannot be efficiently utilized in conventional warehouses and a new structure—often 40 to 50 feet in height—must be constructed to house the new apparatus.

The significant fact is that automated or semiautomated warehouses will sharply curtail the use of relatively unskilled labor formerly required to handle cases of merchandise and will increase the need for skilled operators of highly complex mechanical equipment. This could react unfavorably for Negroes who have limited education and background.

Automatic Checkout and the Universal Code

The automatic checkout depends upon a scanning device at the checkout which reads a code on merchandise and automatically records the price in the register. For maximum effectiveness the code must be applied by manufacturers. At the present time equipment is available for the scanning function and industry leaders are seeking ways to get common agreement among manufacturers, wholesalers, and retailers on the specifications for the code.

If the automatic checkout becomes a reality it will eliminate the need for price-marking at the store level and thus will reduce requirements for relatively unskilled labor in the store. However, this represents only a small percentage of the total work load in a supermarket. At the same time, the automatic features of the scanning and registering equipment would make possible the use of less skilled personnel in the checkout operation. With the addition of automatic changemakers, the previous requirement for ability by checkout personnel in simple arithmetic can be substantially reduced. The girl at the checkout becomes a handler of merchandise and a bagger rather than the operator of a calculating machine.

Whereas the advent of the central meat warehouse and the automatic grocery warehouse may reduce opportunities for employment of unskilled Negroes in the supermarket industry, the automatic checkout may, on balance, eliminate one of the barriers to such employment and make possible the employment of less skilled personnel at the front end. The impact of all three of these innovations will be felt only slowly in the industry because of the heavy costs associated with their introduction, but their influence should be reckoned with in any assessment of the long run opportunities for Negroes in the industry.

INDUSTRIAL LOCATION

Due to its essential nature, food stores are found in every community of the country. Both large supermarkets and small groceries are fairly well distributed, except that large supermarkets are becoming increasingly scarce in heavily black central city areas. (See discussion of black ownership in Chapter VII.) Of the nearly 300,000 food stores recorded by the 1967 Census of Business, 33 percent were in central cities, 26.1 percent in other metropolitan locations, and 40.9 percent in nonmetropolitan areas.[52] The South was characterized by more numerous smaller stores, averaging 7.7 employees per store in 1967, but other regions had only slightly larger stores, ranging from 10.5 to 11.4 employees per store.[53]

Employment Concentration

Supermarket company employment tended to be most heavily concentrated in central city areas, except in the South, where supermarket employment was more evenly distributed among all

---

52. *U.S. Census of Business, 1967*, BC 67-RA1, Retail Trade, Area Statistics, Tables 11 and 12.

53. *Ibid.*, Table 6.

locations. Table 8 shows the distribution among locations for the
various regions in 1967, taken from the sample constructed by
one of the authors. The South had the highest suburban concentration of employment, while the Rocky Mountain region had
the largest proportion of supermarket employment in nonmetropolitan areas, 29.3 percent of the total.

Except in the South, Negro population is concentrated in the
central cities of large metropolitan areas. Although the location
of Negro population appears to correspond well to the location
of substantial supermarket employment opportunities, the dispersion of the industry may result in wide variation in Negro employment, even among stores of the same company. Furthermore,
the concentration of supermarket employment in central cities
does not necessarily mean that the markets are located in the
sections of central cities characterized by predominantly Negro
population. As will be pointed out in subsequent discussion, the
lack of good public transportation from one part of a city to
another can act as an effective barrier to Negro employment.

Small towns and rural areas, outside of the South, are unlikely
to have many black workers in the labor force, thus leading to
lower national aggregates of black supermarket employment than
other factors, such as skill levels, would indicate would be the
case.

The Urban-Suburban Shift

Dr. Charles Perry's study of the department store industry,[54]
noted that there has been a marked exodus of department stores
from central city shopping areas to the suburbs, reflecting the
reaction of department store management to the problems arising from congestion, crime, riots, and other characteristics of
the central city economic and social environment. A somewhat
similar trend is evident in the supermarket industry, reflecting
these factors as well as circumstances peculiar to the supermarket
industry.

An increasing proportion of supermarkets are being opened in
shopping centers. The food shopper apparently enjoys the convenience of "one-stop" shopping. Supermarkets located in shopping centers generally report higher sales per square foot than
solo markets. In 1969, 66 percent of new supermarkets were con-

---

54. See the department store study in the Racial Policies of American
   Industry series, pp. 15-16.

TABLE 8. *Supermarket Industry*
Employment by Region and Location
Selected Chain Companies
United States, 1967

Location	Northeast		South		Midwest		Rocky Mountain		West Coast	
	Total	Percent Distribution	Total	Percent Distribution	Total	Percent Distribution	Total	Percent Distribution	Total	Percent Distribution
Metropolitan [a]										
Central city	58,689	55.4	41,965	36.8	52,705	42.5	6,989	42.7	18,474	30.1
Suburban	12,963	12.2	23,517	20.6	24,915	20.1	2,562	16.2	12,030	19.6
Other metropolitan [b]	18,442	17.4	27,345	24.0	25,795	20.8	1,927	11.8	23,715	38.6
Nonmetropolitan	15,903	15.0	21,238	18.6	20,654	16.6	4,806	29.3	7,185	11.7
Total	105,997	100.0	114,065	100.0	124,069	100.0	16,384	100.0	61,404	100.0

Source: Tables 24, 25, and 26.

[a] Metropolitan areas with 10 percent or more Negro population.

[b] Metropolitan areas with less than 10 percent Negro population.

structed in new shopping centers, up from 61 percent in 1968. Of the units erected in new shopping centers, about one-half were in large centers and about one-half in small centers.[55]

The significant fact about this gravitation of markets to shopping centers is that it reinforces the retail exodus to the suburbs. Few shopping centers are being constructed in central cities (except occasionally as part of an urban redevelopment project) because a shopping center typically requires a large expanse of land for parking and multibuilding construction and such large areas simply are not available at a feasible cost in central cities.

Secondly, the size of the typical supermarket is growing. Reference has already been made to the advent of the super supermarket. It is becoming increasingly difficult to operate economically a store of 15,000 to 20,000 square feet. Industry executives predict that over the next decade the face of the industry will change. Many of the medium-sized markets will go out of business and the industry will be increasingly composed of large numbers of both convenience stores and large markets of 30,000 to 40,000 square feet.[56] Obviously construction of markets of the latter size will be difficult in the congested areas of our central cities. The growth in size of supermarkets, therefore, is another trend which may to an increasing extent remove the supermarket from the locations in which most Negroes live and work.

As described more extensively in Chapter VII, relatively few new markets are being constructed in ghetto areas, while considerable numbers are being shut down—and in some cases burned down. The exodus of supermarkets from the ghetto is of far more serious concern to Negro employment than the urban-surburban shift, for the former removes employment opportunities from the very location where most Negroes would find it most convenient to work.

---

55. Super Market Institute, *Facts About New Super Markets Opened in 1969* (Chicago: The Institute, 1970), p. 8.

56. There is some dissent concerning the hypothesis that the average size of the supermarket will increase in the years ahead. For example, one observer predicts that the impending shortage of electricity in this country will lead to a reduction in size of markets. See *Advertising Age*, November 1, 1971, p. 88. Even if such a shortage should develop, however, it seems likely that a single market of 40,000 square feet would be a more efficient user of electric power than two markets each of 20,000 square feet.

It is obvious that the ubiquity of supermarkets should not mask the very real problems which location presents in terms of Negro employment in this industry. The importance of location will be more fully discussed in Chapters V and VIII. In the following chapter, factors affecting early Negro employment in food stores will be discussed.

CHAPTER III

Negro Retail Food Store Employment to 1960

Negroes have never been totally excluded from retail trade, and have in fact been shopkeepers as well as store employees since at least the 1800's, but in very small numbers. This chapter will examine the development of Negro employment prior to the enactment of the Civil Rights Act of 1964. For the earliest years, only localized studies are available which occasionally mention Negro grocery store merchants. From 1890, census data for retail dealers are available, and for 1940, 1950, and 1960, the census allows a closer look at occupations within the retail food store industry. Separate racial data in these years for supermarkets alone are not available.

EMPLOYMENT, 1800 TO 1940

There are only isolated data on the earliest Negro employment, but these indicate that shopkeeping, particularly grocery or provision stores, was an occupation of northern free Negroes before the Civil War. John Daniels' Boston study found a Negro-owned "provision shop" listed in an 1829 directory.[57] Constance Green's research on Washington, D.C. revealed that free Negroes operated shops and restaurants in that city in the pre-Civil War era, even in the face of city ordinances prohibiting Negro-run businesses.[58] A census survey of two states and two cities in 1850 listed 77 Negro "merchants" in Louisiana, 64 of them in New Orleans. It also showed 2 merchants in Connecticut and 3 in New York City.[59]

---

57. John Daniels, *In Freedom's Birthplace* (1914; reprint ed., The American Negro: His History and Literature Series, New York: Arno Press, 1969), p. 19.

58. Constance McLaughlin Green, *The Secret City: A History of Race Relations in the Nation's Capital* (Princeton: Princeton University Press, 1967), pp. 37, 43, 49.

59. U.S. Bureau of the Census, *Negro Population in the United States, 1790-1915* (Washington: Government Printing Office, 1918), Chapter XIX, Table 14.

It is obvious that the number of Negro-run shops was never very large. As Spear points out, of the few Negro businesses that did develop, most grew out of the traditional service pursuits of black workers, where they had experience and were able to fill accepted roles, and where a much smaller capital investment was required than would be necessary to stock a store.[60] Negro employment data in the latter half of the 1800's and early 1900's are as sketchy as earlier material, although several excellent studies of this period have been made.[61] According to Mrs. Green, the Washington ordinance against Negro businesses was abolished after Emancipation, allowing the growth of stores and shops. Some had two or three Negro employees as well and were patronized by white customers, although white merchants in the late 1800's did not employ Negro store clerks.[62]

In 1896, W.E.B. DuBois surveyed the Seventh Ward in Philadelphia, where 6,611 Negroes with "gainful occupations" lived. He found 4 male and 4 female grocery store merchants among 270 black "entrepreneurs" in the area; for comparison it should be noted that 4,889 of the 6,611 listed themselves as in "domestic and personal service" occupations.[63]

Early census data confirm that a very limited number of Negroes were merchants in grocery and related retail food business. Statistics for 1910 are shown in Table 9. The 5,550 Negro grocery store merchants and dealers comprised 2.8 percent of all such merchants in 1910.[64] No data are available on grocery store employment specifically, but in retail stores in general, the few Negro clerks and sales workers employed were far outnumbered by those working as laborers in such establishments, as Table 9 shows.

60. Allan H. Spear, *Black Chicago: The Making of a Negro Ghetto, 1890-1920* (Chicago: University of Chicago Press, 1967), p. 112.

61. See e.g., Green, *op. cit.*, Spear, *op. cit.*, as well as W.E.B. DuBois, *The Philadelphia Negro*, Political Economy and Public Law Series No. 14 (Philadelphia: Ginn & Co., 1899) ; George Edmund Haynes, *The Negro At Work in New York City* (New York: Arno Press, 1968) ; Lorenzo J. Greene and Carter G. Woodson, *The Negro Wage Earner* (Washington: The Association for the Study of Negro Life and History, 1930) ; and Richard R. Wright, Jr., *The Negro in Pennsylvania: A Study in Economic History* (1912; reprint ed., The American Negro: His History and Literature Series, New York: Arno Press, 1969).

62. Green, *op. cit.*, pp. 60, 89, 94, 132.

63. DuBois, *op. cit.*, pp. 104-108.

64. U.S. Bureau of the Census, *op. cit.*, Chapter XIX, Table 22.

TABLE 9. *Retail Trade and Grocery Store Industry*
Negro Employment by Sex and Occupation
United States, 1910

Occupation	Total	Male	Female
Retail dealers	20,653	17,659	2,994
Grocery merchants and dealers	5,550	4,564	986
Other food store merchants and dealers[a]	1,439	1,146	293
Clerks and sales workers in stores[b]	8,196	5,976	2,220
Laborers, porters, and helpers in stores[b]	37,576	36,906	670

Source: U.S. Bureau of the Census, *Negro Population in the United States,*
1790-1915 (Washington: Government Printing Office, 1918), Chapter XIX, Tables 19 and 22.

[a] Candy and confection, coffee and tea, delicatessen, fruit, milk, and produce
and provision stores.

[b] May include some workers in wholesale as well as retail stores.

Richard Wright reported two incorporated grocery companies
in Philadelphia in the first decade of the twentieth century, as
well as one department store and a bank.[65] According to Daniels,
groceries predominated among Negro-owned businesses in Boston
during this period. One company, Goode, Dunson and Henry, was
so large that it operated both as a retail store and as a wholesale supplier to small Negro grocery stores.[66]
    Census data in the next two decades indicate that Negro gro-
cery store dealers comprised less than 3 percent of the total, although the number grew from 6,339 to 7,547 during the period.
Negroes made up only about 0.7 percent of all sales persons and
"clerks" in all retail stores in 1920 and 1930.[67]

65. Wright, *op. cit.,* p. 86.

66. Daniels, *op. cit.,* pp. 369-370.

67. *U.S. Census of Population: 1920,* Vol. IV, Occupations, Chapter III,
Table 5; *1930,* Vol. V, General Report on Occupations, Chapter III,
Table 3.

NEGRO EMPLOYMENT, 1940 TO 1960

Census data after 1930 enable us to examine both total employment and major occupations within "food and dairy products stores." Table 10 shows total and Negro employment for 1940, 1950, and 1960 for this industry group.

Negro employment was a low 3.6 percent of the total grocery store industry employment in 1940, and the two ensuing decades reflect little improvement. By 1950 Negro employment had risen 0.7 percentage point (to 4.3) and by 1960 Negro employment amounted only to 4.6 percent, a rise of 0.3 percentage point over the 1950 decade and a rise of only one full percentage point for the entire twenty years. Negro employment, however, increased about twice as fast as total employment between 1940 and 1950, largely because of the threefold increase among Negro women workers.

Between 1950 and 1960, total employment declined slightly as over 100,000 males left the industry and were replaced by about 90,000 females. The very small increase in the overall Negro proportion resulted from change in opposite directions among Negro male and female workers relative to the total. There was almost no change in numbers of Negro men employed; thus their percentage of total male employment increased as white men left the industry. White women, however, entered the industry at a much faster rate than Negro women (in sharp contrast to the previous decade), thus bringing a drop from 4.0 to 3.8 percent in the Negro female proportion.

During the period from 1950 to 1960, structural changes in the grocery store industry may have contributed to the limited improvement in opportunities for Negro workers. A growing share of the market was captured by smaller concerns during this period, including members of cooperative and affiliated groups. Located in expanding suburban areas, employing local personnel, often starting with relatives and friends as the nucleus of their labor force, these companies were able to give customers personal service and respond more quickly than the corporate giants to the needs and opportunities in local areas. As a consequence, the independents made substantial inroads on the share of market held by corporate chains, even though total sales of the latter group continued to rise. Between 1949 and 1960 the share of total grocery store sales accounted for by the corporate chains fell from 41 percent to 38 percent. The share of unaffiliated in-

TABLE 10. Retail Food Industry
Employment by Race and Sex
United States, 1940, 1950, and 1960

Year	All Employees			Male			Female		
	Total	Negro	Percent Negro	Total	Negro	Percent Negro	Total	Negro	Percent Negro
1940	1,489,303	53,483	3.6	1,206,548	47,157	3.9	282,755	6,326	2.2
1950	1,719,403	74,190	4.3	1,238,605	55,056	4.4	480,798	19,134	4.0
1960	1,691,982	77,014	4.6	1,121,656	55,568	5.0	570,326	21,446	3.8

Source: *U.S. Census of Population:*

1940: Vol. III, *The Labor Force*, Part 1, U.S. Summary, Table 76.

1950: Vol. II, *Characteristics of the Population*, Part 1, U.S. Summary, Table 133.

1960: PC (2) 7F, *Industrial Characteristics*, **Table 3.**

Note: Tables 10-13 are based on the census definition "Food and dairy product stores and milk retailing." This is more inclusive than the SIC 541-543 groups shown in Tables 4 and 7.

dependents dropped from 28 percent to 13 percent, but the share of affiliated independents rose spectacularly from 30 percent to 49 percent during this period.[68]

Although many observers viewed the rise of the affiliated independent as a healthy trend in the industry, from the point of view of the Negro seeking employment in the industry the net effect of the shift in market power and employment opportunities from the corporate chain to the independent was probably negative. The location of independent-operated stores, the tendency of state fair employment law enforcement agencies to concentrate attention on larger companies (as they and their federal counterparts still do), and the decentralized policy determinations of independents with respect to hiring all combined to restrict employment opportunities for Negro personnel.

Increases in Female Employment

By 1960, women comprised 33.7 percent of total employment, up from 20 percent twenty years earlier. The rapid increase in Negro female employment in the decade of the forties and the stagnation during the fifties appears largely the result of labor market and locational factors. First, the use of women as checkout clerks or cashiers became firmly established during World War II and it was only natural to hire Negro women to fulfill this function, at least in black neighborhoods. At first there was little disposition to use Negro women elsewhere; but as more and more states enacted fair employment practice legislation, supermarkets, particularly in the northern cities, began to employ black female clerks and cashiers. The industry's disposition to do so was furthered by the changing urban labor supply, as the white middle class left cities to dwell in the suburbs and Negro migrants from southern agriculture took their place as urban dwellers.

This out- and in-migration of population, which gathered momentum during the 1950's, affected the locus of supermarket operations which in turn limited the opportunities for Negro female help. An increasing proportion of new supermarket construction was located in suburban towns and in shopping centers on major highways on the outskirts of metropolitan areas. At the same time, older stores in the cities declined in sales and

---

68. Herbert R. Northrup and Gordon R. Storholm, *Restrictive Labor Practices in the Supermarket Industry* (Philadelphia: University of Pennsylvania Press, 1967), Table 2-1, p. 12.

many were closed. Supermarket operators in these new locations found that suburban women and students provided excellent help; the black city dweller tended to look for work closer to home. As a result, although Negro female employment in the grocery store industry rose from 1950 to 1960, it did not increase as rapidly as total female employment, and the Negro female proportion fell to 3.8 percent.

Regional Variations

Some interesting differences are revealed when employment data are broken down by region for 1940, 1950, and 1960, as Table 11 shows. The Northeast, Midwest, and West were characterized by consistent growth in male and female Negro employment, and in one, the Northeast, this occurred while total industry employment actually declined over the two decades, as men left the industry faster than they were replaced by women. In the Midwest, Negro employment grew steadily, though slowly, despite an employment drop between 1950 and 1960. The West Region had steady employment growth in all sectors over the twenty-year period.

The employment picture during this period in the South was quite different. Total employment increased from 1940 to 1960. From 1950 to 1960, however, both Negro men and women declined numerically and proportionally in the industry—male employment declined from 10.1 to 9.9 percent, and female employment from a high of 9.2 to 7.3 percent. This trend was probably a corollary to developments in other regions, since it occurred during the period of Negro northern migration.

KEY OCCUPATIONS, 1950 AND 1960

As was pointed out in Chapter II, the jobs of manager, cashier, and meat cutter represent three numerically important occupations in the industry. Therefore, it is useful to examine data which give some indication of the trend of employment of Negroes in these key positions. Census data cast some light upon the changing status of the Negro in these occupations prior to 1960. The statistics must be interpreted with care, for they relate to the grocery store industry as such and therefore include thousands of small grocery stores as well as supermarkets. Obviously the content of the job of manager in the two kinds of

TABLE 11. *Retail Food Industry
Employment by Race and Sex
Four Regions, 1940, 1950, and 1960*

Region		All Employees			Male			Female		
		Total	Negro	Percent Negro	Total	Negro	Percent Negro	Total	Negro	Percent Negro
Northeast	1940	508,101	6,710	1.3	424,007	6,017	1.4	84,094	693	0.8
	1950	515,834	11,488	2.2	398,214	9,306	2.3	117,620	2,182	1.9
	1960	458,689	13,846	3.0	319,030	10,256	3.2	139,659	3,590	2.6
South	1940	366,533	39,891	10.9	303,187	35,530	11.7	63,346	4,361	6.9
	1950	491,927	48,568	9.9	354,178	35,944	10.1	137,749	12,624	9.2
	1960	512,180	46,460	9.1	346,005	34,333	9.9	166,175	12,127	7.3
Midwest	1940	451,555	6,379	1.4	349,703	5,194	1.5	101,852	1,185	1.2
	1950	501,508	12,086	2.4	335,503	8,266	2.5	166,005	3,820	2.3
	1960	477,672	14,167	3.0	294,507	9,627	3.3	183,165	4,540	2.5
West	1940	163,114	503	0.3	129,651	416	0.3	33,463	87	0.3
	1950	210,134	2,048	1.0	150,710	1,540	1.0	59,424	508	0.9
	1960	241,147	3,082	1.3	163,049	2,295	1.4	78,098	787	1.0

Source: *U.S. Census of Population:*

1940: Vol. III, *The Labor Force,* Part 1, U.S. Summary, Table 77.

1950: Vol. II, *Characteristics of the Population,* Part 1, U.S. Summary, Table 161.

1960: PC(1) 1D, *United States Summary,* Table 260.

establishments is quite different and may require quite different skills and competence.

Negro Managers

The data in Table 12 show that the number of salaried managers increased by about 6 percent during the decade of the 1950's and that self-employed managers declined by about 42 percent. These changes reduced the numerical superiority of self-employed managers from almost 4 to 1 in 1950 to 2 to 1 in 1960.

The miniscule growth in salaried managers was limited to white males, while the Negro group registered losses in both sexes. Both Negroes and white women experienced absolute numerical declines as well as relative declines in this classification. The proportion of salaried managers who were black was already low (2.0 percent in 1950), but the declines among both males and females during the 1950 decade reduced that percent to 1.3 percent in 1960.

The changes in the self-employed manager category detailed in Table 12 explain, to a large extent, the 1950 to 1960 reduction in total industry employment of white males noted in Table 10. Male self-employed managers declined to 133,757 between 1950 and 1960 while industry-wide male employment was declining 116,949. (Compare Tables 10 and 12.) Some of the former entrepreneurs no doubt remained in the industry as salaried managers or clerks, but the increasingly popular practice of hiring women as clerks together with the paucity of openings in managerial ranks probably forced the formerly self-employed managers to seek work in other industries.

As was pointed out in Chapter II, the period from 1940 to 1960 was marked by a substantial decline in the number of store units, partially as a result of acquisitions and mergers, but mostly as a consequence of the advent of the large supermarket which could serve an area formerly supplied by many small independent grocery stores. Some of the formerly self-employed managers left the industry entirely, while others became salaried employees of larger companies. The trend to replacement of the small grocery store by the modern supermarket was slowed in the core city areas because of lack of available land space to accommodate the large building and parking lot which were essential to supermarket operation. As a result, the small grocery store survived and continued to fulfill a useful function in the inner city. Many

TABLE 12. *Retail Food Industry Employment by Race and Sex Three Occupations, 1950 and 1960*

Occupation	Year	All Employees			Male			Female		
		Total	Negro	Percent Negro	Total	Negro	Percent Negro	Total	Negro	Percent Negro
Managers, officials, and proprietors										
Salaried	1950	98,400	1,920	2.0	85,890	1,290	1.5	12,510	630	5.0
	1960	104,286	1,336	1.3	94,849	955	1.0	9,437	381	4.0
Self-employed	1950	379,560	14,520	3.8	309,150	8,640	2.8	70,410	5,880	8.4
	1960	218,903	8,740	4.0	175,393	5,238	3.0	43,510	3,502	8.0
Meat cutters [a]	1950	167,700	6,420	3.8	164,010	6,300	3.8	3,690	120	3.3
	1960	180,302	7,391	4.1	174,955	6,724	3.8	5,347	667	12.5
Sales clerks	1960	499,936	17,976	3.6	270,788	9,812	3.6	229,148	8,164	3.6

Source: *U.S. Census of Population:*

1950: Vol. IV, Special Reports, *Occupational Characteristics*, Table 3.

1960: PC(2) 7A, *Occupational Characteristics*, Table 3.

[a] Meat cutters include about 13 percent non-food store employment.

of these establishments were Negro-operated. Consequently, as the data in Table 12 indicate, Negroes increased their proportion among self-employed managers even though their numbers declined.

The high proportion of Negroes among female self-employed managers in both 1950 and 1960 probably reflects only the greater likelihood of these women working, for the numbers were small in both years. Negro female self-employed managers declined to 3,502 in 1960, less than 2 percent of all such managers. Practically all of the stores represented in this category were probably small food stores in predominantly black neighborhoods in inner city areas.

Negro Meat Cutters

The figures in Table 12 for meat cutters must be interpreted with caution. In the first place, they are not limited to food store operations. They actually include all persons in this category of occupation in establishments other than slaughterhouses and packing houses. About 13 percent of the employment is estimated to be in non-food store establishments. Thus in 1950, meat cutter employment specifically in food stores is estimated to have been about 146,000 of the 167,700 total employment as shown in Table 12.[69] Furthermore, there may also be some misclassification of personnel as a consequence of which women working as wrappers and weighers in meat departments have been included in the meat cutter category, even though their jobs are relatively unskilled and do not normally represent an apprenticeship stage in a meat cutter training program.

Meat cutter employment was overwhelmingly male in 1950 and remained so throughout the decade. The decade opened with men holding over 97 percent of the jobs and closed the same way. Total meat cutter employment increased by 7.5 percent between 1950 and 1960.

Negro meat cutter employment grew about twice as fast and thus increased from 3.8 to 4.1 percent. Although Negro men merely retained their position among male meat cutters, it is obvious from the figures that there was a substantial increase in the number of Negro women working in meat departments. Be-

---

69. See *U.S. Census of Population, 1950*, Vol. IV, Special Reports, *Occupation by Industry*, Table 2. For 1960, the comparable figures are 155,031 employment in food stores compared to 180,302 total employment. *U.S. Census of Population, 1960*, PC (2) 7C, *Occupation by Industry*, Table 2.

tween 1950 and 1960, the percentage of female Negro workers in this category rose over 450 percent from 3.3 to 12.5 percent of the female workers. Since the number of women in this general category is relatively small compared to men, the gain by Negro women had relatively little effect on the overall black proportion in this occupational category.

Negro Food Store Clerks

Clerks, check-out clerks, and cashiers comprise the largest single occupational group in the retail food industry. According to Table 12, they numbered almost one-half million in 1960. This amounted to almost 30 percent of total industry employment shown in Table 10 for 1960. If Negroes are to achieve a significant level of employment in the industry, it is clear that they must attain a high level of employment as sales clerks. They had not done so by 1960; both Negro men and women accounted for only 3.6 percent of both male and female employment in this category.

Overall Distribution, 1960

Table 13 gives the total and Negro distribution among the three occupations mentioned above, and all other occupations, in 1960. It is evident that Negroes were underrepresented in each occupation and in the industry as a whole, compared to their representation in the general population in 1960. Moreover, even given the inadequate level of Negro employment generally in the grocery store industry, that employment was not distributed among the various occupations in the same way in which total industry employment was distributed. For example, 6.2 percent of all industry employment was in the salaried managers category, but only 1.7 percent of Negro employment in the industry was found in this occupation. A similar situation existed for sales clerks, where almost 30 percent of all employment was found, but only 23.3 percent of black employment.

The "all other" occupation accounted for 40.7 percent of industry employment, but 54.0 percent of Negro employment. The concentration of Negroes here arises from the fact that the "all other" occupation was primarily composed of office workers and warehouse workers. The Negroes were in the warehouses, not the offices, and it can correctly be inferred that the warehouses were heavily black.

TABLE 13.   *Retail Food Industry*
Employment and Percent Distribution by Race and Occupation
United States, 1960

Occupation	All Employees			Negro Employees		
	Total	Percent Distri-bution	Total	Percent Negro	Percent Distri-bution
Salaried managers	104,286	6.2	1,336	1.3	1.7
Self-employed managers	218,903	12.9	8,740	4.0	11.4
Meat cutters	180,302	10.7	7,391	4.1	9.6
Sales clerks	499,936	29.5	17,976	3.6	23.3
All others[a]	688,555	40.7	41,571	6.0	54.0
Total	1,691,982	100.0	77,014	4.6	100.0

Source: Tables 10 and 12.

[a] Primarily clerical and blue collar occupations.

From the vantage point of 1960, the outlook for Negro employment in the decade ahead did not seem promising. During the entire period from 1950 to 1960 there had been little improvement in the relative position of the Negro in the grocery store industry. Furthermore, looking ahead into the future, there did not seem to be any industry developments which would cause black employment to grow more rapidly than it had in the past. Even in the meat departments where gains had been made, their position seemed precarious. Industry plans to centralize meat-cutting in meat warehouses seemed to pose a threat of reduced overall employment which would limit opportunities for Negro employment and advancement in this phase of supermarket operations.

Despite this unpromising outlook, the decade of the sixties resulted in a marked improvement in the status of the Negro in the supermarket industry. The circumstances which brought about this change will be examined in more detail in the following chapters.

CHAPTER IV

Negro Supermarket Employment, 1960 to 1970

The decade of the sixties was marked by direct action on the part of Negro and various civil rights groups in support of the drive for equal employment opportunities for Negroes and other disadvantaged groups in the labor market. It is not surprising that a major thrust of such activity was directed against supermarkets. Whereas the plants or headquarters offices of many industrial companies were remote from the centers of civil rights agitation, supermarkets were abundant in large cities, their employment policies were visible even to the casual shopper, and their operations were vulnerable to consumer picketing. In black neighborhoods, supermarkets were frequently the targets of riot activity in those cities which experienced racial upheavals during the 1960's.

The latter half of the decade was characterized by a tight labor market, a situation which generally tends to improve Negro employment opportunities in industry at large. We would therefore expect this trend to be reflected in employment statistics in the supermarket industry, particularly in view of the low skill requirements and high turnover rates which characterize many of the jobs in the industry.

This chapter will examine the changing trend in Negro employment from 1966 to 1970 as evidenced by statistical data provided by the U.S. Equal Employment Opportunity Commission and from a survey conducted by one of the writers. In addition, observations are made concerning the trend in Negro employment in the early seventies, based upon interviews with key companies in the supermarket industry.

SUPERMARKET INDUSTRY DATA

The data referred to in this chapter, unlike the census data examined previously, are more directly related to supermarket operations and exclude small independently operated grocery stores. Although in terms of numbers there are still more small grocery stores in the nation than supermarkets, the majority of employment in the retail food industry is provided by the supermarket segment of the industry. Moreover, this portion of the industry is continuing to grow at the expense of the small grocery store. It is the assumption of this study that the racial employment policies with the most significant impact upon the Negro will emanate from the supermarket industry and in particular from the portion of the industry which is represented by corporate chains and multistore owners.

EEOC data for 1966, 1967, 1969, and 1970 provide the basis for an analysis of overall racial employment trends in the industry. The data cover the entire category of SIC 54: Retail Trade-Food Stores, but almost exclusively represent employment in supermarket chain and multistore companies of various sizes and in especially large independent supermarkets, because only companies with 100 or more employees are required to report to the EEOC. Some companies operating chains of "convenience" stores may also be included. It is believed, however, that supermarket employment statistics dominate the EEOC data. The data are companywide, that is, executive headquarters, warehouse, food processing, and store employment are combined in these tables.

A second group of statistics, used in the following chapter, is based upon selected chain supermarket employment figures from a sample constructed by one of the authors. These data permit a closer look at differences within the supermarket industry, such as variations for store location, than EEOC data can provide. They are, however, limited as to time, since the sample was obtained in 1967. Field investigation conducted in 1971 suggests that a marked change has occurred in the intervening years in the attitude of many supermarket companies toward Negro employment as a result of external social and governmental pressures. Therefore, the 1967 figures should not be interpreted as an index of current employment practice. Taken together, the two groups of data provide for the period of the mid- and late 1960's a fairly clear picture of the status of Negro employment in the supermarket industry, both as to developing trends and regional variations.

EMPLOYMENT OVERVIEW, 1966-1970

Census data indicated that Negro employment in the entire retail food industry had increased very little between 1940 and 1960, and stood at a low 4.6 percent at the beginning of the 1960's. It might be assumed that the supermarket segment of the retail food industry employed a substantially higher proportion of Negro workers, because of such factors as the greater size of stores, company image or visibility in the community, or store location. The data in Table 14, however, indicate that this was not the case. For whatever reasons, supermarket companies and other large food store employees reporting to the EEOC had an aggregate Negro employment level of just 5.0 percent in 1966.

Our occupational discussion must exclude 1966 because of widespread misclassification in that year. In 1967, Negro workers were barely represented in white collar occupations, including sales where most of the work force was concentrated, but more heavily represented among blue collar work. The proportions were 4.1 percent white collar, 9.7 percent blue collar, 5.5 percent overall in 1967. Both Negro men and women barely had a foothold in supermarket employment in mid-1960.

TABLE 14. *Supermarket Industry*
Total and Negro Employment by Major Occupational Group
Chain Companies and Large Independents
United States, 1966, 1967, 1969, and 1970

	All Employees			White Collar			Blue Collar		
Year	Total	Negro	Percent Negro	Total	Negro	Percent Negro	Total	Negro	Percent Negro
1966	583,997	29,149	5.0	92,461	1,249	1.4	491,536	27,900	5.7
1967	755,345	41,697	5.5	568,803	23,561	4.1	186,542	18,136	9.7
1969	731,048	47,295	6.5	558,167	27,773	5.0	172,881	19,522	11.3
1970	731,865	51,905	7.1	555,483	28,135	5.1	176,382	23,770	13.5

Source: Appendix Tables A-1—A-4.

Note: Employment figures vary to some degree because of reporting dfferences. See Appendix Tables for numbers of establishments represented.

Increasing Negro Employment to 1970

Negro employment increased in both blue collar and white collar occupations during the second half of the 1960 decade, despite apparent declines in overall employment in both of these occupational groups. Blue collar gains far outweighed those in the white collar occupations, the Negro proportion rising from 9.7 percent in 1967 to 13.5 percent in 1970 in the former, but only one percentage point, to 5.1 percent, in the latter. Gains in the lowest skill categories led to overrepresentation for both Negro men and women, and largely account for the overall proportions in this industry. The continuing exclusion of black workers from craftsmen jobs deserves a careful examination, as does the opportunities for advancement for lower level blue collar workers. Complete data on all occupational differences and trends will be discussed in detail after an examination of the employment process.

Significance of the Trend

As Table 14 shows, overall Negro employment increased from 5.0 percent of the total work force in 1966 to 5.5 percent in 1967, and to 6.5 percent in 1969 and to 7.1 percent in 1970. This slow but steady upward trend in representation of the Negro in the labor force of the industry is encouraging, but the adequacy of this performance cannot be judged without some consensus as to what would be a satisfactory goal. In 1970, Negroes accounted for about 11 percent of the civilian labor force in the United States.[70] Since the supermarket is found all over the United States, does this mean that the industry should seek to adjust its labor force so that 11 percent of employees are Negroes?

On the other hand, it is also a fact that the supermarket generally functions as a neighborhood institution. Most of its customers live within 2 to 3 miles of the store and many of its employees are drawn from the surrounding neighborhood. Does this mean that the standard of racial balance should be related to the city or to the neighborhood in which the particular market is located?

As we shall see from the discussion in this and following chapters, implementation of an affirmative racial employment policy

---

70. U.S. Bureau of Labor Statistics, *Black Americans: A Chartbook,* Bulletin 1699 (1971), p. 23.

in the supermarket industry is rendered complex because of the large number of geographically scattered outlets, the diversity in population mix which surrounds these outlets, and the relative immobility of Negro labor even within the boundaries of major cities.

But there is a second and even more difficult problem which faces the industry; that is to achieve an equitable distribution of Negroes in the various jobs which constitute the hierarchy of occupations in the supermarket industry. Managers cannot be trained overnight. Some entry jobs are more important than others for upward mobility in the job structure. Changes in these strategic jobs today could forecast important shifts in Negro representation in higher level administrative positions in the future. In the following sections we shall consider supermarket employment policies and practices which ultimately influence the number of Negroes who will be hired and their distribution in the job structure.

EMPLOYMENT POLICIES AND PRACTICES

A significant amount of hiring in the supermarket industry takes place at the store level, sometimes far from company headquarters or regional personnel offices. Although some smaller chains may perform the hiring function at company headquarters and larger chains may hire at division headquarters for all but remote stores, nevertheless the practice of permitting store managers considerable autonomy in hiring is common in the industry. As a consequence, broad policies initiated at the executive level with respect to minority employment practices are difficult to implement and control, as the number of decision makers expands to encompass all the store managers in a chain. Hiring decisions may be made by persons who have neither the time nor the training to make the most objective selection of employees and who may be even less able to apply affirmative action guidelines regarding minority hiring. Decentralized employment procedures may result in a lack of information about such guidelines in those cases where they do exist.

An individual store manager may feel that he is far more able to judge what employment policy is best for his store than staff men at remote headquarters, and since his income and progress depend heavily on the profitability of his own operation, he has economic motives not to discount his own judgment in anything which might affect store profits. Profits of supermarkets are razor thin and the various elements of store operating costs must be controlled to the second decimal point. A frequent complaint of store managers is that the president of the company makes speeches about hiring the disadvantaged and encourages store managers to add blacks and other minority groups to the payroll, but when the periodic report of store profits is due the standards for performance are unchanged. Promotion and recognition within American business—whether it be the supermarket industry or the automobile industry—still go hand in hand with profit performance, not with social consciousness, and typically it is the front-line manager—the store manager in the supermarket industry or the foreman in the plant—who is subjected to the conflicting pressures of hiring other than the best qualified help and of meeting budgeted profit goals.

Some chains have sought to ameliorate this problem by providing some sort of offset to labor cost at the store level when a manager hires a disadvantaged employee who will require special training. Thus one supermarket chain made no charge to stores for two weeks for the salaries paid to such employees; another chain instituted a sliding scale of charges pursuant to which no charge was made to stores for 3 weeks and then in succeeding weeks an escalating proportion of trainees' salaries was assumed by the stores. Such procedures are more likely to be applied when the hiring is done pursuant to a Manpower Development and Training Act contract with the U.S. Department of Labor, since the funding of such contracts provides a "kitty" which can be charged with the trainee's salary. When Negroes or other minority groups are hired in the normal course of business, however, such procedures are not generally utilized.

Several factors, most notably community pressures directed at company executives rather than store managers, are leading to more direction and control over the hiring of store employees from upper level executives. A greater interest in store level hiring, or a partial removel of this function to formal personnel departments could do much to insure that all hiring is done on a nondiscriminatory basis. On the other hand, it is simply impractical, and probably impossible, for a central personnel office to hire for hundreds of stores scattered throughout an area. The basic job of the central personnel office is to provide policy guidance and to train the managers in its utilization.

Sources of Employees

There is little formal recruitment in the industry. Practically all employment needs are met by persons who apply directly at the store, warehouse, or personnel office, either as walk-ins or referrals by employees or customers. Occasionally a chain will run a newspaper ad to staff a new store or to recruit meat cutters, who seem to be in perenially short supply. Such recruitment procedures (or lack of them) do little to alter the prevailing ethnic or racial composition of the work force. Employees or customers are most likely to refer friends for jobs and walk-ins tend to be people who live in the immediate area of the store. Nevertheless, observations certainly show that the racial composition of store employment is often different from that of a neighborhood in which it is located.

Special recruitment efforts directed at the black community and the assistance of community agencies and civil rights organizations have been used in conjunction with special training programs as well as in response to organized demands for increased black employment. These efforts, which have in some instances brought forth a large number of qualified applicants and in other cases have produced only disappointing results, will be discussed in later sections. One fact emerges clearly from interviews by the authors with a broad cross-section of the industry: the most effective recruiters of minority members of the labor force are other minority member employees. This pattern is not surprising. Studies have indicated that in the urban labor market most jobseekers learn of opportunities for employment through friends and relatives.[71] A company which is able to attract a nucleus of qualified Negroes and affords them opportunities for promotion on a fair and open basis is likely to be assured of a steady flow of Negro applicants.

Recruitment of employees with special qualifications for managerial positions has always been a difficult task in the supermarket industry. Some supermarket recruitment has been conducted at colleges throughout the country in search of graduates who are interested in a career in this business. Most companies have experienced considerable difficulty in attracting business and economics majors (the preferred degrees) from the larger, better known colleges and have therefore turned to re-

---

71. See U.S. Department of Labor, *Manpower Report of the President, January 1969* (Washington: Government Printing Office, 1969), p. 181.

cruiting at smaller schools. Very little recruiting effort, however, has been directed toward Negro institutions. In recent
years the pressure to find suitable Negro candidates for managerial and supervisory positions has led to renewed interest
among some chains in the graduates of Negro colleges.

Unfortunately, supermarket companies have found it difficult
to attract such Negro graduates to the industry. There is first
of all the problem of the image of the industry, discussed in
more detail below. The black college graduate who maintains a
satisfactory academic rating can choose among many attractive
offers. The prospect of lugging cases around a store as part of
his basic training is not likely to make him view the supermarket in an attractive light. A second—and perhaps more per-
plexing problem—is that Negro college graduates do not want
to work in stores in black neighborhoods. They do not want to
be "ghettoized;" they are aware of the problems of operating such
stores and they realize that the real opportunities for advancement lie in the new and larger markets which are generally in
the suburban areas. Thus, while on the one hand supermarket
concerns would like to hire Negroes who, after training, could
handle the problems which plague stores in black neighborhoods
and whose presence in such stores would answer the demands of
various action groups who demand that supermarkets in black
neighborhoods have black managers, the men who would have to
fill these jobs have a different viewpoint as to where opportunities
for their future lie. The fear that they may end up in a deter-
iorating store in a black neighborhood may account for the lack
of enthusiasm on the part of many black graduates to join the
supermarket business.

Although supermarkets offer reasonably good pay and attractive working conditions and benefits, the industry has for many
years found it difficult to attract qualified personnel, white or
black. Part of the problem rests in the fact that, to many people, employment in a supermarket conjures up visions of working
in the old grocery store—and it is a fact that the nature of the
labor functions required has not changed materially in the last
thirty years. To most applicants the industry has little glamor
and it does not convey the status of working in an institution
such as a bank, even though the take-home pay may be higher.

Apparently Negro males view the typical entry job in a supermarket as a low-paying position with little hope of advancement,
because they see few black faces among store managers and

middle management. By contrast, warehouse entry jobs, which also offer little promise of advancement but offer initial pay levels of about $4.00 per hour, have an abundant supply of applicants and as has already been pointed out, Negroes represent a high proportion of the total labor force in supermarket warehouses.

The supermarket industry must place more blacks in middle management positions if it wishes to attract qualified Negroes into entry level jobs at the store level. Without the promise of promotion, store level entry jobs in the supermarket industry are apparently viewed by Negroes as relatively unattractive "secondary market" type positions. Recent research has indicated that minority members of the labor force as well as the bulk of the poor in metropolitan areas tend to find work in the secondary labor market where jobs are characterized by low wages, irregular employment, poor working conditions, and low-status work. There are in effect two parallel labor markets, with the disadvantaged members of our society seemingly shut out of the primary market where the highest wages and maximum upward mobility prevail.[72]

It would certainly come as a surprise to most supermarket executives to learn that entry level jobs in the industry might be characterized as "secondary market" positions in the same category as jobs in hospitals, hotels, restaurants, and similar occupations which carry a low status in the job market. Supermarket employment is steady; the pay is adequate; the conditions of work are generally excellent. Nevertheless, its image is low and without reasonable possibilities of promotion it may very well present a dreary picture to the black applicant.

A common complaint made by supermarket executives with respect to Negro employees is that they are undependable; they may work for a few weeks and then disappear. The same phenomenon has been observed in the secondary labor market. According to one recent study,

the instability of secondary jobs is matched by the instability of the work force, with cause and effect difficult to disentangle. The high turnover rates among secondary workers can be seen as a response to the kinds of jobs available to them. The rewards of secondary employment are

---

72. See Michael Fiore, "On-the-Job Training in the Dual Labor Market: Public and Private Responsibilities in On-the-Job Training of Disadvantaged Workers," in Arnold Weber (ed.), *Public-Private Manpower Policies* (Madison: Industrial Relations Research Association, 1969), p. 102.

low and, therefore, the penalty for quitting or otherwise losing one's job is also low.[73]

The writers have talked to personnel directors in various companies who are at a loss to explain why they are unable to attract Negro applicants. Perhaps the industry needs to do a better job of research to determine how potential applicants view jobs in the particular company and in the industry in general. The fact is that today jobs in the industry—for both white and black—are very much in the primary labor market category. But there is a gulf between what *is* and what people *perceive*. If Negroes do not really believe that they can ever advance beyond menial positions in the industry, their conception of the job as falling in the secondary labor market category is understandable.

Qualifications and Testing

Store level entry jobs require reasonable neatness, an ability to meet the public, and a clear record insofar as can be determined. Since arrests are such a common factor in the black community, some supermarket companies have relaxed this standard, although they are likely to draw the line at convictions for other than minor offenses.

As far as tests are concerned, a radical change has occurred in the industry attitude toward and usage of tests as a pre-hire procedure between 1967, when this study was begun, and 1971 when interviewing was completed. In 1967 it was common practice to require that applicants for full-time store level positions perform satisfactorily on some standardized tests. Usually the test battery involved one or more of the following: a dexterity test, a general intelligence test, a mental alertness test, and/or an arithmetic test. Some chains did not become directly involved in testing but relied on tests administered by state employment offices. Other companies used the state tests themselves or utilized tests sold by various firms.

The growing recognition by management that such tests were frequently discriminatory against minority group applicants, a conclusion sustained by the United States Supreme Court in the *Griggs* case,[74] has led most companies in the industry to abandon

---

73. U.S. Department of Labor, *Manpower Report of the President, April 1971* (Washington: Government Printing Office, 1971), p. 97.

74. *Griggs* v. *Duke Power Company*, 401 U.S. 424 (1971).

tests as a pre-hire procedure. Tests are still used, however, as a measure of a particular skill which a job may require—such as ability to use a typewriter or a business machine. Likewise, companies still use testing as an aid in making decisions with respect to promotions for in-house personnel.

At first glance, it would appear that there are no rigid qualification standards which pose a barrier to Negro employment in store entry jobs in the supermarket industry. Generally, no prior skill is required and training is characteristically on-the-job. In actual practice, however, the minimum requirements of appearance, dress, and demeanor, which can be easily met by the white applicant, may cause trauma to some Negroes. The norms which are essential to supermarket operation may be the ones most difficult for the Negro to adapt to, involving as they do such personal matters as his manner of dress, speech, and the way he wears his hair. This problem is aggravated by the fact that some store managers, who have been directed to hire more Negro employees, will subconsciously look for Negroes who look, act, talk, and dress like whites.

In nonstore level positions, the minimum qualifications required for various jobs are also not generally restrictive. For warehousemen, for example, few qualifications are necessary other than strength and minimum reading and arithmetic ability. These employees must be able to follow directions, to read instructions, and to add small numbers on occasion. Stricter qualifications are generally unnecessary since these employees are not usually expected to move up the occupational ladder, although warehousemen do move up to warehouse supervisory jobs. Warehousing often has a 50 percent or more black ratio indicating that, on racial grounds, there can be little complaint about hiring standards.

Truck driver positions involve tests of driving skill, prior attested to by a driver's or chauffeur's license, plus a record of dependability. Since Negro applicants often have a history of prior arrests, some management officials are hesitant about entrusting large trailer trucks to Negro drivers. A number of large food chains, however, report satisfactory experience with them. In its Washington, D.C. division, Safeway Stores has raised its complement of Negro drivers to 60 percent of the total with satisfactory results. The Kroger Company reports a similar experience in Houston where over 50 percent of its drivers are black.[75] Ne-

---

75. Data provided by company executive.

groes employed by the U.S. Post Office Department (now the Postal Service) have for many years demonstrated their competence as tractor trailer and motor vehicle operators, so there is no reason why they should not be able to perform as well in the supermarket business.[76]

Some executives explained that the relatively poor representation of Negroes in the truck driver category was attributable not to unduly rigorous qualification standards but rather to a lack of available supply of applicants. As has already been mentioned, in some areas there is already a high percentage of Negro drivers, but in others a web of restrictions imposed by unions and management may present barriers to Negro entrance into this kind of employment. For example, many Teamster union contracts give part-time drivers the first preference to bid for full-time work when it becomes available, and there are few Negro part-time truck drivers. The reason is that the white driver has greater mobility and can move from company to company and support himself by picking up part-time work as it becomes available. The Negro driver, because of discriminatory barriers in various companies and industries, is less likely to risk this continual confrontation with hostile hiring offices. As a consequence, the vacancies in the ranks of full-time drivers tend to be filled by white part-time drivers. This circumstance illustrates how union contractual provisions which seem patently fair at first glance can nevertheless erect barriers to Negro employment because of the peculiar conditions affecting the employment and eligibility of the Negro applicant.

In the office and clerical area, employment standards are similar to those in other industries. Usually they encompass a high school diploma (although this requirement is now frequently waived), neat appearance, and proficiency on an office machine, particularly a typewriter, as demonstrated by a standard test. The relatively small percentage of black women employed in these jobs by supermarket companies is the result of a combination of factors: lack of adequate training on the part of applicants, competition of other concerns for their services, hesitation on the part of some employers to hire Negroes. Of considerable importance is the fact that information about job openings fre-

---

76. Herbert R. Northrup, *et al.*, *Negro Employment in Land and Air Transport*, Studies of Negro Employment, Vol. V (Philadelphia: Industrial Research Unit, Wharton School of Finance and Commerce, University of Pennsylvania, 1971), Part Three, pp. 43-46.

quently travels fastest by word of mouth; the girls already working in the office tell a friend about a vacancy. Unless affirmative action is taken by management to break this circle, the white group tends to perpetuate itself. Furthermore, many black female applicants are reluctant to work in a company where they will be the only Negro in the office or one of a very few. Supermarket executives have become cognizant of this problem and in the last few years have made considerable progress in breaking down the "lily-white" appearance of headquarters office personnel.

On the whole, and irrespective of what may have been the practice in the past, there is little evidence today that unduly rigorous hiring qualifications impose a barrier to Negro employment in the supermarket industry. If there are barriers, they must be sought in more subtle and complex practices and in the nature of basic demand and supply patterns with respect to the Negro community.

Screening Procedures

Applications for employment, whether obtained at the store level or at division or headquarters offices, are usually processed through a personnel office. The personnel office does little in the way of reviewing an applicant's background except to call one or two former employers to ascertain that the applicant was not dismissed from his former jobs. The application form is, of course, checked for discrepancies and to see that the applicant has not noted a felony charge. Frequently a retail credit check (and sometimes a criminal record investigation) is also used.

In recent years many supermarket companies have entered into Manpower Training Contracts with the U.S. Department of Labor pursuant to the Job Opportunities in the Business Sector (JOBS) plan. Such programs require the employment of disadvantaged members of the labor force under training schedules which typically run for six to nine months. Although some companies began with an altruistic purpose of seeking to help some of the least qualified applicants, most supermarket concerns found that some screening was absolutely necessary in order to prevent complete deterioration of the program. As had already been mentioned, supermarket companies operate on narrow profit margins and typically have a limited number of staff people available for consultation on personnel problems. Companies which hired Negroes with problems such as drug addiction and with emotional and attitudinal problems which interfered with their work perform-

ance found that they had neither the funds nor the staff to deal
with such situations. A number of executives in the industry
commented that they believed supermarkets were better suited to
deal with the "underemployed" than the unemployed—that supermarket personnel simply were not competent to take adults who
had never worked and teach them basic work patterns.

There is the further problem that in the supermarket industry
the penalty for poor performance is immediately seen and retribution may be swift. The effect of sloppy work by a trainee in a
manufacturing plant may not be observed for some time, but in a
supermarket improper pricing or discourtesy may immediately
raise the ire of a shopper. The customer is at the site of the
worker's performance and therefore the tolerance for error is
considerably reduced.

Sensitivity Training

Opinions differed among executives of supermarket concerns as
to the desirability of sensitivity training for white employees as
a prelude to a major program to hire Negroes. Many companies
felt that such sensitivity training for managers, supervisors, and
other executive personnel was necessary when they undertook
hardcore training programs with the U.S. Department of Labor.
For example, a large eastern chain put 100 executives from the
Chairman of the Board on down through a two-day program.
This company even persuaded the union business agents to participate in the sensitivity training course.

Other companies were more skeptical about the value of sensitivity programs, particularly when they consist of "one-shot"
presentations by outside consultants. One executive expressed
the view that singling out black employees as requiring special
handling or treatment tended to be counterproductive in that it
detracted from the dignity of the Negro employee and tended to
prejudice supervision against them.

Nevertheless most companies concurred that some kind of training or briefing of existing employees prior to introduction of
such programs was desirable. An influx of Negro employees is
likely to cause concern among white employees—and particularly
among white males—that their opportunities for promotion will
be curtailed. Management objectives and the value to the company in obtaining a loyal cadre of qualified Negro workers need
to be explained in order to insure an atmosphere of cooperation,
rather than one of distrust.

OCCUPATIONAL DIFFERENCES AND TRENDS

Table 15 presents data on Negro employment by occupation as a percent of total employment for 1967, 1969, and 1970. Black workers were far better represented among the low skill level blue collar jobs than in white collar positions. This is particularly unsatisfactory in light of the fact that the major occupation is sales, followed by managerial and meat cutting for men and clerical for women. Supermarket companies do have extensive warehouse and delivery operations which provide blue collar jobs, but these do not provide particularly major proportions of all employment, nor are they positions which generally lead to promotion to salaried jobs, except to supervisory levels in those departments.

Table 16 compares the occupational distribution of the black work force in 1970 with that of all workers in that year. It is clear that Negroes tended to be best represented in the least numerous jobs. In 1970, only slightly more than one-half of all black employees were white collar workers while over 75 percent of the industry's employment was in these occupational groups.

Officials and Managers

Almost 10 percent of the supermarket work force was in official and managerial positions in 1970 (Table 16). In addition to corporate executives, this category includes all the store managers and assistants which are numerous in the industry, particularly in the male segment, where 13.9 percent of all workers held official or managerial jobs in 1970. From 1967 to 1970, Negro workers advanced to these positions very slowly, as their proportion rose from 1.2 to 2.4 percent of the total (Table 15). Given the long period of development which leads to managerial positions, however, this increase is not insignificant. Any improvement in this category, as long as most such positions are filled from within the industry, will necessarily lag behind increases in the overall Negro work force. At the same time, Negro improvement in this area depends upon the availability of store manager openings to a large extent. Any decline in the total number of stores reduces these possibilities. Movement of stores to suburban locations may also affect the opportunities for would-be Negro managers, if there is greater reluctance to place Negroes at the head of stores with primarily white customers

TABLE 15. *Supermarket Industry*
Percent Negro Employment by Sex and Occupational Group
Chain Companies and Large Independents
United States, 1967, 1969, and 1970

Occupational Group	All Employees			Male			Female		
	1967	1969	1970	1967	1969	1970	1967	1969	1970
Officials and managers	1.2	2.0	2.4	1.1	1.9	2.3	2.1	3.8	4.1
Professionals	5.7	3.4	3.1	5.0	3.3	2.8	13.0	4.9	5.2
Technicians	6.9	7.6	4.5	6.6	7.2	5.2	7.6	8.5	2.7
Sales workers	4.7	5.4	5.5	5.2	5.9	5.9	3.8	4.8	4.9
Office and clerical	3.8	5.2	5.4	6.0	6.6	7.8	2.9	4.6	4.7
Total white collar	4.1	5.0	5.1	4.4	5.1	5.2	3.7	4.7	4.8
Craftsmen	3.4	4.3	6.2	3.4	4.3	6.2	4.3	4.4	4.8
Operatives	10.2	13.4	13.9	12.4	16.1	15.6	5.2	7.4	9.1
Laborers	11.5	13.9	18.3	12.7	14.6	18.8	5.9	10.4	16.3
Service workers	14.9	13.5	15.7	17.7	15.7	16.4	9.5	8.4	14.5
Total blue collar	9.7	11.3	13.5	10.6	12.2	13.9	6.6	8.1	12.1
Total	5.5	6.5	7.1	6.1	7.1	7.7	4.2	5.2	5.9

Source: Appendix Tables A-2—A-4.

TABLE 16. *Supermarket Industry*
Percent Distribution of Employment by Race, Sex, and
Occupational Group
Chain Companies and Large Independents
United States, 1970

Occupational Group	All Employees		Male		Female	
	Total	Negro	Total	Negro	Total	Negro
Officials and Managers	9.8	3.3	13.9	4.1	1.6	1.1
Professionals	0.5	0.2	0.6	0.2	0.2	0.2
Technicians	0.3	0.2	0.4	0.3	0.3	0.1
Sales workers	58.9	45.6	54.4	41.7	67.9	55.7
Office and Clerical	6.4	4.9	2.3	2.3	14.5	11.5
Total white collar	75.9	54.2	71.6	48.6	84.5	68.6
Craftsmen	5.7	4.9	8.1	6.5	1.0	0.8
Operatives	7.9	15.5	8.7	17.8	6.2	9.5
Laborers	5.7	14.7	6.9	17.0	3.3	8.9
Service workers	4.8	10.7	4.7	10.1	5.0	12.2
Total blue collar	24.1	45.8	28.4	51.4	15.5	31.4
Total	100.0	100.0	100.0	100.0	100.0	100.0

Source: Computed from Appendix Table A-4.

than to place them in stores in black or mixed neighborhoods. Intraplant mobility will be discussed further in a later section.

Professionals and Technicians

Negroes seem to have experienced decreases as a proportion of professional and technical occupations between 1967 and 1970. The percentage of black professionals went from 5.7 to 3.1 percent of the total, and of technicians, from 6.9 to 4.5 percent. These changes, however, actually reflect very small numbers, since taken together these two occupations employed less than one percent of the total work force in 1970 (Table 16). All professionals increased only slightly during this period and the number classified as technicians declined. The low number of Negroes who train for professional careers,[77] combined with the high demand for such people and the relatively less glamorous position the supermarket industry offers may help to explain the decreases in Negro technical and professional employment in this period.

Sales Workers

Sales work in the supermarket industry does not require particularly high skill or educational attainment, especially among the female checkout-cashier group, but employs over one-half of the industry's work force. Yet Negro employment lags far behind in this area, both as proportions of the total and in comparative distribution of black and white workers. In 1970, only 5.9 percent of the male sales force was Negro, and only 4.9 percent of female sales personnel, lower than the male and female Negro proportions of the total supermarket industry work force which stood at 7.7 and 5.9 percent, respectively. These proportions represent only small percentage increases over 1967 in both groups. The proportion of Negroes in sales work in the supermarket industry, though quite low, is higher than in the economy in general. Data compiled by the U.S. Bureau of Labor Statistics for the year 1970 indicate that Negroes and other minority races represented only 4 percent of all workers in sales occupations in that year.[78]

Since sales functions account for over one-half of all men in the supermarket industry and nearly 70 percent of women (Table 16), little real improvement can occur in the overall representation until Negroes make up a much larger proportion of sales workers. In 1970, both the male and female black work forces were less concentrated in sales than was characteristic of the total work force—each group lagging over 10 percentage points behind. Since these store clerk positions are the ones which lead to management ranks, this lag makes more difficult the task of securing better representation for Negroes in more responsible administrative positions in the industry.

---

77. About 2 percent of engineering students and 5 percent of technology students are black, according to a study by Robert Kiehl, *Opportunities for Blacks in the Profession of Engineering* (Newark: Foundation for the Advancement of Graduate Study in Engineering, 1970).

78. U.S. Bureau of the Census, *The Social and Economic Status of Negroes in the United States, 1970*, Special Studies, Current Population Reports, Series P-23, No. 38 (July 1971), Table 49, p. 61.

Office and Clerical Workers

Among the occupations, Negroes were relatively well represented in office and clerical jobs if one looks at the percentage distribution of total and Negro workers. The data in Table 16 indicate that 11.5 percent of all Negro women were in office and clerical positions compared to 14.5 percent for all female employees. Less than 5 percent of all female office and clerical workers, however, were black, despite the fact that most company national and regional headquarters are located in urban areas with high Negro populations. Yet the proportion in 1970—4.7 percent—does represent an increase over 1967. Furthermore, field research in 1971 indicates that the percentage representation of female Negro workers in such occupations is continuing to grow. Supermarket executives have learned that although Negro women often do not possess the necessary skills for such jobs, special training programs can yield valuable results. Some current efforts in this regard are discussed in a later section.

The exactly equal proportions of Negro men to all men in the clerical group (2.3 percent) may reflect Negro employment in warehouse operations. In 1970, 7.8 percent of all male clerical workers were Negro, up from 6.0 percent in 1967 (Table 15). Among the large proportions of Negro laborers and operatives in warehouses, some upgrading to the warehouse billing and other clerical positions may have occurred during this period.

Craftsmen and Operatives

The major jobs in the upper-level blue collar groups are meat cutter, truck driver, and warehouseman. The census data in Chapter III indicated that only about 4.1 percent of all meat cutters were Negro in 1960. It is not possible to distinguish meat cutters among the 1970 EEOC occupational data, but Negroes did hold a very high proportion of the operative jobs, 13.9 percent, some of which were meat cutters (Table 15). Among craftsmen, however, they were only 6.2 percent of the total in 1970. Both categories reflect increases over 1967.

Relative Negro employment in these occupations can be seen in the percentage distributions for 1970 in Table 16. Negro workers were far more concentrated in operative positions, where 17.8 percent of all Negro men and 9.5 percent of Negro women worked, than the total work force, which was only 8.7 and 6.2 percent operative. The male proportions especially should be noted in this regard. Clearly Negro men had little difficulty getting operative jobs in the industry, for this was one of the most heavily Negro among the male occupations.

Although these data do not reveal whether Negroes held disproportionately more of the warehouse and other lower skilled and lower paid operative jobs and fewer truck driver or store meat cutter ones, our field work and observations clearly indicate this to be the case. Past employment policies of companies, craft orientation of Meat Cutter and Teamster local unions, and opposition of white workers have all played a role in keeping these better jobs heavily white. There is evidence of change, to be sure; but generally speaking, the warehouse remains heavily black, the meat department and the truck drivers, white.

Laborers and Service Workers

Little more than 10 percent of the supermarket work force is found in laborer and service occupations in stores and warehouses, but these are disproportionately heavily Negro—over 25 percent of all black workers were found in these two groups in 1970. Both groups had Negro proportions over twice as high as their representation in the industry as a whole. Clearly, if Negroes were not so overrepresented in these positions their overall representation in the industry would be much lower.

In terms of improving Negro employment opportunities, it would be desirable to see considerable upgrading from these two occupational groups, but this does not seem to be occurring, judging by Table 15. It is, however, difficult to assess any trend from the EEOC data because of possible misclassifications in this category. EEOC definitions state that service workers include: night watchmen, janitors, porters, snackbar waitresses, cooks, charwomen, and utility clerks. Very few personnel are employed in these categories by most supermarket concerns. Indeed, spot checks made by one of the writers in 1971, which involved reviewing employment records in detail, suggest that employment in this category in the supermarket industry does not normally exceed 2 percent. Yet the data displayed in Table 16 indicate that almost 5 percent of all workers were classified as service in 1970. Part of the problem may rest with the rather ambiguous classification of utility clerk which probably has different meanings in different parts of the country. In any case, it is dangerous to draw any broad generalizations as to trend in this category although it is apparent that Negroes are heavily represented in such jobs.

THE PROCESS OF UPWARD MOBILITY

A large supermarket may employ from 50 to 100 men and women, but the store has only one manager. Although at first glance it might appear that opportunities for advancement are slim, this is not true. There are a large number of intermediate positions of substantial responsibility in a large market: head clerk, department manager, assistant manager, and so forth. Furthermore, the supermarket frequently is the training ground for persons who will fill various staff functions, such as purchasing and personnel, as well as for line supervision.

As has already been pointed out, one of the major challenges facing the supermarket industry is to achieve a better distribution of Negroes in various management functions throughout the company structure. Until this is done, until the Negro clerk can see black faces in management, he is likely to view the job as a deadend position.

It is therefore important to understand how the process of upward mobility works in the industry. Since the store is the heart of the business, we shall direct our attention to this unit of operation, although obviously there are also promotional opportunities in the warehouse and in processing plants. We have seen that entry requirements should not be barriers to Negro employment. In the following discussion we shall review training and promotion procedures with a view to ascertaining their impact upon the upward mobility of Negro employees.

Company and Academic Training

Most of the training and instruction in the supermarket industry is conducted on-the-job, but in recent years an increasing number of concerns have adopted formal training programs for at least some categories of their employees. Such instruction may be given at headquarters or at store level but is part of a structured program which is usually controlled through the personnel office.

A study conducted by Super Market Institute of the training practices of its member companies revealed that, in 1970, 51 percent of the companies provided formal training for at least some of their personnel.[79] As can be seen from Table 17, there has

---

79. Super Market Institute, *The Super Market Industry Speaks, 1970,* Twenty-Second Annual Report (Chicago: The Institute, 1970), p. 29.

TABLE 17. *Supermarket Industry*
Formal Training Courses for Store Employees
Super Market Institute Members
Selected Years, 1955-1970

Employee Group	Percentages of Companies			
	1955	1959	1967	1970
Checkers	25	30	36	41
Baggers	13	18	21	28
Store managers	16	16	25	28
Meat personnel	13	17	26	27
Produce personnel	19	17	22	23
Grocery clerks	14	14	18	19
Store manager candidates	n.a.	15	18	16
Any training course	32	37	43	51

Reprinted from *The Super Market Industry Speaks, 1970*, p. 29, by permission of the Super Market Institute. © 1970 by Super Market Institute, Inc.

been a consistent increase over the years in the percentage of companies conducting such courses for various categories of employees. Most of the courses are for new employees, but a substantial proportion are for old employees, particularly in the case of store managers and produce personnel.[80]

Although such training programs are generally conducted by company personnel, many companies—and particularly smaller concerns—take advantage of courses given for specific job functions by wholesalers, manufacturers, trade associations, and educational institutions. The Super Market Institute itself has developed a well-rounded curriculum of courses and seminars for employees of member companies.

Most companies have a structured program for training future store managers which combines formal off-the-job training with rotation among the various departments of the store. For example, a college graduate who enters a store manager training program can advance from clerk to assistant manager in about two years, if he demonstrates the necessary aptitudes and qualifications along the line. The same progression might take an

---

80. *Ibid.*, p. 29.

ordinary clerk without special educational or other qualifications about five to seven years.

Employees, including store managers, are encouraged to complete home study courses in food retailing. A series of books and courses prepared for home study by Cornell University under the sponsorship of the National Association of Food Chains now take employee-students through a variety of subjects ranging from food retailing to business law. In order to encourage participation by employees in such home study work, a number of companies underwrite part or all of the cost of this seven-part course.

The increasing professionalism in management positions in the industry has been assisted by the establishment of programs leading to degrees in food distribution and marketing in several academic institutions. The first was Michigan State University in 1953, followed by Cornell University and the University of Southern California. Western Michigan University added food distribution to its Distributive Education program under both a four year co-op plan equivalent to two years of college and a regular degree program. St. Joseph's College (Philadelphia) established the Academy of Food Marketing in 1962 and offers a regular degree with a major in food distribution.[81] The number of Negroes enrolled in these various academic courses is quite small.

A number of the larger companies in the industry offer extensive scholarship support for academic training. For example, each year the Jewel Companies offers thirty $750 scholarships to high school seniors who are currently part-time Jewel employees and who agree to work for Jewel the summers following their freshman and sophomore years, for which they earn about $1,000 each summer. Jewel also has a separate $750 per year plan for full-time employees who have completed three to six semesters of work toward a degree and who plan to enroll in a full-time college program the following fall.

There is nothing in the structure of training and instruction in the industry which should impede the upward mobility of blacks to positions of responsibility. The problem is not with the process but with people and attitudes. These problems are not one-sided; they rest with both the Negro employee and his white supervision.

The typical Negro employee works under considerable psychological pressure. He realizes that everyone is watching him. This

---

81. "Specialized College Training to Shape Future Industry Leaders," *Progressive Grocer*, April 1962, pp. 92, 96.

sometimes creates an air of overdefensiveness, but more importantly may lead him to refrain from asking questions when he is faced by a problem which he cannot solve. Too often a Negro will fail to perform satisfactorily in a position because he was afraid to ask a few simple questions which he feared would disclose his lack of knowledge. Supervision must understand that the process of communication is not easy between black and white and that failure of lines of communication can set up as serious barriers to promotion as discriminatory tests. Surprisingly, an equally serious communications problem frequently exists between a black manager and black employees. For example, in a black-owned market chain in Los Angeles it was reported that most of the black employees resent the black store manager and the black supervisors. "They don't want to take orders from another black—they don't give the black managers any respect and they refuse to respond to their authority," the source explained.[82]

From the point of view of the manager, assistant manager, or supervisor who is given the job of training a black employee, a typical attitude is often expressed in the complaint: Why did they have to give me the problem? Most supervisory personnel are sympathetic to the idea of bringing more Negroes into the company, but they would prefer that "someone else" have the responsibility of performing the training function.

This attitude stems in part from a stereotype of the black as lazy, unreliable, and a problem worker. This conception sometimes derives from an unsuccessful training effort on the part of the particular company with hardcore unemployed under various government-sponsored programs. Supervisors need to understand that there can be as much difference between a hardcore trainee and a Negro applicant as there is between the hardcore trainee and the ordinary white applicant. The mere fact that skin coloration of the former and the Negro applicant frequently happens to be the same is no indication of the ability or motivation of the Negro who is assigned for training to the supervisor. The fact is that many Negroes are more capable than many whites and, given the opportunity, can become excellent managerial personnel. Despite this truism, white employees all too frequently tend to damn all blacks for the deficiencies of a minority.

Because day-to-day training in the supermarket business is decentralized, top management must take cognizance of the im-

---

82. *Supermarket News*, October 11, 1971, Section I, p. 4.

pact of supervisory attitudes and must, through sensitivity training and policy directives, make it clear that the company objectives require a fair and understanding approach toward Negro employees. One large chain continually monitors the training of Negro employees through store visits by a black training director who interrogates both employees and supervision as to the progress being made and attempts to bring into the open any problems which may have developed.

The Promotion Process

The four primary entry level job positions in supermarkets are checkout clerk, grocery clerk, meat cutter apprentice, and produce clerk. As a practical matter, however, promotions do not occur equally from all four categories. The prevailing attitude that checkout clerks are only temporary workers has already been explained. In addition, meat cutter apprentices may move up to meat department managers, but their movement through other job categories in the store is impeded in part by the specialized nature of the skill which they are in the process of acquiring and in part by union restrictions. Frequently the members of the meat department may be represented by a different union from other store employees, but even when there is a so-called "wall-to-wall" agreement covering all employees, there is less upward mobility from the meat department to general store manager positions than in the grocery department and produce department. Thus, there are two entry level jobs, grocery clerk and produce clerk, from which promotion is most likely to proceed.

Typically a young man, usually from the neighborhood, will begin working as a part-time employee sacking groceries while in high school. His future depends on the impression he makes on the store manager who initially hired him. If it is good, he will be moved to stocking shelves, weighing produce, and perhaps running a cash register, still as a part-time employee or during summer work.

After high school he can become a full-time employee fairly easily, based on his previous employment, although he may have to take employment tests at the personnel office. Even then, the manager's desire to keep him is the most important qualification —even failing the employment tests may be overlooked.

A full-time store clerk who is considered promotable will be shifted among the various departments over a period of months and perhaps be encouraged to take a home study course. This leads to promotion to department manager, possibly at another store. If he is then considered a managerial candidate, the manager and assistant manager will teach him their work—handling complaints, work schedules, company policies and procedures, and so on. If he proves himself as an assistant manager to the store manager and district manager, he will finally be given a store of his own—the culmination of about five to seven years' effort, on the average.

A process such as this may well tend to maintain existing racial employment patterns unless special efforts are made to bring other workers into the system and to consider them for promotion. The entry level clerk position is likely to go to a white boy in a white neighborhood, and of course, broad company policies may have little effect on store managers who are solely in charge of hiring at their own stores and who are not personally committed to equal employment practices. Once hired, a black employee may find it more difficult to win the necessary approval of the manager that will lead up the job hierarchy, either because of real or assumed customer prejudice or lack of awareness on the manager's part that Negro employees are welcomed by the district and division managers, as well as by corporate executives. Given the present promotion process, the store manager is largely the key to improving Negro occupational distribution in the industry through in-store promotion.

Company policy comes into play at the point of assigning store managers. If the policy is to test the Negro's managerial capabilities by first putting him in a black neighborhood, the number of possible openings is correspondingly reduced, as is the chance for successful performance. Ghetto supermarkets have been plagued by inventory shortages, low gross profits, poor employee productivity, and the constant threat of violence. A large West Coast chain reported that two of its black managers left the company because of constant threats and the hazards of working in ghetto neighborhoods. As has already been mentioned, black college graduates do not want to be assigned to stores in black neighborhoods. Yet management is under considerable pressure to find Negroes who can fill such managerial posts. Indeed, in some companies, the choice may narrow down to closing the stores or finding capable black managers, because white managers are either unable to cope with the problems or do not wish to work in such neighborhoods.

Company policy is also important with respect to assignment of store managers for newly constructed markets. The opening of a new market represents a commitment of a tremendous investment; the success or failure of the store may hinge upon the image it projects in the opening weeks of operation. Should the company risk placing a black manager in a store with all white employees in a white neighborhood? Unless companies are ready to make such judgments on the basis of qualifications without regard to race the openings for Negroes in managerial positions will be restricted, and this will affect opportunities for advancement for Negroes throughout the company, no matter what policies may be enunciated by the chief executive. Fortunately, there is growing evidence that companies are to an increasing extent looking for Negroes for managerial positions and are prepared to place qualified candidates in new stores in white suburban neighborhoods.

A successful store manager will progress horizontally to more profitable stores, where salaries are higher. Above the store manager is the district or zone manager and above him a division manager. The usually small headquarters staff consists of executives supervising functional specialties, such as distribution, merchandising, purchasing, industrial relations, etc. Choices for corporate jobs among store managers or assistant managers are based on the division manager's advice and the candidates' personal files and operating performance. Unfortunately, the relatively few Negroes in managerial positions greatly reduces their availability for the higher managerial ranks. As noted, however, supermarket chains have begun to recruit Negro college graduates as store manager trainees, as well as for headquarters positions.

The data in Table 15 revealed that only 5.9 percent of all male sales workers and only 2.3 percent of all male officials and managers were black in the supermarket industry in 1970. This discussion of the promotion process shows how closely interrelated these two conditions are, at least for male employees. The upper level occupations are likely to lag behind increased Negro employment among male sales workers, i.e., store clerks, unless college level recruitment is greatly expanded. Training programs aimed specifically at increasing Negro employment in sales positions, and special efforts to upgrade black employees, will be discussed in a subsequent chapter.

CHAPTER V

Regional, Locational, and Company Variations

National aggregate data on Negro employment in the supermarket industry in the latter half of the 1960's indicate the direction of change and pinpoint some of the problem areas in increasing black employment. Actual change within the industry, however, has not proceeded evenly among all regions, areas, and companies, and aggregate data fail to show some of the wide variations in employment patterns existing during this period. To understand underlying problems and trends, it is necessary to discuss employment on a more limited scale, particularly in light of the difference between supermarket dispersion and black population concentration.

THE 1967 CHAIN SAMPLE

In order to examine employment patterns more closely, it was found necessary to construct a field sample, since EEOC material only present industry statistics on a statewide and metropolitan area wide basis. (These data will be examined by region and location in later sections of this chapter.) Data were therefore collected from a selected group of chain supermarket companies which permit an analysis of the employment situation in several specific areas. Although data were collected both for 1967 and 1968, the earlier sample was chosen because it contains a larger and more representative portion of the supermarket industry.

These chain company data allow comparison of employment patterns within regions, by urban, suburban, and nonmetropolitan areas, and within companies, by store and nonstore operations. In addition, the extremes in low and high Negro employment can be separated for a comparison of occupational distributions and the impact of regional factors.

Chain Supermarket Overview, 1967

Table 18 shows the total and Negro employment patterns in the selected chain companies in the 1967 sample. A comparison with Table 15 in Chapter IV indicates that the selected chains had higher Negro employment than the average for all companies reporting to the EEOC in 1967. Total employment was 6.2 percent Negro compared to 5.5 percent in the EEOC group, and was higher in sales and clerical and all blue collar occupational groups. In general, however, the chain sample had fairly similar proportions of black employees to the large group, as further shown by Table 19, except for a lower overall proportion of blue collar to white collar workers. It should be further noted that the percentage of service workers to all workers in the 1967 supermarket sample is only 2.3 percent, a figure close to that indicated by detailed research in 1971, and seems more likely to properly reflect industry occupational patterns than the 1970 EEOC figure of 4.8 percent as shown in Table 16.

Store Employment

The vast majority of employment opportunities are located in the supermarket store units themselves. Stores are also important because promotion to corporate executive levels, as discussed earlier, has traditionally come from store managerial ranks. Table 20 shows the store employment distribution for the selected chain companies in 1967, where 81.5 percent of all employment in this sample was concentrated. Female workers were slightly more heavily concentrated in the stores than males— 82.7 percent to 81.0 percent.

Negro supermarket employment, however, does not follow the same distribution as total employment. As was mentioned earlier, warehouses sometimes are 50 percent Negro or more, so lower proportions of Negro males in stores would not be unexpected. A comparison of Tables 18 and 20 reveals that only 71.6 percent of black male supermarket employment was in stores in the 1967 sample, while Negro female proportions were more nearly similar to total female store employment—83.4 percent of all Negro women worked in stores, compared to 82.7 percent of the total.

In actual store operations, 6.2 percent of the male sales workers and only 4.6 percent of the females were Negro in 1967. Since this occupational group has been pinpointed as vital for

TABLE 18. *Supermarket Industry*
Employment by Race, Sex, and Occupational Group
Selected Chain Companies
1,172 Reporting Units
United States, 1967

Occupational Group	All Employees			Male			Female		
	Total	Negro	Percent Negro	Total	Negro	Percent Negro	Total	Negro	Percent Negro
Officials and managers	47,069	642	1.4	45,626	596	1.3	1,443	46	3.2
Professionals	2,069	28	1.4	1,920	25	1.3	149	3	2.0
Technicians	2,586	179	6.9	2,016	133	6.6	570	46	8.1
Sales workers	224,182	12,652	5.6	142,913	8,883	6.2	81,269	3,769	4.6
Office and clerical	31,698	1,303	4.1	9,577	631	6.6	22,121	672	3.0
Total white collar	307,604	14,804	4.8	202,052	10,268	5.1	105,552	4,536	4.3
Craftsmen	31,869	1,349	4.2	30,812	1,295	4.2	1,057	54	5.1
Operatives	39,994	4,160	10.4	28,064	3,551	12.7	11,930	609	5.1
Laborers	32,722	3,857	11.8	24,063	3,427	14.2	8,659	430	5.0
Service workers	9,730	1,965	20.2	7,640	1,742	22.8	2,090	223	10.7
Total blue collar	114,315	11,331	9.9	90,579	10,015	11.1	23,736	1,316	5.5
Total	421,919	26,135	6.2	292,631	20,283	6.9	129,288	5,852	4.5

Source: Data in the authors' possession.

TABLE 19. *Supermarket Industry*
Percent Distribution of Employment by Race, Sex, and
Occupational Group
Selected Chain Companies
United States, 1967

Occupational Group	All Employees		Male		Female	
	Total	Negro	Total	Negro	Total	Negro
Officials and managers	11.2	2.4	15.6	2.9	1.1	0.8
Professionals	0.5	0.1	0.7	0.1	0.1	0.1
Technicians	0.6	0.7	0.7	0.7	0.5	0.8
Sales workers	53.1	48.4	48.8	43.8	62.9	64.4
Office and clerical	7.5	5.0	3.3	3.1	17.1	11.4
Total white collar	72.9	56.6	69.1	50.6	81.7	77.5
Craftsmen	7.5	5.2	10.5	6.4	0.8	0.9
Operatives	9.5	15.9	9.6	17.5	9.2	10.4
Laborers	7.8	14.8	8.2	16.9	6.7	7.4
Service workers	2.3	7.5	2.6	8.6	1.6	3.8
Total blue collar	27.1	43.4	30.9	49.4	18.3	22.5
Total	100.0	100.0	100.0	100.0	100.0	100.0

Source: Calculated from Table 18.

minority employment and advancements, the low proportions found in stores in 1967 are particularly unsatisfactory. It should be noted, however, that efforts to improve Negro employment in sales work were just getting underway at that time. More recent advances in that area of employment will be discussed in the next chapter.

In the blue collar category, craftsmen, operatives, and service workers were concentrated in the stores. Negro men were barely represented among store craftsmen, but held a considerable proportion of the male operative jobs in stores. The high proportion of Negro males in store level operative jobs and the relatively low proportion of Negro women in such jobs is rather surprising and again raises questions as to the accuracy of reporting. The classification of "operative" is intended to cover workers who operate machine or processing equipment which can be mastered

TABLE 20. *Supermarket Industry*
Employment by Race, Sex, and Occupational Group
Selected Chain Company Stores
United States, 1967

Occupational Group	All Employees			Male			Female		
	Total	Negro	Percent Negro	Total	Negro	Percent Negro	Total	Negro	Percent Negro
Officials and managers	37,847	569	1.5	36,691	533	1.5	1,156	36	3.1
Professionals	679	15	2.2	621	14	2.3	58	1	1.7
Technicians	874	147	16.8	790	114	14.4	84	33	39.3
Sales workers	223,302	12,607	5.6	142,420	8,873	6.2	80,882	3,734	4.6
Office and clerical	18,403	794	4.3	7,465	457	6.1	10,938	337	3.1
Total white collar	281,105	14,132	5.0	187,987	9,991	5.3	93,118	4,141	4.4
Craftsmen	23,301	612	2.6	22,767	595	2.6	534	17	3.2
Operatives	22,294	2,536	11.4	12,360	2,076	16.8	9,934	460	4.6
Laborers	9,942	835	8.4	8,313	750	9.0	1,629	85	5.2
Service workers	7,267	1,284	17.7	5,560	1,108	19.9	1,707	176	10.3
Total blue collar	62,804	5,267	8.4	49,000	4,529	9.2	13,804	738	5.3
Total	343,909	19,399	5.6	236,987	14,520	6.1	106,922	4,879	4.6

Source: Data in the authors' possession.

in a few weeks and requires only limited training. A typical operative job at store level would be that of a meat wrapper, but this function is normally more likely to be performed by Negro women than Negro men.

Although service work jobs were more heavily located in the stores than elsewhere, the Negro service work group was more concentrated in nonstore operations, leading to a lower than average black proportion in this occupation. Service work covers such a wide variety of low level, unskilled jobs that it is difficult to say what jobs the Negro workers held.

Table 21 compares storewide occupational distributions. Here the picture is more encouraging, for although the actual number of black workers employed was low, they at least tended to be similarly distributed among the available jobs in comparison to the white work force. Whereas Table 20 showed sharply lower black proportions in the white collar occupations, at the store level Negro women were more concentrated in sales positions than all women employees. The almost complete lack of black officials and managers accounts for the 10.5 percentage points difference between male total and Negro white collar employment, but in other white collar positions the male Negro work force was better represented. Among blue collar occupations, total and Negro female work forces were very similarly distributed, while greater differences can be seen in the male section, where 14.3 percent of black men were in operative positions, compared to only 5.2 percent of all men. These proportions would seem to indicate that, at the store level while upgrading is seriously needed to close the gap in managerial proportions, increases in representation at all levels may be needed more than a redistribution among various occupations. Certainly there do not seem to be barriers to placing Negro store employees, if hired at all, in sales positions.

Headquarters and Warehouse Employment

Supermarket nonstore employment can largely be divided into white collar and blue collar groups. The former work at corporate headquarters, divisional offices, and similar operations. The latter are almost entirely located in central warehouse distribution facilities, although a few may also be in a limited number of food processing operations. When store employment is subtracted from companywide data, these two major remaining groups of workers appear. Employment patterns are shown in

TABLE 21. *Supermarket Industry*
Percent Distribution of Employment by Race, Sex, and
Occupational Group
Selected Chain Company Stores
United States, 1967

Occupational Group	All Employees		Male		Female	
	Total	Negro	Total	Negro	Total	Negro
Officials and managers	11.0	2.9	15.5	3.7	1.1	0.8
Professionals	0.2	0.1	0.3	0.1	0.1	*
Technicians	0.3	0.7	0.3	0.8	0.1	0.7
Sales workers	64.9	65.0	60.1	61.1	75.6	76.5
Office and clerical	5.3	4.1	3.1	3.1	10.2	6.9
Total white collar	81.7	72.8	79.3	68.8	87.1	84.9
Craftsmen	6.8	3.2	9.6	4.1	0.5	0.4
Operatives	6.5	13.1	5.2	4.3	9.3	9.4
Laborers	2.9	4.3	3.5	5.2	1.5	1.7
Service workers	2.1	6.6	2.4	7.6	1.6	3.6
Total blue collar	18.3	27.2	20.7	31.2	12.9	15.1
Total	100.0	100.0	100.0	100.0	100.0	100.0

Source: Calculated from Table 20.

* Less than 0.05 percent.

Table 22 for these groups. It should be kept in mind that there is some overlap due to the presence of some blue collar work at company headquarters and white collar work outside the central offices.

A comparison of Tables 20 (stores) and 22 (headquarters and warehouses) indicates that Negro employment is highest in warehouse blue collar jobs of supermarket companies and lowest in headquarters operations' white collar jobs. In 1967, only 2.5 percent of nonstore white collar employment was Negro; 2.0 percent of the male work force and 3.2 percent of the female work force. There were very small numbers of Negroes in all white collar occupations, with black men filling only 63 of 8,935 managerial positions, 0.7 percent. Although Negro women held 9.0 percent of the female nonstore sales positions, this accounted for

TABLE 22. *Supermarket Industry*
Employment by Race, Sex, and Occupational Group
Selected Chain Company Headquarters and Warehouses
United States, 1967

Occupational Group	All Employees			Male			Female		
	Total	Negro	Percent Negro	Total	Negro	Percent Negro	Total	Negro	Percent Negro
Officials and managers	9,222	73	0.8	8,935	63	0.7	287	10	3.5
Professionals	1,390	13	0.9	1,299	11	0.8	91	2	2.2
Technicians	1,712	32	1.9	1,226	19	1.5	486	13	2.7
Sales workers	880	45	5.1	493	10	2.0	387	35	9.0
Office and clerical	13,295	509	3.8	2,112	174	8.2	11,183	335	3.0
Total white collar	26,499	672	2.5	14,065	277	2.0	12,434	395	3.2
Craftsmen	8,568	737	8.6	8,045	700	8.7	523	37	7.1
Operatives	17,700	1,624	9.2	15,704	1,475	9.4	1,996	149	7.5
Laborers	22,780	3,022	13.3	15,750	2,677	17.0	7,030	345	4.9
Service workers	2,463	681	27.6	2,080	634	30.5	333	47	12.3
Total blue collar	51,511	6,064	11.8	41,579	5,486	13.2	9,932	578	5.8
Total	78,010	6,736	8.6	55,644	5,763	10.4	22,366	973	4.4

Source: Data in the authors' possession.

only 35 employees, so the percentage is hardly significant. Overall, 4.5 percent of all Negro white collar employees were in company headquarters and the nonstore operations compared to 9.4 percent of the total white collar work force in the selected chain companies. In headquarters, as in stores, Negro females actually held a larger proportion of managerial jobs relative to all females than their male counterparts relative to all males, despite the fact that this occupation is overwhelmingly dominated by men. The actual numbers involved, however, were so small that the comparison is not significant. It is clear that very few Negroes—male or female—had made their way from stores to executive-level positions by 1967.

The warehouse segment of the work force, represented by the blue collar group in Table 22 was 11.8 percent Negro in 1967. This is considerably higher than the blue collar segment of the store work force, which was 8.4 percent Negro in 1967 (Table 20). Over three-fourths of the Negroes in warehouses were operatives and laborers, and less than 10 percent of the total (only 578 of 6,064) were Negro women. Both Negro men and women held relatively high proportions of the available craftsmen positions—8.7 and 7.1 percent respectively, but this represents only 737 workers in all. Since truck drivers are usually classified as nonstore operatives, it is noteworthy that a much lower proportion of male warehouse operatives were black than of those in supermarkets—9.4 percent compared to 16.8 percent.

The occupational distributions for nonstore operations (Table 23) show that the total work force was about one-third white collar (headquarters) and two-thirds blue collar (warehouses, etc.). The Negro work force, in comparison, was 90 percent blue collar. These figures tend to bear out earlier observations about the racial compositions of warehouse employment. Negroes are strongly represented among laborers who do the bulk of warehouse work, and underrepresented among the group which includes the more highly paid truck driver positions. Warehouse location may have an important influence on the level of Negro employment, since it has been observed that some such operations are far more heavily Negro than these statistics indicate. It is sometimes more likely for a supermarket warehouse to be nearly all white or all Negro than to reflect the averages shown in Table 22.

TABLE 23. *Supermarket Industry*
Percent Distribution of Employment by Race, Sex, and
Occupational Group
Selected Chain Company Headquarters and Warehouses
United States, 1967

Occupational Group	All Employees		Male		Female	
	Total	Negro	Total	Negro	Total	Negro
Officials and managers	11.8	1.1	16.1	1.1	1.3	1.0
Professionals	1.8	0.2	2.3	0.2	0.4	0.2
Technicians	2.2	0.5	2.2	0.3	2.2	1.4
Sales workers	1.1	0.7	0.9	0.2	1.7	3.6
Office and clerical	17.1	7.5	3.8	3.0	50.0	34.4
Total white collar	34.0	10.0	25.3	4.8	55.6	40.6
Craftsmen	11.0	10.9	14.5	12.1	2.4	3.8
Operatives	22.7	24.1	28.2	25.6	8.9	15.3
Laborers	29.2	44.9	28.3	46.5	31.4	35.5
Service workers	3.1	10.1	3.7	11.0	1.7	4.8
Total blue collar	66.0	90.0	74.7	95.2	44.4	59.4
Total	100.0	100.0	100.0	100.0	100.0	100.0

Source: Computed from Table 22.

CHAIN COMPANY LOCATIONAL VARIATIONS, 1967

The 1967 sample of chain companies also showed interesting variations by company locations. To examine this more closely, the data were divided into metropolitan and nonmetropolitan segments, and those metropolitan areas with substantial Negro populations were then divided into core-city and suburban locations. These data are presented in Tables 24 through 26.

Cities with Negro Population Concentrations

Negro employment in the selected chains in 1967 was highest in the central cities of metropolitan areas where large numbers of Negroes lived, with the exception of the South. None of these areas, however, had especially high Negro employment, except, once again, in the South, where 13.0 percent of all central city

TABLE 24. Supermarket Industry
Employment by Race, Sex, and Region
Selected Chain Companies
Large Metropolitan Areas, 1967

Region and Location	All Employees			Male			Female		
	Total	Negro	Percent Negro	Total	Negro	Percent Negro	Total	Negro	Percent Negro
Northeast									
Central city	58,689	3,482	5.9	39,656	2,252	5.7	19,033	1,230	6.5
Suburban	12,963	495	3.8	8,718	393	4.5	4,245	102	2.4
Total	71,652	3,977	5.6	48,374	2,645	5.5	23,278	1,332	5.7
South									
Central city	41,965	5,451	13.0	30,611	4,665	15.2	11,354	786	6.9
Suburban	23,517	4,359	18.5	17,518	3,573	20.4	5,999	786	13.1
Total	65,482	9,810	15.0	48,129	8,238	17.1	17,353	1,572	9.1
Midwest									
Central city	52,705	4,278	8.1	35,724	3,036	8.5	16,981	1,242	7.3
Suburban	24,915	1,038	4.2	17,033	932	5.5	7,882	106	1.3
Total	77,620	5,316	6.8	52,757	3,968	7.5	24,863	1,348	5.4

Rocky Mountain									
Central city	6,989	162	2.3	5,419	146	2.7	1,570	16	1.0
Suburban	2,662	40	1.5	1,950	29	1.5	712	11	1.5
Total	9,651	202	2.1	7,369	175	2.4	2,282	27	1.2
West Coast									
Central city	18,474	838	4.5	13,569	677	5.0	4,905	161	3.3
Suburban	12,030	506	4.2	8,776	423	4.8	3,254	83	2.6
Total	30,504	1,344	4.4	22,345	1,100	4.9	8,159	244	3.0
Total									
Central city	178,822	14,211	7.9	124,979	10,776	8.6	53,843	3,435	6.4
Suburban	76,087	6,438	8.5	53,995	5,350	9.9	22,092	1,088	4.9
Total	254,909	20,649	8.1	178,974	16,126	9.0	75,935	4,523	5.6

Source: Data in the authors' possession.

Note: These metropolitan areas have substantial (over 10 percent) Negro population.

employment was Negro. Supermarket companies in northeastern central city areas were only 5.9 percent Negro; in the Midwest, 8.1 percent; in the Rocky Mountain region, 2.3 percent; and on the West Coast, 4.5 percent (Table 24). As low as these proportions are, they represent the highest Negro employment levels in each region of all locations, as a comparison with Tables 25 and 26 show.

The supermarket industry employment pattern was quite different in southern large metropolitan areas. There, while about twice as much employment was in central cities as in suburban locations (41,965 to 23,517), Negro employment was almost equally divided (5,451 to 4,359). Thus Negro employment was considerably higher in suburban supermarkets, comprising 18.5 percent of the work force there.

It has already been noted that Negro population is more generally distributed in the South, so that suburbs there are often not the lily-white residential areas often found in metropolitan areas outside the South. The extremely high Negro employment in southern suburban areas, however, seems attributable in part also to the much greater use of Negro men there than in other regions. The highest Negro representation yet seen was among Negro men in southern suburban areas—20.4 percent of the male work force. This may be a result of the tendency to maintain the old customer service patterns longer in the South, together with smaller store units. The service work occupations which Negro men have traditionally held in great numbers may still exist in the South, although they are becoming more and more limited in other areas.

On the West Coast, the difference between suburban and core city Negro employment is only 0.3 percentage points. This is probably a reflection of the fact that cities themselves are less centralized in the West, where both white and Negro populations are dispersed over wide, although not necessarily integrated, areas. In this region, the supermarket industry itself was less concentrated in the central cities, in contrast to other parts of the country, where twice as much or more employment was located in the central cities than in suburbs.

Negro suburban employment in all regions may reflect the fact that warehouses tend to be located on the outskirts of cities, and that these operations have generally offered substantial blue collar employment to Negroes. Warehouse employment offers instant high pay for no previous skill and the opportunity to attain the top rate rather quickly without a long apprenticeship period. With this kind of attraction, Negroes seem to be able to overcome the transportation problems involved in getting from the inner city to suburban warehouse locations. On the other hand, opportunities for store level employment, often much closer to home, frequently fail to attract Negro applicants because the entrance rate is apparently not sufficiently high and the promotional possibilities seem limited to most Negroes.

The relatively low levels of Negro employment in central cities go a long way toward explaining the overall low representation of black workers in the supermarket industry in 1967. It seems likely, however, that supermarkets in central cities recorded the greatest improvement in levels of Negro employment in the latter years of the decade. This came about because of the tight labor market which created pressure on markets to tap a new pool of labor and because of the growing interest of companies in improving their overall racial mix.

Other Metropolitan Areas

Table 25 shows Negro employment by region for those cities which lacked substantial Negro population in the 1960's. Except in the Northeast region, the Negro proportion was about one-half as much in these metropolitan areas as in those shown in Table 24, and was lower than in the suburban component of those metropolitan areas as well. Of all regions, the highest level of black employment was among men in the South, where 6.7 percent of the work force was black. It was lowest in the Rocky Mountain region, where there were only three Negro males among 1,438 men and no Negro females in 1967, and where, of course, few blacks reside.

There is not much difference in Negro employment between the two groups of metropolitan areas in the Northeast region. Those with high levels of black population averaged only 5.6 percent Negro supermarket employment (Table 24), those with average or low Negro population had work forces that were 4.1 percent black in 1967 (Table 25). In this region, Negro white collar employment was higher than blue collar employment (4.1 to 3.7 percent) in the metropolitan areas with smaller Negro populations.[83] This is a reversal of the occupational trends found elsewhere, where blue collar employment tended to be more heavily

---

83. Data in the authors' possession.

TABLE 25. *Supermarket Industry*
Employment by Race, Sex, and Region
Selected Chain Companies
Smaller Metropolitan Areas, 1967

Region	All Employees			Male			Female		
	Total	Negro	Percent Negro	Total	Negro	Percent Negro	Total	Negro	Percent Negro
Northeast	18,442	749	4.1	11,753	506	4.3	6,689	243	3.6
South	27,345	1,662	6.1	19,769	1,326	6.7	7,576	336	4.4
Midwest	25,795	924	3.6	16,047	597	3.7	9,748	327	3.4
Rocky Mountain	1,927	3	0.2	1,438	3	0.2	489	—	—
West Coast	23,715	672	2.8	16,906	515	3.0	6,809	157	2.3
Total	97,224	4,010	4.1	65,913	2,947	4.5	31,311	1,063	3.4

Source: Data in the authors' possession.

Note: These are metropolitan areas without substantial Negro populations.

Negro. This reversal has a significant impact because white collar employment so far outnumbers blue collar work in the supermarket industry. The small numbers involved, however, probably indicate that this reversal is due to unusual conditions in a single company in the region. On a national scale, such a change would be extremely important.

Small Towns and Rural Locations

Supermarkets in nonmetropolitan areas have the lowest levels of Negro employment, as a comparison of Table 26 with the two previous tables shows. Average nonmetropolitan area employment was only 2.1 percent Negro. Not unexpectedly, the South registered considerably higher Negro employment—4.3 percent—than the average, but even this is low in relation to black population distribution. The less than one percent level in the Midwest, Rocky Mountain, and West Coast regions is understandable in light of the previously mentioned far greater dispersion of the industry itself than of Negro population.

The South region's low percentage seems especially unsatisfactory in light of the disparity between male and female employment. Whereas in other regions, male and female Negro employment was equally low, in the South Negro men held a much higher percentage of the male jobs than Negro women (5.3 percent to 1.4 percent). Since it is unlikely that these represent differential population concentrations, it must represent labor market forces such as a greater willingness in the industry to hire Negro men than women or more desirable job opportunities for Negro women outside the supermarket industry.

Urban Concentration of Negro Employment

The data on employment by location in 1967 indicate strongly that Negro employment was more heavily concentrated in central cities than industry employment in general. The breakdown shown in Table 27 makes this very clear. Negro employment was disproportionately concentrated in the central cities and their surrounding suburbs—79 percent of the total—whereas only 60.4 percent of all supermarket jobs were located in that area.

This distribution makes the relatively low employment proportion found in central cities very significant and indicates the extent of the impact on Negro employment in the total industry which would result from even relatively small improvement of

Region	All Employees			Male			Female		
	Total	Negro	Percent Negro	Total	Negro	Percent Negro	Total	Negro	Percent Negro
Northeast	15,903	334	2.1	9,729	207	2.1	6,174	127	2.1
South	21,238	904	4.3	15,618	825	5.3	5,620	79	1.4
Midwest	20,654	183	0.9	13,907	132	0.9	6,747	51	0.8
Rocky Mountain	4,806	10	0.2	3,351	9	0.3	1,455	1	0.1
West Coast	7,185	45	0.6	5,139	37	0.7	2,046	8	0.4
Total	69,786	1,476	2.1	47,744	1,210	2.5	22,042	266	1.2

Source: Data in authors' possession.

Note: These are small towns and rural areas outside of Standard Metropolitan Statistical Areas.

TABLE 27. *Supermarket Industry*
Percent Distribution of Employment by Race and Location
Selected Chain Companies
United States, 1967

Location	All Employees	Negro Employees
Central cities	42.4	54.4
Suburbs	18.0	24.6
Other metropolitan areas	23.1	15.3
Nonmetropolitan areas	16.5	5.7
Total	100.0	100.0

Source: Calculated from Tables 18 and 24-26.

the 8.1 percent Negro work force in central city locations and their suburbs (Table 24). It should be kept in mind that these locational data are based on a 1967 sample and that some dramatic changes have occurred since then. These will be explored further in Chapter VI. First several other aspects of Negro employment in the late 1960's will be discussed.

COMPANY VARIATIONS, 1967

Chain companies sampled by one of the authors in 1967 showed a wide range in employment of black workers, as Table 28 indicates. Of thirty companies, 17 had less than 4 percent Negro employment, and only 7 had more than 8 percent. Two of the latter, however, employed more than 20 percent black workers. There were several differences between those companies with the highest Negro employment. Data for four companies which averaged less than one percent Negro employment are shown in Table 29; four which averaged almost 19 percent Negro employment are shown in Table 30.

Although both groups are made up of relatively small companies, the chains with high Negro employment operate in high Negro population areas—in the South and in an East Coast city with a large black population. Only one of the four chains with low employment operates in areas with substantial Negro employment. This company is also a medium sized chain.

TABLE 28. *Supermarket Industry*
Range of Percent Negro Employment
Thirty Chain Companies, 1967

Percent Negro Employment	Distribution of Companies
0 to 4.0	17
4.1 to 8.0	6
8.1 to 12.0	3
12.1 to 16.0	2
16.1 to 20.0	0
20.1 to 24.0	2
24.1 to 28.0	0
28.1 to 32.0	0
Total	30

Source: Data in the authors' possession.

The companies with high employment had a much superior Negro occupational distribution to those with few black employees as well as to the average in that year. Only about one-fourth of the Negro workers were in white collar occupations in companies with extremely low Negro employment, compared to over one-half of the black workers in high employment companies. Although only 7.3 percent of all black employment in the selected companies in 1967 was in the four companies with large proportions of Negroes, 16.8 percent of all black officials and managers, 10.7 percent of all professionals, and 78.8 percent of all technicians were in these four. (Compare Table 30 with Table 18.)

The national and regional chains, the industry giants, were not represented in either of the two extremes in 1962. Their employment policies and practices, however, have the greatest impact on Negro employment because of their size. During the year 1967, their black proportions were basically confined to the 4.1 to 12.0 percent range, with most at the lower end of the scale.

TABLE 29. *Supermarket Industry*
Employment by Race, Sex, and Occupational Group
Four Chain Companies with Low Negro Employment, 1967

Occupational Group	All Employees			Male			Female		
	Total	Negro	Percent Negro	Total	Negro	Percent Negro	Total	Negro	Percent Negro
Officials and managers	1,390	1	0.1	1,290	1	0.1	100	—	—
Professionals	253	2	0.8	239	1	0.4	14	1	7.1
Technicians	68	—	—	64	—	—	4	—	—
Sales workers	7,161	21	0.3	2,942	11	0.4	4,219	10	0.2
Office and clerical	886	3	0.3	582	—	—	304	3	1.0
Total white collar	9,758	27	0.3	5,117	13	0.3	4,641	14	0.3
Craftsmen	631	4	0.6	582	2	0.3	49	2	4.1
Operatives	519	5	1.0	430	—	—	89	5	5.6
Laborers	3,086	35	1.1	2,807	35	1.2	279	—	—
Service workers	751	28	3.7	326	15	4.6	425	13	3.1
Total blue collar	4,987	72	1.4	4,145	52	1.3	842	20	2.4
Total	14,745	99	0.7	9,262	65	0.7	5,483	34	0.6

Source: Data in the authors' possession.

TABLE 30. Supermarket Industry
Employment by Race, Sex, and Occupational Group
Four Chain Companies with High Negro Employment, 1967

Occupational Group	All Employees			Male			Female		
	Total	Negro	Percent Negro	Total	Negro	Percent Negro	Total	Negro	Percent Negro
Officials and managers	1,469	108	7.4	1,335	93	7.0	134	15	11.2
Professionals	72	3	4.2	59	3	5.1	13	—	—
Technicians	220	141	64.1	179	110	61.5	41	31	75.6
Sales workers	5,471	742	13.6	3,091	487	15.8	2,380	255	10.7
Office and clerical	351	44	12.5	88	17	19.3	263	27	10.3
Total white collar	7,583	1,038	13.7	4,752	710	14.9	2,831	328	11.6
Craftsmen	902	113	12.5	896	113	12.6	6	—	—
Operatives	308	191	62.0	285	191	67.0	23	—	—
Laborers	732	127	17.3	726	127	17.5	6	—	—
Service workers	617	443	71.8	579	420	72.5	38	23	60.5
Total blue collar	2,559	874	34.2	2,486	851	34.2	73	23	31.5
Total	10,142	1,912	18.9	7,238	1,561	21.6	2,904	351	12.1

Source: Data in the authors' possession.

REGIONAL VARIATIONS, 1966-1969

The EEOC data for chains and large independents collected in 1966, 1967, and 1969 are broken down by regions in Table 31. Some important variations from the national trends discussed in the preceding chapter can be seen in this table. Whereas Negro employment increased by about 1.5 percentage points for the industry as a whole, the range of increase among regions was from 0.3 percentage points in New England to 2.2 percentage points in the Midwest. Tables 32-36 summarize the occupational data with respect to the regional changes in Negro employment between 1967 and 1969. Occupational data for 1966 can be found in the appendix, but are not presented for comparison.

New England Region

Negro employment increased almost imperceptibly in the New England states between 1966 and 1969. It is difficult to assess the changes in the actual labor force in this period for this and the other regions because of reporting differences from one year to the next. Yet the overall trend can be fairly reliably determined. In New England, it appears that Negro men gained jobs slightly faster than Negro women, but their total employment was still very low as of 1969. The industry pattern of heaviest Negro representation among laborers was followed in New England, as was that of having larger proportions of black employees in blue collar than in white collar jobs.

Negroes were proportionately better represented among men than among women in the late 1960's in this region, but neither group held more than a tiny fraction of the numerically vital sales jobs—only 1.9 percent of the male and 1.6 percent of the female sales workers were Negro by 1969. This was lower than the overall representation among men, owing to the larger share of male blue collar jobs held by Negroes, while the female proportion among sales was almost exactly the same in all female occupational groups where Negro women were employed.

It should be noted that two of the fifteen largest supermarket companies are headquartered in this region. Corporate efforts to increase black employment levels, though limited perhaps to the major cities by black population concentrations in New England, should be able to improve the occupational picture. The very low levels are somewhat surprising in light of longtime fair employ-

TABLE 31. Supermarket Industry
Employment by Race and Sex
Five Regions, 1966, 1967, and 1969

Region	Year	All Employees			Male			Female		
		Total	Negro	Percent Negro	Total	Negro	Percent Negro	Total	Negro	Percent Negro
New England	1966	40,592	707	1.7	25,912	481	1.9	14,680	226	1.5
	1967	47,110	883	1.9	30,447	600	2.0	16,663	283	1.7
	1969	48,713	958	2.0	30,315	672	2.2	18,398	286	1.6
Middle Atlantic	1966	95,396	4,897	5.1	65,488	3,141	4.8	29,908	1,756	5.9
	1967	141,422	6,349	4.5	93,558	4,051	4.3	47,864	2,298	4.8
	1969	150,569	8,237	5.5	96,988	5,205	5.4	53,581	3,032	5.7
South	1966	161,185	13,369	8.3	117,402	11,636	9.9	43,783	1,733	4.0
	1967	222,265	21,047	9.5	159,853	17,389	10.9	62,412	3,658	5.9
	1969	202,627	20,094	9.9	141,647	15,961	11.3	60,980	4,133	6.8
Midwest	1966	161,294	6,535	4.1	105,741	4,565	4.3	55,553	1,970	3.5
	1967	211,723	9,458	4.5	138,328	6,618	4.8	73,395	2,840	3.9
	1969	224,731	14,110	6.3	143,657	9,611	6.7	81,074	4,499	5.5
West	1966	119,526	3,604	3.0	88,821	2,973	3.3	30,705	631	2.1
	1967	127,741	3,940	3.1	92,991	3,144	3.4	34,750	796	2.3
	1969	95,938	3,479	3.6	68,667	2,723	4.0	27,271	756	2.8

Source: Appendix Tables A-5 to A-19.

Note: Variations in total employment are due to variations in reporting completeness during the three reporting periods. It is felt that the latest data, 1969, most accurately reflect food store employment within the definition of companies with 100 or more employees, although one major company's data are missing in 1969.

TABLE 32. *Supermarket Industry*
Percent Negro Employment by Sex and Occupational Group
Chains and Large Independents
New England Region, 1967 and 1969

Occupational Group	All Negro Employees		Male		Female	
	1967	1969	1967	1969	1967	1969
Officials and managers	0.6	0.6	0.6	0.6	2.4	1.8
Professionals	—	1.5	—	1.8	—	—
Technicians	0.9	—	0.9	—	—	—
Sales workers	1.4	1.8	1.4	1.9	1.4	1.6
Office and clerical	2.4	2.9	7.1	7.4	1.7	1.9
Total white collar	1.4	1.7	1.3	1.7	1.5	1.6
Craftsmen	1.0	1.3	1.0	1.3	0.8	1.0
Operatives	4.3	3.0	5.1	4.8	3.3	1.4
Laborers	3.9	4.7	4.7	5.4	1.2	1.8
Service workers	2.1	2.2	2.9	3.0	0.9	1.1
Total blue collar	3.4	3.0	3.8	3.8	2.5	1.3
Total	1.9	2.0	2.0	2.2	1.7	1.6

Source: Appendix Tables A-6 and A-7.

ment laws in this region and some early interest in improving supermarket racial employment in Connecticut, which will be discussed in the next chapter.

Middle Atlantic Region

The Middle Atlantic states of Pennsylvania, New York, and New Jersey might be expected to have fairly high levels of black employment, due to both early fair employment legislation and the large black population in the major cities there.   Table 33, however, shows neither a high level nor much improvement in the late 1960's.   Negro employment stood at just 5.5 percent in 1969, up one percentage point over 1967, and here again Negro men seem to have made a slightly greater gain.

Occupational levels improved slightly during the period, although blue collar representation rose more than white collar representation, 1.5 percentage points among men and 1.4 percentage points among women. The increase in representation among sales workers, especially important to an assessment of the overall occupational position of Negroes in this region, was even smaller than the overall percentage increases among both men and women—up from 4.4 to 4.9 percent overall between 1967 and 1969.

South Region

Male and female Negro employment registered proportionate gains in the South between 1967 and 1969 even though the actual number of total and Negro employees reported declined (Table 31). As Table 34 shows, Negro women registered larger gains than men, though there was still considerable difference in their relative representation by 1969, with 6.8 percent of the female work force Negro, compared to 11.3 percent of the male work force.

TABLE 33. *Supermarket Industry*
Percent Negro Employment by Sex and Occupational Group
Chains and Large Independents
Middle Atlantic Region, 1967 and 1969

Occupational Group	All Negro Employees		Male		Female	
	1967	1969	1967	1969	1967	1969
Officials and managers	1.4	1.6	1.3	1.5	2.2	2.5
Professionals	2.6	3.7	2.4	3.4	7.7	6.4
Technicians	0.3	12.0	0.3	9.8	0.5	17.3
Sales workers	4.4	4.9	4.4	5.1	4.5	4.7
Office and clerical	4.4	6.3	4.5	6.2	4.3	6.4
Total white collar	4.0	4.7	3.7	4.4	4.4	5.1
Craftsmen	2.5	3.1	2.5	3.0	2.1	4.1
Operatives	6.5	8.7	6.8	9.7	5.9	7.1
Laborers	5.4	9.7	5.4	7.9	5.8	17.1
Service workers	12.0	9.5	12.6	10.1	11.0	7.9
Total blue collar	6.3	7.9	6.2	7.7	6.8	8.2
Total	4.5	5.5	4.3	5.4	4.8	5.7

Source: Appendix Tables A-9 and A-10.

TABLE 34. *Supermarket Industry*
Percent Negro Employment by Sex and Occupational Group
Chains and Large Independents
South Region, 1967 and 1969

Occupational Group	All Negro Employees		Male		Female	
	1967	1969	1967	1969	1967	1969
Officials and managers	1.6	2.4	1.6	2.4	2.3	2.1
Professionals	19.9	2.5	17.7	2.0	38.1	7.1
Technicians	11.8	12.5	12.5	14.5	10.6	8.9
Sales workers	7.3	7.5	8.4	8.2	4.9	6.2
Office and clerical	4.6	5.8	9.2	9.1	2.5	4.4
Total white collar	6.4	6.7	7.2	7.1	4.6	5.8
Craftsmen	6.5	7.3	6.4	7.3	8.7	7.5
Operatives	23.1	28.9	31.2	35.0	7.4	9.2
Laborers	24.7	25.5	25.9	28.0	14.9	13.3
Service workers	34.3	29.7	37.5	30.0	26.5	28.7
Total blue collar	20.5	22.4	22.4	23.8	13.0	15.0
Total	9.5	9.9	10.9	11.3	5.9	6.8

Source: Appendix Tables A-12 and A-13.

The large male Negro proportion results from their extremely high representation in the three lower level blue collar groups. Both men and women, however, also had higher than average sales worker proportions—8.2 percent among men and 6.2 percent among women—and Negro men were considerably better represented among managers and clerical workers than the average as well. Nevertheless, the vast difference between blue collar and white collar employment indicates that serious barriers existed to Negro white collar employment in the South, as in other regions. The increases during the late 1960's, however, indicate a very positive basis for future change.

Midwest Region

The Midwest registered the largest gains in Negro employment in the late 1960's, almost 2 percentage points, both among men and women, and had the highest level of black employment except for the South in 1969 (Table 31). This is particularly interesting because this large area has both heavily Negro metropolitan areas and nearly all white states. Major corporate headquarters are in Chicago, Cincinnati, and Detroit, where heavy concentrations of Negroes are found.

Table 35 indicates that Negroes in the Midwest enjoyed a relatively good occupational distribution, particularly since the black proportions of male and female officials and managers (2.6 and 4.3 percent, respectively) were the best of all regions in 1969. Black proportions in sales, however, were about average—5.5 percent—and the male clerical group had considerably lower than average black employment in 1969.

Between 1967 and 1969, Negro representation increased in all occupational groups, but did not result in such a heavy overrep-

TABLE 35. *Supermarket Industry*
Percent Negro Employment by Sex and Occupational Group
Chains and Large Independents
Midwest Region, 1967 and 1969

Occupational Group	All Negro Employees		Male		Female	
	1967	1969	1967	1969	1967	1969
Officials and managers	1.1	2.7	1.1	2.6	2.4	4.3
Professionals	1.8	4.3	1.7	4.3	3.4	3.5
Technicians	2.7	2.8	2.4	2.8	3.0	2.8
Sales workers	3.9	5.5	4.2	5.9	3.6	5.1
Office and clerical	4.0	5.2	6.0	5.8	3.3	5.0
Total white collar	3.6	5.1	3.6	5.2	3.6	5.0
Craftsmen	2.7	4.2	2.7	4.2	3.8	4.7
Operatives	7.8	12.2	7.9	12.1	7.2	12.5
Laborers	7.4	11.8	8.3	12.1	4.6	10.4
Service workers	9.3	9.6	11.5	13.0	5.9	5.4
Total blue collar	6.8	9.7	7.1	9.9	5.5	8.8
Total	4.5	6.3	4.8	6.7	3.9	5.5

Source: Appendix Tables A-15 and A-16.

resentation among lower blue collar occupations as was found in the South. The sales occupations became a target for increased black employment by Operation Breadbasket in Chicago during this period, which perhaps explains some of the increase in that occupational group. The next chapter will examine developments in individual companies in Chicago and other cities.

West Region

As Table 31 shows, there was a large decline in reported employment between 1967 and 1969 in the West Region, indicating the absence of many reporting units, probably those of a single large firm. Thus it is difficult to assess the changes in the second half of the 1960's in Negro employment. Such employment seems to be low but increasing among both men and women.

Examination of trends in occupational representation (Table 36) reveals Negro gains in all but the two lowest skill occupational groups. Overall, Negro men held 3.1 percent of white collar jobs and Negro women held 3.0 percent, while they occupied 6.1 and 2.0 percent, respectively, of blue collar work in the West region in 1969.

The unusually high proportion of Negro female officials and managers, 10.6 percent, represents 46 of 432 female employees. This may result from a reclassification (or misclassification) of some Negro women, rather than true upgrading, since two years earlier the percentage was only 0.5 percent—2 of 436 female officials and managers. Negro men made up only 0.7 percent of this group by 1969, a very slight increase.

Sales work occupations were less heavily Negro than the industry average in the West in each year, rising to 3.4 percent in 1969. Negro proportions of the upper level blue collar occupations were low, and both the laborer and service occupations showed lower proportions in 1969 than in 1967, possibly an indication of upgrading efforts.

Since this region covers the entire western United States, while blacks tend to be concentrated in Los Angeles and Oakland, overall employment would be expected to be quite low. The following section, on metropolitan areas, permits a look at what was happening during this period in areas where the lack of Negroes in the labor force was not a factor.

TABLE 36. *Supermarket Industry*
Percent Negro Employment by Sex and Occupational Group
Chains and Large Independents
West Region, 1967 and 1969

Occupational Group	All Negro Employees		Male		Female	
	1967	1969	1967	1969	1967	1969
Officials and managers	0.5	1.3	0.5	0.7	0.5	10.6
Professionals	0.6	3.0	0.6	2.8	0.9	4.3
Technicians	1.8	4.6	1.4	1.9	3.1	9.5
Sales workers	2.8	3.4	2.9	3.6	2.6	2.9
Office and clerical	1.5	2.0	1.9	1.9	1.4	2.0
Total white collar	2.3	3.0	2.3	3.1	2.3	3.0
Craftsmen	1.4	1.9	1.4	1.9	1.4	3.4
Operatives	2.5	3.7	3.3	5.2	1.1	1.5
Laborers	8.7	6.4	9.5	7.6	1.5	1.5
Service workers	10.2	8.5	13.0	10.3	3.7	2.6
Total blue collar	5.2	5.3	6.0	6.1	2.2	2.0
Total	3.1	3.6	3.4	4.0	2.3	2.8

Source: Appendix Tables A-18 and A-19.

SELECTED METROPOLITAN AREAS, 1966-1969

EEOC data are available on both a statewide and a metropolitan area wide basis. Twenty metropolitan areas which have large Negro populations in four regions of the country were selected for an examination of racial employment trends in these areas during the latter half of the 1960's.[84] Aggregate data by region are shown in Table 37, summarizing Appendix Tables A-23 to A-34.

---

84. Standard Metropolitan Statistical Areas chosen are Atlanta, Baltimore, Charlotte, Chicago, Cincinnati, Cleveland, Dallas, Detroit, Houston, Indianapolis, Jacksonville, Kansas City, Los Angeles, Memphis, New Orleans, New York, Philadelphia, Richmond, St. Louis, and Washington, D.C.

TABLE 37. *Supermarket Industry
Employment by Race, Sex, and Region
Chains and Large Independents
Twenty Metropolitan Areas, 1966, 1967, and 1969*

Region		All Employees			Male			Female		
		Total	Negro	Percent Negro	Total	Negro	Percent Negro	Total	Negro	Percent Negro
Middle Atlantic a	1966	39,462	2,271	5.8	27,986	1,488	5.3	11,476	783	6.8
	1967	57,530	3,952	6.9	39,433	2,534	6.4	18,097	1,418	7.8
	1969	57,329	4,572	8.0	37,678	2,854	7.6	19,651	1,718	8.7
South b	1966	52,220	7,817	15.0	37,113	6,743	18.2	15,107	1,074	7.1
	1967	74,932	12,403	16.6	53,317	10,022	18.8	21,615	2,381	11.0
	1969	76,665	11,072	14.4	53,515	8,817	16.5	23,150	2,255	9.7
Midwest c	1966	66,508	4,047	6.1	44,430	3,003	6.8	22,078	1,044	4.7
	1967	85,084	6,307	7.4	57,744	4,506	7.8	27,340	1,801	6.6
	1969	113,005	11,084	9.8	73,056	7,603	10.4	39,949	3,481	8.7
West d	1966	24,685	1,515	6.1	18,687	1,257	6.7	5,998	258	4.3
	1967	28,549	1,808	6.3	21,475	1,508	7.0	7,074	300	4.2
	1969	26,326	1,868	7.1	19,413	1,491	7.7	6,913	377	5.5

Source: Appendix Tables A-20—A-34.

a New York and Philadelphia.

b Atlanta, Baltimore, Charlotte, Dallas, Houston, Jacksonville, Memphis, New Orleans, Richmond, Washington, D. C.

c Chicago, Cincinnati, Cleveland, Detroit, Indianapolis, Kansas City, St. Louis.

d Los Angeles.

Regional Comparisons

Negro employment levels were considerably higher in the selected metropolitan areas than regional averages in each year, as a comparison of Tables 31 and 37 shows. Metropolitan employment outside the South was much more similar from region to region than in the all-region aggregates as well. The West trailed far behind the Midwest and Middle Atlantic regions as a whole, whereas the Los Angeles area itself had only slightly lower Negro employment than the average for New York and Philadelphia in 1969—7.1 percent compared to 8.0 percent for the Middle Atlantic areas.

In the Middle Atlantic region, Negro employment in the two metropolitan areas of New York and Philadelphia was 5.8 percent in 1966, compared to 5.1 percent for the region as a whole. By 1969, the difference was much greater, with 8.0 percent black employment in these two urban areas, but only 5.5 percent regional average.

Negro employment was almost twice as high in the ten southern metropolitan areas in 1966 as it was in the region as a whole, 15.0 to 8.3 percent. Although the level stayed very high, by 1969 black employment declined to 14.4 percent in the cities, while it rose to 9.9 percent in the entire region. Once again, reporting differences should be noted. Total employment seemed to increase in the ten cities, while both total and Negro employment reported in the region as a whole declined over the three-year period.

In the midwestern cities, Negro employment rose more, and was at higher levels than the regional averages from 1966 to 1969. In fact, these seven cities had almost as high a level of black employment—9.8 percent—as the average in the South region in 1969—9.9 percent. While Negro men held a relatively higher proportion of male jobs than Negro women, the difference between the two was much less—10.4 to 8.7 percent—than in southern cities, where Negro men had 16.5 percent of the jobs, but Negro women only 9.7 percent.

Metropolitan Averages, 1969

Tables 38 and 39 compare Negro proportions and percent distribution by occupation for the twenty selected metropolitan areas with the national aggregates in 1969. In that year, 60.5 percent of all Negro supermarket industry employment reported to the EEOC was in these twenty metropolitan areas, but only

TABLE 38. *Supermarket Industry*
Percent Negro Employment by Sex and Occupational Group
Chains and Large Independents
Twenty Metropolitan Areas and United States, 1969

Occupational Group	20 Metropolitan Areas			United States		
	Total	Male	Female	Total	Male	Female
Officials and managers	3.5	3.3	7.5	2.0	1.9	3.8
Professionals	4.5	4.4	5.2	3.4	3.3	4.9
Technicians	9.5	9.7	9.0	7.6	7.2	8.5
Sales workers	8.9	9.5	8.0	5.4	5.9	4.8
Office and clerical	7.4	9.1	6.8	5.2	6.6	4.6
Total white collar	8.0	8.1	7.8	5.0	5.1	4.7
Craftsmen	6.8	6.8	8.2	4.3	4.3	4.4
Operatives	21.3	23.4	13.7	13.4	16.1	7.4
Laborers	25.0	25.8	19.7	13.9	14.6	10.4
Service workers	25.3	25.1	26.1	13.5	15.7	8.4
Total blue collar	19.0	19.2	17.4	11.3	12.2	8.1
Total	10.5	11.3	8.7	6.5	7.1	5.2

Source: Appendix Tables A-3 and A-22.

37.4 percent of total industry employment; thus metropolitan
areas had much larger black proportions in the work force. In
these twenty cities, 11.3 percent of all male workers, and 8.7
percent of all females were black in 1969, compared to national
averages of 7.1 and 5.2 percent respectively.

Black women enjoyed slightly better occupational distribution
in cities, with 78.3 percent of these workers in sales or clerical
occupations, compared to 74.7 percent in the national aggregate.
This may result from industry variations such as the location
of company headquarters in these cities, since white collar occupations, particularly managerial, employed slightly more of the
total, as well as the Negro, work force. The metropolitan female
work force was 90.1 percent white collar, compared to 84.9 percent for the industry as a whole. Overall the black metropolitan
work force was only 0.5 percentage points higher than the national average, owing to slightly lower white collar proportions
in the male segment.

TABLE 39. Supermarket Industry
Percent Distribution of Employment by Race, Sex, and Occupational Group
Chains and Large Independents
Twenty Metropolitan Areas and United States, 1969

Occupational Group	20 Metropolitan Areas						United States					
	All Employees		Male		Female		All Employees		Male		Female	
	Total	Negro	Total	Negro	Total	Negro	Total	Negro	Total	Negro	Total	Negro
Officials and managers	10.4	3.5	14.6	4.2	1.7	1.5	10.0	3.1	14.2	3.8	1.7	1.2
Professionals	0.5	0.2	0.7	0.3	0.2	0.1	0.4	0.2	0.6	0.3	0.1	0.1
Technicians	0.4	0.4	0.5	0.4	0.3	0.4	0.5	0.6	0.5	0.5	0.5	0.8
Sales workers	58.6	49.8	52.6	44.0	70.9	65.0	59.0	49.7	54.3	45.0	68.5	62.3
Office and clerical	7.6	5.3	2.9	2.3	17.0	13.3	6.4	5.1	2.5	2.4	14.1	12.4
Total white collar	77.5	59.2	71.3	51.2	90.1	80.3	76.3	58.7	72.1	52.0	84.9	76.8
Craftsmen	6.0	3.9	8.6	5.2	0.6	0.5	5.8	3.8	8.2	5.0	0.9	0.7
Operatives	7.7	15.7	9.0	18.6	5.1	8.0	7.7	16.0	8.0	18.2	7.0	9.9
Laborers	4.6	10.9	5.9	13.4	1.9	4.4	5.3	11.4	6.6	13.6	2.7	5.4
Service workers	4.2	10.3	5.2	11.6	2.3	6.8	4.9	10.1	5.1	11.2	4.5	7.2
Total blue collar	22.5	40.8	28.7	48.8	9.9	19.7	23.7	41.3	27.9	48.0	15.1	23.2
Total	100.0	100.0	100.0	100.0	100.0	100.0	100.0	100.0	100.0	100.0	100.0	100.0

Source:　Computed from Appendix Tables A-3 and A-22.

Data on the metropolitan areas indicate that black workers did hold substantial proportions of supermarket employment in these areas in 1969. They were, however, heavily overrepresented among the lower level blue collar occupations, and barely present in managerial ranks, just as they were in the country as a whole. The sales worker group, which employed more Negroes than all blue collar occupations together, was still considerably behind in Negro employment, only 8.9 percent black (Table 38). Increasing pressures for black employment and upgrading developed in these metropolitan areas during the 1960's. The following chapter will assess the strength, focus, and direction of these developments as they are affecting Negro supermarket employment.

PITFALLS IN STATISTICAL INTERPRETATIONS

The data examined in this and in the preceding chapter give a fair indication of the status of Negro employment in the supermarket industry during the latter part of the 1960's. It would be erroneous, however, to compare the percentage of employment of Negroes in supermarkets with the percentage which Negroes constitute in the population and regard the difference as evidence of the degree of discrimination which exists in this industry. The fact is that national, regional, or metropolitan area figures on population distribution are relatively poor indexes of the availability of Negro labor as far as the supermarket industry is concerned.

On a national basis, Negroes represented approximately 11 percent of the labor force in 1971,[85] but it is obvious that stores located in numerous cities and towns of this nation will have a labor force available with much smaller percentages of Negroes present. The lack of correspondence between minority member population on a national basis and supermarket location is well illustrated by the distribution of Spanish-Americans in this country. Safeway Stores, Inc., a national food chain with stores coast-to-coast, has about 4.9 percent of its retail store positions filled by persons with Spanish-American surnames. This percentage is the same as their representation in the total United States population. This correlation is more an accident of the location of this chain's retail outlets than an indication of Safeway's policies toward this minority group. By the same token,

---

85. U.S. Bureau of Labor Statistics, *Black Americans, A Chartbook*, Bulletin 1699 (1971), p. 23.

if another company should show a percentage of employment of
Spanish-Americans substantially less than their percentage in the
national population, this variance would likewise, by itself, have
little significance.

Somewhat the same problem exists when the area used as the
standard is narrowed to the region, the Standard Metropolitan
Statistical Area, or the city. For example, the Washington, D.C.
SMSA consists of the District of Columbia, the counties of Montgomery and Prince Georges in Maryland, the cities of Alexandria, Arlington, Fairfax, and Falls Church, and the counties of
Fairfax, Prince William and Loudoun in Virginia. There is tremendous variation within the SMSA with respect to the percentage representation by Negroes in the population. Thus, Negroes represent 24.6 percent of the population in the total SMSA,
71.1 percent in the District of Columbia central city, 14.1 percent in Alexandria, and only 1.4 percent in Falls Church.[86] Depending upon the location of a company's stores or facilities, the
concern may have a very large Negro population available for
hire or hardly any at all, since the mobility of Negro labor is
frequently highly restricted.

If Negro percentages are viewed on a city-wide basis, they may
or may not be meaningful depending upon the adequacy of the
public transportation system. In New York City, there is a relatively high degree of mobility which is facilitated by an excellent
subway system. In other cities where such facilities are not available, Negroes may be unwilling to journey from one part of a
city to another by a circuitous route which may involve a number
of streetcar or bus transfers and consume over an hour from
source to destination.

The foregoing statistics, therefore, must be interpreted with
care. The relevance of location to the demand for Negro labor
in the supermarket industry will be considered in more detail in
Chapter VIII.

---

86. U.S. Census of Population, 1970, advance report.

Efforts to Increase Negro Employment: Impact of Government, Civil Rights Groups, Management, and Unions

Increasingly throughout the 1960's special efforts were brought to bear on the supermarket industry to improve Negro representation in employment and to upgrade Negro employees. Early efforts had little widespread impact, but as momentum built up, the combined effect by the late 1960's could be felt across the country. The development of these forces and responses is the subject of this chapter. Although each is treated separately, change was brought about by an interaction of the activities of state and federal government agencies, civil rights organizations, and company-initiated programs.

GOVERNMENT REVIEWS AND PROGRAMS

Because they are major employers, supermarket companies have been responsible for reporting breakdowns of racial employment data to the Equal Employment Opportunity Commission since the mid-1960's. They, as well as smaller employers, have also been subject to state fair employment laws where they have been enacted. Since supermarket chains cross state boundaries, interest in employment practices by any state commission may well have an impact on supermarket policy and practice beyond that state boundary.

Plans for Progress

When some of the nation's largest employers were invited to join the voluntary Plans for Progress program early in the 1960's, the supermarket giants were not overlooked. By the end of 1964, its first year of operation, four national chains had become members—Grand Union, A & P, Kroger, and National Tea [87]—and had signed agreements with the Vice-President of the United States, promising to follow nondiscriminatory employment practices and to take steps to improve black employment. Since they were not government contractors, these voluntary plans represented the extent of federal government control in the supermarket industry at that time.

EEOC Activities

The Equal Employment Opportunity Commission, arising from the Civil Rights Act of 1964, was given powers to review and conciliate issues of fair employment practice. Although it has tended to concentrate its efforts on manufacturing industries, two events in the mid-1960's, while limited in scope, indicated that the EEOC did not intend to ignore the retail trade industries.

Speaking before a joint meeting of the New York City and U.S. Chambers of Commerce in 1966, Stephen N. Shulman, then chairman of the EEOC, gave wide publicity to the results of a Wayne State University study of minority employment in New York City's retail stores.[88] Mr. Shulman pointed to data showing that Negroes continued to be concentrated in the lowest level jobs in retailing, while relatively few could be found in upper level sales positions, "regardless of the stated policy of the firms." [89] He further brought out the findings that black workers in New York City stores were promoted less frequently than other employees, and that relatively well-distributed Negro employment could only be found in firms where employers had made special efforts to insure that black workers held jobs at all levels.[90] Although this report did not single out supermarket firms as particular offenders among retail companies, the major companies, with headquarters or markets in the New York City area, could hardly ignore the publicity given the study by the EEOC.

---

87. Plans for Progress Advisory Council, *Plans for Progress* (Washington: President's Committee on Equal Employment Opportunity, August 1964), pp. 20-21.

88. *Retail Labor Report*, No. 910 (December 9, 1966), p. A-9.

89. *Ibid.*

90. *Ibid.*

A second EEOC activity in the mid-1960's more directly affected supermarkets, although this time the event itself was more localized. The EEOC became involved in a lawsuit brought under Title VII of the Civil Rights Act against the industry giant, A & P, in North Carolina, when Mrs. Annie Brinkley claimed that she was denied a job at A & P because of her race. In February 1966, the EEOC was able to announce that the parties to the suit, A & P and Mrs. Brinkley (represented by the NAACP), agreed to try to work out an agreement out of court. The general terms were to be that employment applications would become more easily available to all persons and that the company would establish better communications with the Negro community of North Carolina.[91]

Connecticut Survey

At about the same time as the EEOC activities were showing the interest of the federal government, the Connecticut Commission on Civil Rights made public a study it had done on the employment of Negroes and Puerto Ricans in Connecticut food stores.[92] Stores chosen for examination represented four national and two regional supermarket chains, as well as smaller chains and independent companies.

The study revealed that only 5 percent of store employment was black or Puerto Rican, despite the fact that those two groups were heavily concentrated in the cities and towns whose stores were examined. Chain company employment was especially low, since a few "exceptional" independents accounted for almost 30 percent of all the Negro and Puerto Rican workers. Among the chain stores, there were no Negro or Puerto Ricans in supervisory jobs, just 4 skilled workers, 2 office workers, and 4 (of 373) "managerial workers." National, regional, and local chains had black and Puerto Rican employment from 1.2 to 9.6 percent, despite the fact that several companies reported having affirmative action plans and long-standing policies of nondiscrimination.[93]

Such specific activities on a state level put supermarket companies on notice that they were considered important in the movement for equal employment opportunity which became more

---

91. *Retail Labor Report*, No. 867 (February 11, 1966), p. A-11.

92. *Retail Labor Report*, No. 886 (June 24, 1966), pp. A-6 to A-7.

93. *Ibid.*

strident as the 1960's progressed. Civil rights and community pressure groups, however, were far more vocal than state and federal agencies during this period, as the following section will show.

CIVIL RIGHTS PRESSURES AND PROTEST TACTICS

Early in the 1960's, supermarket chains were chosen as targets of Negro organizations demanding more jobs and other financial benefits in the black neighborhoods where the stores were doing business. During the decade, the tactics of protest were refined and strengthened and one organization—Operation Breadbasket—became the leader in negotiating and pressuring retail businesses. Earlier activities by a variety of groups helped to define its concept and tactics.

CORE Shop-In in San Francisco

In 1963, the San Francisco area chapter of the Congress of Racial Equality took on Lucky Stores, a major regional chain, in an effort to win promises of increased black employment in the company's Bay area stores. CORE thought it had succeeded in gaining such an agreement with the company, but when only 18 of 320 new clerks hired in a subsequent four-month period were black, CORE instituted a "shop-in" against Lucky.[94] The tactic involved "customers" filling shopping carts and taking the merchandise through the checkout line, and then leaving the full grocery sacks unpaid for at the checkout counters. A second maneuver was to shift goods around within the stores, "cross-filing" merchandise from one shelf to another among the departments.

These protests, which took place early in 1964, were inhibited at the time by criticism and resistance from other organizations within the Negro community, including the Baptist Ministers Union and the *Bay Area Independent*, a Negro weekly newspaper. CORE ultimately called off the shop-ins but continued its picketing.[95] A year later, CORE and the United Civil Rights Committee instituted a boycott of Thriftimart stores in Los

94. Lawrence E. Davies, "New CORE Tactic on Coast Shifts Goods on Stores' Shelves," *New York Times*, February 28, 1964; and "Some Negroes Try Shop-Ins, Clog Stores; Others Object," *Philadelphia Bulletin*, February 28, 1964.

95. *Ibid.*

Angeles over hiring and upgrading practices of the company.[96] The protest was dropped, however, before any definite conclusion was reached. This period was the genesis of a much stronger and more organized protest movement which has claimed major success against the supermarket industry—Operation Breadbasket.

Operation Breadbasket Tactics and Targets

Operation Breadbasket was conceived by the fertile imagination of Dr. Leon Sullivan of Philadelphia.[97] The idea was then picked up by the late Dr. Martin Luther King, Jr., and his Southern Christian Leadership Conference. Its first large-scale success occurred in Chicago in mid-1965, when the Rev. Jesse Jackson put it into operation against one of the city's major supermarket chains. Since then the Movement has become established in several other cities and supermarkets have been one of the primary recipients of Operation Breadbasket's attention.

The philosophical basis of Operation Breadbasket is morality, although the tactics are derived from those of unions. Operation Breadbasket contends that it is immoral for white manufacturers and merchants deriving a substantial portion of their revenues from the black community to fail to utilize the resources of that community in providing goods and services. The morality issue is important because it enhances organizational unity by drawing to it the support of ministers and other religious groups, especially the black pastors in the ghettoes. The ministers are able to rally community support, supplying volunteers necessary to effectuate Operation Breadbasket programs. The moral position also arouses the interest of the news media, creates some sympathy within the white community, and provides a firm basis for bargaining with white businessmen.

The basic purpose of Operation Breadbasket is to improve the economic lot of Negro ghetto residents. This objective breaks

96. "Blacks in L.A. Take on Safeway," *Supermarket News*, December 1, 1969.

97. The writers wish to express their appreciation to Professor Robert McKersie, then of the Graduate School of Business, University of Chicago, for assistance in the preparation of this section and especially for introductions to persons working in the Chicago branch of Operation Breadbasket and for supplying two unpublished research papers by students: J. W. Brod, "My Summer," 1967 and Richard C. Speiglman, "Bargaining for Civil Rights," 1967.

down into three main parts: (1) increasing the employment of Negroes in white-owned establishments in absolute numbers, in relation to total employment, and in status of occupational position; (2) creation of a climate in which Negro businessmen can prosper and grow which involves inducing white-owned businesses to make use of the goods and services provided by black entrepreneurs; and (3) channeling money into black-owned financial institutions in the ghetto—the main source of funds for aspiring Negro businessmen and the rest of the black community.

In dealing with supermarkets, these goals are translated into requests for Negro employment at each hierarchical level, utilization of Negro-owned janitorial and garbage collection services, stocking the products of Negro-owned food manufacturers, use of Negro construction companies in the building of new supermarkets, and depositing a portion of ghetto supermarket revenues in the local Negro-owned bank.

Supermarkets are prime targets because they derive a substantial portion of their business from the black community and because they can utilize the services and market the goods of black-owned businesses. Since economic sanctions are the tactic, the selected company must have policy control over the whole organization.

Hi-Low's Experience with Operation Breadbasket

After some success with soft drink and food manufacturers in the Chicago area, Operation Breadbasket moved to the food chains themselves, selecting Hi-Low Foods as the first company to be approached. Hi-Low operates approximately 50 supermarkets, practically all of them in the Chicago area. Moreover, about 15 of its stores are located in Negro neighborhoods. The other chains with substantial operations in Chicago are A & P, Jewel, and National Tea, all of which are very large in comparison to Hi-Low and thus able to sustain economic sanctions with less difficulty—particularly in view of the fact that their operations extend to a number of other metropolitan areas and states.

Hi-Low was approached on October 25, 1966 and an agreement, or covenant, was signed on November 19, 1966. Hi-Low apparently realized its position and the strength of Operation Breadbasket and wished to avoid a boycott. The agreement provided for hiring or upgrading 183 Negro employees, giving display space and competitive markups to Negro-made products, and placing some funds from at least thirteen stores into Negro-controlled banks. The agreement was hailed by Negro leaders as a major economic development. The late Dr. Martin Luther King, Jr., for example, said, "The development portends dramatic new strides toward economic freedom for American black people." [98] In the ensuing months, agreements were reached peacefully with the other chains with a major interest in the Chicago area—National Tea (December 1966), Jewel (early 1967) and A & P (May 1967).

An agreement between Operation Breadbasket and an employer may require that racial employment statistics be forwarded to Operation Breadbasket at regular intervals so that Operation Breadbasket can see how well an employer is living up to his agreement. The first Hi-Low report on January 20, 1967 was apparently acceptable to Operation Breadbasket since discussions with Hi-Low were not reopened at that time. Subsequent statements, however, indicated a disparity between commitments made to Operation Breadbasket and actual employment results. After further fruitless negotiations, Operation Breadbasket instituted a boycott against the company and Hi-Low responded with a court suit seeking a temporary injunction to halt the boycott. Eventually a new agreement was reached between the parties, and the suit and boycott were terminated.

The terms of the original and final agreement are shown in Table 40. Although the later agreement constitutes a net decrease of one in the number of jobs over the previous agreement, it should be noted that total employment at Hi-Low declined from 2,096 to 1,974 during the original agreement period. The terms of the first agreement, had they been met, would have raised Negro employment from 16.8 percent to 20.1 percent. Based on the lower May employment figures, however, Negro employment would rise to 21.3 percent of the total.

After the situation in Chicago was fairly well stabilized, Operation Breadbasket moved on to other cities. It found, however, that the Hi-Low pattern was to be repeated in its negotiations with A & P in Chicago where once again the company was unable to live up to its employment figures.

---

98. "Food Chain to Aid Chicago Negroes," *New York Times*, November 26, 1966; Murray Wyche, "Hi-Low, Dr. King Pact Ups Jobs for Negroes," *Supermarket News*, December 5, 1966, p. 24.

TABLE 40. *Hi-Low Agreement with Operation Breadbasket Current and Projected Negro Employment by Occupation Chicago, 1966-1967*

Occupation	Nov. 1 Statistics	To Be Added in Six Months	Actually Added by May	Final To-Be-Added Agreement Based on Nov. 1 Statistics
Butchers	10	66	5	57
Managers	1	9	2	8
Asst. Mgrs.	3	6	0	6
Dept. Mgrs.	11	3	5	5
Cashiers	69	6	26	26
Clerks	135	90	17	77
Security	7	0	0	0
Loaders	1	1	1	1
Maintenance	2	0	0	0
Drivers	1	2	0	2
Total Negro	240	183	56	182
Total Employment	2,096		1,974	

Source: Richard C. Speiglman, "Bargaining for Civil Rights," 1967 (unpublished paper prepared for Dr. Robert McKersie, Graduate School of Business, University of Chicago).

The A & P Agreement in Chicago

In its original negotiations, in May 1967, with Operation Breadbasket in Chicago, the A & P had promised to hire and promote 770 Negroes within one year. The chain reported hiring 697 and promoting another 167, but the net gain was far below the agreed upon figure, which the company attributed to substantial turnover.[99]

Operation Breadbasket launched a boycott and picketing which went on for 14 weeks, resulting in a new agreement being signed in October 1968. The new pact called for A & P to hire 268 more Negroes in the coming 12 months and to promote at least 20 to managerial or executive positions, and to create

99. *Retail Labor Report*, No. 1006 (October 11, 1968), p. A-7.

three positions for Negroes who will ensure the agreement is carried out.[100]

By April 1969, A & P had filled 130 of the promised jobs. Forty of the stores in Chicago were marketing products of 25 black manufacturers and using the trucking, garbage collection, and extermination services of another 25. Eighteen Negroes had been promoted to management positions, 12 as store managers and 6 in area and warehouse supervisory positions. Prior to the Breadbasket pact, 25 of A & P's 260 Chicago area stores were managed by blacks.[101]

Agreements in Cleveland

Operation Breadbasket negotiations with Pick-N-Pay Supermarkets, a division of Cook Coffee Company, which operated 60 stores in Cleveland were marked by sporadic picketing over a three-month period. The agreement reached in November 1967 was substantially similar to the Chicago plans, with Pick-N-Pay promising to add 300 Negroes, to use black bank and service companies, and to sell their companies' products.[102] The Pick-N-Pay agreement provided for a reevaluation on January 1, 1969.[103]

In December of 1968, A & P also concluded an agreement with Operation Breadbasket in Cleveland. The covenant called for A & P to hire 55 more Negroes at its 12 inner-city stores: 8 as management trainees, 12 as meat and/or produce managers, 15 as cashiers, 12 as meat clerks and as meat cutter apprentices. This agreement was reached after more than 60 days of picketing and boycotting at the chain's busiest inner-city stores and in the final weeks was extended to all 12 inner-city stores. According to the Rev. Randall T. Osburn, Cleveland's director of Operation Breadbasket, A & P had a black store manager in just one of its 50 stores, and only 196 Negroes among 1,116 employees before the Breadbasket agreement. Besides employment, A & P agreed to deposit $10,000 in a black savings and loan association, to use black models in its advertising, to adver-

---

100. *Ibid.* and "Blacks Wrap Up Slice of Action at Food Chains," *Business Week*, April 26, 1969, p. 162.

101. *Business Week*, pp. 162-163.

102. "Pick-N-Pay to Offer 300 Jobs in Its Stores to Cleveland Negroes," *Wall Street Journal*, November 28, 1967.

103. *Retail Labor Report*, No. 1015 (December 13, 1968), p. A-6.

tise in black-owned newspapers and radio stations, and to sell the products and use the services of black companies.[104]

Other A & P Experiences

As the most widely known and largest national chain, A & P could perhaps be expected to be a prime target of black employment demands. The previous sections indicate its experiences with Operation Breadbasket in Chicago and Cleveland. It also has been the target of localized boycott by that organization in Philadelphia, even though its inner-city stores were already almost completely run by Negroes, and has signed hiring agreements with the National Association for the Advancement of Colored People and the United Negro Protest Committee in Pittsburgh.[105]

In December 1970, the Rev. Jesse Jackson, national director of Operation Breadbasket, announced a 20 city boycott of A & P in a large-scale effort to bring about negotiations on increased Negro hiring and use of black-owned services.[106] The protest centered on the company headquarters city of New York, and the refusal of company president William J. Kane to meet with Breadbasket leaders led to sit-ins at the executive offices, led by Rev. Ralph David Abernathy. In the past, Operation Breadbasket has dealt with regional A & P executives in negotiating agreements for A & P operations in other cities, and the company maintained it must do the same in New York.[107] This boycott did not seem to have evoked the same response from the black communities as earlier ones. Perhaps Operation Breadbasket overreached itself by trying for a national position.

Other Pressure Group Efforts

Other organizations have also sought to obtain agreements with food stores with respect to quality of product, prices, em-

---

104. *Ibid.*

105. *Retail Labor Report,* No. 1010 (November 8, 1968), p. A-8.

106. "Operation Breadbasket Urges Boycott of A & P Food Chain in 20 Cities," *Fair Employment Report,* December 21, 1970, p. 178; and "Support for Breadbasket," *Fair Employment Practices,* No. 159 (March 25, 1971), summary section.

107. "The Sit-In at A & P Was No Tea Party," *Business Week,* February 6, 1971, p. 21; and Lesley Oelsner, "Abernathy Seized at A & P Protest," *New York Times,* April 7, 1971, p. 29.

ployment, purchase of services, and other matters. In Los Angeles, Safeway Stores was threatened with boycotts by a Negro group called the Coalition of Community Groups. The Coalition demanded that Safeway sign a so-called "Covenant Agreement" which in addition to containing the usual demands for better quality, efforts to employ minority members, and similar legitimate requests, also required Safeway to

. . . covenant and agree not to sell, advertise or otherwise deal in any table grapes until the grape boycott sponsored by the American Farm Workers Union has been resolved.
. . . covenant and agree not to advertise their products or their stores in the Los Angeles Herald-Examiner newspaper, or to offer for sale . . . any copies or editions of the said newspaper until the current labor-management dispute between the said newspaper and certain labor unions has been resolved.[108]

Safeway condemned these requests as wholly improper and refused to sign an agreement containing them. The incident indicates how organizations with legitimate goals can easily be led astray into other controversial areas and can strive to use their economic power to bring pressure upon parties and conflicts far removed from the field of minority employment opportunities.

Supermarkets have also been confronted by the Black Panthers, who seek donations of cash or merchandise both for general support and for their children's breakfast program, rather than for jobs. The Panthers' goals and methods are far more controversial and questionable than those of the civil rights organizations. When a Safeway store in California refused to contribute to the breakfast program, it found itself subject to a Panther-led boycott.[109] To some observers, such action seemed close to blackmail.

The various pressure groups in the black community represent a wide spectrum of goals, tactics, and membership, but on the whole they suffer from one common deficiency—a total lack of understanding of the economics of the supermarket industry. A viewpoint commonly held is that the supermarket is "recession-proof." This belief is then apparently equated with the assumption that supermarkets only make profits and never lose money. Indeed the black community—like most of the white community

---

108. See clauses 11 and 12 in the "Covenant-Agreement" reprinted in Appendix B.

109. Earl Caldwell, "Black Panthers Serving Youngsters a Diet of Food and Politics," *New York Times*, June 15, 1969.

—seems to believe that the supermarket is a veritable gold mine and averages about 10 to 20 percent in profits! One Negro group approached a financially troubled eastern food chain and demanded that the company hire a quota of blacks which was equal to the total number of store employees already on the roster of the concern. Although it was well known in financial and trade circles that the company had lost money in recent years, the leaders of the group found such a possibility difficult to accept. Nor could they understand that the policy of the company not to hire any new personnel was essential to the economic survival of the business. The pressures to which supermarkets have been subjected in recent years to some extent represent the fruits of an appalling degree of economic illiteracy which plagues our nation as a whole.

Blackmail Attempts

The line between legitimate pressure and outright blackmail is a thin one, but it seems clear that some groups fall in the latter category. The blackmailers, in contrast to the legitimate civil rights organizations, do not ask for more jobs, lower prices, or cash donations. They demand 50 percent (or more) of profits from stores in Negro areas or tell the owner to sign over his ownership in the store.

The writers were informed by an executive in Boston and by another in Houston that self-styled black leaders had attempted to blackmail them. The Boston man refused and the resultant picketing forced him out of business. The supermarket owner in Houston said that he was threatened with much more than pickets and boycotts and therefore sold his supermarkets in black neighborhoods to the Negro managers of those stores. The writers were also told of similar instances in other cities, but the information was second or third hand. One such blackmail threat is said to have resulted in the sale of about 20 stores by one chain in one large western state.

In Chicago, a street gang forced its way onto the payroll of Red Rooster Super Markets, a seven-store food chain, as a result of pressure brought upon the company by Operation Breadbasket, and eventually forced the concern out of business. The details of the bizarre incident were revealed by the *Chicago Tribune*. According to the newspaper report:

The documents show that the management of Red Rooster Super Markets placed 22 Rangers on their payroll, including 15 members of the "Main 21," the ruling echelon of the city's largest street gang . . . . The Rangers made their move in the midst of an economic boycott and picketing of the Red Rooster stores in March 1969 by Operation Breadbasket, the economic arm of the Southern Christian Leadership Conference.[110]

A letter from the management of the Red Rooster Super Markets to the Rev. C. T. Vivian of the Coalition for Community Action, a local community action group, indicated that the 22 men were being hired at the recommendation of Operation Breadbasket and the Coalition. The men in question have charges pending against them ranging from attempted murder to armed robbery. As a result of the losses which ensued from employment of these gang members, the chain closed seven stores and an estimated 300 blacks lost their jobs.[111]

Proved instances of this type of racketeering are rare, but they are certain to arise as unscrupulous persons are attracted to the tactics of boycott and coercion. Moreover, there is often a fine line between legitimate protest, illegal coercion, and outright attempted blackmail. For example, deliberate food spoilage (putting perishable fruits and vegetables under heavy groceries in a shopping cart and then leaving them) is at very least a questionable tactic.

Indeed the entire concept of extracting a covenant from an employer for a specific number of Negro jobs, although it may have a moral basis, rests upon questionable legal grounds. Demanding an all black supermarket labor force in certain stores would seem *per se* illegal under Title VII of the Civil Rights Act of 1964. Imposing a quota upon an employer with respect to Negro employees causes him to hire on the basis of race and therefore is likely to discriminate against other applicants in violation of law. Demanding that a company stock a black-owned and/or produced product to the exclusion of another may constitute both an unfair trade and an unfair labor practice and be illegal under both trade and labor laws. How proper or legal is it for a civil rights organization to demand that a company buy a particular product which it is alleged to be black owned and then when it receives the order, buy the product from a regular white-owned supplier and repackage it? Yet

---

110. *Chicago Tribune*, March 8, 1970, Section I, p. 2.

111. *Ibid.*

such schemes have been tried. Certainly some searching questions need to be asked about the legality and propriety of certain actions of civil rights organizations in order to clarify the respective rights of such organizations, the employers with whom they seek to obtain covenants, and the employee and potential employees of such concerns.

Results of Operation Breadbasket

Results achieved by Operation Breadbasket have varied in different parts of the country depending upon their bargaining strength versus that of the target employer and upon the tactics utilized. In some cases, Operation Breadbasket has merely sought "moral covenants" with little detailed implementation or follow-up. In other cases, it has used lengthy boycotting and picketing activity to extract specific commitments as to jobs, bank deposits, and service contracts with the requirement of periodic reviews.

Operation Breadbasket has not always been accorded united support by the Negro community. In fact in some areas as many as three or four civil rights organizations have vied with one another in obtaining covenants with supermarket operators. Furthermore, the demands of such organizations have sometimes been viewed by Negro union employees of supermarkets as requests for preferential treatment for unqualified applicants. In one recent confrontation in a large eastern city, a black union leader met with an Operation Breadbasket organizer and in fact told him to "get in line"—that the union would not tear down seniority to satisfy the demands of Operation Breadbasket for specified numbers of Negroes at various levels in the store labor force hierarchy.

On the whole, although the tactics of Operation Breadbasket may at times be questioned, it seems likely that its activities, and the publicity surrounding them, have resulted in a net gain in Negro employment in the chains against which it has acted. Even more important are the job upgradings that have resulted. Operation Breadbasket always places much more importance upon improvements in high pay and high status jobs despite its recognition that in terms of numbers the clerk and cashier jobs have a greater impact on employment as a whole. Of benefit also to the Negro community has been the success of Operation Breadbasket's efforts to involve the chains with Negro entrepreneurs and Negro-made products.

Operation Breadbasket has made the supermarket industry much more conscious of racial problems and undoubtedly has led to a number of policy changes. Thus special affirmative action hiring and promotion activities have been stepped up, and store managers have been trained to recognize the problems which they face in the civil rights area. It is likely that the greatest success of Operation Breadbasket and similar movements has been indirect, through action it has induced in companies to "get their house in order."

Most of the effects of Operation Breadbasket and similar movements are not shown in our latest employment statistics based on data collected in early 1969. Negro employment and occupational distributions—particularly the number of black managers—should, however, show definite improvement in the early 1970's as a result of these external pressures in combination with special efforts to be examined in the following section.

Of even deeper concern is the fact that conflict between such organizations as Operation Breadbasket, Black Panthers, and others purporting to represent the black community on the one hand and the white supermarket operator on the other has tended to wall off the inner city in terms of future expansion possibilities for most supermarket concerns. It is not simply the possibility of financial loss which makes new store construction in such areas unattractive, but also the conflict with Negro organizations which take an inordinate amount of top executive time and the threat of violence and confrontation which overhangs supermarket operation in such areas.

It is the opinion of the writers, gathered from conversations with supermarket executives all over the United States, that the psychological attitude of such executives toward supermarket operation in inner city locations is at an all-time low. Typical attitudes are reported in a recent special study in *Supermarket News,* entitled "Retailers Glum in L.A. Ghetto." [112] The article quotes various executives who operate stores in the predominantly black areas of south-central Los Angeles. One operator is quoted as saying, "I know of no retailer in this community who would come in again if he had it all to do over again. As a matter of fact, most retailers are wondering how they can get out." [113]

---

112. *Supermarkets News*, October 4, 1971, p. 1.

113. *Ibid.*

Not all operators share this pessimistic view. Ralphs Grocery
Co., for example, has instituted a number of innovative procedures in its black neighborhood supermarkets and is remer-
chandising such stores at the rate of one a month in order to
make them more responsive to the particular needs of Negro
shoppers. According to Byron Allumbaugh, executive vice president of the 63-unit chain,

With nine relatively high-volume stores in the black community, we do
as much or more volume than any group of stores in the area. We
therefore have a substantial stake in the community and we want to do
a better job of catering to its needs.[114]

Ralphs has appointed a Negro supervisor to head the nine-store
district and has established a "junior board of directors" composed of Negro employees in these stores to advise management
concerning their operation. Ralphs has found it necessary to
provide better managerial coverage in stores in black neighborhoods with a high proportion of Negro employees. Because of
the long hours that markets are open in the Los Angeles area,
it is not uncommon to have the third assistant manager in charge
of the store at certain times. Ralphs found that discipline and
performance suffered at such times. Furthermore, the company
also concluded that black store managers need additional support
in such stores because of the complex operating and merchandising problems which exist. Therefore, Ralphs has adopted a
policy of backing up a black store manager with two assistant
managers, one of whom is white, even though the customary
store complement might call for only one assistant manager.

Despite its obvious commitment to make its stores in this area
successful, Ralphs has also been afflicted with operational problems. For example, Allumbaugh reports that in this neighborhood losses from bad checks and pilferage are usually more than
twice the average and in some stores triple the average for a
given sales volume.[115] The problems experienced by operators in
the black community of south-central Los Angeles are particularly disturbing because this is not a ghetto area as the term is
normally used. There are no dirty tenements. People do not live
bunched together in squalid rooms. The area is physically not
comparable to the south side of Chicago or to New York's Har-

114. *Ibid.*, p. 4.

115. *Ibid.*

lem. Yet all the problems already referred to which threaten
the profitability of operation of supermarkets are even more serious in those gretto areas where deterioration is rampant and
levels of crime, unemployment, and dope addiction are even
higher.

In the long run, civil rights organizations will achieve more
lasting benefits in terms of Negro employment and maintenance
of vital services for the Negro community if they work with
supermarket concerns rather than against them. One of the first
things that needs to be done is to educate the leaders of such
organizations to the dollar and cents problems of running stores
in such inner city areas. The failure of most black-operated
markets in inner city areas indicates that black capitalism is
no solution, as will be discussed in the following chapter. The
problem lies in the maintenance of law and order, in developing
better performance on the part of employees, and in minimizing
some of the problems which erode profits and make market
operators reluctant to open new stores in such areas or to commit major funds to remodel old stores. Emphasis upon such
issues would bring Operation Breadbasket into confrontation
with powerful groups within the black community. As a political matter, therefore, it is doubtful whether such a change in
emphasis can occur. Attacks on the white chain store operator
for discrimination and exploitation represent an easier road, but
unfortunately in the long run they may simply result in dimin-
ished opportunities for employment by Negroes in their own
neighborhoods and a reduction in facilities capable of marketing
food to low income families at competitive prices.

COMPANY RECRUITMENT, TRAINING, AND UPGRADING PROGRAMS

In response to several factors, not the least of which were
the demands of such organizations as Operation Breadbasket,
chain companies are now actively seeking to improve their black
employment positions. They have enlisted the aid of Negro community agencies in finding prospective employees, and have become extensively involved in training programs.

Training the Hardcore Unemployed

Chain companies, singly or as members of larger organizations, have instituted recruitment and training programs di-

rected at increasing minority employment. As mentioned above, most entry level jobs have traditionally required only on-the-job training, such as for store clerks and cashiers. The hardcore training programs are generally extensions of this type of preparation, with the addition of specialized job-related help geared to insure successful adaptation to the supermarket work force by those with little previous job experience.

Grand Union, a chain headquartered in East Paterson, New Jersey, has been active in special training programs since the early 1960's, but its first efforts met with little success. A four-year effort to train Negro women in the use of various office machines never really got off the ground—the training just was not effective for some reason. Another attempt was to send applicants to regular business schools to teach office skills, but it was abandoned because about 90 percent always dropped out. Advertisements in *Ebony* also proved to be ineffective (no applicants) and expensive ($1,000 for two advertisements). The company even became involved with the Camp Kilmer Job Corps Center, mustering industry support in the form of training equipment. This, too, failed—the young men there just were not interested in food retailing.

After participating in a multi-industry training program in Florida, Grand Union began an experimental training program of its own in 1968, called "Operation Opportunity." The plan was to place four trainees in each of ten training stores. Initial recruitment difficulties in numbers and in finding people who would stay with the program resulted in giving responsibility for the program to Mr. Alfred Jackson, who had been promoted from assistant manager at a Poughkeepsie, N.Y. store to a personnel position at corporate headquarters.

Jackson also had recruitment problems, despite many appearances before many groups, but finally the quality and quantity problems improved. He had to learn to judge which applicants were willing to make an effort, as well as to overcome what he calls the "incredibility gap" that kept many good applicants from bothering to apply.

The essence of the program was deceptively simple. People who appeared to have motivation were tested and then test results ignored. The store manager was given responsibility for on-the-job training (extending the break-in period as required), and was taught to be lenient in cases of tardiness or absence —especially at the beginning of training. Jackson acted as a

backstop and a liason between worker and manager. He emphasized the importance of punctuality, for example, and telephoned
to notify the manager when a problem necessitated an absence;
and he also lent assistance in personal problems (that often
cause the absences).

Grand Union's experiment led to a two-year contract with the
Labor Department in 1969 to train 24 persons as cashiers, clerks,
and meat wrappers in the New York metropolitan area. The
Retail Clerks endorsed the contract, which called for wages after
training ranging from $1.87 to $2.12 an hour.[110] Although the
program produced 24 trained workers, in 1972 only 5 or 6 remained with the company, an indication of the characteristically
high turnover in this industry. In 1972, Grand Union was involved in a new training program for apprentice meat cutters.

In Los Angeles, the effort to make productive citizens of the
heardcore unemployed is primarily a product of the collective
bargaining system between food chain employers and the unions.
The president of the Food Employers Council and others saw
early in 1963 that racial problems in Los Angeles would inten-
sify. A two-day meeting was convened and resulted in a seven
page document entitled "Guide to Merit Employment: A Re-
statement of Industry Principles and Practices." Basically the
document reemphasized the policy of equal opportunity in employment and called for "a vigorous recruitment program for
qualified applicants on a community-wide basis." [117]

Although the document was favorably received by the Urban
League, no specific action plan was instituted until the Congress
of Racial Equality began a picket and boycott campaign at
Safeway aimed at forcing the company to employ more Negroes.
When it was explained to CORE that Safeway would be glad
to hire any qualified Negro applicants that the organization
could locate, CORE said that finding qualified applicants is an
employer's responsibility.

The impasse was placed in the hands of the Food Employers
Council for resolution. There did not seem to be an adequate
number of qualified Negroes available and the other chains did
not wish to share the Safeway experience. The Council solution
was to employ a trainer to set up a school and to seek a Man-

---

116. *Retail Labor Report*, No. 1023 (February 7, 1969), p. A-13.

117. Page 2 of the document (unpublished) supplied by Food Employers
Council.

power Development and Training Act grant from the federal government to underwrite part of the expenses. Union approval was also necessary because pay and other conditions were to be different from the contractual agreement. This could have been an obstacle, but the unions immediately agreed to the program.

Starting up the training involved the logistical problems of finding a trainer and training site, equipping the building, etc. In addition, over 90 ministers and organizations were contacted with requests to send applicants. Initial screening was done by the state employment service and procedures for secondary screening were worked out.

The program was required by the Manpower Development and Training Act to accept only the unemployed and underemployed, yet it has experienced an exceptional success rate. Of the first 40 to begin training—three weeks prevocational training and thirteen weeks of OJT—36 completed the program. Two were lost to the draft, one quit, and one was dropped from the program.

Similar training ventures, all supported by government-industry sponsored National Association of Businessmen JOBS contracts funded by the U.S. Department of Labor, have been run by chain companies in various cities across the country. In Chicago, Jewel Tea trained cashiers and produce department workers through on-the-job training and careful supervision by special "Coaches" who both counseled trainees and worked with store personnel to ensure their success. Although Jewel recruited extensively for this program, it had difficulty finding black males to enter training. Its female cashier training, however, was considered quite successful.[118] In 1970, Jewel had 10 stores in exclusively black neighborhoods, seven of which were managed by Negroes. Of its ten stores in mixed neighborhoods, four were headed by black managers.[119] It may have difficulty increasing these numbers if Negro men are not found to enter the job progressions who could benefit from the specialized training.

Hardcore unemployed persons are being trained by Lucky Stores in several western cities to become journeymen retail clerks. After a year of operation, the program had achieved a

---

118. *Supermarket News*, November 19, 1969, p. 47.

119. Seth B. King, "Food Chain Seeks Involvement in Chicago," *New York Times*, July 21, 1970, p. 47.

66 percent retention rate with its trainees, who averaged 23.7 years old, with previous incomes of $1,000 to $1,700 before entering training. Lucky's program gave two weeks of classroom work and then distributed the trainees among its stores for four weeks of OJT, then returned them to the classroom for another week for job reorientation. Special assistance to the trainees included help with finances and credit problems and police arrests.[120]

King Soopers in Denver, Milgram Food Stores in Kansas City, Ralphs Grocery in Los Angeles, and Penn Fruit in Philadelphia have also been awarded training grants.[121] One major company contracted nationally to train 374 hardcore applicants for jobs in the warehouse, processing plants, and stores. To date, however, only 138 jobs have been filled. Like other supermarket concerns, this company has found that turnover is substantial among such trainees and despite commitment to the program by top officials, operating personnel, who have the ultimate responsibility for the day-to-day detail of training, are constantly diverted by the pressures of other operating problems.

A few contracts have also been awarded to train store managers, assistant managers, meat cutters, and clerks. Once trained, the Small Business Administration planned to help the new managers open their own stores, if they so desired, in or near "problem neighborhoods." [122]

All these training programs hopefully will have an impact on black supermarket employment. They can be especially important where they bring new black workers into sales, managerial, or craft occupations, and where they enable Negroes to join the entry ranks which lead to store manager positions, because these occupations were most noticeably lacking in black workers at the end of the 1960's.

Affirmative Action Programs

In 1965 President Johnson signed Executive Order 11246 [123] requiring that contractors or subcontractors with 50 or more employees and a contract of $50,000 or more with the Federal

---

120. *Retail Labor Report*, No. 991 (June 28, 1968), p. A-5, and *Supermarket News*, April 21, 1969, p. 12 and July 21, 1969, p. 21.

121. *Retail Labor Report*, No. 991 (June 28, 1968), p. A-5.

122. *Retail Labor Report*, No. 1023 (February 7, 1969), pp. A-12 - A-13.

123. 30 *Federal Register* 12319.

Government develop a written affirmative action compliance program for each of its establishments. Rules issued [124] by the U.S. Department of Labor in implementation of this order require that the participating company submit a detailed analysis of job categories with data indicating the number of females and minority members in various classifications. Furthermore, the company must submit figures indicating how the percentage of various minority groups on the payroll compare with the percentage which these groups constitute in the labor areas surrounding the particular facilities. Finally, the company must submit goals, timetables, and affirmative action commitments designed to correct identifiable deficiencies.

Good faith compliance with the Executive Order, therefore, requires a major commitment by a company in terms of time, money, and personnel. The order is not generally applicable to the supermarket industry because relatively few supermarket concerns sell to the government. As one executive pointed out, government contracts are so minor in relation to other revenue producing areas of the business that it would be simple to withdraw from the government contract business and thus eliminate the need for undertaking such a major program with respect to minority employment.

It is not known how many supermarket companies in the United States are currently subject to the terms of the Executive Order. The number is probably small. It is significant, however, that Safeway Stores, Inc., the nation's second largest food chain, has elected to come under the order even though its government contract business is minimal relative to the billions it annually registers in retail sales. Company executives believe that participation in the program provides a useful discipline and will give them an advantage over competition in learning how productively to utilize minority members of the labor force. The company has made a detailed canvas of its minority labor force representation and has established goals— both short run and long run—in terms of employment levels in its various districts and facilities.

Alliances with Negro Organizations and Other Company Activities

Whether they are involved in training programs, supermarket companies generally have relations with local and national civil

----

124. See 41 CFR Part 60-2, *Federal Register*, Vol. 36 (August 31, 1971).

rights and other Negro organizations. Spokesmen for A & P, a company which has had several confrontations with Operation Breadbasket, and is currently being boycotted on a national scale, have been careful to point out their company's links with the Urban League, CORE, NAACP, and the Floyd McKissick Association, as well as other community groups. In addition, A & P recently elected its first black member of the company's board of directors, Hobart Taylor, Jr., a Washington attorney.[125] As pointed out above, other firms have utilized their contacts with black organizations in developing sources of potential Negro employees.

Companies have been involved in other kinds of activities to express their concern for local communities and the problems of black inner city dwellers. Some have contributed to the Black Panther's breakfast program, although this particular activity has been accused by others of being primarily a propaganda effort whose requests for donations have been labeled a "strong arm tactic." [126]

Jewel Food Stores in Chicago wants to be "a major community factor" in that area, according to its president, Harry G. Beckner. In addition to consumer problems which affect its stores in all neighborhoods, such as unit pricing and anti-pollution information about products on its shelves, Jewel is making special efforts with its stores in Chicago black neighborhoods. These efforts include stocking of special foods and extensive modernization of its older, inner city stores. Jewel is particularly sensitive to the need to have black employees in managerial positions. Of its 20 stores in all-black or mixed neighborhoods, 11 were headed by black managers in 1970.[127]

Safeway Stores has provided another example of corporate concern. When a Negro-owned supermarket, the Neighborhood Co-Op, located in a San Francisco Negro neighborhood, was on the point of collapse, Safeway stepped in with managerial help, new stock, and other assistance. As a result, the store was able to reopen with new equipment and a new merchandising pro-

---

125. "The Sit-in at A & P Was No Tea Party," *Business Week*, February 6, 1971, p. 21.

126. "Blacks in L.A. Take on Safeway," *Supermarket News*, December 1, 1969, p. 1.

127. Seth B. King, "Food Chain Seeks Involvement in Chicago," *New York Times*, July 21, 1970.

gram.[128] Safeway continued to support the Co-Op for over two years, lending it a skilled manager without cost. Indications are that the operation is still running on a marginal basis, a primary reason being the lack of consumer support from the black community.

UNION IMPACT

The various unions in the supermarket industry have generally agreed to the special provisions of the company's training programs, thus helping these efforts to succeed. Union approval is necessary because pay and other contractual conditions may differ in these training arrangements from those agreed to in labor contracts. The Retail Clerks; Teamsters, Bakery and Confectionery Workers; Retail, Wholesale and Department Store Union; and the Amalgamated Meat Cutters have all endorsed JOBS training programs where the plans are operating in unionized stores.[129]

In some instances, the unions have adopted an affirmative program. Thus some locals of the Amalgamated Meat Cutters, with national union support and encouragement, have established training programs for minority workers.[130] The Amalgamated has a heavy representation of blacks in its packinghouse worker locals and among its national and local officers and staff, and they obviously exert a strong influence toward equalitarianism. International officers, however, are reluctant to take disciplinary action against local unions and therefore in the Meat Cutters union—as in many other unions—locals pursue discriminatory policies which may be directly contrary to international union policy.[131]

On the whole, it seems likely that the organizational structure of unions in the supermarket industry, and policies which they

---

128. "Food Giant Saves Frisco Co-Op for 2,700 Owners," *New Pittsburgh Courier*, June 29, 1968.

129. *Retail Labor Report*, No. 991 (June 28, 1968), p. A-5; and No. 994 (July 19, 1968), pp. A-5 - A-6.

130. The locals in Detroit, Chicago, New York, and several other areas are involved in these programs.

131. See Walter A. Fogel, *The Negro in the Meat Industry*, The Racial Policies of American Industry, Report No. 12 (Philadelphia: Industrial Research Unit, Wharton School of Finance and Commerce, University of Pennsylvania, 1970), for an analysis of overall Amalgamated racial policies.

pursue, probably have an adverse impact on Negro employment and job improvement, even though the structure and policies are certainly not designed to have this effect. Historically, the meat department has always been, and continues to be, unionized on a separate basis, in most cases by a different union from the balance of the store. Truck drivers are in the same category. Thus the top hourly jobs in the industry are outside any line of progression of typical entry jobs. Workers in unionized stores do not usually acquire storewide seniority, or easily transfer to the meat or driver groups, or to jobs from which they can advance to a butcher or truck driver position. Since Negroes, as a group, are more likely to lack skill or training, they generally are employed as clerks or unskilled grocery workers. They tend to remain in this department, where wages are relatively good but below those of the meat and driver groups.

To be sure the unions neither inaugurated this system, nor intend it to discriminate against minorities. They have, however, institutionalized it. Even where one union maintains a "wall-to-wall" agreement covering all of a company's hourly jobs, separate units are frequently maintained. If the Retail Clerks and the Meat Cutters do merge, as they are considering, one can apparently expect little change in this structure in the immediate future. As in the building construction industry, craft demarcations impede intraplant movements and therefore disproportionately retard any group that is overly concentrated in lower rated jobs.

Other union policies react against Negro employment, again not intentionally, but in fact. The Retail Clerks' insistence that bag boys be paid the basic clerical rate has caused their elimination in many areas. Jobs for which young, unskilled Negroes (or whites, of course) could be employed, were thus eliminated. The Meat Cutters Union has pushed hard to have skilled personnel take over the related unskilled jobs—wrapping, weighing, sweeping, etc.—much as building craftsmen have done.[132] This has not only eliminated jobs for which Negroes without special skills might easily qualify, but it has also reduced the potential for entry level positions from which one might be naturally upgraded.

---

132. For details of these practices, see Herbert R. Northrup and Gordon R. Storholm, *Restrictive Labor Practices in the Supermarket Industry,* Industrial Research Unit Study No. 44 (Philadelphia: University of Pennsylvania Press, 1967), Chapters 5 and 6.

Although the Teamsters Union has many black members and has participated in activities designed to enhance Negro employment, it has generally not supported black aspirations to gain over-the-road or key local truck driving jobs.[133] This seems to be the situation in the supermarket industry, where Negroes comprise a large segment of the warehouse employees and a very small proportion of the truck drivers. The Teamsters Union does not appear to be opposed to this situation, nor especially interested in changing it.

As was mentioned in Chapter II, one of the major technological developments in the supermarket industry is the transfer of the meatcutting operation from individual butcher shops in the back rooms of individual markets to a centralized meat warehouse where meat would be cut, packaged, and shipped to stores either in retail cuts and packages or so-called "block-ready" cuts which require a minimum of further processing prior to packaging for the customer.[134] The result of this transition—which is well underway in the industry—will be to curtail sharply the employment opportunities for meat cutters at the store level. In order to obtain union approval of the change in work, many companies have agreed that store level meat cutters will have the first option for warehouse jobs on a seniority basis. Since a central warehouse is much more efficient than a number of store level meatcutting operations, the establishment of such a facility will overall tend to reduce the total number of meat cutters required. The seniority provision could therefore effectively freeze out Negroes from the new warehouse jobs, since on the whole they tend to be newer hires than the white employees. Furthermore, since the Meat Cutters will control the allocation of work in the central facilities through the application of seniority provisions, they may be able to set up barriers to Negro transferance to higher paying, more attractive jobs. The Meat Cutters Union, even in plants, has traditionally espoused department, rather than plant, seniority. As a consequence, Negroes have often been confined to the departments

---

133. On Teamster policy, see Richard D. Leone, "The Negro in the Trucking Industry," in Herbert R. Northrup, *et al., Negro Employment in Land and Air Transport*, Studies of Negro Employment, Vol. V (Philadelphia, Industrial Research Unit, Wharton School of Finance and Commerce, University of Pennsylvania, 1971), Part Three.

134. See Northrup, *op. cit.*, pp. 171-176 for union policy and company response on this development.

with the more unsavory working conditions.[135] To the extent that separate seniority prevails for butchers, with their employment on a craft basis, Negroes could have difficulty in progressing to these jobs.

Although in theory the substitution of a central facility for numerous backroom operations would seem to narrow the opportunities for Negroes in meat-related jobs in the supermarket industry, in practice the contrary may result. The experience of a number of companies which have set up central meat facilities suggests that white meat cutters are reluctant to transfer to such jobs. Apparently work in a central meat facility is not viewed as "journeyman work." Since there has been a continuing shortage of skilled meat cutters in the trade, those displaced by the closing or curtailment of backroom cutting operations can readily find employment elsewhere in markets which have not adopted this procedure.

On the other hand, blacks have always been accustomed to working in meatpacking plants and readily apply for work in central meat distribution warehouses of supermarket companies. Therefore, as the transition proceeds during the coming decade from store to central facility employment in meatcutting and meat preparation, the net result could very well be an increase in employment opportunities for Negro workers.

On the whole, however, it appears that current union policies are more discouraging than helpful to Negro employment. Management policies, of course, remain far more significant since management does the hiring. Moreover, a sizable segment of the industry—particularly the regional and local chains, and of course the small stores—operate nonunion. We have been unable to assess definitively whether unionized supermarkets employ a higher percentage of Negroes than do nonunion ones, where other factors (for example, store location) are relatively equal. Since, however, the large supermarkets appear to be the leading employers of blacks, and since they are the most heavily unionized, one must conclude that unions have not interfered with the employment of Negroes, but that their policies have precluded further employment and easier access to better jobs.

---

135. Fogel, *op. cit.*, pp. 105-108.

CHAPTER VII

Black Capitalism and Black Supermarkets

The mounting problems faced by corporate chains in operating stores in ghetto areas has led to the closing of many markets in such locations. The availability of such stores coupled with the general interest in the Negro community in the concept of black capitalism has led to a major thrust by Negroes to acquire ownership of supermarkets in the communities in which they live. If this movement were to meet with success, it would have important implications for the economic future of Negroes in our central cities. Not only would Negro owned and operated supermarkets fill a community need for convenient food distribution facilities, but also such markets could provide employment opportunities for Negroes at every level of the occupational ladder.

Success, however, depends upon making a profit, and, as has already been indicated, profits do not come easy in the ghetto environment. Unfortunately, as with black capitalism itself, the interest shown by Negro entrepreneurs in supermarkets reflects a mixture of economic and emotional motivation rather than a cold analytical appraisal of the opportunities for profit which exist in this area of private enterprise. In this chapter, we shall appraise some of the major difficulties which lie in the way of successful Negro ownership and operation of supermarkets in ghetto areas and suggest some tentative solutions for the problems which black businessmen are experiencing.

WHY BLACK SUPERMARKETS?

Why do Negroes want to own their own supermarkets? The reasons are not hard to find.

Portions of this chapter previously appeared in "Black Capitalism in Ghetto Supermarkets: Problems and Potential," by Gordon F. Bloom in *Industrial Management Review*, Spring 1970. © 1970 by the Industrial Management Review Association; all rights reserved. Reprinted by permission.

Foremost perhaps is the fact that the supermarket has become a universal symbol of successful American business enterprise. Even Khrushchev inspected a supermarket when he visited the United States. Likewise in the ghetto the supermarket is a symbol of the white man's world of abundance. Ghetto communities have been compared to underdeveloped nations. While the analogy is imperfect, there is a basic similarity in that both groups suffer from feelings of inferiority which may require a success symbol in order to develop unity and strengthen morale. A busy supermarket is an attractive business; it has the appearance of success even when it is losing money! Furthermore, when located in the ghetto it is likely to be one of the newer structures in the area. Even though ghetto manufacturing plants may afford a less tortuous road to profits—as will be elaborated at a later point in this chapter [136]—the supermarket has a visibility quotient which makes it a focus of entrepreneurial interest in the black community.

The supermarket is a symbol of big business to the average Negro businessman. It must be remembered that until recently the typical black business activity in the ghetto was the small corner grocery store. To the struggling black businessman, big successful business was epitomized by the white supermarket with its thousands of customers and millions of dollars going through the checkout stands. Perhaps that is a major part of the fascination of the supermarket—it is a million dollar business in terms of sales, even though profits are often miniscule.

While the two reasons set forth above are primarily emotional, there is also a sound economic basis for black interest in supermarkets in ghetto areas. This grows out of a recognition that there is a need for markets in such areas. In the first place, almost every ghetto has sufficient population to support a new supermarket, but white chains have been slow to build them. While white suburbs with 25,000 to 30,000 population will frequently have four or five new supermarkets, it is not unusual to drive through densely populated blocks in ghettos containing even greater population concentrations and find not a single new supermarket. The lack of new supermarket construction is not attributable solely to the racial characteristics

---

136. That ghetto manufacturing plants are also experiencing difficulties is confirmed by the writer's field research. The comparison is one of degree. See also John T. Garrity, "Red Ink for Ghetto Industries?" *Harvard Business Review*, May-June 1968, pp. 4 *et seq.*

of these areas. Many other circumstances contribute to this
condition, including the difficulty of finding adequate land at
reasonable cost in a densely populated urban neighborhood.
Nevertheless the fact remains that if we look at the problem
solely on the basis of the ratio of markets to population, there
is an obvious shortage of supermarkets in black neighborhoods.
Moreover, because car ownership is low among black residents
of ghetto areas, the availability of conveniently located supermarkets becomes even more important in such neighborhoods.

In the second place, the need for supermarkets in ghetto areas
is made more urgent by the fact, substantiated by recent investigations conducted by the U.S. Department of Labor, the
U.S. Department of Agriculture, the Federal Trade Commission
and other groups, that the poor do pay more for their food in
such areas.[137] Because large modern chain markets are frequently not available, the ghetto resident often is compelled to
shop in the smaller, less efficient convenience stores which charge
higher prices for their products. Furthermore, where older chain
supermarkets do exist in ghetto neighborhoods, there have been
charges—in most cases unfounded, but nevertheless given wide
credence by the black community—that chains charge more in
ghetto stores than in white neighborhoods for the same products,
that perishable products are generally of poorer quality, and
that prices are deliberately raised just before welfare checks
become available to customers.

Part and parcel of the interest in black supermarkets is the
philosophy that underlies black capitalism generally, namely that
the money earned in business located in the ghetto ought to
stay in the black community, that black ownership is necessary
to give the Negro dignity and status in the mainstream of American economic life, and that examples of accomplishments by
Negroes as successful American business entrepreneurs will afford new motivation to Negro youth to stake out careers in
private enterprise. In St. Louis, James E. Hurt, Jr., one of the

---

137. See, for example, U.S. Bureau of Labor Statistics, National Commission
    on Food Marketing Special Studies in Food Marketing, "Retail Food
    Prices in Low and High Income Areas," *Technical Study No. 10*, June
    1966; U. S. Department of Agriculture, Consumer and Marketing
    Service, *Comparison of Prices for Selected Foods in Chain Stores in
    High and Low Income Areas in Six Cities* (Washington: Government
    Printing Office, June 1968) ; Committee on Government Operations,
    United States House of Representatives, *Consumer Problems of the
    Poor: Supermarket Operations in Low-Income Areas and the Federal
    Response*, Union Calendar No. 755, 90th Cong. 2d Sess., August 7, 1968.

more successful black supermarket operators, built a supermarket and shopping center across the street from the largest high school in the city which has almost 3,000 black students. He puts the motivation argument this way:

Can you imagine what's going to happen to those Black boys and girls consciously and subconsciously as they pass back and forth over the four years that they're in high school, passing this shopping center, passing this supermarket and knowing within themselves, "This belongs to us"? [138]

This line of reasoning assumes that the black supermarket will be successful—and this one may well be. But on the record to date it appears that the majority will fail. If this should happen, then a reverse action could be engendered and the black community could suffer losses, both economic and emotional which might leave scars for years to come. This possibility does not seem to have been adequately weighed by many Negro entrepreneurs who seem to have been unduly swayed by the glamor and volume potential of supermarket operation without appreciating a simple basic fact, well understood by men with long experience in the trade: the supermarket business is a difficult and risky business.

THE RECORD TO DATE

Before we review the experience of black entrepreneurs in supermarket operation, it may be helpful in terms of perspective to consider the overall experience of Negro-operated businesses in the ghetto. While no adequate statistics are available, it is generally recognized that the experience has been unfortunate. The results are what would be expected, given the nature of the business, the nature of the environment, and the handicaps flowing from lack of managerial know-how.

Decline of Negro Business Operations

Most black business operations have been small retail establishments—typically the corner grocery store, variety store, lunch counter, beauty parlor, and so forth. The average life of this type of business—whether managed by a Negro or a white man —is very short. Statistics indicate that 51 percent of all new

---

138. Speech at National-American Wholesale Grocers' Association Executive Conference, Nassau, The Bahamas, September 20, 1968.

retail businesses fail within one and one-half years and 70 percent fail within three and one-half years.[139]

The problems of small business are magnified by the changing and hostile environment of the ghetto. Crime, violence, riots, all raise the risk of doing business in such areas. Furthermore, construction of new highways, urban redevelopment projects, exodus of manufacturing plants, and constantly changing neighborhoods have literally strangled Negro enterprise and turned once prosperous neighborhood shopping areas into rows of vacant stores. To overcome such obstacles the small businessman would need great managerial talent and abundant working capital—neither of which is characteristic of small business enterprise regardless of the color of the owner.

It is not surprising then to find that in the decade from 1950 to 1960 there was actually a 20 percent decline in the number of Negro owned and operated businesses in the United States.[140] Now we have a resurgence of interest in Negro operation of business in ghetto areas. Has the picture changed? Will the pattern of failure be reversed, or will the same difficulties inherent in the nature of the business, the nature of the environment, and the lack of managerial ability produce a new round of failures and disenchantment with private enterprise?

Experience of Black Supermarkets

Despite current interest by black businessmen in supermarket operation, to date only a small number of such enterprises have actually been acquired or newly constructed. According to estimates provided from various industry sources,[141] there are probably less than 100 black-owned supermarkets in the entire United States, if we define as a supermarket a market with self-service meat, grocery, and produce having sales on an annual basis of not less than one million dollars.[142] There are two avenues to black ownership of supermarkets in ghetto areas: acquisition of existing white-owned stores, or construction and operation of

---

139. *Business Management*, May 1969, p. 6.

140. Dan Cordtz, "The Negro Middle Class is Right in the Middle," *Fortune*, Vol. 74 (November 1966), p. 228.

141. It is a sad commentary on the lack of attention to Negro enterprise in this field that there is no up-to-date compilation of the number and location of Negro-owned and operated supermarkets in the United States.

142. This is the accepted definition in common usage in the industry.

new markets in such areas. The black-owned markets which are presently in operation represent both of these approaches, but neither one seems to bring with it the assurance of success.

The fact is that the record of black-owned supermarkets to date has been one of losses, sales below expectations, and in a few cases scandalous mismanagement. Despite these difficulties, trade publications and black journals are inclined to describe the operations in glowing terms which bear little relation to reality. Cosmetic exaggeration has been substituted for analytical appraisal. There is a real need for candid discussion of the nature of the difficulties in order that some solution can be found for the problems that beset the black owner of a ghetto supermarket. At a recent meeting attended by a number of black owners of supermarkets, one ruefully remarked: "I thought that I was the only one losing money and that everyone else was coining money." The fact is that most of the black-owned supermarkets, including those which have received considerable publicity, have been losing money. The time has come to take a long hard look at the reasons.

THE CAUSES OF FAILURE

It is easy to explain away the dismal record of black supermarkets by saying that Negroes do not have the needed managerial skills. If what is "needed" is a skill to make money in the ghetto, then the record of loss proves that the Negro owners did not have it and the statement contains its own explanation. But the problem goes much deeper, because the real question is whether any owner—white or black—can make money in such operations. Obviously the level of management ability is a factor, but the nature of the supermarket business and the peculiarities of the ghetto environment combine to produce a multiplicity of problems which has compounded the task of black management. Let us take a look at each of these factors in turn.

The Nature of the Supermarket Industry

Supermarket operation even under normal conditions is a demanding business. Profits are low, averaging only about one percent on sales. There is little margin for error. Many costs are figured to two decimal places. Not only are profit margins low, but volume is high. The result is that mistakes can be very costly. While it is difficult, and indeed unusual, for a store to earn more than 2 to 3 percent net, after allocation for overhead, it is all too easy to lose 2 to 4 percent on sales if critical ratios get out of line.

The supermarket customer is extremely critical. She will not tolerate inaccurate pricing, or out-of-stock shelves, or poor service. This is true whether she is white or black, and whether the store is black-owned or white-owned. As a matter of fact, most black supermarket operators allege that the Negro customer enters a black-owned market with a built-in skepticism that the black operator can do as well as the white man, and therefore the black operator may actually have to maintain the store at a higher standard than a white operator in order to attract and retain customers. The black operator is particularly at a disadvantage in the opening weeks of operation when he has many untrained employees in the store and few knowledgeable people to train them. Yet the black customer may form an unfavorable image of the store in these early days of operation and consequently take her business elsewhere. Chains, of course, are able to open stores with much less difficulty by transferring a cadre of skilled employees to the new unit while training new employees in other stores of the chain.

Ideally, the black entrepreneur ought to have an umbrella over his business during the first year of operation to enable him to get on his feet. He may be able to get help from a wholesaler or other trade source, but there is no way in the supermarket business that he can contract for business from his customers for a year—or even for a day. One of the advantages of a manufacturing plant operation as a vehicle for black ownership is that it is possible to negotiate a contract either with government or a sponsoring company to take all or a substantial part of the plant's output for the first year of operation. In the retail field, however, the black entrepreneur is exposed to the full blast of the winds of competition from the moment he opens his doors for business. Experience has demonstrated that appeals to the customer on the basis that the store is black-owned and therefore deserves the support of the community fall upon deaf ears when the operation does not measure up to competitive standards.

In a large eastern city, ministers appealed to their congregations to shop at a newly constructed supermarket which was owned by members of the Negro community. Despite such appeals, sales continued at a unsatisfactory level while a nearby white-owned supermarket continued to do almost twice as much business. In a western black-owned supermarket with unsatisfactory sales and heavy losses, most members of the cooperative which owned the store shopped elsewhere. A successful eastern black supermarket operator reported that while his sales were generally satisfactory in the lower economic strata of the Negro community, he was unsuccessful in attracting middle class blacks to his market.

For the reasons enumerated, the supermarket industry is a difficult industry in which to learn the fundamentals of business operation. Retribution for mistakes comes too fast and swift. Moreover even the most successful chains find that at any time a substantial number of their stores may lose money. One investigator has found what he terms is an "S-Curve of Profitability" of stores in the industry with 25 to 30 percent of the stores of the typical chain actually operating at a loss.[143] The point is that in the retail business—and particularly in the supermarket business—even the most experienced company cannot go into a new location, put its best manager in charge of the unit, and be certain that the new store will make money. There are too many sales and cost factors which are wholly or partly beyond the control of the operator. *A fortiori*, when a black owner with less developed managerial skills opens a new store, there is a substantial risk that he will lose money. The real problem lies in the fact that he may not have sufficient capital to enable him to weather the difficult first year or two of operation while he develops a seasoned crew to run the store and an image of value and service with his customers.

If the black supermarket operator fails, he has plenty of company. Pick up any daily newspaper and turn to the pages listing business auctions. You will be surprised at the number of auctions listing sales of supermarket equipment. According to Dun and Bradstreet, in 1970 there were 533 failures reported in the "Food and Liquor" category, 200 of them "grocery" and "grocery and meat" stores.[144] In view of the fact that the black entrepreneur will frequently be undercapitalized and lack an ex-

---

143. William Applebaum, "Chain Store Location Strategy and the Store Profit S-Curve," *Proceedings of American Marketing Association*, June 1965, pp. 283-294.

144. Dun and Bradstreet, *Quarterly Failure Report*, Third Quarter, 1971.

perienced management team, one may seriously question whether the supermarket industry is an appropriate vehicle for experimentation in black capitalism.

Problems of the Ghetto Environment

A Negro marketing consultant remarked at a recent meeting that the problems faced by black owners of supermarkets in the ghetto were really no different from those that were faced by white owners of markets in white urban centers—except that they were worse! There is much truth in this statement, but it overlooks the fact that certain of the problems created by the ghetto environment are really different *in kind*. The black operator is burdened not only with difficult merchandising and operating problems but also with complex social problems which the community and government have been unable to solve.

Violence. Most critical of the problems unique to the ghetto is the atmosphere of violence which has become an everyday part of ghetto living. The black businessman must not only be a good businessman but a very astute politician as well. The ghetto is a forum for conflicting power blocs and any major business enterprise which hopes to operate successfully and without interruption in this arena must learn to deal with these contestants. When one black supermarket operator who was having difficulty hiring skilled black employees was asked why he did not hire white employees he answered that the black militant group in the neighborhood had warned him not to hire white employees if he wanted to avoid trouble. "They will fire bomb me if I do," he stated unequivocally.

Violence evidences itself in many forms in the ghetto. Crimes of a violent nature are frequent occurrences on ghetto streets, especially robbery, aggravated assault, forcible rape, burglary and similar crimes. The National Advisory Commission on Civil Disorders found that low income Negro areas have significantly higher crime rates than low income white areas.[145]

The ever-present threat of riots and bombing makes fire insurance extremely costly. When a wholesaler in a large eastern city sold a supermarket covered by a blanket fire insurance policy to a black operator who was going to operate the one store, the fire insurance rate for the property jumped 300 per cent. De-

---

145. National Advisory Commission on Civil Disorders, *Report* (New York: Bantam Books, 1968), p. 267.

spite the passage by Congress in August 1968 of the FAIR Program (Fair Access to Insurance Requirements), one-third of the states have not adopted FAIR plans and the program is not affording much relief even in the states where it is operating. A Congressional subcommittee was told recently that some Chicago ghetto dwellers are paying five times as much for coverage as they did before the April 1968 riots, when there was no FAIR Program.[146] Similar problems of cost and coverage face the operator of ghetto markets.

Many ghetto markets close early on winter evenings because residents are afraid to go out in the streets after dark. Furthermore, female help are reluctant to work evenings if they have to go home after dark. In certain ghetto areas, markets will not make deliveries to housing projects where trucks have been looted or deliverymen attacked.

Employee Theft and Customer Pilferage. While violence is in many respects almost a unique characteristic of the ghetto environment, employee theft and customer pilferage are problems faced by every retail enterprise. In the ghetto, however, as in many low income white or mixed neighborhoods, their incidence is magnified by the presence of all those factors which tend to foster a disrespect for traditional rights of private property: high unemployment, poverty, dope addiction, lack of parental supervision and discipline, and social disorganization. As a consequence, employee theft and customer pilferage are probably the two most costly burdens imposed by the ghetto environment upon the retailer seeking to operate a business in such areas.

Losses from these two sources can be staggering. The white operator of a relatively new market which recently closed in an urban ghetto reported to the writer that his shortages were running as high as 5 percent of sales! This is quite a cross to bear in a business that normally earns only one percent net on sales. Nor will the color of the black operator's skin shield him from this insidious drain on profits. All over the United States, the experiences of black operators of supermarkets attest to an undeniable fact: blacks will steal from blacks just as whites steal from whites. Appeals to race pride, community ownership, and such popular concepts as "It's your own bag" do not offset the fatal fascination of thousands of dollars passing through the cash registers.

---

146. *Business Week*, May 10, 1969, p. 104.

The ghetto environment not only fosters crime but also makes it difficult for the retailer to take appropriate measures to control losses. When employee theft is suspected in a retail unit, chain operators normally take certain precautions. If theft through the checkouts is suspected, they will transfer certain employees to other units in order to break up cliques which might be working together and also they attempt to hire for cashier positions persons who do not live in the immediate neighborhood and who are therefore less likely to permit orders for friends to go through the checkouts at less than the correct amount. The single store ghetto operator, however, does not have this flexibility. He cannot make transfers to and from other units and to make matters worse he usually finds it difficult to get employees from other areas to come into a particular neighborhood "where they do not belong." The result is that a condition is created and perpetuated which presents an invitation to a kind of employee theft which is extremely difficult to detect.

This kind of situation developed in a ghetto store in an eastern city. The delinquent employees were finally uncovered through use of lie detector tests. It is interesting to note that in this particular case the market was owned by residents of the ghetto community and the Board of Directors was composed of Negro ministers, but this identity of the business enterprise with the black community did not deter employees from stealing thousands of dollars from the company.

What does the black owner of a ghetto supermarket do when he apprehends a black employee stealing? Negro operators say it is a heartrending experience. Most of these operators are struggling to make a success of their businesses not just to make a profit but because of a conviction that the success of the business will benefit the whole community and will uplift the image and morale of the black man. Consequently, when the black owner finds a black employee stealing, it is a little like catching a traitor. Yet most black operators confess that at first they bent over backwards and were exceptionally lenient with such employees, and with black customers caught stealing, as well. Eventually, however, they found that a lenient attitude only encouraged more theft and therefore adopted a policy of turning over such miscreants to the police for prosecution.

Most Negro supermarket operators are acutely aware of the risk of serious inventory shortages and many employ full-time security officers, another costly burden imposed by the ghetto environment. Yet while black operators are aware of the problem, they have practically no idea of exactly how much they are losing through theft. The reason is that their accounting controls are insufficient to reveal anything more than an unsatisfactory gross profit which could be caused by a variety of factors unrelated to theft. The only way that a fairly accurate indication can be obtained of the magnitude of inventory shortages in a retail business is through utilization of the so-called retail method of accounting. At a recent meeting of operators of black-owned markets from various parts of the United States, the writer found that not a single one maintained this kind of inventory control. The failure to use such accounting procedures serves to highlight the fundamental problem produced by the interaction of ghetto environmental conditions and black management. The difficulties of the ghetto environment referred to above require a high degree of sophistication in the application of management controls in order to avoid the risk of ruinous losses, yet on the whole black management has neither the knowledge nor the experience to apply such controls rigorously and effectively.

Employee Productivity and Turnover. Violence and theft are concrete. They are difficult to control yet they can be seen or measured or converted into dollars and cents. More elusive but equally serious is the effect of years and years of discrimination, disappointment and disillusionment on the motivation of black workers. "Employees don't want to work" is a common complaint of all business managers today, but it poses a much more complex problem in the ghetto. Black operators find that they have difficulty convincing black employees that they are really offering them an opportunity for secure employment and advancement in return for hard work. Too often the black employee does not believe the black employer because he has been misled and disappointed too often in the past. He is afraid to set his hopes too high for fear of being disappointed and so as one black entrepreneur put it, "The black employee protects himself with a low level of aspiration."

The result is a lower level of productivity in ghetto stores employing blacks. The problem seems to be more one of motivation and attitude than of skill or intelligence. Most of the jobs at the store level in a supermarket, particularly in the grocery department, do not require a high level of either skill or intelligence. The difficulty is that the image of the hard-working clerk striving to get ahead is a white image and is in many respects foreign to the Negro youth in today's ghetto. Low productivity means high labor costs, a costly handicap in a supermarket. While labor costs in a market are normally less than 10 percent of sales, they typically represent more than 50 percent of variable costs. Management control of productivity can therefore spell the difference between profit and loss in the operation.

A related problem is the high turnover among Negro employees, particularly youth. Turnover of 100 percent of store personnel in the first year of operation was reported by one black operator who recently opened a market in the ghetto of an eastern city. Employee turnover is an affliction that affects all businesses, but it is particularly painful for a one-store operator. When several members of his crew do not turn up, he cannot call up headquarters and ask to have some men transferred to his unit from another store. He has to do the best that he can, even if he is short-handed. The result is frequently poorly stocked shelves, sloppy price-marking, and poor service. The black customer—like her white counterpart—is really not interested in the black operator's problems. All she knows is that there were only two cashiers in the store and she had to wait twenty minutes in line with a small order!

Merchandising Problems. The dynamics of the ghetto community are such that shopping habits and consumer needs are in many ways better served (except with respect to price) by the small grocery store which gives credit than the large cash and carry supermarket. The typical ghetto customer has a low income and a continuing shortage of cash. Whereas in a suburban white market, the typical customer will shop with a car and buy a week's supply of groceries on one trip, in the ghetto the Negro mother may send one of her children to the store several times during the week to pick up a few items on each trip.

This pattern of shopping imposes higher operating costs upon the ghetto supermarket. Costs of running the cashier-checkout operation are inflated because of the high proportion of small transactions. The shortage of cash reflects itself in what may be called the "discarded can syndrome." One operator estimated that it cost him about $25 per week just to put back on the shelves cans of products that are left by customers near the checkouts when they find that they do not have sufficient cash to pay for the order in their shopping carts. These additional costs may seem small, but in a business where profit is measured in pennies, their accumulated effect can add up to losses.

The low income of shoppers distorts the merchandising mix of the ghetto market. The black customer cannot afford expensive specialty items found in the grocery, dairy, frozen food, and produce departments of suburban markets. She buys a high proportion of staple items—sugar, coffee, flour, etc.—which typically provide only a narrow margin of gross profit, if any. While in the meat department the preference of Negroes for cuts of meats not in demand elsewhere tends to result in a higher gross profit, the overall impact of low income is to produce a lower gross profit than would prevail in comparable markets in more affluent neighborhoods.

This is an income problem, rather than an ethnic problem. However, the black operator of a market in the ghetto faces merchandising problems which are uniquely related to the color of his skin and would not exist if the store were operated by a typical national food chain. The source of these problems is the deep skepticism which the black customer holds with respect to the business capability of her black brother.

The kind of problem this attitude can produce is well illustrated by the experience of one black market owner who started in business with the theory that if his service and store condition and prices were as good as his white competitor, the black customer would shop with him because he was black. "It doesn't work out that way," he reported some months later after watching a downward sales trend. He found it necessary to cut the prices of about 200 high volume items below competitive levels in order to offset the built-in image that a black operator can't compete with the big white chain. In another city, a competitive price check indicated that a new black owned and operated supermarket had prices as much as 20 percent lower than a white competitor yet the black-operated store had the image in the community of being high priced! Black operators are slowly learning how to combat this image problem by featuring many low-priced items in ads and through other devices, but the problem is simply another of the difficulties which adds to the profit woes of black supermarkets.

Problems of Management

As in practically all other fields of American business enterprise, there is an acute shortage of competent black managers
in the supermarket business. Indeed in the next few years it
appears that there will be more white-owned markets in ghettoes
for sale than there are black managers capable of operating
them. Funds for purchase and operation can be raised without
too much difficulty from the black community, Small Business
Administration and other governmental agencies, business groups,
banks, and insurance companies. The limiting factor is—and
will continue to be—the scarcity of skilled black managers.

The Scarcity of Black Managers. The reason, of course, lies
in the fact that Negroes have historically been relegated to menial positions in the industry. Consequently, there are few blacks
with administrative experience available. Means must therefore
be developed to train promising blacks as managers in the food
industry or to find them in other industries.

Interestingly enough, there is little unanimity in the retail food
industry as to the best sources for men who can run supermarkets successfully as independent operators, whether they be white
or black. While experience as a store manager is useful in developing administrative skills, the typical store manager in a
large chain organization works within a highly structured environment in which most merchandising decisions are determined
at headquarters. Today, computer programs are increasingly
being used to determine even such things as shelf layout allo-
cations. Pricing, of course, has long been centrally determined
and payroll schedules are also rigorously supervised by headquarters. There is, therefore, a considerable difference in the
decision-making process in operating an independently owned
store and a unit in a large chain.

For this reason, some wholesalers have favored the idea of
taking successful operators of small stores and moving them up
to larger operations. This viewpoint has considerable merit, but
the capability to grow is an attribute which can often not be
measured in advance. While the operator of a successful small
market will often develop considerable merchandising finesse, he
may be completely incapable of managing 50 people, regulating
payroll, maintaining accounting controls, and functioning as the
manager of a sophisticated business venture.

Unfortunately, whether we look to the small successful market
or the manager of a chain unit, there are very few Negroes to
be found in either category. As a consequence, when a black

owner opens a market in a large city he may find it necessary to hire a black manager from a chain in a different metropolitan area simply because there are no black managers available in the immediate locality. Even if a black manager or a Negro with experience as operator of a small market can be found, there is no assurance that the applicant will be successful in the new position in an independent supermarket.

The demands on individual initiative are quite different in the case of the independent supermarket manager as compared with the manager of a ghetto manufacturing plant. In the latter case, a sponsoring company can take a man who has successfully run a printing operation, a fabrication department, electronics assembly, or camera repair, to cite a few examples, install him in a plant in the ghetto, give him orders to fill from the sponsoring company as a starter, and the man is in business in a relatively familiar and stable business environment. The writer is well aware of the red ink that has been spilled in ghetto manufacturing enterprises, but in many cases the losses were incurred because the company ventured into an entirely new and foreign type of operation or did not adequately provide for sufficient orders to make the plant viable during the difficult first few years. While admittedly there are many problems of cost analysis, labor productivity, marketing, quality control, and other factors in a manufacturing operation, it is also true that the operation can be limited to a relatively few products so that controls can be easily understood and applied.

A supermarket must of necessity carry from 6,000 to 8,000 items. The problems of the merchandise mix, of maintaining shelf position, of proper ordering, and of controlling 50 or more employees require a high degree of managerial ability and initiative. Furthermore there is the additional crucial factor of sensing on a day-to-day basis the needs of the consumer and responding promptly to such needs.

The Problem of Communication. Cannot a wholesaler or a chain retailer help a black operator to solve all of these problems, yet give him the advantage of retaining the store profits? The answer is yes, and there are a number of examples where retailers and/or wholesalers have proffered such help. As a matter of fact, most food wholesalers customarily provide various services for their accounts such as bookkeeping, store supervision, fixture purchase and financing, store layout, and other services. But these programs were designed to help white independ-

ent operators in white neighborhoods. Wholesalers are finding
to their dismay that even the best of such programs will not
work with black operators in ghetto stores. Unfortunately racial
differences impose serious barriers in communication between
people. Even well-meaning dedicated whites, who want to help
blacks become successful, are finding the process a test of their
patience and understanding.

A long list of wholesalers (and retailers) have confided to the
writer the same complaint:

> We tried to help Mr. . . . but he wouldn't listen to our advice. When
> our supervisor would go into the store and find certain things were
> wrong, he would tell the store manager and here's the answer he would
> get: "We don't have to do what you say anymore. We own this store."
> Finally we gave up trying to give advice.

How did this breakdown in communication come about? It appears to stem from three sources. First is the difficulty experienced by both blacks and whites in working together on a cooperative but independent arms-length basis. Whites who wish
to help blacks are often overly patronizing in their manner;
blacks on their part are frequently oversensitive to criticism.
Blacks seem to have a fear that if they accept advice from whites
and submit to "restrictions" they are somehow subverting their
independence and becoming "Uncle Toms."

A second source of difficulty is the fact that blacks believe
they know the ghetto community better than whites and that
therefore they do not need advice. "If you know all the an-
swers," the black operator asks, "how come you are closing
stores in the ghetto and not opening new ones?" The black
operator does not believe that the white wholesaler or retailer
has the solutions and therefore he is unwilling to accept many
of the operating formulas and restrictions which are a normal
part of franchise or similar wholesale-retailer arrangements.

A final difficulty springs from what black operators refer to
as "the credibility gap." Black store owners believe that it is
very important for them to get across to the community unequivocally that the store is black-owned and that the black operator
is not acting as a front for a white chain or wholesaler. They
fear that if there are a number of white supervisors going in
and out of the store and appearing to give orders that the community will get the impression the black ownership is merely a
gimmick and that the old power structure has not been changed.

The so-called credibility gap also explains their reluctance to accept controls by a wholesaler. One black operator complained that he could not convince his employees that he really owned the store when checks had to be countersigned at the office of the wholesaler who supplied him.

Despite these difficulties, it seems apparent that white supervisory assistance will have to be given to most black supermarkets if they are to have any chance of success. One technique which has been used with some success is for a chain to grant a leave of absence to a manager or supervisor who is interested in helping a black market get started. He can then be put on the payroll of the new market and spend full time helping it become established, with the option to return at any time to the chain where he may have accumulated substantial seniority and other benefits.

The Role of Black Capitalism. The problem of management of black-owned supermarkets is really part of a more basic problem. That is, what do we mean by black capitalism? Black capitalism in this context could mean: (a) total black ownership; (b) majority black ownership; (c) black ownership and black management; (d) black ownership, black management, and black employees. Obviously there are many other possible combinations of these basic factors. Most black owners of supermarkets tend to think in terms of both ownership and management as necessarily being black, although they will accept department managers who are white during a transition phase until black managers can be trained and qualified. As far as the mix of employees is concerned, to some extent this seems to be influenced by the mix of customers in the store. For example, if the ratio of black and white customers is 90 percent black and 10 percent white, they are inclined to feel that only 10 percent of the employees should be white. This concept of "reverse discrimination" does not rest upon a balancing of costs and productivity, but rather upon vague notions of what is right in the community.

Despite superficial resemblance in physical and economic conditions, the ghetto areas of our large cities vary considerably from one another. They are different basically because the Negro residents vary in their aspirations, their abilities, and their attitudes—even on such critical issues as integration and Black Nationalism. It is therefore dangerous to attempt to lay down any general rules for successful operation of black-owned markets in ghetto areas. Nevertheless, it would seem to make sense

for black entrepreneurs to concentrate on the ownership aspect
of black capitalism and to do everything possible to make their
ventures profitable. Black managers and black employees who
are competent or who can be trained should, of course, be employed, but white managers and employees should be used as
needed, unless there are strong community objections. We still
live in an integrated society and there is considerable evidence
to suggest that most Negroes prefer to shop in an integrated
store and to work in an integrated environment.

POSSIBLE SOLUTIONS

A dispassionate cold appraisal of the prospects for profits by
black owners of supermarkets in American ghettoes can lead
to only one conclusion: a few will make it; the rest will fail.
The nature of the business, the hardships presented by the environment, and their own lack of managerial experience are
against them. Yet the march of events will make black ownership of supermarkets in ghettoes essential to the maintenance
of an economical distribution of foods in these areas. As each
year passes, as violence recurs in various ghettoes, we shall find
an increasing number of white-owned supermarkets closed down,
stark symbols of the inability of the white business establishment to cope with the social problems which years of neglect
have spawned in the dark streets of our ghettoes.

If experienced white corporate chains cannot operate such
stores profitably, if black owners cannot operate them profitably,
what is the solution?

Government Subsidy

It seems likely that some form of government subsidization
will eventually be required to offset the cost differential of doing
business in the ghetto. The question of what type of subsidy
should be used and how it should be applied is complex and
requires detailed consideration. Care must be taken that assistance to ailing markets does not put at a competitive disadvantage those few stores which may be operating profitably in
ghetto areas. Likewise, it would seem unwise to make a distinc-
tion between black-owned and white-owned markets. This may
be more of a problem in theory than in practice. If the needs
of ghetto residents could be taken care of by black-owned markets, it is doubtful if many chains would be eager to open in

these areas even if some subsidy were available. Opening a market in the ghetto today poses very delicate problems of community relations for a white chain and takes a tremendous amount of top executive time. Furthermore, there is always the problem of demands that the market be turned over to the community after it is viable and this poses thorny problems of the proper role of the corporation relative to its stockholders.

Whatever the subsidy, it will have to be substantial to be meaningful. The suggestion made by one observer [147] that as an offset to higher operating costs in the ghetto the investment credit be raised to 10 percent can be compared to tying a band-aid to a running sore. The subsidy would almost certainly have to be related to operating costs to be effective. A tax subsidy would be of little help to the one-store operator who is losing money. Probably the best measure would be some subsidy related to wages. However, the subsidy ought not to increase without limit as payroll increases since this would put a premium on inefficiency. Perhaps the subsidy could be based upon payroll up to 10 percent of sales or some similar measure.

The question may be raised why MA-5 funds under the Manpower Development and Training Act cannot be used for this purpose. The answer is that the basic problem ought to be met squarely and not by indirection: the funds are primarily needed to offset operating handicaps and not for training. The ghetto supermarket, particularly one operated by a black owner, is not a particularly favorable environment in which to train employees. Probably these men and women would get better training in a larger retail chain where there is greater staff support and depth of managerial know-how.

Cooperative Industry Action

By and large the American food industry has a highly developed sense of social responsibility. Next to the automobile industry, it is currently training more hardcore employees than any other industry group. What is needed now is a joint program by wholesalers and retailers to train managers for black-owned ghetto markets. Several retail food chains have undertaken experimental programs of this kind in which Negro managers of various departments will be given a special course to

---

147. Frederick D. Sturdivant, "Better Deal for Ghetto Shoppers," *Harvard Business Review*, March-April 1968, p. 138.

teach them administrative skills. Perhaps some sort of central training agency should be established by the various elements of the industry. There ought to be some central food agency which maintains active contact with the various black-owned markets now in operation and offers trouble-shooting services to help them. Furthermore, interested persons who wish to open a market in a ghetto area should be able to contact one central source and then be referred to a sponsoring company which would "adopt" the new venturer and help him get established in business.

Consultant Organizations

In the years ahead there will be a critical need for competent consultant organizations which can put together men, location and capital to operate supermarkets in ghetto areas and provide continuing supervisory assistance, as required. Such organizations could obtain funding from various government agencies or private foundations and would help avoid many of the mistakes that are now being made by black markets in various parts of the country. The Council of Equal Business Opportunity performs this function to some degree, but its major objective is to serve as a catalyst to activate new black-owned businesses, rather than to provide supervision. The various black consulting or franchise organizations which exist do not appear to have either the experience or the depth of management needed to cope with the difficult problems which exist in ghetto supermarket operations. The ideal arrangement would be a firm composed of both black and white experts who could assist fledgling supermarkets in various stages of development.

CONCLUSION

Black Capitalism is a controversial subject. There are those who believe that it represents a misdirection of effort and that it has no place as a concept in an integrated society. On the other hand, there are those who support it with almost religious zeal and argue that it is essential to uplift the Negro to his proper status in society. Whatever we may think of Black Capitalism, it is important to recognize that as a movement it is gaining in strength and that the Administration in Washington is apparently committed to it as a workable principle. That being the case, it is vital that success and not recrimination result from the experiments now going on. Already some black critics are predicting failure and blaming President Nixon for bequeathing to the black community a concept that no longer works even in the white community.

One black newspaper put it this way:

And why does Mr. Nixon respond so generously? Because he knows what blacks don't know—free enterprise is a worn out institution: it is not what is making the American economy hum; it is not what has brought affluence to the large masses of white Americans. In short, it is not what's happening and thus, as a worn out idea, it can now be given, like an old shoe, to black folk.[148]

We do not believe that free enterprise is a worn out institution, nor that the black-owned independent supermarket in the ghetto is an old shoe, despite all the difficulties alluded to in this article. But it will take a major effort by the food industry, government, and local agencies to overcome the difficulties of conducting a retail food business in the ghetto. If a well-conceived comprehensive program can be developed—backed up by men and money—the black-owned supermarket can become a visible symbol of the opportunities that await black enterprise. If the black owner is given no more help than he is receiving at the present time, there will be a wave of failures, the ghetto resident will suffer by paying more for food, and the darkened supermarket will be a grim reminder of the failure of our society to face the problems of ghetto living with foresight and adequate funds.

---

148. Excerpt from *Manhattan Tribune*, cited in *Business and Society*, Vol. 1 (April 8, 1969), p. 2.

CHAPTER VIII

Determinants of Negro Employment

Some of the factors which affected Negro employment in the past are becoming less important today; some are being replaced by new, more positive forces; others still remain operative in the industry. This chapter will review these determinants and the forces likely to become increasingly important in bringing about change in the industry. Finally, some tentative prognostications concerning the role of the Negro in the supermarket industry will be suggested.

INDUSTRY LOCATION

Supermarkets are fairly well distributed throughout the country. Those of the major chains, however, tend to be located in the larger cities and their surrounding metropolitan areas, rarely completely isolated from areas of Negro population. Indeed, older chains such as A & P may have a substantial portion of their stores in or near Negro neighborhoods.[149]

We have found indications that Negroes are unwilling to commute any substantial distance to work in supermarkets, although they apparently will do so to work in warehouses. It appears that the lower entry rate of pay in markets and the apparent lack of opportunity for rapid advancement tend to deter applications for store level jobs. By contrast, the high pay offered by food warehouses attracts Negroes to warehouse jobs even when facilities are located in the suburbs. Furthermore, Negroes —like other minority groups—tend to apply for work where other Negroes are employed. Therefore, high levels of Negro employment in warehouses tend to perpetuate themselves, while

---

149. The Rev. William Jones of Operation Breadbasket has pointed out that A & P has 900 stores in the New York metropolitan area, 20 percent of which are in black areas. He claims that at least 25 percent of the company's 4,500 stores nationwide are in black neighborhoods. See "Jesse Jackson and Operation Breadbasket," *Black Enterprise*, May 1971, p. 21.

the low level in outlying stores will likewise continue unless management can break through patterns of inertia and convince Negro applicants that the supermarket holds forth real promise of promotion and higher pay.

Within central cities, the transportation problem is less of a barrier and therefore markets in such areas are the natural source of employment opportunities for Negroes in the future. The level of Negro employment in the industry, therefore, to a significant degree is dependent upon the financial health and operating success of supermarkets in black or predominantly black neighborhoods. The exodus of whites and the influx of blacks into our central cities is expected to continue during the balance of the decade of the seventies with the result that many supermarkets now in predominantly white neighborhoods will find that they must now contend with pressures from a predominantly black neighborhood. From 1960 to 1969 in central cities of metropolitan areas of one million or more population, the white population declined 9 percent while the black population increased 41 percent.[150] By 1970, 28 percent of the population of central cities in metropolitan areas of 2 million or more population was black compared to only 20 percent in 1960.[151] The continued successful operation of supermarkets in such central city areas is important not only to insure that food is available to low income families at competitive prices, but also to provide employment opportunities to job seekers living in such neighborhoods.

The operational problems of such stores will unfortunately continue to mount during the decade of the seventies. Of major concern is the tremendous increase which is taking place in the Negro teenage population in central cities. The number of 16 to 19 year old Negroes in central cities rose by nearly 75 percent from 1960 to 1969 while the number of white teenagers rose by only 14 percent.[152] This unprecedented increase in the number of young black people—many of them jobless,[153] out of

---

150. U.S. Department of Labor, *Manpower Report of the President, April 1971* (Washington: Government Printing Office, 1971), p. 85.

151. U.S. Bureau of the Census, *The Social and Economic Status of Negroes in the United States, 1970*, Special Studies, Current Population Reports, Series P-23, No. 38 (July 1971), p. 16.

152. U.S. Department of Labor, *loc. cit.*

153. In 1970, one out of every three Negro teenagers in central cities was unemployed. *Ibid.*

school, and a potential source of delinquency [154] and social un-rest—poses major problems for the supermarkets—and indeed for all retailing—in such neighborhoods.

Since supermarkets have always been a major source of part-time employment for teenagers, the question arises as to whether the supermarket industry can help to convert the superabundance of Negro teenagers into an asset so that these young people can be made productive members of the labor force rather than being left to fester in the ghetto, unemployed, unwanted, and bitter against society. The supermarkets of the central city are located near a great reservoir of labor—the teenage Negro. The sad fact is that there is no coordinated program in the nation designed to bring such teenagers into the main stream of business. Such training and inculcation should begin while they are still in school; arrangements should be made for part-time training during summers; city, state and federal agencies should coordinate efforts with supermarket companies to see what can be done to make Negro youth productive members of society.

Failure to cope with the number of jobless Negro teenagers will mean rising levels of delinquency in the central city and a continuing attrition in the number of supermarkets in such areas. Since more Negroes are moving into these areas every day, maintenance of adequate employment opportunities requires construction of new stores. Although there are isolated examples of such developments—such as Progress Plaza in North Philadelphia—a growing proportion of new construction will tend to be found in outlying areas where land is more plentiful, roads less congested, and operational problems less severe. The continuous increase which has been occurring in the size of new supermarkets is itself a factor working against location in the cities, for high land costs and high real estate taxes will make it increasingly difficult to find locations in central cities which will permit profit-able operation.

Black ownership and operation *per se* is unlikely to provide the solution to profitable operation of supermarkets in the ghetto environment. Negro entrepreneurs, like white businessmen, are more likely to meet with success if they invest in new facilities

---

154. The National Advisory Commission on Civil Disorders found that persons in the 14 to 24 age group were responsible for a disproportionately large share of crime in the United States. For example, in 1966 persons under 25 years of age were responsible for 71 percent of all robberies and 81 percent of all burglaries. See National Advisory Commission on Civil Disorders, *Report* (New York: Bantam Books, 1968), p. 269.

in the suburbs than if they take over small obsolete facilities in the inner city. However, a concerted effort involving a combination of federal aid and retail food industry support might enable a significant number of black-owned markets to survive in ghetto locations while management and employees learn how to cope with the internal and external problems of the business. Such a program could provide a useful training ground for Negroes, particularly in the managerial ranks, while at the same time maintaining a vital service to the community.

The factor of location, therefore, as a determinant of Negro employment can act as a two-edged sword. On the one hand, the migration of the Negro population into major metropolitan areas can operate to lift the level of Negro employment by bringing Negroes into closer proximity to the locus of many of the supermarket facilities in the nation. On the other hand, the growing concentration of new construction of supermarkets in the suburbs can in the long run restrict Negro employment opportunities. Unlike some of the other factors which we shall be considering, there is little that supermarket management can do to offset the basic trends which are inducing this out-migration of markets. Ultimately tax policy, urban renewal measures and possibly even governmental subsidies may be required to render more attractive the development of new supermarket construction in central cities.

DEMAND FOR LABOR

Supermarkets, with their large female work forces and availability of part-time positions, generally tend to have high turnover rates. Supermarkets therefore generate a continuing high demand for labor. At the same time, the industry seems little affected by the business cycle, so that supermarket jobs represent stable employment opportunities.

The high turnover characteristic of supermarket operations enables companies in the industry to react quickly to new policies relative to employment of minority groups, provided that Negro applicants are available. But the relationship between demand and supply has always been tenuous in the labor market and this is particularly so when Negro applicants are sought. There is considerable evidence that Negro males still do not believe that this industry affords them any real opportunity. Two of the most effective ways to bridge this credibility gap are (1) the employment and effective utilization of a Negro personnel officer and (2) the elevation to positions of visible responsibility of a substantial number of Negroes in the organization.

A case in point is the 80-store Waldbaum chain which has its headquarters in Garden City, Long Island. Two Negro twin brothers, who have been with the chain for many years, function respectively as vice president of merchandising and sales, and assistant vice president in charge of store operations, two of the most responsible and challenging positions in a supermarket concern.[155] Despite the fact that only one of the chain's stores is in a predominantly black area, the company has experienced no difficulty in attracting competent Negro help, both male and female. Indeed, the chain presently has 12 Negro store managers and 13 Negro assistant managers.[156] By contrast, other supermarket companies in the New York City metropolitan area with less Negro representation in managerial ranks complain that they are unable to attract qualified Negro applicants.

Since most of the turnover in supermarket employment occurs at the front end, particularly in the cashier and bagger job classifications, the industry may not afford as much opportunity to adult male Negroes as to youths and females. Although both federal and state laws prohibit discrimination in hiring based upon sex, the fact is that females tend to be more dexterous with cash register manipulation than men and are more attracted to this kind of position than male job seekers. Furthermore, store managers prefer to hire female employees for cashier jobs.

Changing technology and practice in the supermarket industry during the decade of the seventies will alter the demand for labor in ways that may significantly affect opportunities for Negro employment. At the front end, the use of the automatic checkout will greatly increase productivity and eliminate the need for hand manipulation of a cash register. The reduction in labor requirements for front-end operation may therefore curtail employment opportunities, particularly for Negro women. As has already been mentioned, the transfer of meat operations to central meat warehouse facilities will result in an overall reduction of jobs in the meatcutting and packaging operations of the supermarket industry but will probably result in a higher percentage of Negro male employees in such operations than

---

155. *Ebony*, June 1968, pp. 29-39.

156. Letter from Waldbaum executive.

now exists. The growing size of the supermarket and the closing of the small and middle-sized markets will eliminate many job opportunities as manager and department head. At the same time, the large volumes handled through the super supermarket will require a highly talented professional manager. Unless efforts are made now to upgrade and train Negro employees for the greater responsibilities that lie ahead in the industry, some of the Negroes now serving as store managers will find that they have been rendered obsolete by the rapidly changing demands of the business.

If Negroes are to play an important role in supermarket management in the future, company executives must begin now to select and train Negro employees who will be able to assume the responsible positions of the future. Rapid technological change will alter the demand for labor in all facets of the industry and it is management's responsibility to be prepared to adapt its personnel to new job requirements. Safeway Stores, Inc., for example, is already looking ahead to even greater automation in its bakery operations and is making plans so that Negroes will be able to find a place among the few highly trained technical people who will be needed in the bakery of the future. The same kind of foresight needs to be exercised in warehousing operations. At the present time, many warehouses in the industry are predominantly black; the Negro employees perform relatively unskilled work moving cases around the warehouse. The automated warehouses of the future will drastically restrict the use of this kind of labor. Therefore, unless advance planning and adequate training is undertaken by firms in the industry, technological developments in warehousing could substantially curtail opportunities for Negro male employment in such facilities.

NATURE OF THE WORK

Despite pending technological developments in the supermarket industry, the nature of the work in most jobs will for many years in the future continue to be primarily unskilled. The typical store level jobs in the supermarket require little skill or training and therefore would seem to afford opportunities for the great bulk of Negro applicants who likewise lack skill and training.

This apparent correspondence between demand requirements and supply characteristics overlooks one most significant fact about supermarket employment. Although job content is simple, there is a premium upon getting work done on time and according to schedule. A supermarket handles and stocks 6,000 or more items in a rather small area. In order to accommodate the mass movement of a broad line of products through a limited facility, trucks must be unloaded on time, shelves must be stocked on time, and customers must be served efficiently and promptly. The emphasis is therefore on timeliness and it is here that many black applicants fail to perform adequately. The single most important reason for dismissal of Negro employees in the industry is tardiness and absenteeism.

This circumstance raises some fundamental questions about the ability of the supermarket industry to hire persons who have not developed sound work patterns, or who are continually late because of transportation difficulties or other personal reasons. As an industry, the supermarket business does not have the depth of staff nor the competitive margins to enable it to do an adequate job in training disadvantaged persons to work. Other industries—such as the automobile industry—have found it necessary to assign personnel whose sole function is to make certain that hardcore employees awake in time in the morning, have transportation to work, and arrive at the job in time. The supermarket industry is unlikely to devote this kind of manpower to the inculcation of basic work habits.

Because profit margins are so thin in the industry and continue to decline, supermarkets must to some extent seek to screen the market and hire only the best applicants. The industry can cope with lack of training but not with lack of reliability. The nature of the work in supermarkets, therefore, poses some problems for unemployed Negroes; for a number of studies have indicated that lack of established work patterns is a common characteristic of the Negro unemployed, particularly in ghetto areas. Thus, one writer concludes:

While low levels of education and training can limit productivity and do affect the attractiveness of workers to prospective employers, unreliability on the job, rather than lack of skill, appears to be a more serious cause of ghetto unemployment.[157]

Work patterns should be learned early in life, especially by youth of high school age. Supermarkets can help in this process

---

157. Peter B. Doeringer, "Programs to Employ the Disadvantaged: A Labor Market Perspective," in P. B. Doeringer (ed.), *Programs to Employ the Disadvantaged* (Englewood Cliffs, N.J.: Prentice-Hall, 1969), p. 249.

through the development, in cooperation with urban school systems, of part-time employment programs for Negro high school students. For the most part, however, supermarket concerns can be expected primarily to provide relatively simple on-the-job training for Negro applicants who through past experience, background, or motivation have already developed sound work habits which enable them to adapt to the time-oriented schedules essential to supermarket operation.

CONSUMER ORIENTATION AND PRESSURES

Supermarkets, like all retail industries, are necessarily sensitive to the desires and biases of their customers. Such orientation can lead, and apparently has in the past led, to oversensitivity to the presumed reactions of customers to black employment. Today, however, most supermarket executives believe that the color of an employee's skin makes little difference in terms of the continued patronage of most customers. This liberal view, however, is not necessarily shared by all store managers. One executive, while noting the strong feelings of some store managers on the subject, related an experiment he had conducted with a Negro cashier. Over the objections of the store manager, he placed this Negro employee in a store where customer reaction was presumed to be negative toward Negro employment. The experiment demonstrated that customers soon became accustomed to the new worker and displayed little reluctance to being served by her.

It is an unfortunate condition of our times that in some communities an increasing degree of polarization has developed between white and black communities. Such issues as school busing, crime in the streets, and competition for jobs have exacerbated these differences. The supermarket has not caused these differences to develop but it can easily be caught in the crossfire of community discord. The dependence of the store manager on successful community relations and good will is likely to affect the rate at which these men are willing to risk their assumptions about customer likes and dislikes and can therefore slow top management efforts to increase Negro employment in some areas.

On the other hand, community demands for increased opportunities for Negroes have been much more explicit and have accelerated the rate of employment of blacks in many supermarket companies. In some cases, however, continued picketing, confrontation and violence have simply resulted in an abandonment of supermarket locations in ghetto areas. Furthermore, as we have seen from an earlier discussion, legitimate pressure tactics have sometimes been converted into outright coercion and racketeering.

Supermarkets are sensitive to changes in community attitudes and therefore they will probably continue to be the target of civil rights and other pressure groups. But supermarkets are also sensitive to changes in profit margins. With a narrow 2 percent pretax margin separating a profitable venture from a losing one, supermarkets cannot long withstand community pressures, racial strife, and high levels of crime and delinquency which erode profits. The history of the migration of the textile and shoe industries from the North to the South as a result of pressures which raised costs and sapped profits is a stern reminder that in the long run capital is extremely mobile and will seek out those areas and opportunities which afford the promise of the greatest profits.

The continued operation of supermarkets in central city areas depends upon the development of an understanding by community leaders of the problems faced by supermarket operators and of a joint effort by industry and community to hire and train Negro workers under a rational schedule which will not impose unreasonable cost burdens upon supermarket concerns.

GOVERNMENTAL PRESSURES AND TRAINING ACTIVITIES

So far, state and federal civil rights agencies have had a significant, if limited, impact on supermarket operations. Since supermarket concerns are not normally contractors for government supply, the strongest federal sanction—contract withdrawal —is not a threat. Neither are supermarkets subject to federal regulatory agencies in any direct way (meat inspection, for example, is a function of food processing, rather than of retailing). Increased federal and state interest in retailing would undoubtedly have an impact on racial employment policies in the supermarket industry, particularly in the light of the sensitivity of companies in the industry to unfavorable publicity.

Governmental subsidized training programs, such as the MA-3, MA-4, and MA-5 programs, have been undertaken by many companies in the industry, but the overall effect has been minimal. Nevertheless, even though the turnover among employees hired for such programs has been high, such programs need to be improved and expanded. They provide a useful escape valve in the black community, providing an opportunity for the Negro with poor education and no skill to help himself out of the vicious cycle of welfare, unemployment, and despair, if he evidences the necessary motivation to stick with the program for the duration of the training period. Some concerns report that after the first two-to-three week period of massive turnover, the rate of turnover among hardcore employees is actually less than that of white employees. As one executive put it, "The hardcore trainee works harder at his job, and appreciates his pay check because he doesn't have as good alternatives elsewhere."

There is also an urgent need for better coordination between supermarkets and various federal and state training and employment offices in clearly specifying the types of skills and abilities which are required in the industry. Some executives stated that so-called Skill Centers performed a satisfactory job in training Negroes for positions as cashiers and other supermarket functions, while others complained that such centers seemed to spend training funds on jobs for which there were no vacancies. A common complaint among companies which had made commitments under various Manpower programs is that state and federal agencies—as well as local civil rights organizations—made promises of sending numbers of Negro applicants but their performance fell far short of their promises.

The relationship between supermarket concerns and various local agencies and organizations interested in promoting the employment of minority groups is rendered complex by the dispersion of supermarket locations. If, as is often the case in manufacturing, Company A could deal exclusively with Agency B in working out a program to hire and train Negroes, there would probably be a better understanding on the part of both employer and agency of the nature of the problem and the chances of successful accomplishment would be improved. In the supermarket industry, however, large chains may have stores in hundreds of cities and towns. Frequently such companies find that they must deal with a variety of agencies, each with a somewhat different policy and approach to the problem. Even within the same city it is not uncommon for four or five agencies plus numbers of informal action groups to contact management concerning programs to hire Negroes. Some executives complained to the writers that the formal agencies tend to be overly defensive and seek to build up statistics to justify their existence. Frequently it is found that the various agencies are working with the same group of people—the so-called "hustlers"—who move from one training program to another but never seem to acquire permanent employment. Certainly the cause of Negro employment would be materially improved by better coordination among the various agencies and groups concerned with this problem.

Mention has already been made of the critical role which could be played by a carefully formulated and supervised training program for Negro youth to be commenced while they are still in high school. Such a program would require some funding and coordination by governmental agencies and the support of the supermarket industry. Another constructive program would involve expansion at central city universities of programs such as that offered at Northeastern University in Boston, wherein students attend class for a given period of weeks, then work for a period of time with an employer who is cooperating with the program, and then return to classroom study again. Such programs fulfill a two-fold purpose of enabling disadvantaged members of our population to continue their educations while earning supplementary income and also give them an opportunity to learn about business and develop sound work habits while still in school. The formation of constructive work habits at an early age, the understanding of the promotional opportunities which the supermarket—and other industries—provide for ambitious Negroes, and the opportunity to earn good pay while still in school could change the outlook on the business world of many young Negroes who might otherwise drop out of high school or university and become a burden to society.

UNION POLICIES

The general impact of union organization upon Negro employment in the supermarket industry is probably, on the whole, adverse. In the first place, the image of the unions in some local areas is such that the potential applicant visualizes that there are now two barriers he must overcome—the company and the union. This attitude, plus the existence of high initiation fees, may deter Negroes from applying for jobs in the industry. Secondly, as has already been mentioned, the restrictions imposed by unions on intrafacility movement and the existence of seniority provisions in union contracts may make it more difficult for Negroes to rise to managerial and supervisory positions in the industry. Furthermore, one of the basic fears of the black is: Am I going to be the first to be laid off? Although the supermarket industry as a whole represents a rather stable employment pattern, the fortunes of individual stores and companies vary, and every locality has seen some companies compelled to close stores and/or curtail their labor force because of competitive conditions. To the Negro job seeker, seniority provisions seem to subject his employment to all the vicissitudes of fluctuations in business.

The impact of these various union policies on the level of Negro employment is quite difficult to assess and it moreover varies considerably from one area to another, depending to a large extent upon the fears and prejudices of local union leaders and their membership. Even in the Teamster Union-dominated trucking industry, which has frequently been the object of accusations of racism by Negro civil rights leaders, there are many locals with high percentages of black drivers where it is obvious that no such prejudice exists.

Although union policies viewed *in toto* may tend to retard the rate of advance of Negro employment, it does not follow that relaxation of various restrictive rules would lead to a marked improvement in the position of the Negro in the industry. In the final analysis it is management which makes the hiring decision and it is to a change in management policy that we must look for real progress in Negro employment.

MANAGEMENT POLICY

Supermarket executives as a group seem to be sincerely interested in increasing the representation of Negroes at every level of the employment roster. Accomplishment of this objective, however, has been retarded by the fragmented nature of hiring practices in the industry and by the lack of sound centralized long range planning in the manpower area.

The Need for Centralized Control

The delegation of hiring responsibilities differs from company to company in the industry depending upon size, geographical location and dispersion, and similar factors. Nevertheless, as a

rule, the hiring responsibility is typically decentralized because
of the variety and geographical dispersion of facilities that are
included in a supermarket company's normal operation. Thus, a
division of a large chain may encompass manufacturing plants,
warehouses, headquarters office, and a large number of stores,
some near to the office and some situated at a considerable distance. Usually each facility and each store does its own hiring,
although because warehouse and headquarters offices are often
combined, the personnel department may assist in screening applicants for jobs in the warehouse. In some chains, the division
personnel office will handle hiring for stores within a convenient
radius of the office, leaving to store managers of outlying units
the responsibility for hiring for their own stores. Frequently
chains permit store managers to hire all employees, full-time and
part-time, but reserve to the division headquarters the preroga-
tive of selecting staff for any new store.

The decentralization of actual hiring decisions makes it difficult
to implement top management objectives in the area of personnel
policy. The store manager may hire a white man and pass by a
better qualified Negro, yet the personnel office will be told that
there were no qualified blacks available. The word can easily
get out in a neighborhood that there is no use for a black to
apply for a job in a particular market, even though at headquarters miles away the division manager is enunciating a detailed plan for promotion of Negroes in the company.

Although centralization of hiring decisions is not generally
considered practical in the industry, modifications of hiring patterns are possible—and may be necessary—to insure that there
is an adequate inflow of qualified Negro trainees. This is particularly true in central cities where supermarket companies
often have headquarters or division offices and where there are
frequently a number of stores located in black neighborhoods.
One East Coast chain, whose store managers normally do all of
their own hiring, selected a number of in-city stores which were
accessible to public transportation facilities and had its personnel
department assume the function of hiring all part-timers for
such stores. In this way, the company was able to make certain
that Negroes would be fairly considered for jobs in the stores
which were most readily accessible to them.

If, however, the hiring function is left with the store managers, it is still possible to implement management plans to increase levels of Negro employment by giving to the personnel

department the staff and the authority to develop with store managers and the directors of various company facilities realistic goals in terms of jobs for Negro applicants. The role of the personnel department in such goal-setting must, of course, be subtle, since the line people are in the last analysis responsible for profits and therefore must be satisfied with the persons they hire. Nevertheless, a firm statement of management commitment plus the establishment of a procedure providing for regular field review by the personnel department to evaluate progress being made toward attainment of goals can give concrete evidence to managers and supervisors that the company really means what it preaches. Such procedures should be supplemented with a training program designed by the personnel department to assist the store managers and directors of facilities in becoming more effective in interviewing and screening candidates for employment. Despite the difficulties presented by the decentralization of the hiring function in the supermarket industry, these and similar measures can help to make progress toward the achievement of company objectives. A sound Negro employment policy can be implemented if the same thought and time is devoted to it as is customarily given to promotional and other operational problems.

The Need for Long Range Manpower Planning

Comprehensive manpower planning is not a well developed management practice in the industry. In view of the technological changes which face the industry and the mass migrations which are altering the ethnic and demographic composition of the populations which compose its major markets, the supermarket industry needs to devote more attention to the future composition of its own work force. Such attention is essential if Negroes are to gain a fair representation in the corporate hierarchy. Periodic review of the corporate roster with respect to the distribution of Negro employees would enable executives to see precisely the progress, if any, which Negroes are making in the industry and would indicate the need for further program changes or better implementation of existing policies. Thus, a manpower review which revealed only one Negro among 500 total store managers and no presently employed Negro who appeared to have the qualifications to eventually become a store manager would strongly suggest that errors were being made somewhere in the company with respect to the hiring, training, and/or evaluation of Negro employees.

The Need for a Special Program to Hire and Train
Black Managers

As has already been mentioned earlier in this text, it is doubtful whether supermarket employment can be made attractive to Negro males unless visible evidence exists of promotional possibilities to store manager and other administrative positions. Because there are so few Negro males in sales positions, the industry cannot rely on normal promotional channels to cure this deficiency in upper echelon representation. A major effort is called for to attract, train, and retain qualified blacks in managerial positions.

This is easier said than done. Negro graduates from the better white colleges and the larger black colleges seem to have more attractive opportunities available to them elsewhere so that relatively few are interested in joining supermarket companies. Furthermore, several companies reported that some graduates come to work for a supermarket company only to gain the work experience and then are wooed away to other industries where jobs are seemingly more glamorous. A number of chains are now concentrating on smaller black colleges in the hope of attracting Negroes who may not have as many other opportunities for employment offered them.

The shortage of qualified Negro graduates who are interested in careers in the retail food industry needs to be viewed as an industry problem and will require concerted industry effort to solve. Perhaps the various trade associations in the industry in cooperation with the various colleges providing training in food retailing can develop an effective promotional program designed to give to Negroes in high schools and colleges a better understanding of the opportunities which are available in the supermarket industry today for qualified Negro applicants.

If supermarket companies are really interested in attracting black college graduates to the industry, they should begin their promotional work early in the college term by providing summer employment for black college students. In Boston, the NAACP's Positive Program for Boston has instituted a "Management Internship Training Program" for college youth which has been highly successful in providing summer employment and enabling students to learn more about particular companies while they are still in school. According to Star Markets, which recruited 10 black students under the program in the summer of 1971, the program has been rewarding. In the words of Ed Buron, Vice President of Human Resources for the company, "The big plus is that it establishes ground rules for both the company and the students, so that it becomes a cooperative work experience." [158] Under this program, cooperating companies undertake the responsibility not only to provide summer employment for qualified applicants, but also to give the trainee some understanding of how the overall business functions.

Despite the need for college-trained blacks in the supermarket industry, the chairman of the Positive Program for Boston reported that he had 287 qualified Negro applicants representing a variety of colleges and universities, but only 100 job offers.[159] Of course not all of such "interns" would necessarily return to the hiring company after graduation, but nevertheless the cooperating employer has the opportunity to explain to the interns how the supermarket business works and what opportunities for promotion exist within the particular company. Programs of this sort would seem to provide an excellent avenue for attracting more black college students to a career in business and to the supermarket business in particular. They deserve the support of the supermarket industry.

One of the basic reasons for the shortage of qualified Negro college graduates in the supermarket business is that relatively few Negro graduates plan to seek a career in business. A long history of discriminatory barriers has created an image of lack of opportunity in the typical Negro college graduate's mind. As a consequence, 60 to 70 percent of Negro college students usually intend to seek employment upon graduation in social work or teaching or to go on to the professions.[160] This is a problem which American business as a whole must tackle, but the supermarket industry can do its part by providing an opportunity for Negro college youth to learn about business in a personal, constructive way.

---

158. *Boston Herald Traveler*, May 2, 1971.

159. *Ibid.*

160. Statement to writers by Director of Positive Program for Boston.

The Need for Industry Commitment

The results of Operation Breadbasket show that there does not have to be a wholesale revolution in social attitudes among a company's store managers for executive commitment to equal employment opportunity to bear fruit. Once a supermarket company develops an active recruitment program for Negroes, the results can be impressive. Jewel increased its Negro employment by 250 percent over a two-year period (1967 and 1968). Of this increase, almost two-thirds were what Jewel terms "disadvantaged employments" (persons who either had two or more periods of employment during the past totalling at least 15 weeks or had no employment history, or who had family histories of dependents on welfare). The retention rate of 60 percent in 1967 and 80 percent in 1968 for new Negro employees in those years is remarkable in light of the high proportion of "disadvantaged employments" to total Negro employments that are still on the job.[161]

This and other successful programs in the industry indicate that to a substantial extent the level of Negro employment in individual companies—despite all of the difficulties already referred to in locating and retaining qualified black employees—is in the final analysis a matter of the extent of commitment by the company itself. Despite its low level of profits, the industry has taken on many expensive programs where consumer pressures and threatened governmental action demanded it. A case in point is the reaction of the industry to various consumerist measures such as unit pricing, open dating, etc. All of these programs entail extra costs; nevertheless the industry has evidenced a statesmanlike attitude in taking the lead in introducing such policies on a voluntary basis.

The same may well be true of Negro employment. What seems to be lacking today is a sense of urgency and a major commitment by the industry. But some companies—perhaps with more vision than others—are already embarking on major programs at considerable expense. One of the largest of the national chains has already upped its minority group representation to over 12 percent at the store level. Other companies are making similar efforts. Their motivation is strictly profit-oriented, which is sound. Executives in such companies believe that ultimately,

---

161. Letter from L. D. Smith, Vice President for Personnel Development, Jewel Food Stores, April 14, 1969.

through legislation or other pressures, companies in the industry will be compelled to increase their ratios of black employees, and they would prefer to move first so as to have the opportunity to select the more qualified employees. It is to be hoped that other companies will also follow this policy and obviate the need for ill-considered legislation.

THE FUTURE OF NEGRO EMPLOYMENT

It seems likely that in the years immediately ahead, Negro employment in the supermarket industry will continue to expand. Given locational problems, the rate of expansion will probably be more rapid in the metropolitan areas than in other areas, and given intrafacility movement difficulties, less rapid in the meat and truck driving departments than in the stores. Warehouses are likely to remain heavily black for some time. Upward movement into managerial positions, however, will be slow because of the small number of male clerks who form the base of the promotion ladder and because of the difficulty of attracting black Negro college graduates to the business.

On the whole, in the immediate future there is reason for cautious optimism with respect to the prospects for improved levels of Negro employment in the industry. The supermarket business, however, is on the threshold of radical changes in almost every facet of its operation. These changes are likely to alter the nature of the work to be performed and in the long run will require changes in personnel at every level of the business. If the industry is to continue to provide improved employment opportunities for Negroes, it is important that long range manpower planning together with adequate training programs be undertaken now or else Negroes may find themselves victims of change in this industry, in much the same way as they have in other industries.

Appendix A

BASIC STATISTICAL TABLES, CHAIN COMPANIES AND LARGE INDEPENDENTS, 1966, 1967, 1969, AND 1970

TABLE A-1. *Supermarket Industry*
Employment by Race, Sex, and Occupational Group
4,489 Establishments
United States, 1966

Occupational Group	All Employees			Male			Female		
	Total	Negro	Percent Negro	Total	Negro	Percent Negro	Total	Negro	Percent Negro
Officials and managers	62,214	562	0.9	59,863	514	0.9	2,351	48	2.0
Professionals	1,155	13	1.1	1,054	13	1.2	101	—	—
Technicians	468	10	2.1	435	8	1.8	33	2	6.1
Sales workers [a]	18,086	441	2.4	12,541	319	2.5	5,545	122	2.2
Office and clerical	10,538	223	2.1	1,824	51	2.8	8,714	172	2.0
Total white collar	92,461	1,249	1.4	75,717	905	1.2	16,744	344	2.1
Craftsmen	40,855	1,094	2.7	39,589	1,064	2.7	1,266	30	2.4
Operatives	5,521	675	12.2	4,679	606	13.0	342	69	8.2
Laborers	5,039	808	16.0	4,515	738	16.3	524	70	13.4
Service workers [b]	440,121	25,323	5.8	282,887	19,508	6.9	157,234	5,815	3.7
Total blue collar	491,536	27,900	5.7	331,670	21,916	6.6	159,866	5,984	3.7
Total	583,997	29,149	5.0	407,387	22,821	5.6	176,610	6,328	3.6

Source: U.S. Equal Employment Opportunity Commission, *Job Patterns for Minorities and Women in Private Industry, 1966*, Report No. 1 (Washington: The Commission, 1968), Part II.

Note: Reporting units in many cases are combined on an areawide basis in 1966, 1967, and 1969.

[a] Actual number of sales workers should be about 418,000. Food industry classified grocery checkers as service workers in 1966, as sales workers in subsequent years.

[b] Actual number approximately 40,000. See note a, above.

TABLE A-2. Supermarket Industry
Employment by Race, Sex, and Occupational Group
2,877 Establishments
United States, 1967

Occupational Group	All Employees			Male			Female		
	Total	Negro	Percent Negro	Total	Negro	Percent Negro	Total	Negro	Percent Negro
Officials and managers	80,480	952	1.2	77,216	885	1.1	3,264	67	2.1
Professionals	3,188	183	5.7	2,912	147	5.0	276	36	13.0
Technicians	5,004	347	6.9	3,539	235	6.6	1,465	112	7.6
Sales workers	431,399	20,226	4.7	275,173	14,249	5.2	156,226	5,977	3.8
Office and clerical	48,732	1,853	3.8	14,030	848	6.0	34,702	1,005	2.9
Total white collar	568,803	23,561	4.1	372,870	16,364	4.4	195,933	7,197	3.7
Craftsmen	46,445	1,602	3.4	44,035	1,499	3.4	2,410	103	4.3
Operatives	61,497	6,280	10.2	42,724	5,299	12.4	18,773	981	5.2
Laborers	42,875	4,946	11.5	35,271	4,496	12.7	7,604	450	5.9
Service workers	35,725	5,308	14.9	23,533	4,155	17.7	12,192	1,153	9.5
Total blue collar	186,542	18,136	9.7	145,563	15,449	10.6	40,979	2,687	6.6
Total	755,345	41,697	5.5	518,433	31,813	6.1	236,912	9,884	4.2

Source: U. S. Equal Employment Opportunity Commission, Job Patterns for Minorities and Women in Private Industry, 1967, Report No. 2 (Washington: The Commission, 1970), Vol. 1.

TABLE A-3. *Supermarket Industry*
Employment by Race, Sex, and Occupational Group
3,598 Establishments
United States, 1969

Occupational Group	All Employees			Male			Female		
	Total	Negro	Percent Negro	Total	Negro	Percent Negro	Total	Negro	Percent Negro
Officials and managers	73,327	1,485	2.0	69,122	1,326	1.9	4,205	159	3.8
Professionals	3,051	105	3.4	2,784	92	3.3	267	13	4.9
Technicians	3,439	262	7.6	2,310	166	7.2	1,129	96	8.5
Sales workers	431,506	23,508	5.4	264,424	15,553	5.9	167,082	7,955	4.8
Office and clerical	46,844	2,413	5.2	12,480	824	6.6	34,364	1,589	4.6
Total white collar	558,167	27,773	5.0	351,120	17,961	5.1	207,047	9,812	4.7
Craftsmen	42,287	1,818	4.3	40,160	1,725	4.3	2,127	93	4.4
Operatives	56,385	7,562	13.4	39,198	6,293	16.1	17,187	1,269	7.4
Laborers	38,747	5,369	13.9	32,125	4,682	14.6	6,622	687	10.4
Service workers	35,462	4,773	13.5	24,613	3,857	15.7	10,849	916	8.4
Total blue collar	172,881	19,522	11.3	136,096	15,557	12.2	36,785	2,965	8.1
Total	731,048	47,295	6.5	487,216	34,518	7.1	243,832	12,777	5.2

Source: U. S. Equal Employment Opportunity Commission, 1969.

TABLE A-4. Supermarket Industry
Employment by Race, Sex, and Occupational Group
10,575 Establishments
United States, 1970

Occupational Group	All Employees			Male			Female		
	Total	Negro	Percent Negro	Total	Negro	Percent Negro	Total	Negro	Percent Negro
Officials and managers	71,617	1,695	2.4	67,656	1,531	2.3	3,961	164	4.1
Professionals	3,653	113	3.1	3,168	88	2.8	485	25	5.2
Technicians	2,525	113	4.5	1,813	94	5.2	712	19	2.7
Sales workers	431,095	23,685	5.5	265,104	15,600	5.9	165,991	8,085	4.9
Office and clerical	46,593	2,529	5.4	11,057	858	7.8	35,536	1,671	4.7
Total white collar	555,483	28,135	5.1	348,798	18,171	5.2	206,685	9,964	4.8
Craftsmen	41,491	2,560	6.2	39,174	2,445	6.2	2,417	115	4.8
Operatives	57,734	8,019	13.9	42,523	6,635	15.6	15,211	1,384	9.1
Laborers	41,788	7,644	18.3	33,809	6,346	18.8	7,979	1,298	16.3
Service workers	35,269	5,547	15.7	23,011	3,774	16.4	12,258	1,773	14.5
Total blue collar	176,382	23,770	13.5	138,517	19,200	13.9	37,865	4,570	12.1
Total	731,865	51,905	7.1	487,315	37,371	7.7	244,550	14,534	5.9

Source: U.S. Equal Employment Opportunity Commission, 1970.
Note: Establishments represent uncombined reporting units in 1970. Data by region and metropolitan area not available.

TABLE A-5. *Supermarket Industry*
Employment by Race, Sex, and Occupational Group
152 Establishments
New England Region, 1966

Occupational Group	All Employees			Male			Female		
	Total	Negro	Percent Negro	Total	Negro	Percent Negro	Total	Negro	Percent Negro
Officials and managers	4,205	15	0.4	4,116	15	0.4	89	—	—
Professionals	42	2	4.8	41	2	4.9	1	—	—
Technicians	11	—	—	11	—	—	—	—	—
Sales workers	395	—	—	270	—	—	125	—	—
Office and clerical	902	26	2.9	185	5	2.7	717	21	2.9
Total white collar	5,555	43	0.8	4,623	22	0.5	932	21	2.3
Craftsmen	2,289	41	1.8	1,988	40	2.0	301	1	0.3
Operatives	728	19	2.6	572	16	2.8	156	3	1.9
Laborers	496	31	6.2	469	23	4.9	27	8	29.6
Service workers	31,524	573	1.8	18,260	380	2.1	13,264	193	1.5
Total blue collar	35,037	664	1.9	21,289	459	2.2	13,748	205	1.5
Total	40,592	707	1.7	25,912	481	1.9	14,680	226	1.5

Source: U.S. Equal Employment Opportunity Commission, *Job Patterns for Minorities and Women in Private Industry, 1966*, Report No. 1 (Washington: The Commission, 1968), Part II.

Note: Massachusetts, Maine, and Connecticut. The sum of regional totals is less than United States totals because EEOC did not publish data for those states with less than ten reporting establishments unless the state had at least five establishments with at least 2,000 employees.

TABLE A-6. Supermarket Industry
Employment by Race, Sex, and Occupational Group
172 Establishments
New England Region, 1967

Occupational Group	All Employees			Male			Female		
	Total	Negro	Percent Negro	Total	Negro	Percent Negro	Total	Negro	Percent Negro
Officials and managers	5,320	34	0.6	5,235	32	0.6	85	2	2.4
Professionals	66	—	—	63	—	—	3	—	—
Technicians	112	1	0.9	112	1	0.9	—	—	—
Sales workers	26,986	379	1.4	16,546	233	1.4	10,440	146	1.4
Office and clerical	2,580	63	2.4	368	26	7.1	2,212	37	1.7
Total white collar	35,064	477	1.4	22,324	292	1.3	12,740	185	1.5
Craftsmen	1,943	20	1.0	1,824	19	1.0	119	1	0.8
Operatives	6,047	262	4.3	3,448	177	5.1	2,599	85	3.3
Laborers	2,175	84	3.9	1,665	78	4.7	510	6	1.2
Service workers	1,881	40	2.1	1,186	34	2.9	695	6	0.9
Total blue collar	12,046	406	3.4	8,123	308	3.8	3,923	98	2.5
Total	47,110	883	1.9	30,447	600	2.0	16,663	283	1.7

Source: U.S. Equal Employment Opportunity Commission, Job Patterns for Minorities and Women in Private Industry, 1967, Report No. 2 (Washington: The Commission, 1970), Vol. 1.

TABLE A-7. *Supermarket Industry*
Employment by Race, Sex, and Occupational Group
204 Establishments
New England Region, 1969

Occupational Group	All Employees			Male			Female		
	Total	Negro	Percent Negro	Total	Negro	Percent Negro	Total	Negro	Percent Negro
Officials and managers	5,041	31	0.6	4,927	29	0.6	114	2	1.8
Professionals	66	1	1.5	56	1	1.8	10	—	—
Technicians	45	—	—	24	—	—	21	—	—
Sales workers	30,653	544	1.8	17,932	345	1.9	12,721	199	1.6
Office and clerical	2,568	74	2.9	459	34	7.4	2,109	40	1.9
Total white collar	38,373	650	1.7	23,398	409	1.7	14,975	241	1.6
Craftsmen	1,997	25	1.3	1,603	21	1.3	394	4	1.0
Operatives	2,624	80	3.0	1,258	61	4.8	1,366	19	1.4
Laborers	3,084	144	4.7	2,463	133	5.4	621	11	1.8
Service workers	2,635	59	2.2	1,593	48	3.0	1,042	11	1.1
Total blue collar	10,340	308	3.0	6,917	263	3.8	3,423	45	1.3
Total	48,713	958	2.0	30,315	672	2.2	18,398	286	1.6

Source: U.S. Equal Employment Opportunity Commission, 1969.

TABLE A-8. *Supermarket Industry*
Employment by Race, Sex, and Occupational Group
312 Establishments
Middle Atlantic Region, 1966

Occupational Group	All Employees			Male			Female		
	Total	Negro	Percent Negro	Total	Negro	Percent Negro	Total	Negro	Percent Negro
Officials and managers	9,526	130	1.4	9,252	122	1.3	274	8	2.9
Professionals	184	2	1.1	174	2	1.1	10	—	—
Technicians	115	2	1.7	106	1	0.9	9	1	11.1
Sales workers	2,432	35	1.4	2,078	19	0.9	354	16	4.5
Office and clerical	2,788	79	2.8	594	13	2.2	2,194	66	3.0
Total white collar	15,045	248	1.6	12,204	157	1.3	2,841	91	3.2
Craftsmen	5,286	312	5.9	5,269	311	5.9	17	1	5.9
Operatives	751	76	10.1	628	51	8.1	123	25	20.3
Laborers	427	15	3.5	406	15	3.7	21	—	—
Service workers	73,887	4,246	5.7	46,981	2,607	5.5	26,906	1,639	6.1
Total blue collar	80,351	4,649	5.8	53,284	2,984	5.6	27,067	1,665	6.2
Total	95,396	4,897	5.1	65,488	3,141	4.8	29,908	1,756	5.9

Source: U.S. Equal Employment Opportunity Commission, *Job Patterns for Minorities and Women in Private Industry, 1966*, Report No. 1 (Washington: The Commission, 1968), Part II.

Note: Pennsylvania, New York, and New Jersey.

TABLE A-9. Supermarket Industry
Employment by Race, Sex, and Occupational Group
437 Establishments
Middle Atlantic Region, 1967

Occupational Group	All Employees			Male			Female		
	Total	Negro	Percent Negro	Total	Negro	Percent Negro	Total	Negro	Percent Negro
Officials and managers	15,120	207	1.4	14,626	196	1.3	494	11	2.2
Professionals	268	7	2.6	255	6	2.4	13	1	7.7
Technicians	1,187	4	0.3	978	3	0.3	209	1	0.5
Sales workers	79,572	3,539	4.4	48,761	2,155	4.4	30,811	1,384	4.5
Office and clerical	14,053	614	4.4	5,529	247	4.5	8,524	367	4.3
Total white collar	110,200	4,371	4.0	70,149	2,607	3.7	40,051	1,764	4.4
Craftsmen	6,677	164	2.5	6,303	156	2.5	374	8	2.1
Operatives	15,361	1,000	6.5	10,121	689	6.8	5,240	311	5.9
Laborers	4,424	241	5.4	3,906	211	5.4	518	30	5.8
Service workers	4,760	573	12.0	3,079	388	12.6	1,681	185	11.0
Total blue collar	31,222	1,978	6.3	23,409	1,444	6.2	7,813	534	6.8
Total	141,422	6,349	4.5	93,558	4,051	4.3	47,864	2,298	4.8

Source: U.S. Equal Employment Opportunity Commission, *Job Patterns for Minorities and Women in Private Industry, 1967*, Report No. 2 (Washington: The Commission, 1970), Vol. 1.

TABLE A-10. *Supermarket Industry*
Employment by Race, Sex, and Occupational Group
455 Establishments
Middle Atlantic Region, 1969

Occupational Group	All Employees			Male			Female		
	Total	Negro	Percent Negro	Total	Negro	Percent Negro	Total	Negro	Percent Negro
Officials and managers	15,974	254	1.6	15,245	236	1.5	729	18	2.5
Professionals	571	21	3.7	524	18	3.4	47	3	6.4
Technicians	1,165	140	12.0	824	81	9.8	341	59	17.3
Sales workers	82,797	4,076	4.9	48,932	2,493	5.1	33,865	1,583	4.7
Office and clerical	12,348	780	6.3	3,706	231	6.2	8,642	549	6.4
Total white collar	112,855	5,271	4.7	69,231	3,059	4.4	43,624	2,212	5.1
Craftsmen	7,565	233	3.1	7,295	222	3.0	270	11	4.1
Operatives	18,451	1,614	8.7	11,572	1,128	9.7	6,879	486	7.1
Laborers	5,819	562	9.7	4,717	374	7.9	1,102	188	17.1
Service workers	5,879	557	9.5	4,173	422	10.1	1,706	135	7.9
Total blue collar	37,714	2,966	7.9	27,757	2,146	7.7	9,957	820	8.2
Total	150,569	8,237	5.5	96,988	5,205	5.4	53,581	3,032	5.7

Source: U.S. Equal Employment Opportunity Commission, 1969.

TABLE A-11. *Supermarket Industry*
Employment by Race, Sex, and Occupational Group
1,461 Establishments
South Region, 1966

Occupational Group	All Employees			Male			Female		
	Total	Negro	Percent Negro	Total	Negro	Percent Negro	Total	Negro	Percent Negro
Officials and managers	18,333	184	1.0	17,382	172	1.0	951	12	1.3
Professionals	266	2	0.8	251	2	0.8	15	—	—
Technicians	36	—	—	34	—	—	2	—	—
Sales workers	3,258	89	2.7	2,060	70	3.4	1,198	19	1.6
Office and clerical	2,074	34	1.6	413	15	3.6	1,661	19	1.1
Total white collar	23,967	309	1.3	20,140	259	1.3	3,827	50	1.3
Craftsmen	11,468	444	3.9	11,092	430	3.9	376	14	3.7
Operatives	1,461	449	30.7	1,393	424	30.4	68	25	36.8
Laborers	1,235	554	44.9	1,015	497	49.0	220	57	25.9
Service workers	123,054	11,613	9.4	83,762	10,026	12.0	39,292	1,587	4.0
Total blue collar	137,218	13,060	9.5	97,262	11,377	11.7	39,956	1,683	4.2
Total	161,185	13,369	8.3	117,402	11,636	9.9	43,783	1,733	4.0

Source: U.S. Equal Employment Opportunity Commission, *Job Patterns for Minorities and Women in Private Industry, 1966*, Report No. 1 (Washington: The Commission, 1968), Part II.

Note: Arkansas, West Virginia, Virginia, Texas, Tennessee, South Carolina, North Carolina, Mississippi, Maryland, Kentucky, Louisiana, Delaware, District of Columbia, Florida, Georgia, Alabama and Oklahoma.

TABLE A-12. *Supermarket Industry*
Employment by Race, Sex, and Occupational Group
1,060 Establishments
South Region, 1967

Occupational Group	All Employees			Male			Female		
	Total	Negro	Percent Negro	Total	Negro	Percent Negro	Total	Negro	Percent Negro
Officials and managers	25,549	414	1.6	24,186	383	1.6	1,363	31	2.3
Professionals	769	153	19.9	685	121	17.7	84	32	38.1
Technicians	2,718	321	11.8	1,757	219	12.5	961	102	10.6
Sales workers	130,844	9,536	7.3	89,883	7,531	8.4	40,961	2,005	4.9
Office and clerical	13,655	629	4.6	4,268	393	9.2	9,387	236	2.5
Total white collar	173,535	11,053	6.4	120,779	8,647	7.2	52,756	2,406	4.6
Craftsmen	14,049	919	6.5	13,258	850	6.4	791	69	8.7
Operatives	15,766	3,638	23.1	10,401	3,242	31.2	5,365	396	7.4
Laborers	10,956	2,705	24.7	9,752	2,526	25.9	1,204	179	14.9
Service workers	7,959	2,732	34.3	5,663	2,124	37.5	2,296	608	26.5
Total blue collar	48,730	9,994	20.5	39,074	8,742	22.4	9,656	1,252	13.0
Total	222,265	21,047	9.5	159,853	17,389	10.9	62,412	3,658	5.9

Source: U.S. Equal Employment Opportunity Commission, *Job Patterns for Minorities and Women in Private Industry, 1967*, Report No. 2 (Washington: The Commission, 1970), Vol. 1.

TABLE A-13. *Supermarket Industry*
Employment by Race, Sex, and Occupational Group
1,141 Establishments
South Region, 1969

Occupational Group	All Employees			Male			Female		
	Total	Negro	Percent Negro	Total	Negro	Percent Negro	Total	Negro	Percent Negro
Officials and managers	22,571	539	2.4	21,027	506	2.4	1,544	33	2.1
Professionals	606	15	2.5	550	11	2.0	56	4	7.1
Technicians	711	89	12.5	454	66	14.5	257	23	8.9
Sales workers	122,882	9,255	7.5	80,204	6,612	8.2	42,678	2,643	6.2
Office and clerical	14,022	820	5.8	4,253	389	9.1	9,769	431	4.4
Total white collar	160,792	10,718	6.7	106,488	7,584	7.1	54,304	3,134	5.8
Craftsmen	11,364	826	7.3	10,886	790	7.3	478	36	7.5
Operatives	12,368	3,579	28.9	9,469	3,311	35.0	2,899	268	9.2
Laborers	9,864	2,520	25.5	8,221	2,301	28.0	1,643	219	13.3
Service workers	8,239	2,451	29.7	6,583	1,975	30.0	1,656	476	28.7
Total blue collar	41,835	9,376	22.4	35,159	8,377	23.8	6,676	999	15.0
Total	202,627	20,094	9.9	141,647	15,961	11.3	60,980	4,133	6.8

Source: U.S. Equal Employment Opportunity Commission, 1969.

TABLE A-14. *Supermarket Industry*
Employment by Race, Sex, and Occupational Group
887 Establishments
Midwest Region, 1966

Occupational Group	All Employees			Male			Female		
	Total	Negro	Percent Negro	Total	Negro	Percent Negro	Total	Negro	Percent Negro
Officials and managers	15,326	144	0.9	14,788	124	0.8	538	20	3.7
Professionals	393	7	1.8	343	7	2.0	50	—	—
Technicians	239	3	1.3	221	2	0.9	18	1	5.6
Sales workers	10,543	301	2.9	6,991	221	3.2	3,552	80	2.3
Office and clerical	3,317	71	2.1	381	14	3.7	2,936	57	1.9
Total white collar	29,818	526	1.8	22,724	368	1.6	7,094	158	2.2
Craftsmen	11,656	193	1.7	11,547	186	1.6	109	7	6.4
Operatives	1,977	107	5.4	1,550	92	5.9	427	15	3.5
Laborers	2,301	157	6.8	2,097	152	7.2	204	5	2.5
Service workers	115,542	5,552	4.8	67,823	3,767	5.6	47,719	1,785	3.7
Total blue collar	131,476	6,009	4.6	83,017	4,197	5.1	48,459	1,812	3.7
Total	161,294	6,535	4.1	105,741	4,565	4.3	55,553	1,970	3.5

Source: U.S. Equal Employment Opportunity Commission, *Job Patterns for Minorities and Women in Private Industry, 1966*, Report No. 1 (Washington: The Commission, 1968), Part II.

Note: Wisconsin, South Dakota, Ohio, Missouri, Nebraska, Michigan, Minnesota, Illinois, Indiana, Iowa, and Kansas.

TABLE A-15. *Supermarket Industry*
Employment by Race, Sex, and Occupational Group
750 Establishments
Midwest Region, 1967

Occupational Group	All Employees			Male			Female		
	Total	Negro	Percent Negro	Total	Negro	Percent Negro	Total	Negro	Percent Negro
Officials and managers	19,281	221	1.1	18,415	200	1.1	866	21	2.4
Professionals	814	15	1.8	755	13	1.7	59	2	3.4
Technicians	414	11	2.7	249	6	2.4	165	5	3.0
Sales workers	121,116	4,767	3.9	68,946	2,879	4.2	52,170	1,888	3.6
Office and clerical	11,183	442	4.0	2,661	159	6.0	8,522	283	3.3
Total white collar	152,808	5,456	3.6	91,026	3,257	3.6	61,782	2,199	3.6
Craftsmen	12,975	351	2.7	12,584	336	2.7	391	15	3.8
Operatives	14,606	1,140	7.8	12,488	987	7.9	2,118	153	7.2
Laborers	21,027	1,557	7.4	16,072	1,328	8.3	4,955	229	4.6
Service workers	10,307	954	9.3	6,158	710	11.5	4,149	244	5.9
Total blue collar	58,915	4,002	6.8	47,302	3,361	7.1	11,613	641	5.5
Total	211,723	9,458	4.5	138,328	6,618	4.8	73,395	2,840	3.9

Source: U.S. Equal Employment Opportunity Commission, *Job Patterns for Minorities and Women in Private Industry, 1967*, Report No. 2 (Washington: The Commission, 1970), Vol. 1.

TABLE A-16. *Supermarket Industry*
Employment by Race, Sex, and Occupational Group
1,024 Establishments
Midwest Region, 1969

Occupational Group	All Employees			Male			Female		
	Total	Negro	Percent Negro	Total	Negro	Percent Negro	Total	Negro	Percent Negro
Officials and managers	20,620	557	2.7	19,237	497	2.6	1,383	60	4.3
Professionals	1,102	47	4.3	1,017	44	4.3	85	3	3.5
Technicians	797	22	2.8	579	16	2.8	218	6	2.8
Sales workers	133,000	7,347	5.5	74,629	4,395	5.9	58,371	2,952	5.1
Office and clerical	12,121	625	5.2	2,385	139	5.8	9,736	486	5.0
Total white collar	167,640	8,598	5.1	97,847	5,091	5.2	69,793	3,507	5.0
Craftsmen	14,112	594	4.2	13,455	563	4.2	657	31	4.7
Operatives	17,010	2,069	12.2	13,310	1,607	12.1	3,700	462	12.5
Laborers	15,948	1,883	11.8	13,476	1,626	12.1	2,472	257	10.4
Service workers	10,021	966	9.6	5,569	724	13.0	4,452	242	5.4
Total blue collar	57,091	5,512	9.7	45,810	4,520	9.9	11,281	992	8.8
Total	224,731	14,110	6.3	143,657	9,611	6.7	81,074	4,499	5.5

Source: U.S. Equal Employment Opportunity Commission, 1969.

TABLE A-17. *Supermarket Industry*
Employment by Race, Sex, and Occupational Group
1,621 Establishments
West Region, 1966

Occupational Group	All Employees			Male			Female		
	Total	Negro	Percent Negro	Total	Negro	Percent Negro	Total	Negro	Percent Negro
Officials and managers	14,044	88	0.6	13,558	80	0.6	486	8	1.6
Professionals	269	—	—	245	—	—	24	—	—
Technicians	67	5	7.5	63	5	7.9	4	—	—
Sales workers	1,458	16	1.1	1,142	9	0.8	316	7	2.2
Office and clerical	1,393	13	0.9	241	4	1.7	1,152	9	0.8
Total white collar	17,231	122	0.7	15,249	98	0.6	1,782	24	1.2
Craftsmen	9,674	101	1.0	9,264	94	1.0	410	7	1.7
Operatives	582	24	4.1	514	23	4.5	68	1	1.5
Laborers	553	51	9.2	501	51	10.2	52	—	—
Service workers	91,486	3,306	3.6	63,293	2,707	4.3	28,193	599	2.1
Total blue collar	102,295	3,482	3.4	73,572	2,875	3.9	28,723	607	2.1
Total	119,526	3,604	3.0	88,821	2,973	3.3	30,705	631	2.1

Source: U.S. Equal Employment Opportunity Commission, *Job Patterns for Minorities and Women in Private Industry, 1966, Report* No. 1 (Washington: The Commission, 1968), Part II.

Note: Wyoming, Washington, Utah, Oregon, New Mexico, Montana, Nevada, Idaho, California, Colorado and Arizona.

TABLE A-18. Supermarket Industry
Employment by Race, Sex, and Occupational Group
434 Establishments
West Region, 1967

Occupational Group	All Employees			Male			Female		
	Total	Negro	Percent Negro	Total	Negro	Percent Negro	Total	Negro	Percent Negro
Officials and managers	14,620	75	0.5	14,184	73	0.5	436	2	0.5
Professionals	1,264	8	0.6	1,147	7	0.6	117	1	0.9
Technicians	549	10	1.8	419	6	1.4	130	4	3.1
Sales workers	70,156	1,990	2.8	49,481	1,444	2.9	20,675	546	2.6
Office and clerical	7,182	105	1.5	1,193	23	1.9	5,989	82	1.4
Total white collar	93,771	2,188	2.3	66,424	1,553	2.3	27,347	635	2.3
Craftsmen	10,483	147	1.4	9,768	137	1.4	715	10	1.4
Operatives	9,449	239	2.5	6,165	204	3.3	3,284	35	1.1
Laborers	4,123	359	8.7	3,720	353	9.5	403	6	1.5
Service workers	9,915	1,007	10.2	6,914	897	13.0	3,001	110	3.7
Total blue collar	33,970	1,752	5.2	26,567	1,591	6.0	7,403	161	2.2
Total	127,741	3,940	3.1	92,991	3,144	3.4	34,750	796	2.3

Source: U.S. Equal Employment Opportunity Commission, Job Patterns for Minorities and Women in Private Industry, 1967, Report No. 2 (Washington: The Commission, 1970), Vol. 1.

TABLE A-19. *Supermarket Industry*
Employment by Race, Sex, and Occupational Group
766 Establishments
West Region, 1969

Occupational Group	All Employees			Male			Female		
	Total	Negro	Percent Negro	Total	Negro	Percent Negro	Total	Negro	Percent Negro
Officials and managers	8,057	102	1.3	7,625	56	0.7	432	46	10.6
Professionals	706	21	3.0	637	18	2.8	69	3	4.3
Technicians	239	11	4.6	155	3	1.9	84	8	9.5
Sales workers	55,397	1,871	3.4	38,205	1,364	3.6	17,192	507	2.9
Office and clerical	5,710	114	2.0	1,615	31	1.9	4,095	83	2.0
Total white collar	70,109	2,119	3.0	48,237	1,472	3.1	21,872	647	3.0
Craftsmen	7,227	140	1.9	6,899	129	1.9	328	11	3.4
Operatives	5,887	220	3.7	3,589	186	5.2	2,298	34	1.5
Laborers	4,032	260	6.4	3,248	248	7.6	784	12	1.5
Service workers	8,683	740	8.5	6,694	688	10.3	1,989	52	2.6
Total blue collar	25,829	1,360	5.3	20,430	1,251	6.1	5,399	109	2.0
Total	95,938	3,479	3.6	68,667	2,723	4.0	27,271	756	2.8

Source: U.S. Equal Employment Opportunity Commission, 1969.

TABLE A-20. Supermarket Industry
Employment by Race, Sex, and Occupational Group
883 Establishments
Twenty Metropolitan Areas, 1966

Occupational Group	All Employees			Male			Female		
	Total	Negro	Percent Negro	Total	Negro	Percent Negro	Total	Negro	Percent Negro
Officials and managers	18,344	313	1.7	17,668	293	1.7	676	20	3.0
Professionals	676	9	1.3	609	9	1.5	67	—	—
Technicians	260	4	1.5	238	3	1.3	22	1	4.5
Sales workers	9,785	326	3.3	6,796	233	3.4	2,989	93	3.1
Office and clerical	4,894	151	3.1	892	36	4.0	4,002	115	2.9
Total white collar	33,959	803	2.4	26,203	574	2.2	7,756	229	3.0
Craftsmen	13,528	487	3.6	13,372	481	3.6	156	6	3.8
Operatives	1,893	320	16.9	1,561	283	18.1	332	37	11.1
Laborers	1,880	395	21.0	1,714	368	21.5	166	27	16.3
Service workers	131,615	13,645	10.4	85,366	10,785	12.6	46,249	2,860	6.2
Total blue collar	148,916	14,847	10.0	102,013	11,917	11.7	46,903	2,930	6.2
Total	182,875	15,650	8.6	128,216	12,491	9.7	54,659	3,159	5.8

Source: U.S. Equal Employment Opportunity Commission, Job Patterns for Minorities and Women in Private Industry, 1966, Report No. 1 (Washington: The Commission, 1968), Part III.

Note: Atlanta, Baltimore, Charlotte, Chicago, Cincinnati, Cleveland, Dallas, Detroit, Houston, Indianapolis, Jacksonville, Kansas City, Los Angeles, Memphis, New Orleans, New York, Philadelphia, Richmond, St. Louis, Washington, D. C.

TABLE A-21. *Supermarket Industry*
Employment by Race, Sex, and Occupational Group
606 Establishments
Twenty Metropolitan Areas, 1967

Occupational Group	All Employees			Male			Female		
	Total	Negro	Percent Negro	Today	Negro	Percent Negro	Total	Negro	Percent Negro
Officials and managers	25,587	654	2.6	24,411	610	2.5	1,176	44	3.7
Professionals	1,196	169	14.1	1,080	137	12.7	116	32	27.6
Technicians	3,077	330	10.7	2,029	226	11.1	1,048	104	9.9
Sales workers	134,337	11,431	8.5	86,933	7,747	8.9	47,404	3,684	7.8
Office and clerical	19,280	1,087	5.6	5,439	465	8.5	13,841	622	4.5
Total white collar	183,477	13,671	7.5	119,892	9,185	7.7	63,585	4,486	7.1
Craftsmen	16,418	1,162	7.1	15,608	1,086	7.0	810	76	9.4
Operatives	21,865	3,664	16.8	16,835	3,132	18.6	5,030	532	10.6
Laborers	12,675	2,784	22.0	10,922	2,650	24.3	1,753	134	7.6
Service workers	11,660	3,189	27.3	8,712	2,517	28.9	2,948	672	22.8
Total blue collar	62,618	10,799	17.2	52,077	9,385	18.0	10,541	1,414	13.4
Total	246,095	24,470	9.9	171,969	18,570	10.8	74,126	5,900	8.0

Source: U.S. Equal Employment Opportunity Commission, *Job Patterns for Minorities and Women in Private Industry, 1967*, Report No. 2 (Washington: The Commission, 1970), Vol. 2.

TABLE A-22. Supermarket Industry
Employment by Race, Sex, and Occupational Group
770 Establishments
Twenty Metropolitan Areas, 1969

Occupational Group	All Employees			Male			Female		
	Total	Negro	Percent Negro	Total	Negro	Percent Negro	Total	Negro	Percent Negro
Officials and managers	28,392	995	3.5	26,855	879	3.3	1,537	116	7.5
Professionals	1,460	65	4.5	1,325	58	4.4	135	7	5.2
Technicians	1,164	111	9.5	852	83	9.7	312	28	9.0
Sales workers	160,194	14,234	8.9	96,655	9,141	9.5	63,539	5,093	8.0
Office and clerical	20,593	1,526	7.4	5,329	483	9.1	15,264	1,043	6.8
Total white collar	211,803	16,931	8.0	131,016	10,644	8.1	80,787	6,287	7.8
Craftsmen	16,334	1,114	6.8	15,797	1,070	6.8	537	44	8.2
Operatives	21,024	4,480	21.3	16,469	3,856	23.4	4,555	624	13.7
Laborers	12,505	3,123	25.0	10,749	2,777	25.8	1,756	346	19.7
Service workers	11,659	2,948	25.3	9,631	2,418	25.1	2,028	530	26.1
Total blue collar	61,522	11,665	19.0	52,646	10,121	19.2	8,876	1,544	17.4
Total	273,325	28,596	10.5	183,662	20,765	11.3	89,663	7,831	8.7

Source: U.S. Equal Employment Opportunity Commission, 1969.

TABLE A-23. *Supermarket Industry*
Employment by Race, Sex, and Occupational Group
73 Establishments
Two Middle Atlantic Metropolitan Areas, 1966

Occupational Group	All Employees			Male			Female		
	Total	Negro	Percent Negro	Total	Negro	Percent Negro	Total	Negro	Percent Negro
Officials and managers	3,985	62	1.6	3,916	61	1.6	69	1	1.4
Professionals	87	2	2.3	85	2	2.4	2	—	—
Technicians	94	—	—	90	—	—	4	—	—
Sales workers	903	10	1.1	890	10	1.1	13	—	—
Office and clerical	1,253	52	4.2	285	7	2.5	968	45	4.6
Total white collar	6,322	126	2.0	5,266	80	1.5	1,056	46	4.4
Craftsmen	1,649	18	1.1	1,648	17	1.0	1	1	100.0
Operatives	121	12	9.9	83	2	2.4	38	10	26.3
Laborers	129	6	4.7	122	6	4.9	7	—	—
Service workers	31,241	2,109	6.8	20,867	1,383	6.6	10,374	726	7.0
Total blue collar	33,140	2,145	6.5	22,720	1,408	6.2	10,420	737	7.1
Total	39,462	2,271	5.8	27,986	1,488	5.3	11,476	783	6.8

Source: U.S. Equal Employment Opportunity Commission, *Job Patterns for Minorities and Women in Private Industry, 1966,* Report No. 1 (Washington: The Commission, 1968), Part III.

Note: New York and Philadelphia.

TABLE A-24. *Supermarket Industry*
Employment by Race, Sex, and Occupational Group
90 Establishments
Two Middle Atlantic Metropolitan Areas, 1967

Occupational Group	All Employees			Male			Female		
	Total	Negro	Percent Negro	Total	Negro	Percent Negro	Total	Negro	Percent Negro
Officials and managers	6,548	139	2.1	6,387	135	2.1	161	4	2.5
Professionals	90	6	6.7	87	6	6.9	3	—	—
Technicians	228	1	0.4	225	1	0.4	3	—	—
Sales workers	33,479	2,387	7.1	21,746	1,442	6.6	11,733	945	8.1
Office and clerical	5,434	416	7.7	1,720	150	8.7	3,714	266	7.2
Total white collar	45,779	2,949	6.4	30,165	1,734	5.7	15,614	1,215	7.8
Craftsmen	2,816	129	4.6	2,764	124	4.5	52	5	9.6
Operatives	5,628	500	8.9	3,777	369	9.8	1,851	131	7.1
Laborers	1,518	143	9.4	1,343	124	9.2	175	19	10.9
Service workers	1,789	231	12.9	1,384	183	13.2	405	48	11.9
Total blue collar	11,751	1,003	8.5	9,268	800	8.6	2,483	203	8.2
Total	57,530	3,952	6.9	39,433	2,534	6.4	18,097	1,418	7.8

Source: U.S. Equal Employment Opportunity Commission, *Job Patterns for Minorities and Women in Private Industry, 1967*, Report No. 2 (Washington: The Commission, 1970), Vol. 2.

TABLE A-25. *Supermarket Industry*
Employment by Race, Sex, and Occupational Group
90 Establishments
Two Middle Atlantic Metropolitan Areas, 1969

Occupational Group	All Employees			Male			Female		
	Total	Negro	Percent Negro	Total	Negro	Percent Negro	Total	Negro	Percent Negro
Officials and managers	6,663	139	2.1	6,370	132	2.1	293	7	2.4
Professionals	164	5	3.0	152	4	2.6	12	1	8.3
Technicians	103	4	3.9	99	4	4.0	4	—	—
Sales workers	33,870	2,778	8.2	20,733	1,722	8.3	13,137	1,056	8.0
Office and clerical	6,072	537	8.8	2,036	163	8.0	4,036	374	9.3
Total white collar	46,872	3,463	7.4	29,390	2,025	6.9	17,482	1,438	8.2
Craftsmen	2,730	108	4.0	2,637	106	4.0	93	2	2.2
Operatives	3,901	506	13.0	2,544	369	14.5	1,357	137	10.1
Laborers	1,966	280	14.2	1,506	162	10.8	460	118	25.7
Service workers	1,860	215	11.6	1,601	192	12.0	259	23	8.9
Total blue collar	10,457	1,109	10.6	8,288	829	10.0	2,169	280	12.9
Total	57,329	4,572	8.0	37,678	2,854	7.6	19,651	1,718	8.7

Source: U.S. Equal Employment Opportunity Commission, 1969.

TABLE A-26. *Supermarket Industry*
Employment by Race, Sex, and Occupational Group
388 Establishments
Ten Southern Metropolitan Areas, 1966

Occupational Group	All Employees			Male			Female		
	Total	Negro	Percent Negro	Total	Negro	Percent Negro	Total	Negro	Percent Negro
Officials and managers	5,548	125	2.3	5,308	119	2.2	240	6	2.5
Professionals	178	1	0.6	172	1	0.6	6	—	—
Technicians	6	—	—	5	—	—	1	—	—
Sales workers	944	20	2.1	418	3	0.7	526	17	3.2
Office and clerical	981	26	2.7	279	12	4.3	702	14	2.0
Total white collar	7,657	172	2.2	6,182	135	2.2	1,475	37	2.5
Craftsmen	3,929	267	6.8	3,891	267	6.9	38	—	—
Operatives	539	219	40.6	519	206	39.7	20	13	65.0
Laborers	414	224	54.1	350	197	56.3	64	27	42.2
Service workers	39,681	6,935	17.5	26,171	5,938	22.7	13,510	997	7.4
Total blue collar	44,563	7,645	17.2	30,931	6,608	21.4	13,632	1,037	7.6
Total	52,220	7,817	15.0	37,113	6,743	18.2	15,107	1,074	7.1

Source: U.S. Equal Employment Opportunity Commission, *Job Patterns for Minorities and Women in Private Industry, 1966*, Report No. 1 (Washington: The Commission, 1968), Part III.

Note: Atlanta, Baltimore, Charlotte, Dallas, Houston, Jacksonville, Memphis, New Orleans, Richmond, Washington, D. C.

TABLE A-27. *Supermarket Industry*
Employment by Race, Sex, and Occupational Group
256 Establishments
Ten Southern Metropolitan Areas, 1967

Occupational Group	All Employees			Male			Female		
	Total	Negro	Percent Negro	Total	Negro	Percent Negro	Total	Negro	Percent Negro
Officials and managers	8,552	317	3.7	8,090	296	3.7	462	21	4.5
Professionals	506	148	29.2	434	116	26.7	72	32	44.4
Technicians	2,394	319	13.3	1,470	217	14.8	924	102	11.0
Sales workers	38,102	5,255	13.8	25,943	3,926	15.1	12,159	1,329	10.9
Office and clerical	6,197	292	4.7	1,935	177	9.1	4,262	115	2.7
Total white collar	55,751	6,331	11.4	37,872	4,732	12.5	17,879	1,599	8.9
Craftsmen	5,453	654	12.0	5,041	599	11.9	412	55	13.3
Operatives	6,594	2,193	33.3	4,746	1,915	40.3	1,848	278	15.0
Laborers	3,765	1,477	39.2	3,240	1,421	43.9	525	56	10.7
Service workers	3,369	1,748	51.9	2,418	1,355	56.0	951	393	41.3
Total blue collar	19,181	6,072	31.7	15,445	5,290	34.3	3,736	782	20.9
Total	74,932	12,403	16.5	53,317	10,022	18.8	21,615	2,381	11.0

Source: U.S. Equal Employment Opportunity Commission, *Job Patterns for Minorities and Women in Private Industry, 1967*, Report No. 2 (Washington: The Commission, 1970), Vol. 2.

TABLE A-28. Supermarket Industry
Employment by Race, Sex, and Occupational Group
315 Establishments
Ten Southern Metropolitan Areas, 1969

Occupational Group	All Employees			Male			Female		
	Total	Negro	Percent Negro	Total	Negro	Percent Negro	Total	Negro	Percent Negro
Officials and managers	8,425	323	3.8	8,001	302	3.8	424	21	5.0
Professionals	392	12	3.1	346	8	2.3	46	4	8.7
Technicians	413	84	20.3	298	62	20.8	115	22	19.1
Sales workers	45,031	4,839	10.7	28,823	3,358	11.7	16,208	1,481	9.1
Office and clerical	5,901	384	6.5	1,748	183	10.5	4,153	201	4.8
Total white collar	60,162	5,642	9.4	39,216	3,913	10.0	20,946	1,729	8.3
Craftsmen	3,628	418	11.5	3,485	405	11.6	143	13	9.1
Operatives	5,299	2,085	39.3	4,393	1,960	44.6	906	125	13.8
Laborers	3,004	1,311	43.6	2,738	1,266	46.2	266	45	16.9
Service workers	4,572	1,616	35.3	3,683	1,273	34.6	889	343	38.6
Total blue collar	16,503	5,430	32.9	14,299	4,904	34.3	2,204	526	23.9
Total	76,665	11,072	14.4	53,515	8,817	16.5	23,150	2,255	9.7

Source: U.S. Equal Employment Opportunity Commission, 1969.

TABLE A-29. *Supermarket Industry*
Employment by Race, Sex, and Occupational Group
237 Establishments
Seven Midwest Metropolitan Areas, 1966

Occupational Group	All Employees			Male			Female		
	Total	Negro	Percent Negro	Total	Negro	Percent Negro	Total	Negro	Percent Negro
Officials and managers	6,132	77	1.3	5,926	67	1.1	206	10	4.9
Professionals	287	6	2.1	240	6	2.5	47	—	—
Technicians	132	3	2.3	116	2	1.7	16	1	6.2
Sales workers	7,512	293	3.9	5,069	217	4.3	2,443	76	3.1
Office and clerical	2,157	66	3.1	236	14	5.9	1,921	52	2.7
Total white collar	16,220	445	2.7	11,587	305	2.6	4,633	139	3.0
Craftsmen	6,072	164	2.7	6,023	159	2.6	49	5	10.2
Operatives	1,007	74	7.3	779	60	7.7	228	14	6.1
Laborers	1,100	130	11.8	1,040	130	12.5	60	—	—
Service workers	42,109	3,234	7.7	25,001	2,348	9.4	17,108	886	5.2
Total blue collar	50,288	3,602	7.2	32,843	2,697	8.2	17,445	905	5.2
Total	66,508	4,047	6.1	44,430	3,003	6.8	22,078	1,044	4.7

Source: U.S. Equal Employment Opportunity Commission, *Job Patterns for Minorities and Women in Private Industry, 1966*, Report No. 1 (Washington: The Commission, 1968), Part III.

Note: Chicago, Cincinnati, Cleveland, Detroit, Indianapolis, Kansas City, St. Louis.

TABLE A-30. Supermarket Industry
Employment by Race, Sex, and Occupational Group
209 Establishments
Seven Midwest Metropolitan Areas, 1967

Occupational Group	All Employees			Male			Female		
	Total	Negro	Percent Negro	Total	Negro	Percent Negro	Total	Negro	Percent Negro
Officials and managers	7,860	159	2.0	7,402	141	1.9	458	18	3.9
Professionals	378	10	2.6	356	10	2.8	22	—	—
Technicians	257	5	1.9	151	3	2.0	106	2	1.9
Sales workers	48,142	2,992	6.2	28,340	1,776	6.3	19,802	1,216	6.1
Office and clerical	5,804	342	5.9	1,556	126	8.1	4,248	216	5.1
Total white collar	62,441	3,508	5.6	37,805	2,056	5.4	24,636	1,452	5.9
Craftsmen	5,597	280	5.0	5,478	269	4.9	119	11	9.2
Operatives	7,963	859	10.8	7,151	750	10.5	812	109	13.4
Laborers	6,294	1,040	16.5	5,306	981	18.5	988	59	6.0
Service workers	2,789	620	22.2	2,004	450	22.5	785	170	21.7
Total blue collar	22,643	2,799	12.4	19,939	2,450	12.3	2,704	349	12.9
Total	85,084	6,307	7.4	57,744	4,506	7.8	27,340	1,801	6.6

Source: U.S. Equal Employment Opportunity Commission, *Job Patterns for Minorities and Women in Private Industry, 1967*, Report No. 2 (Washington: The Commission, 1970), Vol. 2.

TABLE A-31. *Supermarket Industry*
Employment by Race, Sex, and Occupational Group
267 Establishments
Seven Midwest Metropolitan Areas, 1969

Occupational Group	All Employees			Male			Female		
	Total	Negro	Percent Negro	Total	Negro	Percent Negro	Total	Negro	Percent Negro
Officials and managers	11,020	458	4.2	10,321	414	4.0	699	44	6.3
Professionals	745	45	6.0	680	43	6.3	65	2	3.1
Technicians	573	20	3.5	397	15	3.8	176	5	2.8
Sales workers	66,984	5,648	8.4	37,213	3,335	9.0	29,771	2,313	7.8
Office and clerical	7,048	552	7.8	1,241	118	9.5	5,807	434	7.5
Total white collar	86,370	6,723	7.8	49,852	3,925	7.9	36,518	2,798	7.7
Craftsmen	7,920	505	6.4	7,664	484	6.3	256	21	8.2
Operatives	10,371	1,780	17.2	8,617	1,427	16.6	1,754	353	20.1
Laborers	6,394	1,416	22.1	5,517	1,242	22.5	877	174	19.8
Service workers	1,950	660	33.8	1,406	525	37.3	544	135	24.8
Total blue collar	26,635	4,361	16.4	23,204	3,678	15.9	3,431	683	19.9
Total	113,005	11,084	9.8	73,056	7,603	10.4	39,949	3,481	8.7

Source: U.S. Equal Employment Opportunity Commission, 1969.

TABLE A-32. *Supermarket Industry*
Employment by Race, Sex, and Occupational Group
185 Establishments
One West Coast Metropolitan Area, 1966

Occupational Group	All Employees			Male			Female		
	Total	Negro	Percent Negro	Total	Negro	Percent Negro	Total	Negro	Percent Negro
Officials and managers	2,679	49	1.8	2,518	46	1.8	161	3	1.9
Professionals	124	—	—	112	—	—	12	—	—
Technicians	28	1	3.6	27	1	3.7	1	—	—
Sales workers	426	3	0.7	419	3	0.7	7	—	—
Office and clerical	503	7	1.4	92	3	3.3	411	4	1.0
Total white collar	3,760	60	1.6	3,168	53	1.7	592	7	1.2
Craftsmen	1,878	38	2.0	1,810	38	2.1	68	—	—
Operatives	226	15	6.6	180	15	8.3	46	—	—
Laborers	237	35	14.8	202	35	17.3	35	—	—
Service workers	18,584	1,367	7.4	13,327	1,116	8.4	5,257	251	4.8
Total blue collar	20,925	1,455	7.0	15,519	1,204	7.8	5,406	251	4.6
Total	24,685	1,515	6.1	18,687	1,257	6.7	5,998	258	4.3

Source: U.S. Equal Employment Opportunity Commission, *Job Patterns for Minorities and Women in Private Industry, 1966*, Report No. 1 (Washington: The Commission, 1968) Part III.

Note: Los Angeles.

TABLE A-33. *Supermarket Industry*
Employment by Race, Sex, and Occupational Group
51 Establishments
One West Coast Metropolitan Area, 1967

Occupational Group	All Employees			Male			Female		
	Total	Negro	Percent Negro	Total	Negro	Percent Negro	Total	Negro	Percent Negro
Officials and managers	2,627	39	1.5	2,532	38	1.5	95	1	1.1
Professionals	222	5	2.3	203	5	2.5	19	—	—
Technicians	198	5	2.5	183	5	2.7	15	—	—
Sales workers	14,614	797	5.5	10,904	603	5.5	3,710	194	5.2
Office and clerical	1,845	37	2.0	228	12	5.3	1,617	25	1.5
Total white collar	19,506	883	4.5	14,050	663	4.7	5,456	220	4.0
Craftsmen	2,552	99	3.9	2,325	94	4.0	227	5	2.2
Operatives	1,680	112	6.7	1,161	98	8.4	519	14	2.7
Laborers	1,098	124	11.3	1,033	124	12.0	65	—	—
Service workers	3,713	590	15.9	2,906	529	18.2	807	61	7.6
Total blue collar	9,043	925	10.2	7,425	845	11.4	1,618	80	4.9
Total	28,549	1,808	6.3	21,475	1,508	7.0	7,074	300	4.2

Source: U.S. Equal Employment Opportunity Commission, *Job Patterns for Minorities and Women in Private Industry,
1967*, Report No. 2 (Washington: The Commission, 1970), Vol. 2.

TABLE A-34. Supermarket Industry
Employment by Race, Sex, and Occupational Group
98 Establishments
One West Coast Metropolitan Area, 1969

Occupational Group	All Employees			Male			Female		
	Total	Negro	Percent Negro	Total	Negro	Percent Negro	Total	Negro	Percent Negro
Officials and managers	2,284	75	3.3	2,163	31	1.4	121	44	36.4
Professionals	159	3	1.9	147	3	2.0	12	—	—
Technicians	75	3	4.0	58	2	3.4	17	1	5.9
Sales workers	14,309	969	6.8	9,886	726	7.3	4,423	243	5.5
Office and clerical	1,572	53	3.4	304	19	6.2	1,268	34	2.7
Total white collar	18,399	1,103	6.0	12,558	781	6.2	5,841	322	5.5
Craftsmen	2,056	83	4.0	2,011	75	3.7	45	8	17.8
Operatives	1,453	109	7.5	915	100	10.9	538	9	1.7
Laborers	1,141	116	10.2	988	107	10.8	153	9	5.9
Service workers	3,277	457	13.9	2,941	428	14.6	336	29	8.6
Total blue collar	7,927	765	9.7	6,855	710	10.4	1,072	55	5.1
Total	26,326	1,868	7.1	19,413	1,491	7.7	6,913	377	5.5

Source: U.S. Equal Employment Opportunity Commission, 1969.

Appendix B

This agreement entered into, by and between the Coalition of Community Groups (referred to hereinafter as "The Coalition"), acting on the behalf of minority groups; and ————————; ————————; ————————; and — ——————— (collectively referred to hereinafter as "The Markets") including any and all branches of each and every one of The Markets, is as follows:

WHEREAS, certain unsanitary, unhealthy and otherwise deplorable and undesirable conditions exist within and about the premises of The Markets; and

WHEREAS, The Coalition seeks to obtain abatement and total elimination of such conditions; and

WHEREAS, The Markets desire to obtain reasonable efforts on the part of The Coalition to the end that The Coalition will encourage all patrons and persons in the immediate market communities to patronize or continue to patronize The Market;

WHEREFORE, each Market, in consideration of the promises of each other Market a party hereto, and in consideration of the promises of The Coalition, and The Coalition, in consideration of the promises of each and every Market a party hereto, and for the benefit of customers, potential customers and all other persons residing in the communities serviced by The Markets, mutually agree as follows:

1. DEFINITIONS. The parties hereto convenant and agree that the following definitions will govern the interpretation of, and performance of all obligations pursuant to, the Covenant-Agreement:

    a. COMMUNITY. "Community" refers to those physical areas which are serviced by The Markets and from The Markets derive their customers.

    b. GROUP OF MINORITY PERSONS. A "group of minority persons" is any group comprised of any of the following persons:

        (1) Black (or Negro) persons; or

        (2) Chicanos (or Mexican-Americans); or

        (3) Orientals; or

        (4) American Indians.

    Whenever used herein, the phrase "minority group" shall mean the same as "a group of minority persons."

217

    c. MINORITY PERSON. A "minority person" is any person who, together with one or more other persons, constitutes a minority group.

    d. GROUP. A "group" consists of two or more persons.

    e. MINORITY COMMUNITY. "Minority community" means any community wherein there reside a group of minority persons and the number of persons in such minority groups constitutes at least thirty percent (30%) of the total number of residents in the community.

2. The Markets covenant and agree that:

    a. They will not discriminate, and will inform their personnel that there is to be no discrimination, against any minority group with respect to price or quality of foods and other products sold by The Markets; and

    b. Wherever a minority group reside within any particular community, spoiled or adulterated products or products otherwise unfit for human consumption are not to be offered for sale by The Markets; nor

    c. Will The Markets at any time sell within any community wherein there reside a minority group, any marinated or tainted meats, and in any such community, The Markets will price lower grade meats and other lower grade products so as to reflect such lower grade, it being expressly recognized that lower grade products do not warrant prices at which products of the best possible quality are sold.

The parties understand that by "discriminate against" is meant, among other things, that the displays and advertising of foods shall *clearly* indicate the true quality of the foods as to grade and other indices of quality; that no attempt will be made to represent food of low or inferior quality as being of a quality other than that which it is, by expressions contained in displays, signs or advertising, such as: "The Best," "Top Quality," "First," "Top Grade," or similar misleading expressions; that unservicable or inedible foods or other products not otherwise marketable in the *general* Los Angeles area will not be sold in stores owned by The Markets at any time.

3. The Markets further covenant and agree that they will immediately correct any and all conditions of uncleanliness that exist on the premises of the subject stores, and will diligently maintain the stores, the parking lots, the food preparation areas, machinery and equipment, the food displays, storage areas and all other areas within the control of The Markets and adjacent to and surrounding their stores, in a neat and clean condition.

4. The Markets covenant and agree that they will afford equal opportunity to all purveyors of products to offer for sale and sell their products to The Markets, and will not discriminate against any product on account of the race of the manufacturer or seller with respect to display or advertising.

5. The Markets will maintain a current, full-time, affirmative program of hiring, training, and up-grading of minority persons on a store-wide basis, as well as affording equal opportunities to minority persons, whether or not then employed, to make applications to fill any and all positions and jobs as they become available in any store by giving all such persons, whether or not then employed, ample notice of the availability of said positions, and means of applying for same.

   Should any Market a party hereto own or operate, in a community that is not a minority community, any stores, branches or divisions in the grocery business, such Market covenants and agrees that it will within any such stores, branches and divisions adopt all reasonable, affirmative efforts to hire, train and up-grade a reasonable number of minority persons to be employed at such stores, branches and divisions.

6. Whenever outside services or products or both are required in the normal and efficient operation of the stores, The Markets, will make a diligent and affirmative effort to utilize and purchase services and products offered by companies owned by minority persons, to the end that so long as such service or product companies as are qualified exist in any minority community, they will be used. Such services and products shall include, but shall not be limited to, accounting and auditing services, legal services, maintenance and cleaning services, construction and repair services and medical services (except that medical services shall be exempted to the extent that a contract with any labor union adequately provides for the rendition of medical services).

7. The Markets covenant and agree that they will as soon as is reasonably possible, contact companies which are owned by minority persons and which sell or distribute newspapers or advertising circulars or other advertising materials in the market community, to discuss buying advertising space therein on a regular basis to the end that they will be utilized whenever possible.

8. The Chairman of The Coalition will arrange for a meeting of the owners of The Markets and the appropriate Officer of the Bank of Finance, or any other black-owned financial institution, to discuss and explore available means for The Markets to utilize the services of said Bank or financial institutions to the end that to the extent that said Bank or financial institutions can provide needed banking services, said Bank or financial institutions will be utilized by The Markets for purposes related to the operation, maintenance and expansion of stores which The Markets (or any of them) maintain within a community, the black residents of which constitute at least thirty percent (30%) of the total population.

   The parties hereto agree and covenant that the phrase "banking services" includes, but is not limited to, the use of the Bank of Finance as the depository for all monies realized from the sales by The Markets (or any of them) of products of any kind whatsoever at any and all branches of The Markets now operated, or in the future to be operated, by The Markets within any community, the black residents of which constitute at least thirty percent (30%) of the total population.

9. Representatives of The Markets and of The Coalition will consult with each other periodically, and at least every thirty (30) days, to discuss means, efforts and plans to accomplish their mutually desired goals; and The Markets agree and covenant to allow any representative of The Coalition to enter, at any and all reasonable hours, market premises for the purpose of ascertaining whether or not The Markets have complied, and are complying, with all covenants and agreements made herein by The Markets.

10. The Markets covenant and agree that they will at all times fully comply with any and all Municipal, State and appropriate Federal laws and regulations pertaining to safety, health and labor standards, conditions and policies.

11. The Markets covenant and agree not to sell, advertise or otherwise deal in any table grapes until the grape boycott sponsored by the American Farm Workers Union has been resolved.

12. The Markets covenant and agree not to advertise their products or their stores in the Los Angeles Herald-Examiner newspaper, or to offer for sale on the Markets' premises any copies or editions of the said newspaper until the current labor-management dispute between the said newspaper and certain labor unions has been resolved.

13. So long as The Markets make a good faith, diligent effort to comply with the covenants and agreements contained herein,

    a. The Coalition will stop, desist and abstain from picketing The Markets or otherwise publicizing, or demonstrating against, grievances against The Markets; and

    b. The Coalition will encourage all patrons and persons in the market community to patronize or continue to patronize each and every non-defaulting Market a party hereto; and

    c. The Coalition will cause to be displayed within The Markets, signs notifying the community that The Markets are signatories to this Covenant-Agreement; except that

    d. At any time that The Markets fail to perform any of their promises made herein, The Coalition may refuse to encourage patronage of the particular Markets failing to comply with any provision of this agreement, and The Coalition may also remove from any defaulting Markets the signs designated in paragraph 13. a., above.

14. The Markets covenant and agree that The Coalition may, within The Markets and by appropriate means, summarize or set forth in

full the terms of this Covenant-Agreement, together with the following notification:

Any complaints of violations of the promises of the Market should be made to

THE COALITION OF COMMUNITY GROUPS
5208 West Pico Blvd.
Los Angeles, California

Phone: 938-3857

or

5527 So. Main Street
Los Angeles, California

Phone: 232-8164

15. PERFORMANCE BOND. Each Market a party hereto, as additional assurance for the faithful performance of its covenants and promises made herein, further covenants and promises:

a. In the event that The Market should violate, or be in default with respect to, any obligations owed by it under this Covenant-Agreement, to pay to The Coalition, the sum of

(1) $2,500.00; plus

(2) Reasonable attorneys' fees and other costs incurred in enforcing this Agreement; and

b. To enter into, and procure, an undertaking with and by a sufficient corporate surety, which shall not substantially vary from the following:

"A certain Covenant-Agreement, having been entered into, by and between (name of Market) and the Coalition of Community Groups, dated _____ and attached hereto as part of this undertaking; and the (name of Market), having promised in said Covenant-Agreement to enter into, and procure, an undertaking for the purpose of assuring faithful performance of the obligations of (name of Market) under that Covenant-Agreement; therefore, (name of surety) undertakes that should (name of Market) ever be in violation of, or in default with respect to, any of its obligations under the said Covenant-Agreement, (name of Market) will pay to the Coalition of Community Groups the penal sum specified hereinafter or if (name of Market) fails to perform any of its obligations under the said Covenant-Agreement and also fails to pay to the Coalition of Community Groups the penal sum, that (name of surety) will pay to the said Coalition the penal sum, which shall be the sum of the following:

(a) $2,500.00; and

(b) Reasonable attorneys' fees and other costs incurred in enforcing the said Covenant-Agreement and this undertaking."

The undertaking required by this paragraph shall otherwise be in the form required by law.

The remedy provided by this paragraph is not to be construed as limiting other remedies available in law for the enforcement by The Coalition of the obligations owed hereunder by The Markets.

16. The Markets covenant and agree that within five (5) days from the signing of this agreement they will begin performance of all covenants and agreements hereinbefore made, and further that within thirty (30) days from the signing of this agreement, the Markets will have fully complied with and performed all covenants and agreements contained herein.

17. This agreement shall be binding upon, and all covenants and agreements shall be performable by, each respective promisor and covenantor and the successors, delegatees, and assignees of each and every covenantor and promisor; and the benefits of each and every covenant and agreement shall accrue to, and be enforceable by, the successors, delegatees and assignees of each promisee and covenantee.

This agreement shall become effective immediately upon signing.

Dated this _____ Day of _____, 1969.

By: _____   By: _____

Title: _____   Title: _____

By: _____   By: _____

Title: _____   Title: _____

THE COALITION OF COMMUNITY GROUPS

By: _____

Title: _____

Source: Copy in authors' possession.

Index

223

PART FIVE

CONCLUDING ANALYSIS

by

GORDON F. BLOOM

TABLE OF CONTENTS

LIST OF TABLES

Concluding Analysis

The preceding studies in this volume describe and analyze the racial employment patterns in three service industries—department store, drugstore, and supermarket. Analysis of racial employment patterns in these major fields of business activity is important not only for the information it conveys concerning employment opportunities in these three industries, but also for the insight it provides concerning the insufficiently investigated sector of wholesale and retail trade which today employs approximately one out of every five wage earners. Future employment opportunities for Negroes—like employment opportunities for all workers—lie primarily in the area of service industries. The trends with respect to black employment revealed in the studies of these three industries may shed some light on the problems and the prospects of Negro employment in the service economy of the future.

EMPLOYMENT IN 1970

Table 1 presents employment by race, sex, and occupation for the department store, drugstore, and supermarket industries combined for comparison with the all-industry data in Table 2. These are both based on reports to the Equal Employment Opportunity Commission in 1970. Examination of these tables indicates that although the three industries combined had higher ratios of Negro employees in both white collar and blue collar categories than the average of all industries reporting to EEOC, nevertheless the percentage of total employment represented by Negro workers was less in the three industries combined than in industry at large. This result stems in part from the fact that in the three industries combined blue collar employment represents only 22 percent of all workers whereas among the companies reporting to EEOC in the all industry compilation, blue collar employment represents 54 percent of the total. Negroes are heavily concentrated in blue collar employment in American industry and the difference in significance of blue collar employment in the three industries studied versus industry at large accounts for the variation in total employment ratios.

TABLE 1. Three Retail Trade Industries
Employment by Race, Sex, and Occupational Group
United States, 1970

Occupational Group	All Employees			Male			Female		
	Total	Negro	Percent Negro	Total	Negro	Percent Negro	Total	Negro	Percent Negro
Officials and managers	192,091	5,252	2.7	143,476	3,694	2.6	48,615	1,558	3.2
Professionals	17,568	619	3.5	11,304	392	3.5	6,264	227	3.6
Technicians	10,962	629	5.7	7,144	393	5.5	3,818	236	6.2
Sales workers	941,096	49,939	5.3	365,688	20,780	5.7	575,408	29,159	5.1
Office and clerical	242,130	20,591	8.5	35,107	3,683	10.5	207,023	16,908	8.2
Total white collar	1,403,847	77,030	5.5	562,719	28,942	5.1	841,128	48,088	5.7
Craftsmen	66,295	4,152	6.3	57,646	3,577	6.2	8,649	575	6.6
Operatives	105,152	14,998	14.3	67,844	10,651	15.7	37,308	4,347	11.7
Laborers	87,012	17,180	19.7	64,131	12,495	19.5	22,881	4,685	20.5
Service workers	139,237	32,169	23.1	68,070	17,639	25.9	71,167	14,530	20.4
Total blue collar	397,696	68,499	17.2	257,691	44,362	17.2	140,005	24,137	17.2
Total	1,801,543	145,529	8.1	820,410	73,304	8.9	981,133	72,225	7.4

Source: Tables 6, 7, and 8.

TABLE 2. All Industries
Employment by Race, Sex, and Occupational Group
United States, 1970

Occupational Group	All Employees			Male			Female		
	Total	Negro	Percent Negro	Total	Negro	Percent Negro	Total	Negro	Percent Negro
Officials and managers	2,541,542	47,395	1.9	2,280,621	36,515	1.6	260,921	10,880	4.2
Professionals	2,432,779	61,002	2.5	1,822,772	31,146	1.7	610,007	29,856	4.9
Technicians	1,279,482	79,799	6.2	934,431	35,161	3.8	345,051	44,638	12.9
Sales workers	2,213,806	98,100	4.4	1,273,568	47,998	3.8	940,238	50,102	5.3
Office and clerical	4,879,694	359,035	7.4	1,158,884	79,556	6.9	3,720,810	279,479	7.5
Total white collar	13,347,303	645,331	4.8	7,470,276	230,576	3.1	5,877,027	414,955	7.1
Craftsmen	3,943,886	222,031	5.6	3,670,113	194,548	5.3	273,773	27,483	10.0
Operatives	6,926,572	982,657	14.2	4,866,287	711,470	14.6	2,060,285	271,187	13.2
Laborers	2,664,243	583,776	21.9	1,904,872	450,685	23.7	759,371	133,091	17.5
Service workers	2,000,550	531,308	26.6	1,001,825	269,819	26.9	998,725	261,489	26.2
Total blue collar	15,535,251	2,319,772	14.9	11,443,097	1,626,522	14.2	4,092,154	693,250	16.9
Total	28,882,554	2,965,103	10.3	18,913,373	1,856,898	9.8	9,969,181	1,108,205	11.1

Source: U.S. Equal Employment Opportunity Commission, 1970.

Review of the data for the individual retail industries shown in Table 3 indicates that the percentage of Negroes employed in the drugstore industry was actually higher than the all industry average proportion 12.7 compared to 10.3 percent. Since employment reported in this industry to the EEOC (less than 70,000) is less than one-tenth of that in supermarkets or department stores, the overall figure for percentage of Negro employment in the three industries combined reflects the lower ratios of Negro employment in the department store and supermarket industries, 8.5 and 7.1 percent, respectively.

Supermarkets had the lowest total percentage of Negro employment of the three industries. Likewise the supermarket industry had the lowest percentage of Negroes in blue collar employment and was the only one of the three industries whose percentage in this regard was less than the average for all industries. The ratio of employment of Negroes to total work force was almost twice as great in the drugstore industry as in the supermarket industry, with department stores falling in between.

What are the factors which have produced these particular ratios in three industries which we have examined? In Volume I of these studies [1] a series of hypotheses were listed which might explain the particular configuration of Negro employment which develops in various industries. It is useful to summarize the results of the studies in the three industries in the light of these basic hypotheses.

DEMAND FOR LABOR

Periods of rising demand for labor in particular industries have generally been associated with major gains by Negroes in number of jobs and character of employment. Increasing demand has characterized the recent development of these three industries, as all of them experienced rising sales during the period from 1947 to 1970. However, the impact of rising demand upon employment—and in particular the employment of Negroes—has been profoundly affected by the fundamental changes which were occurring during this period in the nature of the selling establishments in these three industries.

---

1. Herbert R. Northrup *et al., Negro Employment in Basic Industry,* Studies of Negro Employment, Vol. I (Philadelphia: Industrial Research Unit, University of Pennsylvania, 1970), Parts One and Eight.

TABLE 3. Three Retail Industries
Percent Negro Employment by Sex and Occupational Group
United States, 1970

Occupational Group	Department Stores (SIC 531)			Drugstores (SIC 591)			Supermarkets (SIC 54)		
	Total	Male	Female	Total	Male	Female	Total	Male	Female
Officials and managers	2.9	2.8	3.1	3.6	3.2	7.2	2.4	2.3	4.1
Professionals	2.9	2.9	2.9	5.7	5.0	9.5	3.1	2.8	5.2
Technicians	6.0	5.6	6.6	8.1	5.3	12.1	4.5	5.2	2.7
Sales workers	5.0	4.8	5.0	7.7	8.6	7.3	5.5	5.9	4.9
Office and clerical	9.2	11.7	8.9	9.5	12.9	8.6	5.4	7.8	4.7
Total white collar	5.7	4.9	5.9	7.2	6.7	7.6	5.1	5.2	4.8
Craftsmen	6.4	6.1	7.4	7.0	8.0	4.3	6.2	6.2	4.8
Operatives	14.5	15.6	13.2	23.7	20.9	36.2	3.9	15.6	9.1
Laborers	20.7	19.8	22.5	27.0	26.8	27.7	8.3	18.8	16.3
Service workers	25.5	30.2	21.6	13.3	35.1	21.8	15.7	16.4	14.5
Total blue collar	19.7	20.4	18.8	25.8	30.5	22.2	13.5	13.9	12.1
Total	8.5	10.5	7.6	12.7	13.8	11.8	7.1	7.7	5.9

Source: Tables 6, 7, and 8.

In the department store industry, total employment grew substantially until the latter part of the sixties, at which time it
commenced to diminish. Changing conditions in the labor market
appear to have been primarily responsible for increased employment of Negroes during the period from 1940 to 1960 but the
growing importance of Negroes in the product market seems to
have been of more significance in recent years in gaining Negroes' acceptance in department store employment, particularly
in sales positions. Negroes were generally first introduced into
white collar clerical jobs in this industry between 1948 and 1955.
During this period there was an increasing demand for clerical
labor in the cities on the part of insurance companies, banks,
and other establishments at the same time as the migration of
the white middle class to the suburbs reduced the supply of such
labor. The low wage department stores found that they could
not retain an adequate supply of white clerical workers and
therefore began to hire qualified Negro applicants.

During the postwar period, the competitive position of the
department store industry in the labor market has tended to
worsen as its wages have failed to keep pace with the rising
level in industry in general. Furthermore, its emphasis upon
part-time female help has also tended to restrict the size of the
labor pool upon which it could draw. The localization and limitation of the labor supply upon which the industry depends has
magnified the impact of changing residential patterns on the
racial composition of the supply of labor to individual stores.
The labor market upon which department stores can draw in
urban locations has become more and more constricted to a
secondary labor force, heavily represented by Negroes living in
the area.

In the drugstore industry, sales rose 200 percent from 1948
to 1967, but employment increased only 58 percent. The drugstore during this period was undergoing a fundamental change
from a seller of services to a seller of products. Self-service
was introduced, eliminating the need for thousands of clerks;
most important, the fountain which had typified the conventional
neighborhood drugstore gave way to rows of gondolas of merchandise. In 1947 fountains accounted for 18 percent of drugstore sales: by 1968 the proportion had dropped to 3.4 percent.
The impact of this change substantially diluted the salutary
aspects of the increase in sales since Negroes—particularly Negro women—had been heavily concentrated in fountain service.

On the other hand, the shift of business from the small neighborhood drugstore to the large chain establishment probably on balance resulted in a net increase in Negro employment. Neighborhood drugstores typically employed only 2 or 3 people who frequently were family members. By contrast, the large corporate chain drugstore was dependent for help on the general labor market and also was apparently more sensitive to community pressures and governmental exhortations to employ Negro labor. Since in the 1960's the chains grew substantially faster than the independent drugstores, the increase in demand in the industry was in effect funneled through larger corporate establishments which, on the whole, favored Negro employment.

A somewhat similar trend in employment has probably characterized the supermarket industry. We know that total employment in the grocery store industry actually dropped from 1,719,-403 in 1950 to 1,691,982 in 1960. However, Negro employment in grocery stores increased both in absolute numbers and proportions of the total between the two years, reflecting in part the shift of business from the small independent corner grocery stores to the large chain markets. Although comparative figures are not available for the supermarket industry, it can be assumed that employment in supermarkets increased substantially during this same period as the new large self-service units replaced the older conventional service establishments. As a growth industry, the supermarket business undoubtedly generated an increasing demand for labor to work in the new larger stores.

While the shift from small independents to large chain supermarkets benefited Negro employment, the same transition converted a major segment of hours worked in supermarkets to part-time employment. Likewise, women formed a larger part of the personnel of the typical supermarket as female dexterity prevailed at the checkout. Thus, increasing demand for labor was at the same time reflected in some contraction of opportunities for full-time male employment in supermarkets.

NATURE OF THE WORK

Comparison of the three industries gives a graphic illustration of the importance of the character of work in affecting Negro employment opportunities. Here are three service industries, all involving retail operations and subject to a number of common trends, such as the spread of self-service marketing and the de-

velopment of shopping centers. Yet the levels of Negro employment differ markedly in the three industries: in department
stores Negroes constituted only 8.5 percent of the labor force,
in drugstores 12.7 percent, and in supermarkets 7.1 percent.
What is the reason for this variation in employment experience?

Occupational Distribution

A clue is provided by an examination of the occupational distribution of jobs in the three industries, as shown in Table 4.
All have a high proportion of white collar employment. In department stores 79.9 percent of workers are white collar, in
drugstores 70.7 percent, and in supermarkets 75.9 percent.
Within the white collar classification there is relatively little
variation among the three industries in the proportion of Negro
employment, although the figures indicate that supermarkets have
done a better job than department stores or drugstores in ad-
justing the distribution of Negroes in sales jobs to approximate
the overall distribution of such jobs among all employees. In
1970 Negroes held 5.7 percent of the white collar jobs in department stores, 7.2 percent in drugstores, and 5.1 percent in
supermarkets (Table 3). These percentages are so similar that
it is apparent the much larger differences in ratio of overall
Negro employment must be found in variations in the blue collar
category.

The three industries do in fact differ markedly in their ratios
of Negro employment in the blue collar classifications and these
differences account for much of the differential in overall Negro
employment. In department stores 19.7 percent of blue collar
workers are Negro; in drugstores 25.8 percent, and in supermarkets only 13.5 percent. (Table 3) The major cause of these
differences is the concentration of Negroes in service occupations. In the drugstore industry, not only is the black percentage
of service jobs higher than in department stores or supermarkets (26.3 percent vs. 25.5 and 15.7 percent respectively) but
more importantly service jobs represent 23.1 percent of all jobs
and almost 50 percent of all Negro jobs in that industry (Table
4). By contrast, service jobs are relatively unimportant in the
supermarket industry, constituting only 4.8 percent of the total
and 10.7 percent of Negro employment, while the department
store industry falls between these two extremes with service
jobs constituting 8.8 percent of all jobs and 26.5 percent of
Negro employment (Table 4).

TABLE 4. Three Retail Trade Industries
Percent Distribution of Total and Negro Employment
United States, 1970

Occupational Group	Department Stores		Drugstores		Supermarkets	
	Total	Negro	Total	Negro	Total	Negro
Officials and managers	11.4	3.9	9.7	2.8	9.8	3.3
Professionals	1.0	0.3	5.4	2.4	0.5	0.2
Technicians	0.8	0.6	0.8	0.5	0.3	0.2
Sales workers	47.8	28.1	45.0	27.3	58.9	45.6
Office and clerical	18.9	20.5	9.8	7.3	6.4	4.9
Total white collar	79.9	53.4	70.7	40.3	75.9	54.2
Craftsmen	2.4	1.8	0.7	0.4	5.7	4.9
Operatives	4.6	7.9	1.8	3.5	7.9	15.5
Laborers	4.3	10.4	3.7	7.9	5.7	14.7
Service workers	8.8	26.5	23.1	47.9	4.8	10.7
Total blue collar	20.1	46.6	29.3	59.7	24.1	45.8
Total	100.0	100.0	100.0	100.0	100.0	100.0

Source: Computed from Tables 6, 7, and 8.

Discrimination, lack of education, and other handicaps historically have created overrepresentation of Negroes in service
occupations. Although Negroes have made substantial progress
during the last decade in breaking down barriers in white collar
and skilled occupations, the concentration in service jobs still
continues. Today, despite antidiscrimination legislation and various affirmative action programs, one out of every five service
workers in private industry is black.[2]

A key factor affecting the employment of Negroes in these
three industries has been the high proportion of sales jobs.
These vary from 45 percent of all employees in drugstore employment to 47.8 percent in department stores and 58.9 percent
in supermarkets (Table 4). Managers have been reluctant to
place Negroes in selling positions because of fears—usually exag-
gerated—that customers would object to being served by a Negro
and might take their patronage elsewhere. None of these industries measures up very well in the proportion of Negroes in
sales positions. Lowest is the department store industry with
5.0 percent representation; next supermarkets with 5.5 percent;
and highest drugstores with 7.7 percent (Table 3).

Although these ratios are hardly commendable, it must be
remembered that they represent national statistics, and that in
many of the smaller towns and suburbs where such retail stores
are located there may be few Negroes available for such jobs.
Actually, these three industries—or at least the larger employers
represented by the EEOC statistics for these industries—measure
up as better than average relative to national statistics for the
entire economy. As Table 2 indicates, in 1970 only 4.4 percent
of sales jobs were held by Negroes in all firms reporting to the
EEOC.

The Level of Pay

Another aspect of the nature of the work in these three industries which has affected Negro employment is the level of
pay for various occupations. For example, most of the jobs in
drugstores have provided relatively low compensation. As a consequence, as better opportunities have opened up in other areas,
Negroes—and Negro males in particular—have left this industry.

---

2. U.S. Bureau of the Census, *The Social and Economic Status of Negroes
   in the United States, 1970*, Special Studies, Current Population Reports,
   Series P-23, No. 31 (July 1971), Table 49, p. 61.

As far as male Negro employment is concerned, a decline in employment in this industry may actually be viewed as a positive factor if it truly reflects a transfer to better-paying jobs elsewhere.

Likewise in both supermarkets and department stores, the relatively low entrance rates and the apparent lack of advancement opportunities have made the jobs relatively unattractive to Negro males. By contrast, warehouse employment has had heavy concentration of Negroes in all three industries because of the high initial pay and the minimum skill required. An indication of this is shown by the high percentage of Negro employment in operative, laborer, and service worker occupations in headquarters and warehouses of drugstores and supermarkets (Table 5). Comparable data are not available for department stores but the distribution of employment is believed to be similar.

The pattern of response to wage rates in the department store and supermarket industries attests to the imperfections in the labor market and the complexity of decisions relating to choice of employment. Department stores offer a bundle of benefits to a prospective employee—status, convenient location, flexible hours, employee discounts. These fringes are apparently of considerable significance to white members of the labor force, particularly in the suburbs. Negroes, however, because of stringent needs for income apparently appraise their jobs primarily in form of the wage paid and in this respect find them wanting. Supermarkets, on the other hand, pay relatively high wages to employees who have acquired some years of service, but nevertheless apparently still retain a low wage image in the community. Furthermore, whereas work in a department store tends to convey status, for some inexplicable reason comparable work in a supermarket does not, and this is a further deterrent to Negro job-seekers.

Part-time Employment

An unusual characteristic of the work in these three industries is the high proportion of part-time employment. In the department store industry, most of the firms studied have indicated a desire to increase the ratio of part-time to full-time nonsupervisory employees to three to one. Data are not available for drugstores but it is known to be substantial and contributes to the high turnover rate experienced by some chains which re-

TABLE 5. *Two Retail Trade Industries*

Percent Negro Employment by Occupational Group and Industry Sector
United States, 1967-1968

Occupational Group	Drugstores (1968)			Supermarkets (1967)		
	Stores Only	Headquarters and Warehouses	Total Company	Stores Only	Headquarters and Warehouses	Total Company
Officials and managers	3.1	1.7	2.9	1.5	0.8	1.4
Professionals	2.5	2.5	2.5	2.2	0.9	1.4
Technicians	3.3	3.1	3.2	16.8	1.9	6.9
Sales workers	4.6	3.6	4.6	5.6	5.1	5.6
Office and clerical	8.7	5.4	7.2	4.3	3.8	4.1
Total white collar	4.5	3.9	4.4	5.0	2.5	4.8
Craftsmen	2.2	4.3	3.3	2.6	8.6	4.2
Operatives	24.1	29.7	25.3	11.4	9.2	10.4
Laborers	19.4	31.4	26.0	8.4	13.3	11.8
Service workers	26.7	29.3	26.8	17.7	27.6	20.2
Total blue collar	26.1	28.1	26.3	8.4	11.8	9.9
Total	10.5	10.7	10.5	5.6	8.6	6.2

Source: Part Three, Table 19; Part Four, Tables 18, 20, and 22.

port that they have a complete turnover among nonprofessional store employees every three months! In the supermarket industry the proportion of part-timers has grown steadily over the years and today stands at about 56 percent of total store personnel.

In view of the large number of women and youth in the Negro labor force, it might be thought that the high ratios of part-time jobs in these industries would enable such industries to raise significantly their proportions of black employees. Furthermore, because of the high turnover which is customary in such part-time jobs, firms in these industries should be able to adjust more rapidly than manufacturing concerns to increasing governmental and community pressures to hire more Negroes.

The relatively low total proportions of Negro employees in these three industries, however, indicate that this has not happened. The reasons lie with the influences of a whole list of factors previously discussed. For example, much of the increase in part-time employment has occurred in suburban locations where fewer blacks reside and where the jobs are apparently more attractive to white females than to Negroes. Furthermore, most of the part-time jobs in these industries are in sales categories, and, as has already been mentioned, there is still some reluctance on the part of managers to fill such positions with Negroes, particularly in suburban locations.

Female Employment

The three industries studied are unique in their high proportion of women employees. Sales work is the major occupation in all three industries and women have especially found a niche in this category. The nature of the work and the high component of female employees has to some extent given jobs in retail stores the connotation of women's work. In supermarkets this is true of checkout cashiers who are almost exclusively women; in department stores it is true of a high percentage of the sales personnel; and in drugstores it is true of fountain help and sales personnel, though not of pharmacists. Tables 6, 7, and 8 permit a comparison by sex and race for the three industries.

The highest ratio of female help is found in the department store industry where almost 70 percent of employment is female. Next in line is the drugstore industry where the ratio is approximately 60 percent. In the supermarket industry EEOC data indicate that women constitute 33 percent of the work force. An

TABLE 6. Department Store Industry
Employment by Race, Sex, and Occupational Group
United States, 1970

Occupational Group	All Employees			Male			Female		
	Total	Negro	Percent Negro	Total	Negro	Percent Negro	Total	Negro	Percent Negro
Officials and managers	113,804	3,314	2.9	69,915	1,975	2.8	43,889	1,339	3.1
Professionals	10,198	295	2.9	4,966	145	2.9	5,232	150	2.9
Technicians	7,883	471	6.0	5,008	282	5.6	2,875	189	6.6
Sales workers	479,103	23,882	5.0	91,266	4,377	4.8	387,837	19,505	5.0
Office and clerical	188,835	17,428	9.2	22,692	2,650	11.7	166,143	14,778	8.9
Total white collar	799,823	45,390	5.7	193,847	9,429	4.9	605,976	35,961	5.9
Craftsmen	24,262	1,561	6.4	18,146	1,106	6.1	6,116	455	7.4
Operatives	46,158	6,680	14.5	24,296	3,802	15.6	21,862	2,878	13.2
Laborers	42,671	8,847	20.7	28,386	5,631	19.8	14,285	3,216	22.5
Service workers	88,114	22,460	25.5	39,713	11,991	30.2	48,401	10,469	21.6
Total blue collar	201,205	39,548	19.7	110,541	22,530	20.4	90,664	17,018	18.8
Total	1,001,028	84,938	8.5	304,388	31,959	10.5	696,640	52,979	7.6

Source: U.S. Equal Employment Opportunity Commission, 1970.

TABLE 7. *Drugstore Industry*
Employment by Race, Sex, and Occupational Group United States, 1970

Occupational Group	All Employees			Male			Female		
	Total	Negro	Percent Negro	Total	Negro	Percent Negro	Total	Negro	Percent Negro
Officials and managers	6,670	243	3.6	5,905	188	3.2	765	55	7.2
Professionals	3,717	211	5.7	3,170	159	5.0	547	52	9.5
Technicians	554	45	8.1	323	17	5.3	231	28	12.1
Sales workers	30,898	2,372	7.7	9,318	803	8.6	21,580	1,569	7.3
Office and clerical	6,702	634	9.5	1,358	175	12.9	5,344	459	8.6
Total white collar	48,541	3,505	7.2	20,074	1,342	6.7	28,467	2,163	7.6
Craftsmen	442	31	7.0	326	26	8.0	16	5	4.3
Operatives	1,260	299	23.7	1,025	214	20.9	235	85	36.2
Laborers	2,553	689	27.0	1,936	518	26.8	617	171	27.7
Service workers	15,854	4,162	26.3	5,346	1,874	35.1	10,508	2,288	21.8
Total blue collar	20,109	5,181	25.8	8,633	2,632	30.5	11,476	2,549	22.2
Total	68,650	8,686	12.7	28,707	3,974	13.8	39,343	4,712	11.8

Source: U.S. Equal Employment Opportunity Commission, 1970.

TABLE 8. Supermarket Industry
Employment by Race, Sex, and Occupational Group
United States, 1970

Occupational Group	All Employees			Male			Female		
	Total	Negro	Percent Negro	Total	Negro	Percent Negro	Total	Negro	Percent Negro
Officials and managers	71,617	1,695	2.4	67,656	1,531	2.3	3,961	164	4.1
Professionals	3,653	113	3.1	3,168	88	2.8	485	25	5.2
Technicians	2,525	113	4.5	1,813	94	5.2	712	19	2.7
Sales workers	431,095	23,685	5.5	265,104	15,600	5.9	165,991	8,085	4.9
Office and Clerical	46,593	2,529	5.4	11,057	858	7.8	35,536	1,671	4.7
Total white collar	555,483	28,135	5.1	348,798	18,171	5.2	206,685	9,964	4.8
Craftsmen	41,491	2,560	6.2	39,174	2,445	6.2	2,417	115	4.8
Operatives	57,734	8,019	13.9	42,523	6,635	15.6	15,211	1,384	9.1
Laborers	41,788	7,644	18.3	33,809	6,346	18.8	7,979	1,298	16.3
Service workers	35,269	5,547	15.7	23,011	3,774	16.4	12,258	1,773	14.5
Total blue collar	176,382	23,770	13.5	138,517	19,200	13.9	37,865	4,570	12.1
Total	731,865	51,905	7.1	487,315	37,371	7.7	244,550	14,534	5.9

Source: U.S. Equal Employment Opportunity Commission, 1970.

even larger proportion is suggested by data compiled by the Super Market Institute which for the year 1969 showed that in reporting companies women constituted 36 percent of all full-time store employees and 38 percent of part-timers.[3]

These high percentages would lead one to expect that a high percentage of Negro women would be employed in these industries. However, this is not the case. Table 6 shows that, in the department store industry, despite the high percentage of jobs filled by women, Negro females in 1970 held only 7.6 percent of total jobs held by women. In the sales category Negro female representation was very poor, amounting to only 5 percent. The Negro female work force did have a relatively better occupational distribution than that for men, more nearly parallel to the distribution for all women than was the case for Negro males. Data for the industry for 1970 indicate that whereas only 29.5 percent of Negro men were in white collar positions, 67.9 percent of Negro women held such positions.

In drugstores, shown in Table 7, although over half of all women are sales workers, most Negro women are blue collar workers, largely food service workers at luncheon counters and soda fountains. In 1970, only 7.3 percent of female sales workers in drugstores were black females. Actually, Negro men hold a disproportionately number of sales jobs in this industry compared to Negro women. Were it not for service work, the black female proportion in drugstore employment would be substantially less than the 11.8 percent ratio which the data show for 1970.

In the supermarket industry in 1970, Negro females held only 5.9 percent of all female jobs although one out of every three jobs was filled by a woman (Table 8). The distribution of Negro females between white collar and blue collar jobs was more akin to the overall distribution for women than the Negro distribution was for all men. These EEOC data for 1970 indicate that 68.6 percent of Negro females were in white collar work compared with 84.5 percent of all women. By contrast only 48.6 percent of Negro males were in white collar employment compared with 71.6 percent of all males. The concentration of Negro males in blue collar work reflects the high percentage of blacks in warehouse jobs. The ratio of Negro females

---

3. Super Market Institute, *The Super Market Industry Speaks, 1970* (Chicago: The Institute, 1970), p. 26.

to all women in sales work was only 4.9 percent, about the same as the comparable ratio in the department store industry, but substantially less than the ratio in the drugstore industry.

Pattern of Occupational Progression

The pattern of occupational progression in companies usually depends upon the industrial or business structure. The drugstore industry is unique in that a major barrier to normal upward progression has been established by state laws which require the licensing of pharmacists and establish minimum educational requirements for the position. Therefore even if entry to the drugstore industry were completely free of discriminatory barriers, it would still be difficult for Negroes to attain managerial positions, because most managers in the industry are pharmacists, except in very large stores. Despite this fact, it is surprising to note that the percentage of officials and managers who are Negro in the drugstore industry is actually higher than in either the department store or supermarket industries where such a statutory barrier does not exist.

In the department store and supermarket industries, management has in the past frequently come up through the organization by progression from the store level. In recent years, however, both industries have tended increasingly to look to college graduates as a source for management personnel. The implications of this policy will be discussed more fully in the section of this summary dealing with managerial policies. Suffice it to say that both industries have very low percentages of Negroes in managerial positions—department stores only 2.9 percent and supermarkets only 2.4 percent (Table 3). It must be recognized that training managers takes time; perhaps the increasing proportions of Negroes employed in white collar positions will gradually be reflected in a better representation in the managerial category.

TIME AND NATURE OF INDUSTRY'S DEVELOPMENT AND COMMUNITY MORES

All three of these industries developed in an economic environment in which Negroes were primarily consigned to service work. By reason of some totally illogical social custom, Negroes could serve a customer food at a lunchcounter but could not sell him a tube of toothpaste in the store. Prior to the late 1960's these industries, therefore, placed relatively few Negroes in sales positions, which represent the major category of job opportunities. The competitive nature of these industries and the continuing fear that racial policies might offend certain segments of the buying public made management lag behind changes which were occurring in community attitudes toward Negroes.

The more recent development of these industries has been marked by intense competition and major changes in size, character, and location of facilities. In many respects, the decade of the sixties was not a propitious period for gains to be scored in Negro employment ratios in these industries.

In the department store industry, employment in general merchandise stores actually declined in the latter part of the sixties and employment of Negroes declined at the same time in absolute numbers. In major metropolitan areas, the drop in total employment was particularly marked. Negro employment declined more than proportionately in such areas with Negro female employment being particularly hard hit.

In the drugstore industry, stores continued to evolve and took on the character of variety stores with further elimination of fountain facilities, thus narrowing opportunities for Negro employment. Even more critical was the number of drugstore closings in urban areas, reflecting the impact of pilferage, robberies, and other urban ills. For example, the number of drugstores in New York State actually declined by 100 from 1963 to 1968, as a consequence of closings in the New York City area exceeding the number of openings in suburban areas.

The supermarket industry was engulfed by a wave of cutthroat competition—euphemistically called discounting—which reduced net earnings after taxes as a percentage of sales for food chains from 1.26 percent in 1961 to 0.86 percent in 1970-71.[4] Although employment figures are not available for supermarkets during this period, it is safe to assume that employment did increase, but much of the increase was absorbed by part-time workers and females.

The fact that Negroes generally scored gains in ratios of employment in these three industries during this difficult period attests to the strength of governmental, community group, and product market pressures which made their influence felt dur-

---

4. New York State College of Agriculture and Life Sciences, *Operating Results of Food Chains, 1970-71* (Ithaca: Cornell University, 1972), p. 11.

ing this period. Were it not for these factors, it seems likely that relatively little progress would have been made in raising ratios of Negro employment. The economics of the respective industries discouraged experimentation in employment policy during this period while the shifting location of new facilities moved the center of management interest from the cities where the Negroes lived to the white suburbs where growth and shopping centers beckoned.

CONSUMER ORIENTATION AND IMAGE CONCERN

In an earlier volume of this series, *Negro Employment in Basic Industry*, Professor Herbert R. Northrup observed:

> Companies which sell to consumers usually align their marketing and racial policies very carefully. They are more likely to be on the lookout for means to avoid offending any group, and especially majority opinion. [5]

This conclusion is particularly appropriate in connection with employment policies in the three industries under examination. The department store industry historically has catered to a predominantly white, primarily middle-class, consumer group. Obviously there has been considerable diversity in attitude among white middle-class Americans toward Negro employment. Department store management has tended to make very conservative estimates of the tolerance of customers for change in order to minimize the possibility of adverse reaction among their traditional clientele. This attitude has prevailed despite the fact that in central cities the percentage of Negro customers served by department stores has continued to grow.

In the drugstore industry, field research disclosed a difference in attitude toward anticipated consumer reaction as between independent drugstore operators and chain organizations. In the former, a majority in all regions except in the Northeast and Midwest expressed the opinion that sales would be lost in some retail stores if Negroes were hired as sales clerks. Chains, on the other hand, have been much more willing to experiment with the use of Negroes in such positions and have generally been pleasantly surprised by the consumer acceptance accorded such changes.

Supermarket managers have also been reluctant to advance too quickly in terms of employment of Negroes for fear of of-

---

5. Northrup *et al., op. cit.,* Part Eight, p. 734.

fending important segments of the buying public. Such fear has been more characteristic of store managers than of top corporate management, but because employment decisions tend to be made for the most part by the store manager who does not wish to endanger his profit margins, employment ratios with respect to minority groups tend to lag behind changes in population mix and consumer attitudes.

Although such restrictive action with respect to Negro employment is not to be condoned, it is important to understand the institutional environment in which such decisions have been made in these three industries. All three are highly competitive, with many competing units, particularly in the supermarket and drugstore business. A consumer who is offended by poor service or does not approve of managerial employment policies can easily take business to a competitor with little inconvenience resutling from the shift. This produces an atmosphere in which managers are reluctant to innovate in policies which may run counter to what they perceive to be community mores. The prevailing attitude is to "let someone else be the hero." Sometimes the only way to break this impasse is through uniform action by all stores in an area at the same time. Such a step was taken by southern and border state retailers to desegregate lunchcounters in the early 1960's.

Concern over company image and product market reactions is a two-edged sword. On the one hand it can cause management to lag behind attitude changes occurring in the community for fear of alienating what it perceives still to be the majority mores. On the other hand, as militant minority groups begin to express their resentment against company policies, this same sensitivity to product market reaction can induce rapid changes in management attitudes toward employment policies.

The concern over product market reactions marks an important difference between service industries and manufacturing industries. Practically all service industries must weigh the effect of employment policies upon customer acceptance. In manufacturing, on the other hand, product market reactions are generally of little concern where the product is a basic material incorporated in other products, but of more concern where the product is marketed under a brand or company name identifying the company to the consumer. Thus, there is evidence that consumer reactions exerted some influence on racial employment policies of automobile, oil, and tobacco companies but had little relationship to the policies of the steel and chemical producers. In the paper industry, most firms have not been concerned about consumer reactions to employment policies except for Scott Paper which is the only large company to market its products under the company name and has been a leader in developing equal employment opportunity programs.[6]

There is another facet of consumer reaction which is unique to the service industries. That is that the consumer is actually present at the point of job performance by the employee. Although not often articulated, field research indicates clearly that in the service industries examined in the foregoing studies concern over the ability of Negroes to perform services at a satisfactory level to meet consumer demands was and is a major factor affecting employment decisions with respect to Negroes. In a manufacturing plant the ultimate consumer does not witness the mistake made by the Negro trainee; in a supermarket would be a face-to-face confrontation with the Negro employee who errs in making change. A lack of confidence in the ability and dependability of Negro hires is a major psychological barrier, particularly among store managers and supervisors. Unless top management takes firm steps to ensure open hiring, many managers will resolve such doubts by finding reasons not to hire the Negro applicant.

MANAGEMENT ETHNIC ORIGIN

There does not seem to be any evidence of a relationship between management ethnic origin and the character of managerial racial employment policies in these industries.

COMMUNITY CRISES

Community crises, picketing, and other forms of community pressures have influenced Negro employment in varying degrees in the three industries. The riots of 1965-1968 and pressure tactics of various militant groups have caused executives to reexamine their employment policies and to develop new programs to increase the number of Negro hires. Civil rights pressure

---

6. *Ibid.*, and Herbert R. Northrup, Richard L. Rowan, *et al.*, *Negro Employment in Southern Industry*, Studies of Negro Employment, Vol. IV (Philadelphia: Industrial Research Unit, Wharton School of Finance and Commerce, University of Pennsylvania, 1970), Part Six, p. 20.

has been particularly effective in securing placement of Negroes in highly visible management positions. Executives in firms in these three industries have also been active in various urban coalition groups which have worked together to improve Negro prospects for employment in metropolitan areas.

Although all three industries have been subjected to community pressures, the supermarket industry has been the major target. Markets have been picketed, boycotted, bombed, and threatened as a result of community action. Organizations such as Operation Breadbasket have exacted "covenants" with respect to Negro employment through the use of threats of withdrawal of community patronage. Such action has had considerable effect in communities with a high proportion of Negro customers. On the other hand, the consequence of such action in some instances has been to subject marginal stores to increased losses with the result that the stores were closed and Negro employment suffered.

Whereas in the supermarket industry much of this community pressure has been directed against the large chains, in the department store field independent department stores seem to have been singled out for more attention. Independent firms in that industry have shown much greater sensitivity to civil rights pressures than have chain organizations, presumably because of greater dependence upon single-unit downtown locations which were becoming increasingly dependent upon the Negro community for both workers and customers. In the department store industry, as a whole, field research suggests that civil rights pressures have exercised a significant effect in breaking down employment barriers and in leading employers to introduce training programs designed to develop Negroes in management ranks. Historically civil rights pressures were responsible for introducing Negroes into sales positions, especially in the South, but these pressures have not been spread evenly over the stores in the industry. In most metropolitan areas, major impact has been restricted to downtown and neighborhood stores, while suburban stores have been little affected. Likewise, carriage trade stores have more often been the object of community pressures than so-called budget stores.

Drugstores, perhaps because of their smaller size and lower level of visibility in the community, have not been subjected to as much direct civil rights action as have supermarkets and department stores. However, the lesson of what can happen to a store's business when the Negro community institutes a boycott or sets up picket lines has not been lost on drugstore operators. Therefore, community pressures have undoubtedly affected managerial decisions with respect to employment policy in this industry, even though it does not bear as many scars of actual conflict as department stores or supermarkets.

NATURE OF UNION ORGANIZATION

Unions have had little impact upon the level of Negro employment in the three industries studied in this volume. Drugstores are not organized to any substantial degree except in New York City and California. The department store industry which is also generally nonunion, except in New York City and San Francisco.

The supermarket industry, however, is more highly organized, particularly among large national chain companies. In 1969, about 60 percent of the companies reporting to Super Market Institute were unionized in whole or in part of their operations. In over 70 percent of the companies with their own warehouse, nonstore employees worked under union contracts. Although unions exert a significant impact upon other managerial policies, unions in this industry have had relatively little effect upon the hiring of Negro employees. International officials, particularly in the Amalgamated Meat Cutters union, have advocated special training programs for Negroes but some locals have dragged their feet in this regard.

Although union policies toward Negro employment have in general been passive in the supermarket industry, the institutional fabric of unionism, by tending to institutionalize the status quo, has probably established unintentional barriers to Negro employment and advancement. Initiation fees, seniority provisions, and restrictions on intrafacility movement may make it more difficult for Negroes to enter, retain employment, and to secure advancement in this industry.

IMPACT OF TECHNOLOGY

All three industries, like retail trade in general, are labor intensive. Relatively little progress has been made in terms of devising sophisticated equipment to replace human effort in sales work and other major occupations in these industries. On the other hand, if we view technology in the broadest sense of the application of applied science to the solution of industrial problems, the development of self-service has itself been a major breakthrough in technology which has drastically altered the system of distribution in these industries and has had conflicting effects upon Negro employment.

The drugstore experience indicates the varied cross-currents of influence which have affected the level of Negro employment. On the one hand, self-service has restricted Negro employment. It has made it possible to handle the mushrooming volume of business with relatively few additional workers, and the additional jobs created have been primarily in the cashier category which many employers seem unwilling to give to a Negro. On the other hand, the transfer of business from small family-owned and operated drugstores to the larger facilities which self-service requires has opened up new opportunities for Negroes.

In the supermarket industry, self-service changed the nature of employment opportunities in the industry as over 100,000 males left the grocery industry between 1950 and 1960. Likewise, the continuing spread of the large self-service market led to the progressive closing of smaller service stores which in turn reduced the number of managerial positions held by blacks in such small neighborhood operations. Although self-service has given birth to an entirely new kind of department store—the discount department store—it is not apparent how this innovation in merchandising has affected net employment opportunities for Negroes in the industry.

In the decade of the seventies all three industries will be experimenting with sophisticated semiautomatic warehousing operations which can eliminate many of the unskilled jobs presently involved in selecting, storing, and loading merchandise. The impact of such changes upon Negro employment could be serious, because blacks hold a high percentage of such positions and Negro employment in warehouses in such industries has accounted for a substantial part of their total representation in each industry.

INDUSTRIAL LOCATION

In terms of long run pervasive influence, the most important single determinant of Negro employment in these three industries is probably the changing locus of employment opportunities. In each industry the significant growth in employment opportunities is occurring in the suburbs, while Negroes are crowding in ever-increasing numbers into the central cities. Central city employment in department stores has already reached a stage of decline. Current figures are not available for central city employment in drugstores and supermarkets but a similar trend may be imminent there as well.

The movement of these industries to the suburbs is attributable to a number of factors which seem to dictate an even more accelerated exodus from the central cities in the future. Of paramount importance has been the development of the shopping center with its requirement of huge land areas for parking. In 1969, 66 percent of new supermarkets were opened in shopping centers. Land costs and real estate taxes make such developments prohibitively expensive in most urban areas.

A related factor has been the growth in size of physical units. In the department store business huge discount department stores of 100,000 square feet or more are now commonplace in our suburbs. Conventional department stores also require tremendous building areas. In the drugstore industry the advent of self-service has changed the drugstore into a mass merchandiser selling a wide variety of products from candy to soft goods. Drugstore size as measured by number of employees grew from 5.5 in 1948 to 7.6 in 1967. In the supermarket business the continued increase in number of items has caused an expansion in size of store from 10,000 to 30,000 square feet. And over the horizon lies the super supermarket with even greater floor areas in prospect.

Even if land costs and real estate taxes in central cities could be brought to a lower level through some kind of subsidy, it is doubtful if corporate executives in these industries would switch expansion plans back to the central city. The fact is that suburban stores tend to be more profitable than central city stores. The reasons relate to both income and expense. By and large, incomes of customers are higher in the suburbs. This makes possible a better merchandising mix of higher gross items and therefore a larger profit. The central city not only poses a less attractive market in terms of income level, but also pilferage losses, burglary and robbery experience, and the incidence of loss from fire and riot are considerably higher.

In recent years a new threat to central city business has arisen—the fear of violence. In many of America's large cities, customers are afraid to go out on the streets at night to shop. Whereas shopping hours are lengthening in suburban shopping centers to accommodate the needs of family shopping, in central cities they are being curtailed as business volume falls off after dark.

Our examination in the opening chapter of this book of the apparent fit between the characteristics of Negro labor supply and the employment needs of retail trade concerns suggested that retail trade could provide a growing field for Negro employment. Unfortunately, the factors above mentioned are moving important centers of retail trade out of the orbit of Negro accessability in much the same way as manufacturing has left the central city. Few new supermarkets, drugstores, or department stores are being constructed in our central cities.

This ominous and clearly obvious trend poses a dual threat to our society. In the first place, it deprives the central city resident of employment opportunities. In the second place it implies a continued deterioration in the quality of retail service available in the central city. In effect, we are building the newest and most efficient distribution outlets in areas farthest removed from our poor and needy who are the very consumers who require food, clothing, drugs, and other consumption items at the lowest possible cost.

The factor of location has a multipronged effect upon the level of employment in the three industries. First there is the urban-suburban location factor. Except in the South, the proportion of Negro employees is higher in urban than in suburban stores in all three industries. (See Table 9.) This result is not unexpected; the labor markets upon which these three industries draw are typically highly restricted in area and localized. Typically, many applicants for jobs are persons who walk in off the street. Since in most parts of the country there are many Negroes in the central cities and relatively few in the suburbs, the job patterns tend to reflect this distribution. In the South, Negroes are generally more dispersed through the suburban areas and as a consequence employment patterns differ markedly from the rest of the country.

Although percentages are higher for urban locations outside of the South, they are not as high as might perhaps have been expected in view of the concentration of Negroes in our major cities. For example, in the supermarket industry, except in the South, Negro employment ratios did not exceed 8.1 percent

TABLE 9.　*Three Retail Industries*
Percent Negro Employment by Urban/Suburban Location
Selected Areas, Four Regions, 1967-1968

Region	Department Store (1968)		Drugstore (1968)		Supermarket (1967)	
	Urban	Suburban	Urban	Suburban	Urban	Suburban
Northeast	15.5	6.1	7.0	2.0	5.9	3.8
South	21.8 a	8.0 a	17.9	17.7	13.0	18.5
Midwest	20.9	6.3	14.2	5.7	8.1	4.2
Rocky Mountain	b	b	2.5	—	2.3	1.5
Far West	12.1	4.6	5.2	2.2	4.5	4.2
United States	18.1	6.3	13.3	8.4	7.9	8.5

Source:　Part Two, Tables 23 and 24 and data in author's possession; Part Three, Table 13; and Part Four, Table 24.

Note:　All are from authors' samples and thus are not comparable in terms of size of sample or range of units represented. Department store group, for example, represents only selected companies in 12 cities.

aIncludes St. Louis, normally classified as Midwest.

b No data available.

(Table 9). (It should be noted that the figures cited in Table 9 are for the years 1967 and 1968 and considerable progress has been made in raising Negro employment ratios in all three industries since those years.)

The level of Negro employment cited indicates that location, while important, is not necessarily a controlling factor in determining the extent of Negro employment in these industries. Other critical factors also make their influence felt. If entry wage rates were higher in these industries and if public transportation facilities were better, the ratios of Negro employment might be higher. We have already observed how Negroes will commute substantial distances to obtain jobs in warehouses but apparently will not do so for jobs in supermarkets which offer lower entry wage rates with what Negroes perceive as relatively little opportunity for advancement. Likewise if facilities are in central city locations but far removed from those areas where most Negroes live, the availability of efficient and rapid public transportation facilities may spell the difference between a high and a low percentage of Negro representation.

Regional location factors also influence the level of employment as well as its division between male and female workers. We have already noted that in supermarkets in the South black employment is actually higher as a percentage of total employment in suburban than in urban areas. On the other hand in the Rocky Mountain and Far West regions there is relatively little difference between the percentages for urban and suburban stores. These figures reflect the difference of dispersion of Negro population in the various sections of the country as well as differences in community mores concerning Negro employment— and in particular male employment. As has been mentioned, Negro employment in the South and in the Rocky Mountain and Far West areas is more generally distributed between central city and suburb than in the North where the lily white suburb is all too typical. In the South an additional significant factor is the greater use of Negro men in supermarket operation. This may be attributable to a tendency to maintain service patterns longer in the South than in other regions and also possibly to greater prevalance of smaller units.

In the drugstore industry a somewhat similar pattern prevails. Again in the South there is a high percentage of employment of Negroes in both urban and suburban locations. By contrast, other areas of the country show substantially higher percentages of Negro employment in urban than in suburban areas (Table 9).

In the department store industry, the pattern is much more uniform nationwide with substantially higher ratios of Negro employment in urban areas. The failure of this industry to follow the pattern of drugstores and supermarkets with high ratios of Negro employment in suburban areas in the South may, in part, reflect the continuing hesitancy of managers in this industry to utilize Negroes as sales clerks in this area of the country. This tendency is probably countered by pressure from the product market in the major cities but asserts itself more strongly as one moves out into the suburbs.

BLACK CAPITALISM IN RETAIL TRADE

The exodus from central cities of many retail businesses has left a void which advocates of Black Capitalism had hoped black ownership might fill. In many ghetto areas shuttered stores, formerly housing a drugstore, supermarket, or other retail establishment, are available at low rents—but there are no takers. Despite efforts of the federal government to stimulate black enterprise, the problems of operation, management, and financing have been too great and therefore it is unlikely that black ownership will in the foreseeable future function as a major source of employment opportunities for Negroes in retail trade.[7]

In the drugstore industry there have been a number of limiting factors. In the first place, the economics of drugstore operation are such that it is ordinarily impractical to own a drugstore unless one is a pharmacist. As we have already observed, the number of Negro pharmacists is extremely limited. Those who are qualified seem more likely to take jobs with large chain drugstore companies than to risk operating a drugstore in a highly competitive industry. In the second place, drugstores are growing larger in size with a consequent increase in minimum investment requirements. As a result, the small independent drugstore operator is rapidly disappearing from the scene. In the third place, drugstores in central cities have been subject to a rash of robberies because they are a repository for drugs. As a consequence, operation of such stores in these areas, even by well-managed chains, has become increasingly unprofitable. In view of these circumstances, the decision of black pharmacists to seek employment in drugstore chains and forego owner-management is understandable and probably in their own best interests.

In the supermarket industry, a number of black entrepreneurs have attempted to operate supermarkets in ghetto areas which white owners had found unprofitable. Experience to date indicates clearly that the problems posed by a hostile environment do not disappear simply because the color of the store operator has changed. High customer pilferage, poor labor productivity, and low gross margins all render profitable operation extremely difficult. Furthermore there are few black managers who have the skill requisite to operate a supermarket under such trying conditions. On the whole, graduates of both Negro and white colleges see more of a future as a member of management in large chain organizations than in fighting a losing battle in central city stores. A field survey conducted by one of the authors

---

7. See Burt Schorr, "Black Leaders' Plans to Build Ghetto Stores Often End in Defeat," *Wall Street Journal*, May 1, 1972, p. 1 which describes the vandalism, shoplifting, and credit problems of black-owned shopping centers.

suggests that most black operators of inner city supermarkets are losing money. The razor-thin profits in this industry simply do not leave sufficient margin to absorb the higher operating costs produced by the ghetto environment. In view of these facts, black ownership cannot be relied upon to provide any significant number of job opportunities for Negroes in the supermarket industry.

Although the drugstore industry and the supermarket industry have at least witnessed some experiments in black ownership, such efforts are practically nonexistent in the department store industry. The reasons are obvious: investment requirements are huge; Negro management talent to operate such large establishments is not available; and it is doubtful whether Negro ownership could retain the patronage of many whites in large cities of the nation. In addition, the chain or federated pattern of management is dominant in the industry and has made the operation even of independent white-owned department stores increasingly difficult. If black ownership of retail establishments should some day become a significant force in the economic scene—perhaps because of major subsidies provided by government—it is likely that the department store field would be the last to witness any significant inroads by Negro-owned organizations. The size and complexity of department store operations militates against the success of operation and ownership by largely inexperienced Negro groups.

THE ROLE OF GOVERNMENT

Government action has been less important in directly influencing racial employment policies in these three industries than in manufacturing industries, because the ultimate sanction of taking away government business conveys no penalty to the typical department store, drugstore or supermarket. On the whole, companies in these industries either do not sell to the federal government at all or if they do it represents a minor share of their total revenue so that the possibility of withdrawal of such business for failure to comply with governmentally imposed standards does not carry much weight. Some firms have voluntarily adopted affirmative action programs, but on the whole such programs are not widespread among companies in these three industries.

It would be a mistake to assume, however, that governmental action has not had a significant effect upon employment policies in these industries. Governmental pressures have made their influence felt in various ways. In the first place, the very requirement of reporting numbers of minority member employees to a governmental agency has probably had a salutary effect on management in making it more attentive to racial imbalances within the personnel structure. Secondly, some companies have been brought before governmental boards, either state or federal, for actions alleged to be discriminatory in hiring or dismissal of employees. Again, such actions have had a salutary effect in making management take a more critical view of its established employment procedures. Finally, and perhaps most important, the passage of the Civil Rights Act of 1964 unquestionably stimulated direct action by various minority groups. From the mid-1960's on, retail outlets in these three industries felt the increasing tempo and pressure of various civil rights organizations which chose to make the highly visible jobs in these industries targets for increased Negro employment and Negro occupational upgrading.

At the same time, however, other governmental legislation may have limited Negro employment opportunities in these industries. In the drugstore industry, the opening by the Office of Economic Opportunity of health centers in low income areas which dispense prescriptions has led to the closing of hundreds of drugstores in these areas. Since drugstores in low income areas typically employ a greater proportion of Negroes than in high income areas, such action has had the effect of depriving many Negroes of jobs in this industry. In all three industries, the continued climb of the federal minimum wage standard has led to the curtailment of many service-type jobs—carry out boy, elevator operator, etc.—and thus foreclosed employment opportunities to some of the marginal members of the Negro work force. It can, of course, be argued that these were undesirable jobs anyway and their elimination should cause no concern. This point of view, however, overlooks the fact that there are many members of the labor force, both white and black, who because of economic, social, or educational handicaps lack skills; such jobs at least provided an opportunity for productive work whereas the only alternative presently available in our society seems to be welfare.

MANAGERIAL POLICIES

The level and character of Negro employment in a firm and in an industry represents the result of the combined influence of a wide spectrum of forces—the location of facilities, the nature of the work, the image of the industry, and so forth. Many of these external and internal influences are beyond the direct control of the individual manager. For example, it is difficult for a department store manager to expand employment of Negro men when the bulk of jobs are female and the nature of the work does not appeal to Negro male job seekers.

Nevertheless the wide variations in employment policies among firms within the same industry suggest that there is a considerable area of latitude in which affirmative action by forceful and socially conscious executives can make a significant impact upon the level of Negro employment. The scope of managerial discretion is particularly noticeable when the effect of scale of operation is examined in these three industries in relation to Negro employment practices, although here too external circumstances impinge upon managerial decision-making.

Whereas in the supermarket industry the regional and national chains have been leaders in employment of Negroes relative to the smaller independents, in the department store industry the opposite seems to be true. In the latter industry on a national basis, independent local companies show a higher total percentage of Negro employment than the federations or national chains. In the drugstore industry the results are not entirely clear but here again, as in the supermarket industry, it seems that the chains have been more aggressive in hiring Negroes.

These varying trends reflect differences in philosophies of management, but they also reflect the influence of the various external factors which we have already considered. For example, it seems likely that the independent department store is frequently a large family owned facility in the downtown of a central city. Obviously community pressures, concern for the stability of the central city area, and considerations of social responsibility may motivate the actions of the chief executives of such institutions. The chain department stores have relied upon representation outside the urban centers to generate profits and have been less concerned about such inner city problems. By contrast, many of the independent supermarkets and smaller

supermarket chains are suburban-based and therefore are more
remote both from sources of Negro labor supply as well as community pressure to employ Negroes.

A contributing factor to the relatively low level of Negro
employment in these three industries is the decentralization of
branch units and the weak control exercised by central headquarters with respect to racial employment policies. A somewhat similar situation was observed in the insurance industry [8]
where the central home office exercised virtually no control over
agency office hiring policies and relatively little influence on
branch office employment policies with respect to hiring of salesmen.

Undoubtedly the geographical dispersion of individual operating units which characterizes the drugstore, supermarket, and
department store industries has made it more difficult for management in these industries to implement hiring policies dictated
at headquarters. Despite obvious problems of communication
and control, employment policies in branch offices can be effectively controlled from headquarters if top management really
makes an effort in this regard. A good example of such practice
is provided by the banking industry where branch office hiring
is under tight control of the home office.[9] One consequence of
this effective control procedure in that industry is that branch
offices of multiunit banks exhibit a higher proportion of Negro
employees than independent banks of the same size as the branch.

Although management appears to be making progress in all
three industries in raising employment ratios of Negroes, there
has been relatively little improvement in moving Negroes into
managerial ranks. A development which must be of increasing
concern to Negroes interested in maintaining upward mobility
in these industries is the increasing reliance by management on
evidence of a college degree as an admission requirement for
managerial training programs. As has already been observed,
this is common practice in the department store industry and is
becoming more common in the supermarket and drugstore industries as the size of stores grows.

---

8. Armand J. Thieblot, Jr. and Linda P. Fletcher, *Negro Employment in
   Finance*, Studies of Negro Employment, Vol. II (Philadelphia: Industrial
   Research Unit, Wharton School of Finance and Commerce, University
   of Pennsylvania, 1970), Part Two, pp. 23-25.

9. *Ibid.,*, Part One, p. 92.

The increasing use of inflated educational requirements in industry at large represents a major concern to the Equal Employment Opportunity Commission. William H. Brown III, Chairman of the Commission, has expressed the view that American
business is fast becoming a "credential society," judging the
worth of people by the number of certificates and seals of approval to which they can lay claim.[10] Unfortunately, just as
testing operated as a bar to Negro entry to lower level jobs,
so can the requirement of a college degree operate to bar many
Negroes who might otherwise be qualified for managerial positions.

The tendency among executives to equate educational achievement with performance on the job has grown despite the fact
that executives generally have made little effort to substantiate
whether there is in fact any correlation between performance
on the job and formal educational background. As a matter of
fact, some recent studies have tended to indicate that in many
classes of jobs where college degrees are required or preferred
there is little or no correlation between educational achievement and job performance.[11] In view of the difficulties encountered by the supermarket, drugstore, and department store
industries in attracting qualified Negro college graduates, management should consider carefully whether a college degree is
really a valid prerequisite for admission to managerial training
programs.

Although there are notable exceptions in each industry, it
appears from the data examined previously that the three industries studied have not been marked by a high degree of management commitment to the cause of Negro employment. Other
business problems, such as consumerism, discounting, and inroads
by other kinds of merchandising institutions have been given
higher priority than considerations of racial composition in the
labor force. In part, this reflects managerial policy which is
impelled by low profit margins and intense competition to avoid
taking positions in the social field which might alienate customers. Although managerial reading of public opinion may have
in fact been wrong and unwarranted, the fact remains that
concern over such reactions with its concomitant effect upon

10. *M B A*, January 22, 1972, p. 16.

11. Ivar Berg, *Education and Jobs: The Great Training Robbery* (New
York: Praeger Publishers, 1970), pp. 85-94.

sales and profits is an important influence in the decision-making process.

High turnover, extensive use of part-timers, and dispersed location of facilities have all militated against a coordinated and well conceived long range manpower policy in these three industries. As a consequence there has been little appreciation of the changing nature of the labor force and of the product market, both of which must dictate the utilization of larger numbers of Negro workers in the future. Training has been of short duration and frequently has lacked the depth of staff support required for a satisfactory experience with minority personnel.

PROSPECTS FOR THE FUTURE

Although ratios of Negro employment are still low in the three industries examined, particularly in white collar occupations, progress continues to be made each year in increasing Negro representation. From 1969 to 1970, according to EEOC data, Negro representation in the drugstore industry increased from 11.1 to 12.7 percent; in the supermarket industry from 6.5 to 7.1 percent; and in the department store industry from 8.1 to 8.5 percent.[12] Overall percentages are expected to continue to grow; the slower and more difficult process involves the training and upgrading of Negroes for managerial positions.

It is to be hoped that top management in these industries will make review and improvement of racial employment policies and practices a matter of high corporate priority. Although ratios of Negro employment in the critical category of sales are higher in these industries than for all industries reporting to the EEOC, much more needs to be done both in terms of upgrading and overall employment ratios. Retail trade represents one of the few businesses which is located where Negroes reside and therefore it is of major importance for the future of Negro employment that progress continue to be made in the proportion and character of Negro employment in these industries.

---

12. Compare 1969 data in Part Two, Table 21, Part Three, Table 23, and Part Four, Appendix Table A-3, with Tables 6, 7, and 8 in this section.